USŪL AL-FIQH

USŪL AL-FIQH

Methodology of Islamic Jurisprudence

RECEP DOĞAN

NEW JERSEY • LONDON • FRANKFURT • CAIRO

TUGHRA BOOKS
New Jersey

18 17 16 15   3 4 5 6

Published by Tughra Books
335 Clifton Avenue, Clifton
New Jersey 07011, USA

www.tughrabooks.com

Library of Congress Cataloging-in-Publication Data

Dogan, Recep.
Usul al-fiqh : methodology of Islamic jurisprudence / Recep Dogan.
pages cm
ISBN 978-1-59784-349-2 (alk. paper)
1. Islamic law--Interpretation and construction. I. Title.
KBP440.32.D64A38 2014
340.5'94--dc23
2014037278

ISBN: 978-1-59784-349-2

Printed by
Çağlayan A.Ş., Izmir - Turkey

Contents

Chapter Six

Istiḥsān (Juristic Preference), *Qawli Saḥābah* (The Statement of the Companions) and Revealed Law Preceding the *Shari'ah* of Islam

Chapter Seven

'Urf (Custom) and *Maslaḥah Mursala* (Consideration of Public Interest)

Chapter 12
***Ijtihād* (Personal Reasoning)**

Transliteration Table

	ح = ḥ	ص = ṣ	ك = k
ا = a	خ = kh	ض = ḏ	ل = l
ء = ‘	د = d	ط = t	م = m
ب = b	ذ = dh	ظ = z̲	ن = n
ت = t	ر = r	ع = ‘	ة,ه = h
ث = th	ز = z	غ = gh	و = w
ج = j	س = s	ف = f	ي = y
	ش = sh	ق = q	

Transliterations of Arabic expressions in this book are arranged according to the table above. In addition, (ū ī ā) are used for long vowels.

Preface

The religion of Islam aims to bring happiness to the life of humans both in this world and in the afterlife by offering them the most suitable lifestyle as decreed by Allah (God). Islam is not a religion that can be imposed on people; no one is forced to accept it, rather it leaves humans free, respects their decisions and is to be practiced by their free will. Sound and healthy worship is only possible with the benefit of sound knowledge. Muslims refer to two main sources to learn about worship and duty: the Qur'an and Sunnah (words and practise of Prophet Muhammad, peace and blessings be upon him). Islam is a set of rulings that have been conveyed to human kind from Allah and practiced by Prophet Muhammad, peace and blessings be upon him, in the most exemplary way.

Not all Muslims are able to have a detailed knowledge of the Qur'an and Sunnah therefore they must refer to the *mujtahid* (jurist) imams whose function is to know the religion at the utmost level. Legal schools were established by imams such as Abū Ḫanīfa, Mālik, Shāfi'ī and Ahmad ibn Hanbal to address this need. Their legal schools were based on the methodology and principles of Islamic jurisprudence. The *mujtahid* imams created their own unique *uṣūl* (methodology) and principles to extract the rulings from the sources which include the Qur'an, the Sunnah, *ijma'* (consensus), *qiyāṣ* (analogy), *maslaḫah mursala* (considering the public benefit), *istiḫsān* (juristic preference), *'urf* (custom), *and sadd dharā'ī* (blacking the means), etc.

This book deals with the sources of Islamic jurisprudence and their importance in deducing the religious rulings. It covers the concept of *ijtihād* (independent reasoning), its conditions and application and illustrates why it is a practice for experts rather than laymen. It also explains the differences in the levels of expertise of the *mujtahids*. In fact, there are seven distinct classifications of *mujtahid*.

The book also covers the communication of God as Lawgiver with regard to the conduct of liable persons. It details the difference in probative value of communication based on the extent to which it binds an individual be it absolutely binding, a recommendation or mere permissibility.

The reader will be able to understand the difference between *fiqh* (law) and *Uṣūl al-Fiqh* (methodology of law). *Fiqh* is the law itself whereas *Uṣūl al-Fiqh* is the methodology utilized to extract the law. The relationship between the two disciplines resembles that of the rules of grammar to a language, or of logic to philosophy. *Uṣūl al-fiqh* in this sense provides the standard criteria for the correct deduction of the rulings of *fiqh* from the sources of Shari'ah (the Qur'an and Sunnah).

The *mujtahids* follow a strict methodology in order to extract the rulings from their sources and scholars have produced some works to explain this methodology with two aims:

a) To be able to examine whether a jurist is qualified as a *mujtahid* and has the necessary qualifications to make *ijtihād* (producing new legal rulings based on Islamic sources) as the previous *mujtahids* did.
b) To provide a person who does not have the qualifications for *ijtihād* a source of reference from which they will be able to understand the evidences which the *mujtahid* used in their *ijtihāds*. As a result, they will accept the work of the *mujtahids* and follow their findings without hesitation.

Uṣūl al-fiqh contains two types of rulings; *aḫkām taklifiyya* (defining law) and *aḫkām wad'iyya* (declaratory law). This book explains both categories and shows the differences between them. It also contains an in-depth explanation of the definition of legal capacity and the necessary conditions to be responsible for carrying out religious duties as well as identification of the ultimate sources of Islamic law.

I would like to thank those who helped me in the preparation of this book. May God make this book beneficial for those interested in learning Islamic law and its methodology.

Recep Doğan, PhD, Lecturer
Centre for Islamic Sciences & Civilization (CISAC)
Faculty of Arts, Charles Sturt University

Chapter One

Introduction to *Uṣūl al-Fiqh*

Introduction to *Uṣūl al-Fiqh*

The religion of Islam is made up of two main categories: the theoretical and the practical. The theoretical aspect is the belief system, which is the topic of *Kalām*. The practical aspect mainly consists of two parts: worship and life. Islamic rulings, which liable Muslims are obliged to perform, are extracted from two main sources; the Qur'an and the Sunnah. These sources contain universal principles that serve to regulate people's individual, familial, social, moral and religious lives.

Any study of Islamic law must begin with the definition of *uṣūl-al fiqh*. The term has two components: *uṣūl* and *fiqh*. The definitions of these two terms help us identify the role and function of the specialists within the Islamic legal system. The terms also elaborate the relationship that exists between the fully empowered jurist and the person who is a pure layman, the nature of the rulings of Islamic law, and the nature of the sources from which the rulings are derived.

The Literal Meaning of *Fiqh*

Fiqh means understanding and discernment. It implies an understanding of Islam in a general way. It may also mean what a prudent person is likely to conclude from obvious evidence. The word has been used in the Qur'an:

> ...Yet, when some good happens to them, they say: 'This is from God;' and when an evil befalls them, they say: 'This is because of you.' Say: 'All is from God.' But how is it with these people that they do not grasp the truth of anything said (or anything that has happened)![1]

In this verse, the Arabic word *'yafqahuun'* means to grasp the truth and comprehend it. This word is derived from the letters f-q-h, which is the same root as *fiqh*.

---

1 Qur'ān 4:78. The copy of the Qur'ān used for translations was: Ünal. A. *The Qur'ān with annotated interpretation in modern English.* S"Umarset, N.J.: The Light, 2006.

> Surely, among the jinn and humankind are many that We have created (and destined for) Hell (knowing that they would deserve it). They have hearts with which they do not *seek the essence of matters to grasp the truth*, and they have eyes with which they do not see, and they have ears with which they do not hear. They are like cattle (following only their instincts)—rather, even more astray (from the right way and in need of being led). Those are the unmindful and heedless.[2]

This verse condemns some human beings for not using their reason and therefore not grasping the truth. The Arabic word '*yafqahuun*', which is derived from f-q-h, is used here to explain the same point.

> He for whom God wills His blessings is granted the understanding of the religion.[3]

In this hadith the word '*yufaqqihhu*' is used, which is also derived from f-q-h, meaning to comprehend and grasp the religion.

The term *fiqh* came to be used exclusively for knowledge of the law. Abu Ḥanīfa defined *fiqh* as: a person's knowledge of his rights and duties.[4] *Fiqh* is to know what is for and against a person who is liable to carry out his or her religious obligations. Imam Shāfi'ī defined *fiqh* as: the knowledge of the legal rulings pertaining to conduct that have been derived from their specific evidences.[5] Al-Ghazzalī defined *fiqh* as: an expression for the knowledge of legal rulings established specifically for human conduct.[6] Fakhraddin al-Rāzī defined *fiqh* as: the knowledge of the legal rulings, pertaining to conduct with reference to their sources, when this knowledge is not obtained by way of necessity in religion.[7]

The expression "not obtained by way of necessity" means that every subject must have some knowledge of *aḥkām* (legal rulings) by necessity, because without such knowledge a liable person will not be able to perform certain obligatory acts, or abstain from those that are prohibited. The knowledge of a liable person is not *fiqh* as it has not been derived from the Shari'ah sources; it is necessary for a person to possess this knowledge. It can be obtained from the jurists and *madhabs* (legal schools).

---

2 Qur'ān 7:179.
3 Bukhari, *Saḥīḥ, Kitāb al-Ilm*, 69.
4 Ṣadr al-Shari'ah, *al-Tawḍīḥ Fi Hall Jawamid al-Tanqīh*, p. 22.
5 Wahba Zuhaylī, *Uṣūl al-Fiqh al-Islāmī*, p. 1/19.
6 Ghazālī, *al-Muṣtaṣfā min Ilm al-Uṣūl*, p. 3.
7 Rāzī, *al-Maḥsul Fi 'Ilm Uṣūl al-Fiqh*, p. 1/78.

As previously mentioned, *fiqh* is the law itself whereas *Uṣūl al-Fiqh* is the methodology used to extract the law. *Uṣūl al-fiqh* in this sense provides the standard criteria for the correct deduction of the rulings of *fiqh* from the sources of Shari'ah. An adequate knowledge of *fiqh* necessitates close familiarity with its sources. This is borne out in the definition of *fiqh*, which is 'knowledge of the practical rulings of Shari'ah acquired from the detailed evidence in the sources.'[8]

Scholars followed a strict methodology in order to extract the rulings from their sources. They produced works to explain this methodology, which served two distinct purposes. Firstly, they helped Muslims to understand whether a contemporary jurist was sufficiently qualified, as his predecessors had been, in order to make *ijtihād* and solve the problems of his day. Secondly, they established trust in the strict methodology of the jurists so that those unqualified would accept their work and follow the rulings without needing to question them.

For this reason, the leading *mujtahids* established the general principles and methodologies of *Uṣūl al-Fiqh* to enable ordinary people to understand how religious rulings are extracted from their sources. They mentioned the conditions that a *mujtahid* must possess in order to be fully qualified for this work, and they also mentioned the conditions for the imitation and its rulings. These principles, methodologies and conditions for being qualified as a *mujtahid* are incorporated in the study of *Uṣūl al-Fiqh*.

Summary: The Literal Meaning of *Fiqh*

1. *Fiqh* means understanding and discernment; it implies an understanding of Islam in a general way; it may also mean what a prudent person is likely to conclude from obvious evidence.
2. The term *fiqh* came to be used exclusively for knowledge of the law. Abu Ḫanīfa defined *fiqh* as: a person's knowledge of his rights and duties. *Fiqh* is to know what is for and against a person who is liable to carry out his or her religious obligations.
3. *Fiqh* is the law itself whereas *Uṣūl al-Fiqh* is the methodology used to extract the laws. *Uṣūl al-fiqh* in this sense provides the standard criteria for the correct deduction of the rulings of *fiqh* from the sources of Shari'ah.
4. Scholars follow a strict methodology in order to extract the rulings from their sources. Their works helped Muslims to understand whether a con-

---

8 Āmidī, *Iḫkām, al-Maktab al-Islāmī*, Beirut, 1982, 1/6.

temporary jurist was sufficiently qualified to make *ijtihād* and they established trust in the strict methodology of the jurists in those unqualified.

5. The leading *mujtahids* established the general principles and methodologies of *Uṣūl al-Fiqh*. These principles, methodologies and conditions for being qualified as a *mujtahid* are incorporated in the study of *Uṣūl al-Fiqh*.

The Definition of *Uṣūl al-Fiqh*

Uṣūl al-fiqh is the science in which a *mujtahid* extracts the religious rulings pertaining to liable Muslims from their detailed evidences based on specific methodology and principles. In other words, the rulings of *fiqh* are derived from the Qur'an and the Sunnah in conformity with a body of principles and methods, which are collectively known as *Uṣūl al-Fiqh*.[9] For a better understanding of this definition, it will be explained further. There are many principles, a few of which are given below with some related rulings.

Each of the principles (*qawā'id*) includes many individual rulings. An example of a principle is: 'Every command is used for demand and it is binding.' There are many examples of this principle:

> O you who believe! Bow down and prostrate yourselves, (thus performing the Prayer), and fulfil all your other duties of worship to your Lord, and do (all the other commands of your Religion, which are all) good, so that you may prosper.[10]
>
> Establish the Prayer, and pay the Prescribed Purifying Alms.[11]

These verses are commands from God and binding on Muslims. The same principle can be used in many instances to determine whether the command is binding for Muslims or not.

Another principle: 'Every prohibition (*nahy*) is used to indicate *haram* (forbidden-unlawful)' can be applied when examining verses or hadiths that prohibit something. Examples of this include:

> O you who believe! Let not some people among you deride another people, it may be that the latter are better than the former; nor let some women deride other women, it may be that the latter are better than the former. Nor defame one another (and provoke the same for yourselves

---

9 M. H. Kamali, *Principles of Islamic Jurisprudence*, the Islamic Text Society, Cambridge, 2003, p. 12.

10 Qur'ān, 22: 77.

11 Qur'ān, 2: 43

> in retaliation), nor insult one another with nicknames (that your brothers and sisters dislike).[12]
>
> Do not consume your wealth among yourselves in false ways.[13]
>
> Do not kill any soul, which God has made sacred and forbidden.[14]

The forbidden acts are extracted from these verses with the help of this principle which can be applied in many different instances. The methodology and the principles used by the *mujtahid* enable them to produce new rulings. This topic will be explained more fully later in the book.

The expression 'The rulings of *fiqh*' (*ḫukm* pl. *aḫkām*) is explained as follows; the ruling is defining something positively or negatively. For example, when we say 'The sun rose' or 'The sun has not risen yet' we are giving information of the result, in this case, whether or not the sun has risen.

The Arabic word *ḫukm* (pl. *aḫkām*) literally means a command. Muslim jurists define *ḫukm* as a communication from God related to the acts of the liable human beings through a demand, an option and a declaration.[15]

There are various ways that the *aḫkām* (rulings) can be established. The first method is through reasoning and the use of the intellect. These rulings are named as the reason-based rulings (*al- aḫkām al-'aqliyya*). Examples of *this* type of ruling are: 'One is half of two' and 'Two contradicting things cannot be true at the same time.' A second method is for the ruling to be understood by using the senses. These are named the sense-based rulings, for example; 'The fire burns' and 'The sun set.' In other instances, the rulings are extracted from the religious sources and are named religious-based rulings (*aḫkām shar'iyya*). Examples of this type of ruling include: 'Five Daily Prayers are obligatory upon the Muslims' and 'Usury is forbidden.' The principles of Islamic law are set up to extract these types of rulings from their sources. In order to exclude the reason-based and the sense-based rulings from the definition of *Uṣūl al-Fiqh*, the term 'religious rulings' (*aḫkām shar'iyya*) is used in the definition.

The religious rulings are further classified into different categories. The rulings related to the five Daily Prayers, fasting, trade, marriage, wills and estates, etc. fall under the category of practise-based rulings (*aḫkām 'amaliyya*) as they are related to the deeds of the servants of God. The rulings about believing in

---

[12] Qur'ān, 49: 11

[13] Qur'ān, 2: 188.

[14] Qur'ān, 6: 151.

[15] Ṣadr al-Shari'ah, *al-Tawḏīḫ*, p. 1/28.

God, the afterlife, the angels, the Prophets, etc. fall under the category of rulings pertaining to belief (*aḫkām i'tiqādī*). The rulings about truthfulness, abstaining from lies, helping poor people, etc. are classified as ethical rulings (*aḫkām akhlaqiyya*).

The science *Uṣūl al-Fiqh* focuses solely on the rulings related to the conducts of a servant as is defined in the expression 'rulings related to the liable Muslims.' As a result, the rulings pertaining to belief and ethics are excluded from the scope of this science.

The expression 'the detailed evidences' refers to the specific evidence for each individual religious ruling. They are used to explain the rulings for each case. For example, the verse; "*Forbidden to you (O believing men) are your mothers*"[16] is an individual piece of evidence for a specific case, because it is related to the specific case and explains its ruling as *haram* (forbidden) in Islam. Another example; "*Do not draw near to any unlawful sexual intercourse*"[17] is also an individual piece of evidence, because it is related to a specific matter (unlawful sexual intercourse) and it explains the ruling (*haram*) for it.

There are also brief, general evidences (*ijmalī-kullī adillah*), however, these are not only related to one specific matter and do not explain its ruling. For example, the Qur'an, Sunnah, *ijma'* (general consensus) and *qiyāṣ* (analogy) are sources for the religious rulings and they are brief, general evidences.

Kamali holds that the methodology is separate from the sources of Islamic jurisprudence and he explains this as follows:

> Some writers have described *Uṣūl al-Fiqh* as the methodology of law, a description which is accurate but incomplete. Although the methods of interpretation and deduction are of primary concern to *Uṣūl al-Fiqh*, the latter is not exclusively devoted to methodology. To say that *Uṣūl al-Fiqh* is the science of the sources and methodology of the law is accurate in the sense that the Qur'an and Sunnah constitute the sources as well as the subject matter to which the methodology of *Uṣūl al-Fiqh* is applied. The Qur'an and Sunnah themselves, however, contain very little by way of methodology, but rather provide the indications from which the rulings of Shari'ah can be deduced. The methodology of *Uṣūl al-Fiqh* really refers to methods of reasoning such as analogy (*qiyāṣ*), juristic preference (*istiḫsān*), presumption of continuity (*istiṣḫāb*) and the rules of interpretation and deduction. These are designed to serve as an aid to the correct understanding of the sources and *ijtihād*.[18]

---

[16] Qur'ān, 4: 23.

[17] Qur'ān, 17: 32.

[18] Kamali, *Principles of Islamic Jurisprudence*, p. 12.

Summary: The Definition of *Uṣūl al-Fiqh*

1. *Uṣūl al-fiqh* is the science in which a *mujtahid* extracts the religious rulings pertaining to liable Muslims from their detailed evidences based on specific methodology and principles.
2. Each of the principles (*qawā'id*) includes many individual rulings.
3. The expression 'the rulings of *fiqh*' (*ḫukm* pl. *aḫkām*) is explained as follows; the ruling is defining something positively or negatively.
4. The Arabic word *ḫukm* (pl. *aḫkām*) literally means a command. The Muslim jurists define *ḫukm* as a communication from God related to the acts of the liable human beings through a demand, an option and a declaration.
5. There are various ways that the *aḫkām* (rulings) can be established. The first method is through reasoning and the use of the intellect. A second method is for the ruling to be understood through using the senses.
6. In order to exclude the reason-based and the sense-based rulings from the definition of *Uṣūl al-Fiqh*, the term 'religious rulings' (*aḫkām shar'iyya*) is used in the definition.
7. However, the religious rulings are further classified into different categories. The rulings about five Daily Prayers, fasting, trade, marriage, wills and estates, etc. fall under the category of practise-based rulings (*aḫkām 'amaliyya*) because they are related to the deeds of the servants.
8. The rulings about believing in God, the afterlife, the angels, the Prophets, etc. fall under the category of belief-wise rulings (*aḫkām i'tiqādī*).
9. The rulings about truthfulness, abstaining from lies, helping poor people, etc. are classified as ethical rules (*aḫkām akhlaqiyya*).
10. The science *Uṣūl al-Fiqh* focuses solely on the rulings related to the deeds of a servant of God.
11. The expression 'the detailed evidences' refers to the specific evidence for each individual religious ruling. They are used to explain the rulings for each case.
12. There are also brief, general evidences (*ijmalī-kullī adillah*), however, these are not only related to one specific matter and do not explain its ruling.

The Differences between *Mujtahid and Faqīh*

As mentioned earlier, the purpose of the science *Uṣūl al-Fiqh* is to provide the methodology and general principles in order to extract the religious rulings from the primary sources for Muslims who are religiously liable. If a scholar is knowledgeable in this science and has the necessary qualifications to perform *ijtihād* he can extract the religious rulings from their specific evidences. Necessary qualifications include a detailed knowledge of the Qur'an and the Sunnah, applying *qiyāṣ* to the different cases, the knowledge of the general purpose of Islamic Shari'ah and many more.

A person who is not a qualified *mujtahid* but chooses to embark on the journey to gain knowledge of this science is called *faqīh.* There are some benefits in this:

1) A *faqīh* gains a full understanding of the process by which *mujtahid* extracted the rulings therefore enabling them to accept these rulings with confidence. In other words, on gaining knowledge of this science a *faqīh* understands that the *mujtahids* do not make rulings based on their own opinions; rather they produce them based on religious sources and they follow the general principles that are extrapolated from the Quran and the Sunnah.
2) If there are some cases on which the *mujtahids* remain silent, the *faqīh* can use their knowledge of the science to apply reason according to the methodology of the *mujtahid.* The same methodology of the *mujtahid* can be applied for new cases.
3) They become capable of comparing the different *ijtihāds* on the same matter and can choose the strongest one from among them with the help of *Uṣūl al-Fiqh.* They can identify which evidence is the strongest and which methodology is most suitable for the application of *ijtihād* in the new case. In order to compare the *ijtihāds* that relate to the same matter, one must know the strength of the available evidences and the methods of preference so he can prefer the strongest *ijtihād.* This cannot be achieved without the knowledge of the methodology and general principles of *Uṣūl al-Fiqh.*

Summary: The Differences between *Mujtahid* and *Faqīh*

1. The science *Uṣūl al-Fiqh* provides the methodology and general principles in order to extract religious rulings from the primary sources.
2. Necessary qualifications for a jurist include a detailed knowledge of the Qur'an and the Sunnah, applying *qiyāṣ* to the different cases, the knowledge of the general purpose of Islamic Shari'ah and many more.
3. A person who is not qualified as a *mujtahid* but chooses to embark on the journey to gain knowledge of this science is called *faqīh.*

The Development of *Uṣūl al-Fiqh*

Uṣūl al-fiqh has been in existence for the same amount of time as *fiqh*. *Fiqh* could not have come into existence in the absence of its sources or in the absence of methodologies used to extract the rulings from these sources. *Uṣūl al-fiqh* appeared as a separate science at the end of the second century of the *Hijrī* calendar. At the time of the Companions and Successors, this science was not necessary, as they had learnt the rulings from the noble Prophet himself or from his contemporaries. Despite this, *fiqh* and *Uṣūl al-Fiqh* originated with and were taught by the Prophet together and the need to separate the two did not arise for a long time.

When the Prophet passed away the task for issuing fatwas (opinions concerning religious rulings) and applying *ijtihād* to new problems was undertaken by the well-known Companions. They knew the Arabic language—the language of the Qur'an and Sunnah, they had witnessed the occasions behind the revelation and the reasons behind the hadith of the noble Prophet and they had experienced the history of Qur'anic revelation. Moreover, they were very intelligent and had very strong memories. They were supreme examples of Islamic morality in the best way as they had lived with the Prophet for a long time and learned these values directly from him.

Whenever a need arose to extract the rulings for new cases related to worldly or otherworldly matters, the Companions and Successors checked the Qur'an first. If they could not find what they were looking for, they looked into the Sunnah of the Prophet. If this too was unyielding, they would make use of their own juristic opinion (*ijtihād*). During this process, they would compare the new issue to pre-existing cases in the Qur'an and Sunnah. In the event of similarities between the two cases, they would implement *qiyāṣ* (analogy) whereby they could apply the same ruling to the new cases. If there was no similarity between the two cases, they would make *ijtihād* based on the purpose and aims of Shari'ah whilst taking into consideration the needs of the Muslims.

Tabi'in, the generation following the Companions, followed the same process of *ijtihād* when generating solutions to new problems. Well-known *mujtahids* from this generation include Said ibn Musayyib, 'Urwa ibn Zubayr, Qādi Shurayh and Ibrahim Nakhāī.

Muslims faced new issues after the first century of the *Hijrī* calendar. Non-Arabian and Arabian Muslims lived together and the intermingling of different cultures resulted in the significant weakening of the Arabic language. Muslim linguists addressed this issue by establishing grammar rules to protect Arabic from the influence of different cultures. Similarly, Muslim jurists established guidelines and methodology to protect Islamic law from corruption.

Despite this, there were at the time many different *mujtahids* each of whom followed his own unique methodology. The profound *mujtahids* of this time recognised the threat of this situation in being able to cause disunity and conflict amongst Muslims. They identified the need to set general guidelines and proper methodology for the work of *ijtihād* to prevent both internal conflicts and baseless personal opinions of scholars appearing in legal rulings. These *mujtahids* established the rules, principles, guidelines and the methodology for Islamic jurisprudence. In their work, they benefitted from the expressive styles of the Qur'an, Sunnah and the Arabic language. They deduced the guidelines from these sources and established the science of *Uṣūl al-Fiqh*.

Summary: The Development of *Uṣūl al-Fiqh*

1. *Uṣūl al-fiqh* has been in existence for the same amount of time as *fiqh*. As a separate science, *Uṣūl al-Fiqh* appeared at the end of the second century of the *Hijrī* calendar.
2. When the noble Prophet passed away the task for issuing fatwas and applying *ijtihād* to new problems was undertaken by the well-known Companions.
3. Whenever a need arose to extract the rulings for new cases related to worldly or otherworldly matters, the Companions and Successors checked the Qur'an first. If they could not find what they were looking for, they looked into the Sunnah of the Prophet. If this too was unyielding, they would make use their own juristic opinion (*ijtihād*).
4. *Tabi'in* followed the same process of *ijtihād* when generating solutions to new problems.
5. New issues were faced by Muslims after the first century of the *Hijrī* calendar.
6. Muslim linguists established grammar rules to protect Arabic from the influence of different cultures. Similarly jurists established guidelines and methodology to protect Islamic law from corruption.
7. There were many different *mujtahids* each with a unique methodology. These *mujtahids* established the rules, principles, guidelines and the methodology for Islamic jurisprudence and established the science of *Uṣūl al-Fiqh*.

The First Work in the Field of *Uṣūl al-Fiqh*

Imam Shāfi'ī (d. 204 AH), was the first scholar to produce an inclusive and comprehensive work in the field of *Uṣūl al-Fiqh.* His work, '*al-Risāla*' was commissioned by the hadith scholar Abdurrahman ibn Mahdi (d. 198 AH). Mahdi asked Imam Shāfi'ī to write a letter (*Risāla*) including the aspects and specifications of the Qur'an, conditions for the acceptance of the reports (coming from the noble Prophet, the Companions and the Successors), the validity of *ijma'* and the abrogated and the abrogating verses (*nāsikh and mansūkh*) contained in the Qur'an. On completion, Imam Shāfi'ī's work was named *Risāla* (letter) by the people of his time.

Ibn Nadīm holds that the first scholar to establish the principles and methodology of Islamic jurisprudence (*Uṣūl al-Fiqh*) as a separate science was Abū Yusuf (d. 182 AH), the student of Imam Abū Ḫanīfa (d. 150 AH). However, Ḫanafī scholars maintain that Abū Ḫanīfa collected all the principles and methodology of Islamic jurisprudence in his work '*Kitāb al-Ray*' (the Book of *Ijtihād*).[19]

In his book *al-Risāla*, Imam Shāfi'ī discussed the following topics: the Qur'an and its style for the explanation of the rulings, the Sunnah and its place as a source of *ijtihād*, the necessity of following the Sunnah, *nāsikh-mansūkh* (the abrogating and abrogated verses in the Qur'an), the problems in the hadith reports, *khabar wāḫid* (single source report), *ijma'* (general consensus), *qiyāṣ* (analogy), the discussion around the proof value of *istiḫsān* (juristic preference) and the circumstances in which conflicts are permissible among the *mujtahids.* As a result, Imam Shāfi'ī's book *al-Risāla* is accepted as the first major work establishing the science of *Uṣūl al-Fiqh* as a separate discipline. However, he was not the first to discover these principles and guidelines. In fact, these principles and methodology were established and used by early *mujtahids* before Imam Shāfi'ī. Previously, each imam followed his own unique methodology in his *ijtihāds* and used these principles respectively. They deduced these principles by studying the sources of Islamic jurisprudence and established their own unique methodology, but they did not write an inclusive work in the field of *Uṣūl al-Fiqh* per se, rather they simply applied them in their *ijtihāds*. Following Imam Shāfi'ī's example, other scholars wrote books in this field and discussed its various components. For example, Ahmad ibn Hanbal wrote *Kitāb Tāat al-Rasūl, Kitāb an-Nāsikh wal Mansūkh* and *Kitāb al-'Ilal.* Later, Ḫanafī and theology (*Kalām*) scholars discussed the issues of *Uṣūl al-Fiqh* in detail and set sound rules for this science.

---

[19] Ibn Nadīm, *al-Fihrist*, Cairo, no date, p. 14.

All the scholars agreed that this science was to be used for extracting the religious rulings from their sources. If there is a ruling relating to the liability of Muslims there is also evidence to support that ruling, identifiable through *ijtihād* by the *mujtahid*. For this reason the scholars of *Uṣūl al-Fiqh* focused on four topics;

1) The categories of the religious rules (*aẖkām shar'iyya*): *fard, haram, mubah, makruh,* etc.
2) The sources of Islamic jurisprudence: Qur'an, Sunnah, *qiyāṣ, ijma',* etc.
3) The methodology for extracting the rulings and their indications to them.
4) The scholar (*mujtahid*) who extracts the rulings.

Due to the variance in methodology, focus and objective of the scholars, two different types of work were produced:

1) The methodology of *mutakallimīn* (theologs): The majority of scholars producing this type of work were *Kalām* (theology) scholars, hence the name of the methodology. This methodology was also named as the methodology of (Imam) Shāfi'ī, after the author of the first book in this style.
2) The methodology of Ḫanafī: this style was established by the Ḫanafī scholars.

Summary: The First Work in the Field of *Uṣūl al-Fiqh*

1. Imam Shāfi'ī (d. 204 AH), was the first scholar to produce an inclusive and comprehensive work in the field of *Uṣūl al-Fiqh* - '*al-Risāla*.'
2. His book covers a wide range of topics and is accepted as the first work to establish the science of *Uṣūl al-Fiqh* on its own.
3. These principles and methodology were established and used by early *mujtahids* before Imam Shāfi'ī.
4. Following Imam Shāfi'ī, other scholars wrote books in this field and discussed its various components.
5. All the scholars agreed that this science was to be used for extracting the religious rulings from their sources.
6. Scholars of *Uṣūl al-Fiqh* focused on four topics;
    1) The categories of the religious rules (*aẖkām shar'iyya*): *fard, haram, mubah, makruh,* etc.
    2) The sources of Islamic jurisprudence: Qur'an, Sunnah, *qiyāṣ, ijma',* etc.
    3) The methodology for extracting the rules and their indications to them.
    4) The scholar (*mujtahid*) who extracts the rulings.

7. Due to the variance in methodology, focus and objective of the scholars, two different types of work were produced in *Uṣūl al-Fiqh*: works which are produced by *mutakallimīn* (theologs) scholars and works which are produced on the methodology of Ḥanafī scholars.

The Methodology of *Mutakallimīn*

The characteristic of this methodology was to establish its principles according to the sources of Islamic jurisprudence and the evidences. This is the theoretical approach to the study of *Uṣūl al-Fiqh* and it is mainly concerned with the exposition of principles. It is also inclined to engage in complex issues of a philosophical nature that may or may not contribute to the development of the practical rulings of *fiqh*.

Imam Shāfi'ī was mainly concerned with articulating the theoretical principles of *Uṣūl al-Fiqh* without necessarily attempting to relate these to the *fiqh* itself. He enacted a set of standard criteria that he expected to be followed during the detailed formulation of the rules of *fiqh*. His theoretical exposition of *Uṣūl al-Fiqh* did not take into consideration its practical application in the area of the detailed rulings.[20]

The scholars who wrote according to this methodology were not inclined to any legal school and were not worried if there was a conflict between their methodology and the *ijtihāds* of their *madhab* (legal schools). Their concern was to identify the primary sources of Islamic jurisprudence and the evidences contained within them. If the principles contradicted these sources, they were rejected. For them, *Uṣūl al-Fiqh* is not in the service of the detailed rulings (*furu' fiqh*), it is dominant over them. As a result, their books contain only a brief section of examples for the sole purpose of explaining these principles.

Summary: The Methodology of *Mutakallimīn*

1. Established principles according to the sources of Islamic jurisprudence and the evidences.
2. A theoretical approach to the study of *Uṣūl al-Fiqh*.
3. Engages in complex philosophical issues.
4. Imam Shāfi'ī enacted a set of standard criteria which he expected to be followed during the detailed formulation of the rulings of *fiqh* but did not take into consideration its practical application.

---

20 Kamali, pp. 17–18.

5. The scholars who wrote according to this methodology were not inclined to any legal school
6. Their concern was to identify the primary sources of Islamic jurisprudence and the evidences contained within them. If the principles contradicted these sources, they were rejected.

The Methodology of Ḫanafī

The characteristic of Ḫanafī methodology was to discover the principles and the methodology of the imams in their *ijtihāds*. This methodology is related to the detailed rulings and tends to develop a synthesis between the principles and the requirements of a particular case. Ḫanafī scholars followed this methodology because Abū Ḫanīfa did not leave a comprehensive work containing all the principles and guidelines to produce a new law; rather he left many *ijtihāds* and solutions relating to many different issues.

When studying *Uṣūl al-Fiqh,* Ḫanafī scholars focused on the *ijtihāds* of Abū Ḫanīfa who followed his own particular methodology. If some were similar to each other, they deduced a general principle based on those examples. They collected the general principles and methodology of Abū Ḫanīfa with the aim of defending him and his *fiqh* against other schools.

Ḫanafī scholars tried to expound the principles of *Uṣūl al-Fiqh* in conjunction with the rulings of *fiqh* itself. This methodology is more pragmatic in its approach to the subject. When a principle of *uṣūl* is found to be in conflict with an established principle of *fiqh*, the inclination is to adjust the theory to the extent that the conflict in question is removed, or else an exception is made so as to reach a compromise.[21]

The two examples below clarify the differences between these two methodologies. The first example explains the methodology of *mutakallimīn*. The second example deals with the methodology of Ḫanafī and how *Uṣūl al-Fiqh* was deduced through the examination of Abū Ḫanīfa's *ijtihāds*.

The first example deals with the rulings related to Daily Prayers. Prayer becomes obligatory upon a liable Muslim as soon as the specific time which is assigned for each Prayer begins. All the scholars are in agreement that each allocated time for each Prayer is the reason (*sabab*) for its obligation and is a precondition for its validity. The Noon (*Ẕuhr*) Prayer does not become obligatory

[21] Kamali, p. 18.

before the time for *Ẓuhr*. Similarly, before evening time, the *Maghrib* (Evening) Prayer does not become obligatory. If a Muslim performs the Prayers before their due times, the Prayers are not valid. The scholars also agreed that the Prayers can be performed at any time within the allocated time frames. However, they differed in opinion as to which segment of time brings the absolute obligation that the person is responsible and has no excuse for not performing it.

The *mutakallimīn* hold the view that the commencement of the allocated time for Prayer brings with it the responsibility for performing the Prayer, but that Muslims are able to perform it during any part of the allocated time. Therefore, if a person is liable for the Prayer when the Prayer time starts, he has to perform the Prayer during its allocated time, even if he loses the condition of liability later during the Prayer time. For instance, if a person is liable at the beginning of the Prayer time but becomes insane during that time, but before he has performed the Prayer, he still has the responsibility of performing that particular Prayer. If however, he loses liability from the beginning until the end of the Prayer time, he is not held responsible for performing that Prayer. Similarly, if a person is not liable to pray at the beginning of the allocated Prayer time, however he meets the conditions of liability sometime during the allocated time, the responsibility for Prayer begins at this point and he is accountable for this Prayer. It has to be prayed before the allocated time ends.

Ḫanafī scholars differ from the *mutakallimīn* on this topic. They hold that the responsibility for performing the Prayer actualizes at the point that the person begins the Prayer. This can be at any time during the allocated Prayer time. Time is the reason (*ṣabab*) for the obligation of the Prayer and each Prayer has a specific period of time within which it can be prayed. After that time, the Prayer cannot be prayed. So, if a person performs the Prayer at the beginning of the Prayer time, the responsibility for praying it also begins at that time. If the Prayer is left until later in the allocated time, the responsibility also comes at that time. If a person postpones praying until the last part of the allocated time, the responsibility also actualizes at that time because there is no other time to perform that Prayer. If a person delays performing the Prayer and then loses the conditions of liability, he is not held responsible for that Prayer. This is because it is allowable to pray at any point of the Prayer time. Therefore, the responsibility doesn't occur until the point at which the person begins to pray during that time.

The *mutakallimīn* scholars rely on the following verse for their opinion on this issue;

> Establish the Prayer in conformity with its conditions, from the declining of the sun to the darkness of the night, and (be ever observant of) the recitation of the Qur'an at dawn (the Dawn Prayer). Surely the recitation of the Qur'an at dawn is witnessed (by the angels and the whole creation awakening to a new day).[22]

God made 'the declining of the sun to the darkness of the night' a reason for the Prayer and the Sunnah explained its beginning and end. As a result, the liable person is afforded an option, as a means of leniency, to perform the Prayer at any time within the specified period. From this evidence, they established the following principle; 'If a liable person is present in any part of the fixed time for the Prayer without any obstacle, the responsibility of the Prayer is prescribed upon them. However, if they meet with obstacles (whereby their liability is nullified) and this obstacle lasts for the duration of the fixed time of the Prayer, they are not responsible for the performance of this Prayer.'

As well as studying the primary sources, Ḫanafī scholars also rely on the *ijtihād* of their imams on this issue. The *ijtihād* of their imams revealed a principle for this matter, according to which; 'If a person is liable at the beginning of the Prayer time but loses the conditions of liability later and this obstacle lasts during the rest of the Prayer time, they are not responsible to perform this Prayer.' The following reasoning was the basis for the fatwa; 'The beginning of the allocated time for the prescribed Prayers does not necessarily bring the responsibility, if it does, performing the Prayers during the last part of the Prayer time wouldn't be valid, because time is a precondition for the Prayer.'

If the first part of the allocated Prayer time was a precondition for performing the Prayer it would not be legitimate to perform it in other parts of the allocated time. The fatwa is supported by the hadith; the noble Prophet said, "Whoever makes it to any *rak'ah* (cycle of Prayer) of *'Asr* before the sun sets his *'Asr* Prayer is valid."[23] This makes it clear that, although the time beginning 45 minutes before the sun sets is considered to be an unfavourable time for performing the *'Asr* Prayer, it is still valid to perform it at that time. As a result, the first part of the Prayer time does not bring the responsibility exclusively; the Prayer can be performed during any part of the allocated time. If the duty is delayed until the last segment of time, the reason (*sabab*) which brings the responsibility actualizes during that last segment.

---

[22] Qur'ān, 17: 78.

[23] *Kutub-u sitta* (Bukhari, Muslim, Abu Dāwud, Tirmidhi Ibn Mājah, Nasāī).

The second example deals with the following principle that Ḫanafī scholars have in their *uṣūl*; 'Homonym (*mushtarak*) words do not include all their meanings at the same time.' Words that are homonyms have multiple meanings; they are initially used with one specific meaning but later gain other meanings and are classified as *mushtarak*. For example, the Arabic word '*mawlā*' means a master who frees his slave, but it is also used to mean a freed slave. In order to separate one meaning from another the scholars used '*mawlā a'lā*' for the master and '*mawlā asfal*' for the freed slave. According to Ḫanafī *fiqh*, if a person makes a will to give some of his inheritance to his '*mawlā*' and he has both types of *mawlā*, the master and the freed slave, this will is not valid, because it is impossible to know which one is intended in the will. From this fatwa, Ḫanafī scholars deduced the principle; 'Homonyms do not include all their meanings at the same time.'

Later, some Ḫanafī scholars discovered that some of the fatwas of their imams did not comply with this principle. For example, the fatwa relating to oaths; 'If one makes an oath not to speak to one's *mawlā*' and the intended person has both types of '*mawlā*' (the master and the freed slave), the oath is broken if he speaks to any of them.' Here, the homonym includes both meanings, contradicting the previous principle. On recognition of this Ḫanafī scholars examined and changed the principle to avoid conflict between the fatwas and the principle; 'Homonym (*mushtarak*) words do not include all their meanings at the same time unless they come after a prohibition.' This amendment removes the conflict between the principle and the previous *ijtihād* because the homonym comes after the prohibition.

The examples demonstrate that Ḫanafī scholars used many *ijtihād* examples to constitute the foundations of their *uṣūl*. They discovered the methodology of their imams through collating and examining their *ijtihāds*, which were scattered in different places.

Summary: The Methodology of Ḫanafī

1. Scholars discovered the principles and the methodology of the imams in their *ijtihāds*.
2. This methodology is related to the detailed rulings and tends to develop a synthesis between the principles and the requirements of a particular case.
3. When studying *Uṣūl al-Fiqh*, Ḫanafī scholars focused on the *ijtihāds* of Abū Ḫanīfa who followed his own particular methodology.
4. Ḫanafī scholars tried to expound the principles of *Uṣūl al-Fiqh* in conjunction with the rulings of *fiqh* itself.

5. As well as studying the primary sources, Ḫanafī scholars also rely on the *ijtihād* of their imams as shown by the examples of the Prayer times and homonym words.

The Books Written according to the Methodology of *Mutakallimīn:*

The classical works that were written according to the methodology of *mutakallimīn* are:

1) Qādi Abdul-Jabbār (d. 415 AH), *'al-'Umda.'*
2) Abū Husayn al-Basrī (d. 436 AH), *'al-Mu'tamad.'*
3) Imam al-Haramayn al-Juwaynī (d. 478 AH), *'al-Burhān.'*
4) Abū Hāmid Muhammad al-Ghazzalī (d. 505 AH), *'al-Muṣtaṣfā.'*

Later works which were written according to this methodology were essentially a summary of these four books.

The Books Written according to the Methodology of Ḫanafī:

The famous works which were written according to the methodology of Ḫanafī include:

1) Abū Bakr Ahmad ibn 'Ali al-Jassās (d. 370 AH), *'al-Uṣūl.'*
2) Abū Zayd 'Ubaydullah ibn 'Umar al-Dabūsī (d. 430 AH), *'Taqwīm al-Adillah.'*
3) Shams al-Aimma Sarakhsī (d. 483 AH), *'al-Uṣūl.'*
4) Fakhr al-Islam Ali ibn Muhammad al-Bazdawī (d. 482 AH), *'al-Uṣūl.'*

Later scholars combined both methodologies in their books with the aim of achieving two benefits:

a) To serve Islamic jurisprudence better by applying both principles of *uṣūl.*
b) To ascertain (and prove with evidence) that the principles of *Uṣūl al-Fiqh* rely on strong foundations.

The following scholars produced works that combine both methodologies:

1) Muzaffar ad-Din Ahmad ibn 'Ali (Ibn as-Sā'atī) (d. 694 AH), *'Badi' al-Nizam al-Jami Bayn al-Uṣūl al-Bazdawī wa al-Iḫkām.'*
2) Sadr al-Shari'ah, 'Abdullah b. Mas'ud al-Bukhari (d. 747), *'al-Tawdih.'* This book is a summary of *Uṣūl al-Bazdawī, al-Maḫṣul* (Rāzī's book), and the *Mukhtasar al-Muntaha* of the Maliki jurist Abū 'Umar Uthman b. al-Hājib (d. 646 AH).
3) Tājaddin al-Subkī (d. 711 AH), *'Jam' al-Jawāmī.'*
4) Kamāladdin b. al-Humam al-Ḫanafī (d. 860), *'al-Tahrir.'*
5) Muhibbiddin ibn 'Abd al-Shakūr (d. 1119 AH), *'Musallam al-Thubūt.'*

The Sources of Islamic Rulings

Humankind was created by God to fulfil a mission on earth and was given guidance for this in the form of the Qur'an and the Sunnah. These sources contain rulings pertaining to life on earth and the afterlife. The rulings are categorised as *halal, haram* and *mubah* according to their nature and responsibility. Evidence to support these rulings is contained in the sources and is used by Muslim jurists to extract and apply rulings to address the issues of their time. Scholars generally agree on the majority of this evidence although there are occasions when the evidence is disputed.

Evidences Agreed Upon (Sources)

The scholars unanimously agreed on the four primary sources of evidence of Islamic jurisprudence;

1) *Kitāb* (the Qur'an)
2) The Sunnah
3) *Ijma'* (general consensus)
4) *Qiyāṣ* (analogy)

It is a religious requirement for liable Muslims to carry out the rulings which are based on evidence or extracted from these sources. However, not all the evidences are of the same binding level and they do not all raise responsibility on the same scale. Another issue that differentiates these sources and their ability to create binding rulings is whether the evidences for rulings are definite (*qat'ī*) or probable (*ẕannī*). The sources of evidence are ranked as follows in order of strength; the Qur'an, Sunnah, *ijma'* and *qiyāṣ*.

When a jurist acquires a new case and wants to ascertain the ruling for it, the first source of evidence to which he will apply is the Qur'an. This is the first place for searching and if the answer is found here, the search does not continue in any of the other sources. However if the answer cannot be found in the Qur'an, the jurist investigates the Sunnah. If unsuccessful here, he applies to *ijma'* and so on. *Qiyāṣ* is the last of the sources to which the jurist can apply. The report of Mu'adh ibn Jabal proves the authenticity of the order of these evidences and the steps taken to determine the rulings for the new case;

> When the Messenger of God intended to send Mu'adh ibn Jabal to Yemen, he asked: 'How will you judge when the occasion of deciding a case arises?' He replied: 'I shall judge in accordance with God's Book. He asked:

> '(What will you do) if you do not find any guidance in God's Book?' He replied: '(I shall act) in accordance with the Sunnah of the Messenger of God.' He asked: '(What will you do) if you do not find any guidance in the Sunnah of the Messenger of God and in God's Book?' He replied: 'I shall do my best to form an opinion and I shall spare no effort.' The Messenger of God then patted him on the breast and said: 'Praise is to God Who has helped the envoy of the Prophet to find something which pleases the Messenger of God.'[24]

Abū Bakr applied the same method to find a solution whenever he encountered a new problem. When the plaintiffs applied to him to find a solution, he first searched for the solution in the Qur'an and if he found it there he would judge according to it. If a solution couldn't be found here he would search for it in the Sunnah. If he couldn't find it there, he would convene the well-versed Companions to discuss the matter. If the Companions reached a general consensus on this matter, Abū Bakr would judge in light of their decisions.

'Umar followed same methodology in legal matters as Abū Bakr. He also utilized the *ijtihād* of Abū Bakr. If he could not find a solution for a specific matter in the previous sources, he would convene the well-versed Companions to discuss the matter with them and if they reached an agreement on the matter, he would judge according to it.

Summary: Evidences Agreed Upon (Sources)

1. Scholars unanimously agreed on the four primary sources of evidence of Islamic jurisprudence; the Qur'an, Sunnah, *Ijma'* and *Qiyāṣ*
2. Liable Muslims must carry out the rulings which are based on evidence or extracted from these sources but not all evidences are of the same binding level and they don't all raise responsibility on the same scale.
3. When making rulings jurists apply to the Qur'an first. If the answer cannot be found, they apply to each of the other sources in order until the answer can be deduced.
4. Abū Bakr applied the same method to find a solution whenever he encountered a new problem.
5. 'Umar followed same methodology in legal matters as Abū Bakr. He also utilized the *ijtihād* of Abū Bakr.

---

24 Abu Dāwud, *Sunan, the Office of the Judge*, 3585.

The Disputed Evidences

There are some types of evidence that are accepted by some of the scholars but rejected by others. These evidences are *masālih mursala* (the public benefits), *istiḥsān* (juristic preference), *istiṣḥāb* (presumption of continuity), *'urf* (custom), *shar'u man qablanā* (the law of previous nations), *sadd al-dharā'ī* (blocking the means which lead to evil) and the fatwa of the Companions.

General Information about the Evidences

These evidences will be discussed separately but it is important here to mention some of the common points between them. The aim of all the evidences is to provide the necessary information for the servants of God about their responsibilities. It is for this reason that God sent His Messenger, Muhammad, peace and blessings be upon him, to guide humanity by explaining to them their duties. Similarly, the common mission for all the sources of Islamic jurisprudence is to define the nature of human responsibility.

The commonalities between the evidences include:

First, the evidences are divided into two categories in Islamic law; *shar'ī* (religion based) and *'aqlī* (reason based). The *shar'ī* evidences are those which are achieved through the authentic reports without any involvement by the jurist. For example, the definite rulings from the Qur'an, Sunnah and *ijma'* are found ready by the *mujtahids* and they are separate from their works. The case is the same for *'urf* (custom), *shar'u man qablanā* (the law of previous nations) and the fatwa of the Companions, because they are known through the reports and the *mujtahids* does not have a role in their derivation.

On the other hand, *aqlī* (reason-based) evidences are achieved through the work of the *mujtahids*. For example *qiyāṣ* (analogy), *masālih mursala* (the public benefits) and *istiḥsān* (juristic preference) are evidences which are achieved through the work of *mujtahids*. In this classification, the criteria is their origin and their nature, therefore they are classified as *shar'ī* and *'aqlī* evidences. However, from the perspective of extracting the rulings and utilizing the sources of Islamic law, each category needs the work of the *mujtahids* because there is a need to use reason and logic to extract the rulings from their sources regardless of the nature of the evidences themselves.

Ruling by reason is only permissible if it depends on divine sources and the general principles which are extracted from them. In other words, human intellect alone is not the source of Islamic jurisprudence but it works according to the objectives of the Qur'an and Sunnah.

The second commonality between the evidences is that the *shar'ī* evidences do not contradict reason and logic. If there is a contradiction, it is because of one of the following;

1) The evidence may not be authentic
2) The evidence may not be understood as intended by the Shāri (Lawgiver-God)
3) The reason might be afflicted by mental diseases, or the person uses his reason according to his whims, personal desires and corrupt ideas.

The reason behind this principle is: 'The *shar'ī* evidences do not contradict sound logic.' God revealed His message to the Prophets and guided humankind through them so they can investigate if these verses are true. If people cannot understand the revelation or see the truth in it, there is no wisdom in holding them responsible through these evidences. For this reason, children and those who are mentally incapacitated are not deemed religiously liable in Islamic law because they do not have the capacity to be responsible. If the evidences were contrary to reason, human beings would not accept them and would not be able to carry out their duties. If it was the case, there would not be any wisdom in sending Prophets and informing people about their responsibilities. All would be in vain, but God is free from meaningless acts.

The third commonality between the evidences is that the *shar'ī* evidences are known as the primary sources of Islamic law and some of them are independent sources such as the Qur'an, Sunnah and *ijma.' Masālih mursala* (the public benefits), *istiḥsān* (juristic preference), *istiṣḥāb* (presumption of continuity), *'urf* (custom), *shar'u man qablanā* (the law of previous nations) and the fatwa of the Companions are extracted from the Qur'an and Sunnah and can be included in the *shar'ī* evidences. In Islamic law, *qiyāṣ* (analogy) is not considered a source on its own. The first sources of evidence (the Qur'an, Sunnah and *ijma'*) are independent sources, because they do not need to refer to any other sources when making a ruling, however *qiyāṣ* relies on the primary sources. It also requires requisite knowledge of the original case (*asl*), the underlying reason (*'illah*) behind the ruling in that case and the information regarding why the rulings were issued. As a result, *qiyāṣ* is not an independent source, rather it is evidence that shows that the Qur'an, Sunnah and *ijma'* include the ruling of the new case as well. For this reason, the scholars said that '*qiyāṣ* discovers the ruling but it does not create a new one.' The following examples clarify this statement:

a) God prohibited all kinds of business at the time of the Friday Prayer with the following verse:

> O you who believe! When the call is made for the Prayer on Friday, then move promptly to the remembrance of God (by listening to the sermon and doing the Prayer), and leave off business (and whatever else you may be preoccupied with). This is better for you, if you but knew.[25]

Ḥanafī jurists understood from this verse that it is disliked to perform business during the time of the Friday Prayer. According to the majority, it is forbidden (*haram*). The underlying reason for the prohibition of business during the time of the Friday Prayer is that it averts people from the performance of the Prayer. The jurists analogized the other things which avert from the performance of the Friday Prayer to this verse and gave the same ruling (prohibition) to them. If there wasn't an original ruling (*asl*) about business during the time of Friday Prayer and the underlying reason (*'illah*) for this ruling was unknown, the ruling of the original case could not be passed on to the new case (*far'*) through analogy (*qiyāṣ*). Through the use of analogy it can be discovered that the new case is also included in the ruling of the original case, because both have the same underlying reason, therefore we can determine that whatever prevents liable Muslims from performing the Friday Prayer is also included in the ruling for this verse.

b) The noble Prophet said; "The murderer cannot be heir (to the one whom he killed)."[26] Using this hadith as evidence, the Muslim jurists ruled that a murderer could not be heir to the one whom he murdered. The underlying reason for this rule is that the murderer wanted to gain rights to the inheritance before its proper time and used an illegal avenue to attain this purpose. As such, deprivation of the inheritance is a punishment for his illicit conduct. The jurists analogized the case 'a bequeathed one kills the one who bequeaths' comparing it to the previous case and issued the same ruling for it, because both cases have the same underlying reason. The jurists are able to pass on the ruling from the original case to the new case and judge so as to deprive the murderer from the inheritance. The ruling for the new case is not created by *qiyāṣ*; it is discovered because the ruling of the original case includes the new case as well. The *mujtahid* looks at the ruling for the original case first and learns the underlying reason behind this ruling. After that he compares the new case to the old one and, if they share an identical underlying reason, he passes the same ruling on to the new case

---

25 Qur'ān, 62: 9.

26 Ibn Majah, *Sunan, Farāiz (the inheritance)*, 2735.

through *qiyāṣ*. Without the original case and it's ruling, *qiyāṣ* is impossible; therefore the mission of *qiyāṣ* is discovering the scope of the ruling of the original case.

Based on the previous evaluations it could be argued that *ijma'* is prevented from being an independent source for the same reason that prevents *qiyāṣ*. The scholars of *Uṣūl al-Fiqh* state that the Qur'an and Sunnah are necessary for the *mujtahids* in order to come to a general consensus on a ruling. At this point, the following question is raised; 'should not *ijma'* be accepted as a dependant source of Islamic jurisprudence rather than independent one?' The answer relates to the two-step process of *ijma.'*

The first step is the occurrence and actualizing of *ijma'* and the second step is using the *ijma'* as evidence for other cases. *Ijma'* is only dependent on the other sources in the step of actualizing but it does not need them when it is used as evidence for new cases. If *ijma'* is valid and is already established through authentic methods, there is no need to mention the whole process of *ijma'* when it is used as evidence for another case. In other words, if a *mujtahid* says, 'The evidence for this ruling is such and such *ijma'*, and it is known that the *ijma'* is real in that matter, it is permissible to make a new ruling based on this *ijma.'* However, this is not the case for *qiyāṣ*. In both steps of *qiyāṣ*, its occurrence and its use as evidence, there is a need to mention the underlying reason (*'illah*) for which the ruling is made. A *mujtahid* cannot say 'The evidence for this ruling is such and such analogy', this is not sufficient to make a new ruling. He has to mention the ruling of the original case as found in the Qur'an, Sunnah or *ijma'* and the underlying reason (*'illah*) of a ruling.

In conclusion, *qiyāṣ* depends on the other sources and an explanation of its process when it is used as evidence for other cases, but *ijma'* does not depend on them in its use as evidence for new cases (in the second step). For this reason, *qiyāṣ* is accepted as a dependent source of Islamic law.

Summary: General Information about the Evidences

1. The aim of all the evidences is to provide the necessary information for the servants of God about their responsibilities.
2. The evidences are divided into two categories in Islamic law; *sharʿī* evidences are those which are achieved through the authentic reports without any involvement by the jurist; *aqlī* evidences are achieved through the work of the *mujtahids.*
3. *Sharʿī* evidences do not contradict reason and logic.

4. *Sharʿī* evidences are known as the primary sources of Islamic law and some of them are independent sources such as the Qur'an, Sunnah and *ijma.'*
5. *Masālih mursala* (the public benefits), *istiḥsān* (juristic preference), *istiṣḥāb* (presumption of continuity), *'urf* (custom), *shar'u man qablanā* (the law of previous nations) and the fatwa of the Companions are extracted from the Qur'an and Sunnah and can be included in the *sharʿī* evidences.
6. *Qiyāṣ* (analogy) is not considered a source on its own because it relies on the primary sources and requires knowledge of the original case and rulings and the reason for the rulings.
7. *Ijma'* is only dependent on the other sources in the step of actualizing but it does not need them when it is used as evidence for new cases. If *ijma'* is real and is already established through authentic methods, there is no need to mention the whole process of *ijma'* when it is used as evidence for another case.

Chapter Two

Kitāb (The Qur'an)

Kitāb (The Qur'an)

Definition of the *Kitāb*

The *Kitāb* (Qur'an) is already very well-known and does not need definition as such; however, it was necessary for the scholars of *uṣūl* to define it to identify important issues pertaining to belief, worship and Islamic law. For example, they needed to understand what makes a person an unbeliever when they deny it and what does not, what parts of it can be recited in the Daily Prayers and what can be used as a source to extract rulings in Islamic law. Their aim was to separate the Qur'an from the hadith (the traditions of the Prophet) and the *mutawātir* readings of the Qur'an from the other readings.

According to the majority of scholars, the word 'Qur'an' is an infinitive form of the verb *'qa-ra-a'* meaning reading or reciting. Therefore, it literally means a thing recited by adding letters and words to one another. The verb *'qa-ra-a'* has another infinitive form, '*qar'u*', which means 'to collect' and, based on this form, some scholars are of the opinion that 'Qur'an' means 'the thing which collects.' Moreover, there are other scholars who affirm that the word 'Qur'an' was not derived from any word; it is the proper name given to the book which God sent to His last Messenger.[27] The Qur'an has other titles, each of which describes one of its aspects and therefore can be regarded as one of its attributes; these include the Book, the Criterion, the Remembrance, the Advice, the Light, the Guidance, the Healer, the Noble, the Mother of the Book, the Truth, the Admonishment, the Good Tiding, the Book Gradually Revealed, the Knowledge and the Clear.

We can define the Qur'an as being a book which was sent by God to Prophet Muhammad, peace and blessings be upon him, by means of the angel Gabriel over the course of 23 years. On receiving a verse, the Prophet would order it to be written by scribes as he recited. These scribes collectively wrote every single revealed verse of the Qur'an. It was transmitted by the most authentic narrations (*mutawātir*) and has been preserved up until the present day without any alteration. It is considered by Muslims as the direct speech of God which has multi-

[27] Rāghib al-Isfahānī, *Mufradaat*, p. 402.

ple aspects and its recitation is considered worship in Islam. The Qur'an describes itself as follows:

> Alif. Lam. Mim. This is the (most honoured, matchless) Book: there is no doubt about it (its Divine authorship and that it is a collection of pure truths throughout). It is a guidance for the God-revering, pious who keeps their duty to God.[28]

The noble Prophet used the following words to describe the Qur'an:

> The superiority of the Qur'an over all other words and speeches is like God's superiority over His creatures. The Qur'an is a definite decree distinguishing between the truth and falsehood. It is not for pastime. Whoever rejects it because of his or her despotism, God breaks his or her neck. It contains the history of previous peoples, the tiding of those to come after you, and the judgment on the disagreements among you. Whoever searches for guidance in something other than it, God leads him or her astray. It is God's strong rope. It is the wise instruction. It is the Straight Path. It is a book which desires cannot deviate and tongues cannot confuse, and which scholars are not fed up with, never worn-out by repetition, and has uncountable admirable aspects. It is such a book that they could not help but say: "We have indeed heard a wonderful Qur'an, guiding to what is right in belief and action and so we have believed in it." Whoever speaks based on it speaks truth; whoever judges by it judges justly and whoever calls to it calls to truth.[29]

Prophet Muhammad, peace and blessings be upon him, received the first revelation when he was forty years old in 610 C.E. The following verse makes it clear that this event occurred during the holy month of Ramadan: "*The month of Ramadan, in which the Qur'an was sent down as guidance for people and as clear signs of Guidance and the Criterion (between truth and falsehood*)."[30] Over a period of just 23 years, the Qur'an instructed the polytheist people of the Arabian Peninsula the belief in *tawḫīd* (the unity of God) and saved them from their deviated pagan practices. As well as being the holy book of Muslims, the Qur'an also represents the finest example of Arab literature. Within its pages, the Qur'an itself proves the authenticity of the Prophethood of Muhammad, peace and blessings

28 Qur'ān, 2: 1–2.
29 Tirmidhi, *Sunan, Thawab al-Qur'ān*, 14.
30 Qur'ān, 2: 185.

be upon him: *"If humanity and jinn banded together to produce the like of this Qur'an, they would never produce its like, even though they backed one another."*[31]

Regarding its style, parables, eloquence, information about the sciences, descriptions of the attributes, the qualities and names of God, guidance, knowledge of the unseen world and many other topics, the Qur'an is not comparable to any other existing work on earth. Bediüzzaman Said Nursi phrases this reality as follows:

> The Qur'an is an eternal translation of the great Book of the Universe and everlasting translator of it multifarious tongues reciting the Divine laws of the universe's creation and operation; the interpreter of the books of the visible, material world and the World of the Unseen; the discloser of the immaterial treasuries of the Divine Names hidden on the earth and in the heavens; the key to the truths lying behind events; the World of the Unseen's tongue in the visible, material one; the treasury of the All-Merciful One's favours and the All-Glorified One's eternal addresses coming from the World of the Unseen beyond the veil of this visible world; the sun of Islam's spiritual and intellectual world, as well as its foundation and plan; the sacred map of the worlds of the Hereafter; the expounder, lucid interpreter, articulate proof, and clear translator of the Divine Essence, Attributes, Names and essential Qualities; the educator and trainer of the world of humanity and the water and light of Islam, which is the true and greatest humanity; and the true guide of humanity leading them to happiness. For humanity, it is both a book of law, and a book of prayer, and a book of wisdom, and a book of worship and servanthood to God, and a book of command and call to God, and a book of invocation, and a book of thought and reflection. It is a comprehensive, holy book containing books for all spiritual needs of humanity; a heavenly book that, like a sacred library, offers numerous booklets from which all saints, eminently truthful people, all discerning and verifying scholars, and those well-versed in knowledge of God have derived their own specific ways, and which illuminate each way and answer their followers' needs.[32]

SUMMARY: DEFINITION OF THE *KITĀB*

1. Scholars of *uṣūl* defined the Qur'an to identify important issues pertaining to belief, worship and Islamic law.
2. Their aim was to separate the Qur'an from the hadith and the *mutawātir* readings of the Qur'an from the other readings.

---

[31] Qur'ān, 17: 88.

[32] Nursi, *The Words, The Twenty-fifth Word*, p. 388.

3. The word 'Qur'an' is derived from the infinitive *'qa-ra-a'* meaning reading or reciting. The verb *'qa-ra-a'* has another infinitive form, *'qar'u'*, which means 'to collect.' Other scholars affirm that 'Qur'an' is a proper name only used for this divine book.
4. The Qur'an is a book revealed through spoken revelation from God to Prophet Muhammad, peace and blessings be upon him, by means of the angel Gabriel over 23 years.
5. It is considered by Muslims as the direct speech of God which has multiple aspects and its recitation is considered worship in Islam.
6. The revelation began during Ramadan in the year 610 C.E. when the noble Prophet was 40.
7. The Qur'an is not comparable to any other existing work in its style, eloquence, content, guidance and knowledge.

The Specifications of the *Kitāb* (The Qur'an)

The Qur'an is clearly different from the hadith of the Prophet and also stands out from the previous religious scriptures. It has its own unique aspects, outstanding qualities and distinguishing features.

The Qur'an is unique compared with all the other revealed books with regard to the time it was revealed, its effectiveness on the people of that time, its style, language and transmission. God blessed His Prophets with miracles that were the most suitable for their time and place. He gave the miracles of the staff and the bright hand to Moses, peace be upon him, whereas to Jesus, peace be upon him, he gave the ability to heal sick people and raise the dead. In 7th Century Arabia, eloquence was a most highly prized skill due to the illiteracy of the majority of the population, so God made the Qur'an the chief miracle of Prophet Muhammad, peace and blessings be upon him. Arabs preserved their tribal pride, history and proverbs in the form of poetry, thus it held a high rank in society alongside the poets who wrote and memorized it. Eloquence was extremely important; any meaningful or unique expressions were memorized for their poetic form and eloquence and handed down to posterity. Eloquence and fluency were in such great demand that a tribe treated its eloquent literary figures as national heroes. This articulacy was so esteemed that two tribes would sometimes go to war over a saying of a literary figure and then be reconciled by the words of another. They even inscribed in gold the odes of seven poets and hung them on the walls of the Ka'ba; they were called the 'Seven Suspended Poems.' With the revelation of the Qur'an came a challenge to these literary figures of Arabia: "*If you doubt what We have sent down on Our servant, produce a surah like it."*[33] It defeated and humbled all of them as no one was able to produce even a sentence of the same literary level as the Qur'an.

One of the unique attributes of the Qur'an it its ability to speak to all levels of people, from the layman to the profound sage, at the same time. This ensures its timelessness and universality. Without ignoring or causing injustice to anyone, the Qur'an addresses different people with different intellectual capacities simultaneously as it is a guide for everyone and the speech of God. The aim of the Qur'an is to guide all people to the truth. It has four main purposes; to demonstrate the existence and unity of God, to establish Prophethood, to prove and elucidate the afterlife with all its aspects and dimensions and to promulgate the worship of God and the essentials of justice. The verses of the Qur'an are mainly based on these themes. They deal with the principles of creed, the rules to govern human life, detailed information on the resurrection and afterlife, prescript for the worship of God, moral standards, direct or indirect information on some scientific facts, principles for the formation and decay of civilizations, outlines of the histories of many previous peoples, and so on. Additionally, the Qur'an is also a source of healing. Its application in life provides a cure for almost all psychological and social illnesses. It is also book of cosmology, epistemology, ontology, sociology, psychology, and law. As a book for all peoples for all of time, it was revealed to regulate human life on earth and is not limited to any time, place or people. It is both universal and timeless.[34]

The most distinguished miracle of the Qur'an is in its letters, words and verses. Using the Arabic alphabet, the Qur'an brings together letters to form words, verses and *surah* (chapters). Despite the seemingly easy task of imitating the Qur'an, even the most eloquent Arabs in all of history such as Walid, Labīd, Ā'shā and Ka'b ibn Zuhayr were unable to produce even similar words, let alone similar chapters, attesting to its impossibility. The Qur'an was sent to an unlettered Prophet; *"You did not recite before it any scripture, nor did you inscribe one with your right hand. Otherwise the falsifiers would have had cause for doubt."*[35]

Despite their lack of belief in the Qur'an, the polytheist leaders in Mecca could not resist listening to its recitation. They would visit the Ka'ba and secretly listen to the Prophet reciting the verses during his Prayers. On one particular occasion, 'Umar ibn al-Khattāb was equipped to kill the Prophet yet upon hear-

[33] Qur'ān, 2:23.

[34] Ali Ünal, The Qur'ān with Annotated Interpretation, foreword.

[35] Qur'ān, 29: 48.

ing the recitation from Surah Ta-ha, his heart was illuminated with the words of the Qur'an and he consequentially converted to Islam. 'Utba ibn Rabia set out to the Prophet's house with the sole purpose of defeating the Prophet in a debate. The noble Prophet listened silently to all of 'Utba's arguments. When he had finished, the Prophet recited the first 13 verses of Surah Fussilat. 'Utba listened in shock and awe. When he returned to his friends who were awaiting news of the outcome of the debate, 'Utba responded: 'I have listened to such words from him that I have never heard before. This is neither poetry, nor magic, nor the words of soothsayers. It is not like any of these. O Quraysh! Pay attention and listen to me, leave him alone. If he cannot be successful the Arabs will destroy him, but if he is successful, his success is your success.[36]

Once Tufayl ibn Amir went to Mecca and was told by the polytheist leaders: 'O Tufayl, you've come to our land, where people who listen to Muhammad are separating from us. Our unity is being dissolved because of him. His words are very effective, like magic which separate the man from his father, his brother and even his wife. We are worried about you and your tribe. Be careful and never listen to him.' Tufayl was alarmed by their warnings and whenever he went to the Ka'ba, he wouldn't listen to Muhammad, peace and blessings be upon him. He would even cover his ears so as to not hear the words of the Prophet. One day he said to himself, 'I am in false belief, what is the harm of listening to his words? If the words are true, I have the capacity to understand it.' After listening to the Qur'an, he converted to Islam. He was the first Muslim guide in his tribe.[37]

The eloquence of the Qur'an was such that sometimes one verse was enough for people to understand and appreciate its value. When Sa'sa the uncle of Farazdaq heard the following verse; "So whoever does an atom's weight of good will see it, and whoever does an atom's weight of evil will see it" he said, 'It is enough for me' and he became Muslim.[38] The Qur'an enabled the Arabs to achieve deep levels of understanding, for example, when Asma'i heard a nice poem from a girl who lived in a village, he said 'What a beautiful poem, how eloquent it is.' Thereupon the girl said, 'What a bad man you are, my words are not more eloquent than this verse; "*We inspired to the mother of Moses, 'Suckle him; but when you fear for him, cast him into the river and do not fear and do not grieve. Indeed, We*

---

36 Ibn Hishām, *as-Sīrah an-Nabawiyya*, 1/294.

37 Ibn Hishām, *as-Sīrah an-Nabawiyya*, 1/382.

38 Qurtubī, *al-Jāmi al-Aḥkām al-Qur'ān*, 20/153.

will return him to you and will make him one of the Messengers."[39] *This verse contains two commands, two prohibitions and two good tidings.'*[40]

Summary: The Specifications of the *Kitāb*

1. The Qur'an is unique. It is the main miracle given to Prophet Muhammad, peace and blessings be upon him, to prove his Prophethood.
2. One of the miracles of the Qur'an it in its eloquence, a highly prized attribute in 7th Century Arabia. The Qur'an challenged the unbelievers to produce even a verse comparable to it but this challenge has never been met.
3. The Qur'an speaks to all people of all levels of knowledge at the same time, without causing any injustice to anyone. It is timeless and universal.
4. The aim of the Qur'an is to guide all people to the truth.
5. The Qur'an has four main purposes; to demonstrate the existence and unity of God, to establish Prophethood, to prove and elucidate the afterlife with all its aspects and dimensions and to promulgate the worship of God and the essentials of justice.
6. The Qur'an is also a source of healing. Its application in life provides a cure for almost all psychological and social illnesses.
7. The most distinguished miracle of the Qur'an is in its letters, words and verses. Just listening to it could cause people to convert to Islam.

The General Features of the Qur'an

As opposed to the other religious scriptures, the Qur'an was revealed in pure Arabic and is not considered to be the Qur'an in any other language. Other scriptures were translated into different languages, and subsequently re-translated, thus losing meaning and content in the process. In Islam, the result of the translation of the Qur'an is not changed if the translation is literal[41] or in meaning.[42]

---

39 Qur'ān, 28: 7.

40 Qurtubī, *al-Jāmi al-Aḫkām al-Qur'ān*, 13/252.

41 Literal translation; the purpose of this translation is to compromise the words, structure and their meanings in both languages. In this translation, an attempt is made to translate the text exactly into another language by finding equal expressions in the other language and replacing the original words with them. This type of translation is difficult as it generally found that the translator cannot find words of equal weight in another language to translate the meaning inferred by the original text.

42 Translation in meaning; in this translation the purpose is not to compromise the words, structure and meanings in both languages. The most important aim in this type of translation is to express the meaning of the original text with words close to or similar in meaning. This type

It is not permissible for the *mujtahid* to make rulings based on a translation of the Qur'an because a translation may not reflect the exact intended meaning and may also contain mistakes. Similarly, the recitations in the prescribed Daily Prayers must be in Arabic or the Prayer is invalidated. Every liable Muslim must learn in Arabic at least the minimum amount of the Qur'an that is necessary for the performance of the Prayers.

The creative style of the Qur'an, rich in the arts, is one of the elements of its unique eloquence. It frequently speaks in parables and adopts a figurative, symbolic rhetoric using metaphors and similes. This natural way of expression conveys knowledge of everything and at the same time addresses people of all levels of understanding and knowledge. Anyone who has encountered or attempted to learn a foreign language is witness that a language is not merely a set of moulds made up of letters and words. Language is intrinsically linked with the history, religion and culture of a nation, the character of the people and the land to which it is tied. It is almost impossible for any word used in a language to have an exact counterpart in another language. Another difficulty in translating the Qur'an directly is being able to match the grammatical structure and the richness of the text. Arabic is a strictly grammatical language and the richest language in the world with regards to its conjugation and derivation. For example, there are three different types of infinitive in Arabic and each verb has 35 different forms, each with a different connotation and implication.[43] It is impossible to match this with a direct word for word translation into any other existing language.

The words and meanings of the Qur'an were revealed by God to the noble Prophet and his mission was to convey and explain it to the people. This is different to the hadith (sayings of the Prophet), which were also divinely inspired, and therefore a different form of *waḫy* (revelation), but were conveyed in his own words.[44] The Qur'an itself is the direct word of God and is on a different level than the hadith.

The Qur'an is manifest revelation (*waḫy ẕāhir*), which is defined as the very word of God, communicated via the angel Gabriel to Prophet Muhammad, peace and blessings be upon him. The hadith are internal revelation, (*waḫy bātin*), which means the inspiration (*ilhām*) of concepts only. With this type of revelation, God

---

of translation is not exact translation as the translator finds ways to give the meaning to the original text in another language, and as such doesn't search for exact words or structures.

43 Ali Ünal, *The Qur'ān with Annotated Interpretation, Foreword.*

44 The meaning from God, but the wording belongs to the Prophet.

inspired the noble Prophet and he in turn conveyed the concepts in his own words.[45] Therefore, no hadith may be ranked as on an equal footing with the Qur'an. The Prayers cannot be performed by reciting hadith, nor is the recitation of hadith considered as of the same spiritual merit as the recitation of the Qur'an.[46]

When attempting to understand the Qur'an, the first step is to understand its language; this is to the text what bodily features are to a human being. The essential essence of the text lies in its meaning, just as the essence of a human being lies in his spirit. The bodily features of a human being are the externalised form of this spirit and serve as a window or mirror in which to see his character. In the same way, the language and style of the Qur'an reflect its meaning and cannot be separated from it. It is due to its miraculous eloquence that the Qur'an has such depth and richness of meaning.

The Qur'an was transmitted by the most authentic narrations (*mutawātir*) and has been preserved until the present day without a single change. It has been retained both in memory and in written record throughout the generations. The definition of *mutawātir* is something reported without alteration by a large number of people from each generation in such a way as to prevent the possibility of their collusion to propagate a lie.[47] Such a possibility is impossible due to their large numbers, diversity of residence and proven reliability. The authenticity of the report is proven by universally accepted testimony.

Each generation after the Prophet preserved the Qur'an with the same enthusiasm and transmitted it to the next generation without changing a single word, therefore it provides binding knowledge and ensures every verse is *qat'ī* (definite). The personal *Muṣḥāf* (copies/readings of the Qur'an) of the Companions are not considered to be the authentic Qur'an, because they have not been transmitted to us through reliable reports. For example, the variant readings of some words in a few verses attributed to 'Abdullah ibn Mas'ud are not established by *mutawātir* narration and therefore are not part of the Qur'an. In the context of atonement (*kaffārah*) of a false oath, the standard copy of the Qur'an shows this to be three days of fasting whereas Ibn Mas'ud's copy shows it to be three consecutive days of fasting. Since the additional element (i.e. consecutive) in the relevant verse in surah Ma'idah (5:92) is not established by *mutawātir*, it is not part of the Qur'an and is therefore of no effect. A Prayer is not valid if one of these

---

45 Hashim Kamali, *Principles of Islamic Jurisprudence*, p. 23.

46 Abū Zahrah, *Uṣūl al-Fiqh*, p. 59.

47 Shawkānī, *Irshād al-Fuhūl*, p. 46; Abū Zahrah, *Uṣūl al-Fiqh*, p. 84.

Muṣḫāf is used for the recitation, and unlike denying the Qur'an, denying the personal *Muṣḫāf* does not make one an unbeliever.

Summary: The General Features of the Qur'an

1. The Qur'an was revealed in Arabic and is not considered the Qur'an in any other form.
2. It is not permissible for the *mujtahid* to make rulings based on a translation of the Qur'an.
3. Every liable Muslim must learn at least the minimum amount of the Qur'an in Arabic necessary for the performance of the Prayers.
4. The creative style of the Qur'an, rich in the arts, is one of the elements of its unique eloquence which enables it to address all levels of understanding and knowledge.
5. It is impossible to translate the Qur'an word for word without losing meaning, especially due to the grammatical structure and richness of the text.
6. The Qur'an is the direct word of God to the noble Prophet through revelation and is different from the hadith which were divinely inspired and conveyed in the Prophet's own words. Therefore, the Qur'an holds the highest spiritual merit.
7. The Qur'an was transmitted by the most authentic narrations (*mutawātir*) and has been preserved until the present day without a single change.

The Dispute over Personal Copies of the Qur'an

Scholars agree that personal copies of the Qur'an that are not transmitted as *mutawātir* are not considered part of the Qur'an. They differ however, in their views as to whether they can be used as evidence for extracting the rulings in Islamic law. Ḫanafī scholars accept them as a source of evidence in the same way that they accept the hadith of the Prophet because both the personal copies and the hadith were transmitted by the Companions. On the other hand, Hanbalī, Maliki and some Shāfi'ī scholars do not accept the personal copies as evidence. Ḫanafī scholars hold that the Companions marked their *Muṣḫāf* with non-*mutawātir* readings of the Qur'an as a result of hearing this from the noble Prophet or as a result of their own personal *ijtihād*. The former reason is more likely as the Companions are accepted as just and trustworthy by all scholars and are unlikely to have written anything they hadn't heard directly from the

Prophet himself. As they were not transmitted as *mutawātir,* the strongest possibility is that they were explanations of the Qur'an by the Prophet and are therefore, evidence of Sunnah. Sunnah is not disputed as a source of evidence on which to base Islamic rulings, therefore, the personal *Muṣḥāf* can be used by the *mujtahid.* The most important criterion when transmitting hadith was not for the Companions to mention whether they were transmitting Sunnah, but whether the report was from the Prophet. This is the same for *mutawātir* and non-*mutawātir* hadith reports and so all the *mujtahid* used them as evidence in their *ijtihād.*

The practical result of this dispute is that Ḥanafī scholars stipulated three consecutive days of fasting as atonement (*kaffārah*) for a false oath based on the *Muṣḥāf* of 'Abdullah ibn Mas'ud. Other jurists and those who share their opinion however, do not take this reading into consideration and they do not apply this condition in their ruling; rather the person can fast three days at different times as atonement.

SUMMARY: THE DISPUTE OVER VARIANT READINGS OF THE QUR'AN

1. Scholars agree that personal copies of the Qur'an which are not transmitted as *mutawātir* are not considered part of the Qur'an.
2. Scholars differ in opinion as to whether personal copies can be used as evidence for extracting the rulings in Islamic law.
3. Ḥanafī scholars accept them because they were transmitted by the Companions.
4. Hanbalī, Maliki and some Shāfi'ī scholars do not accept them as evidence.

The Stages of Revelation

Muslim scholars generally classify the revelation of the Qur'an in three stages; the recording of the divine plan on a Preserved Tablet; *inzāl* (to descend), the descent of the Tablet to the lower realms of the Heavens; and *tanzīl* (to send down), the revelation in stages over 23 years.

> Indeed it is a glorious Qur'an (a sublime Book revealed and recited), in a Preserved Tablet (guarded from every accursed devil, and secure from any falsehood).[48]

This verse describes the first stage of revelation. God wrote on a Preserved Tablet the divine project for the whole of creation, events and destiny. He then

[48] Qur'ān, 85: 21–22.

created, and continues to create, according to this record which never changes. It determines everything that will happen in the creation of the Heavens and Earth until the end of time. The noble Prophet said:

> The first thing that God created was the Pen. He said to it: write, it responded, 'O my Lord! And what shall I write? God said: write the destiny of all things, until the Day of Judgement.[49]

The second stage (*inzāl*-to descend) is when the Preserved Tablet is sent down complete from the upper heavens to the abode of glory, or lower heaven, (from *lawḫ al-maḫfūz* to *bayt al-'izzah*). The Qur'an mentions that the revelation began during the month of Ramadan:

> The month of Ramadan, in which the Qur'an was sent down as guidance for people and as clear signs of Guidance and the Criterion (between truth and falsehood).[50]

> We have surely sent it (the Qur'an) down in the Night of Destiny and Power.[51]

The second verse references angel Gabriel hearing and understanding the revelation and revealing what he heard. He descended with the revelation from a higher place (the upper heavens) to a lower place (*bayt al-'izzah*).

The Prophet said:

> Whenever God desires to inspire a matter (to His servants), He speaks with the inspiration, and (because of this) the heavens themselves shake out of fear of God. When the people of the Heaven (i.e., the angels) hear of it, they fall down in a swoon and prostrate to Him. The first one to raise his head is Gabriel and God speaks to him with the inspiration that He wishes. Then Gabriel passes by the angels; whenever he goes by any heaven, the angels of that heaven ask him 'What did our Lord say, O Gabriel?' He answers, 'He has spoken the truth, and He is the Most High, the Most Great.'[52]

The final stage (*tanzīl*), referred to by many verses of the Qur'an, is the revelation being sent down from the heavens to earth during the 23 years of Muhammad's Prophethood as displayed in the following verse:

---

49 Tirmidhi, *Sunan, the Destiny*, 94.
50 Qur'ān, 2: 185.
51 Qur'ān, 97: 1.
52 Bukhari, *Saḫīḫ, Kitāb at-Tawḫīd*, 14.

This (Qur'an) is indeed the Book of the Lord of the world's being sent down by Him (in parts). The Trustworthy Spirit brings it down on your heart, so that you may be one of the warners (entrusted with the Divine Revelation), in clear 'Arabic tongue.'[53]

SUMMARY: THE STAGES OF REVELATION

1. Scholars classify the revelation in three stages: the recording of the divine plan on a Preserved Tablet, The descent (*inzāl*) of that Tablet to the lower Heavens and the sending down (*tanzīl*) through revelation over 23 years.

The Wisdom behind the Gradual Revelation of the Qur'an

The revelation of the Qur'an occurred over a period of 23 years rather than as a complete book in one act of revelation. There are many reasons for this showing the wisdom behind this method, the most significant of which are listed here.

1) The gradual revelation of the verses served to strengthen the heart of the Prophet who faced many difficulties and suffered severe persecution. The revelation was a constant source of support to both him and the early believers and gave them guidance whenever the need arose.

2) Revelation itself was a difficult and demanding experience for the Prophet. To support him God mentioned the stories of past nations and Prophets, showing Prophet Muhammad, peace and blessings be upon him, that he was not alone on this path. He gave the message that He always helped the Messengers and did not leave them alone. He informed the noble Prophet of his impending success.

3) On a practical level, the revelation of the Qur'an in stages allowed for the gradual implementation of the new laws and way of life. It was necessary for the Muslims to have time to adapt to the new rules and rid themselves of old beliefs, customs and bad habits. The prohibition of alcohol, for example, happened in four stages after many years of Prophethood. The fact that human nature needs time to change was taken into consideration.

4) In order to both understand and memorize the verses easily, the Companions would learn ten verses at a time, memorize them and apply them in their everyday life. The revelation in stages ensured a firm grounding in the new faith and practises and a deep knowledge and understanding in the followers.

---

[53] Qur'ān, 26: 195–195.

Summary: The Wisdom behind the Gradual Revelation of the Qur'an

1. To strengthen the heart of the noble Prophet against the difficulties he encountered.
2. To support the Prophet with anecdotes of Prophets who had undergone the same suffering and to assure him of future success.
3. To allow for a gradual implementation of the new laws and way of life.
4. To ensure a firm grounding of the new faith by helping the followers both memorise the verses and deepen their knowledge.

Transmission of the Qur'an

The main mission of Prophet Muhammad, peace and blessings be upon him, was to convey the revelation to people and preserve it from change. To fulfil this mission he employed strict procedures. After memorizing the verses from the angel Gabriel, he would teach them to his Companions and encourage them to repeat and memorize them.[54] The Companions were eager to memorize the verses and read them throughout their days and nights. However, the Prophet did not think their enthusiasm alone was enough to preserve the Qur'an so whenever he received a revelation he ordered scribes to write it down. On completion, he would listen to the verses being read and would correct any mistakes, thus protecting the Qur'an from any kind of change. Zayd ibn Thabit reports:

> The Prophet ordered me to write the verses and when I finished writing, he would order me to read what I had written. If I skipped or mispronounced any word, the Prophet would correct them. After this process I would inform the Muslims about the new verses.[55]

Additionally, the Prophet ordered copies to be made. These were taken by the Muslims who would disseminate them for more people to memorize. Those who could write would copy the verses for their own personal usage. The original copy was returned to the Prophet for safekeeping in his home.[56] Through this method, the Qur'an was transmitted untainted by multiple people both orally and in written form.

---

54 Bukhari, *Fadāil al-Qur'ān*, 20, Ahmad ibn Hanbal, *Musnad*, 6/66.

55 Haythamī, *Majma' az-Zawā'īd*, 8/257.

56 Zarqānī , *Manāhil*, 1/247.

The Qur'an was transmitted and completed in the form we know today in three stages. Firstly it was collected during the life of the noble Prophet. It was collected for a second time during Abu Bakr's reign and again during the caliphate of 'Uthman.[57] During the Prophet's lifetime, it was impossible to collect the Qur'an into one single book as the revelation continued up until his death. However, it was preserved in his memory first and checked each year by the angel Gabriel during Ramadan and twice in his last year of life. By the time of his death, the whole Qur'an was memorized by multiple Companions and preserved on uncollated written materials.

Many reasons compelled Abu Bakr to collect the Qur'an into one single book during his caliphate. During his life, the Prophet was the assurance for the Muslims in all their affairs, including the protection of the Qur'an. No one else could possess this quality and with his death came a need to protect the Qur'an in another way. The scattered pieces of writing were collated and placed in order in book form. This gave the Muslims insurance and enabled them to unite under the authority of the Qur'an.[58]

Abu Bakr recognised the need to produce one official copy (*Imam Muṣḥ̮āf*) of the Qur'an which would be used as the authority under which all Muslims could unite. He could have collated this from the pieces of script that the scribes had produced under the dictation of the Prophet but the possibility of inaccuracies or variations between them made him deem this insufficient. Additionally, the existence of personal copies enhanced this danger and Abu Bakr feared that disputes would arise due to these differences. The fact that certain verses were only in the possession of a limited number of scribes and could be lost forever if not collected was at the forefront of his mind. In addition, there was the issue of verses which had been abrogated which would no longer be included in the Qur'an. Knowledge of these was limited and it was necessary to inform those who did not know the true text of the Qur'an. Abu Bakr established a committee to produce one official *Imam Muṣḥ̮āf.* This would be used as the authority and all personal copies would be corrected accordingly to prevent conflict. Zayd ibn Thabit was given the weighty responsibility of collecting the Qur'an and he did so by employing meticulous and scrupulous methodologies. Rather than relying on the memories of the Companions or written papers alone, he accredited both the papers which were written in the presence of the Prophet and the memories of the

---

57 Zarkashī , *al-Burhān*, 1/237; Suyūtī, *al-Itqān*, 1/76.

58 Suat Yıldırım, *Kur'an İlimlerine Giriş*, p. 63.

Companions.[59] He first checked whether the material was written in the presence of the noble Prophet and he then compared the compatibility of those materials with the memories of the Companions. In addition to this, he required two witnesses for each scribe to verify the specific verses presented to him were written in the presence of the Prophet. Zayd performed this duty under the close instruction of both Abu Bakr and 'Umar who told him: 'Sit at the entrance to the [Prophet's] Mosque. If anyone brings you a verse from the Book of God along with two witnesses, then record it.'[60]

Some scholars hold that the two witnesses were considered as the written material and the memories of the Companions,[61] but this doesn't fit the reality. If we accept this opinion, we accept the idea that Zayd would approve material from any Companion who memorised and wrote the Qur'an by himself for inclusion in his collection. However, the criterion for verses to be accepted was that they would have to have been recited and dictated by the Prophet himself and the two witnesses must testify to this account.[62] Zayd did not take any verses into Qur'an if they did not meet this condition. This methodology eliminated any doubt concerning the authenticity of the Qur'an. As such, the Qur'an was collected into one single book under strict conditions and the supervision of Abu Bakr, 'Umar and Zayd ibn Thabit.

One of the most important activities for the preservation of the Qur'an was the publication of true copies. 'Uthman succeeded the caliphate on 'Umar's death and ruled for ten years.[63] During this reign, his most significant service was the publication of copies of the Qur'an and their distribution to different Islamic cities to ensure unity and prevent conflict among the Muslims. There were many underlying reasons that led to the publication and distribution of the Qur'an during 'Uthman's caliphate.

Abu Bakr's collection of the Qur'an and production of the *Imam Muṣḥāf* addressed the immediate needs of the Muslims and was sufficient at that time.

---

59 Ar-Rāfi', *I'jāz al-Qur'ān*, p. 18.

60 Zarqānī , *Manāhil*, 1/252.

61 Ibn Ḥajar, *Fatḥ al-Bāri*, 19/16, Ibn Ḥajar says; As if what is meant by two witnesses are memory [backed by] the written word. Or, two witnesses to testify that the verse was written verbatim in the Prophet's presence. Or, meaning they would testify that it was one of the forms in which the Qur'ān was revealed. Their intention was to accept only what had been written in the Prophet's presence [and, therefore, also checked by him], not [what had been penned] from their memory.

62 Suyūtī, *al-Itqān*, 1/77.

63 Suyūtī, *Tarīkh al-Khulafa*, p. 153.

Until 'Uthman's caliphate there was no need to copy or distribute it. However, as the Muslim empire expanded into vast territories there was an increasing need to publish and send copies of the Qur'an to the new Islamic cities. It was necessary to address disputes that were arising due to the concept of the seven readings of the Qur'an.

Abu Qilaba reports;

> The Qur'an teachers were teaching the Qur'an according to the different readings (seven letters); one would teach from another. The students began disputing and having disagreements among themselves because of the reading issue. They would take these matters to their Qur'an teachers, and every one began denying the others reading style. When 'Uthman was informed about this, he gave a sermon and said, 'If you dispute in our presence, the Muslims in far cities would dispute more. O Companions of the Prophet! Come together and write one *Imam Muṣḥāf* (one official and authority Qur'an).'[64]

The disputes and disagreements among the Muslims reached very dangerous levels which, if not immediately addressed, would result in serious consequences, even war, between Muslim communities.

Summary: Transmission of the Qur'an

1. The Prophet's mission was to convey the revelation to people and preserve it from change.
2. On receiving the revelation he taught it to his Companions.
3. He also ordered scribes to write it, after which he would listen and check the writing for accuracy.
4. The noble Prophet would order copies to be made and distributed amongst the believers. These were again copied by those who could write.
5. The Prophet held an original copy of the verses in his home for safekeeping.
6. Through this method, the Qur'an was transmitted untainted by multiple people both orally and in written form
7. The Qur'an was checked every year by the angel Gabriel until the Prophet died. It was then collected into a single book during Abu Bakr's caliphate and then again during 'Uthman's caliphate.
8. Abu Bakr collected the Qur'an into an official *Imam Muṣḥāf* to provide an authority under which all Muslims could unite.

---

[64] Ibn Abī Dāwud, *al-Masāḥif*, p. 21.

9. He established a committee under Zayd ibn Thabit which followed strict procedures to ensure accuracy. He only accepted verses written in the presence of the Prophet and two witnesses were required to affirm them.
10. During 'Uthman's reign the Qur'an was again collected, copies were made and distributed to the major cities of the new Islamic empire to help avoid conflict and disputes.

The Methodology in the Collection of 'Uthman

Islamic sources record that 'Uthman empowered a committee to collect and copy the Qur'an according to strict criteria which were:

1) The collection of Abu Bakr was the true and correct starting point for making a copy of the Qur'an.
2) The Qur'an would be written according to the last recitation of the Prophet to the angel Gabriel (*arḏ ākhira*); i.e. in the Quraysh dialect. This would maintain one letter and exclude the other six.[65]
3) Abrogated verses no longer included in recitation would be excluded; for example, the verse about prohibition because of suckling 10 times (being milk mother and related rules) which was reduced to five times and later abrogated.[66]
4) If any dispute arose among the members of the committee, the Quraysh dialect would take precedence and the verses would be written according to it.[67]
5) The Qur'an would be copied in several numbers and each copy would be sent to the Islamic centres. If any personal copy was found to have any discrepancy it would be burnt.[68]
6) The *surah* (chapters of Qur'an) would be arranged in the order we know today. In Abu Bakr's collection the verse order was the same but the *surah* (chapter) order was different. 'Uthman ordered the committee to arrange the *surah* order too.
7) Any additional words for the purpose of explanation would be excluded from these copies.[69]

[65] Bukhari, *Fadāil al-Qur'ān*, 3; Ibn Abī Dāwud, *al-Masāḫif*, p. 21.

[66] For these verses see Muslim, *Saḫīḫ, ar-Radā'*, 24; Imam Malik, *Muwatta, ar-Radā'*, 18, Tirmidhi, *Sunan, ar-Radā'*, 3.

[67] Bukhari, *Saḫīḫ, Fadāil al-Qur'ān*, 3.

[68] Manāil Kattān, *Mabāhis*, p. 131.

[69] Zarqānī, *Manāhil*, 1/257–260.

Relying entirely on primary sources, including the Companions' parchments and additional material held by A'isha, 'Uthman prepared an independent copy of the Qur'an. In the five years it took the committee to complete its work, under the direction of Zayd ibn Thabit, there was only one disagreement. This disagreement was regarding how the last letter of the word *'al-tābūt',* in 2:248 should be written. Zayd said this letter should be written as circle 'ta' (ة) but when this matter was referred to 'Uthman he ordered them to write it as open 'ta' (ت).[70] This problem regarding the script of one word in the official Qur'an was solved by the intervention of 'Uthman. The committee wrote several copies of Qur'an during these years and they were distributed to Mecca, Kūfa, Basra, Damascus, Yemen, and Bahrain with one copy remaining in Medina.[71] This copy was named the *'Imam Muṣḥ̮āf.'*[72]

With the task now completed, the ink on the final copy dry, and all duplicate copies sent to the major Islamic cities, there was no longer a need for the numerous fragments of the Qur'an still in the possession of people. After consultation with the remaining Companions, 'Uthman ordered the burning of these fragments.[73] There were no objections made to this decision; Ali ibn Abī Tālib reports; "By God, he only did what he did with these fragments in clear view of us all [i.e. and with our consent]."[74]

Summary: The Methodology in the Collection of 'Uthman

1. The starting point for the collection was Abu Bakr's *Imam Muṣḥ̮āf.*
2. The Qur'an would be written in the Quraysh dialect and exclude the other six readings.
3. Certain abrogated verses would be excluded.
4. The Quraysh dialect would be the determining factor in any committee disputes.
5. The Qur'an would be copied and distributed to Islamic centre.
6. The *surah* would be ordered.
7. Additional explanations would be excluded.
8. An independent copy of the Qur'an was collated entirely from primary sources over a period of five years and witnessing just one disagreement.

70 Ibn Abī Dāwud, *Masāḥ̮if,* p. 20.
71 Ibn Abī Dāwud, *Masāḥ̮if,* p. 34.
72 Manāil Kattān, *Mabāhis,* p. 131.
73 Qurtubī, *al-Jāmi' al-Bayān.* 1/52.
74 Ibn Abī Dāwud, *Masāḥ̮if,* p. 22.

9. Copies were distributed to Mecca, Kūfa, Basra, Damascus, Yemen, and Bahrain with one copy, the *Imam Muṣḥāf*, remaining in Medina.
10. Remaining fragments of the Qur'an were burned with the agreement of the Companions.

Qur'anic Script

The 'Uthman *Muṣḥāf* was written in the old Kūfī script which is almost incomprehensible to modern-day Arabic readers. There was no demarcation on the letters such as *hamzahs*, dots (*nuqat*)[75] or vowel marks (*tashkil*).[76] This was the traditional manner of writing at that time. Therefore, a straight line could represent the letter *baa*, *taa*, *thaa* and *yaa*, and each letter could have had any of the vowel marks assigned to it. Letters and vowels could only be differentiated by context, something the Arabs at that time were accustomed to.[77] There were no indications signifying the ending of the verses and the only sign that a *surah* had ended was the *basmala* at the beginning of the following *surah*. There were also no textual divisions (into thirtieths, sixtieths, etc.).[78]

After immigrating to Medina, encouraged by the noble Prophet, many Muslims began to learn how to read and write a primitive style of writing without demarcation. As native Arabic speakers, it was not difficult for them to read or understand this writing, however, from the first century after *Hijrah* many non-Arabs converted to Islam and struggled to read the Qur'an correctly. It was very common to hear reading mistakes among these non-Arab Muslims. To protect the Qur'an from these mistakes it was necessary to introduce a demarcation system to make it easier to read.

The first change occurred with the addition of the diacritical marks; the *tashkeel*. Abu al-Aswad ad-Dualī (d. 69 A.H.), was the first to codify the science of Arabic grammar, (*naḥw*). According to one report, 'Ali ibn Abī Tālib asked him to make the *Muṣḥāf* easier for the people to read but he declined deeming it unnecessary. However, on hearing the wrong recital of a verse he changed his mind. The verse was: أَنَّ اللهَ بَرِيءٌ مِنَ الْمُشْرِكِينَ وَرَسُولُهُ

[75] The nuqat are the dots that are used to differentiate between different letters that have the same base structure.

[76] They are the diacritical marks of the *fatḥa*, *kasra*, and *zamma* and other marks (such as the *shadda*) that are used to pronounce the particular letters correctly.

[77] Abu Ammaar Yasir Qadhi, *the Sciences of Qur'ān*, p. 141.

[78] Qadhi, *the Sciences of Qur'ān*, pp. 141–14.

"God disavows those who associate partners with Him (and break their treaty), and His Messenger likewise (disavows them)."[79]

With the mistake in reading, the meaning changed to 'God disavows all ties with the pagans and His Messenger.' This drastic change in meaning occurred with the change of just one vowel. Abu al-Aswad said, 'I did not think the state of the people had degenerated to this level!' He remembered the advice of 'Ali ibn Abī Tālib and went to Ziyad ibn Abīhī, the governor of lraq, and requested a scribe. Ziyad sent 30 scribes to Abu al-Aswad, from which he chose just one and started his work. He instructed the scribe to use a different colour ink for each of the marks, 'If I pronounce (the vowel) 'a', then write a dot above the letter. If I pronounce it as 'u', then write a dot in front of the letter. If I pronounce 'e', then write it below the letter.'[80] Abu al-Aswad personally oversaw the work and corrected any mistakes. He marked the whole Qur'an from beginning to end very carefully.[81]

Introducing this type of marking could prevent mistakes in *I'rab* (the placement of words in the sentence, known by the sound of last letter of each word). However, it was very difficult for non-Arabs to understand the Arabic letters without dots. For example, the Arabic letters *'baa'*, *'taa'*, *'tha'*, *'jim'*, *'haa'*, *'faa'* and *'qaf'*, look similar without dots and it is very difficult for a non-native speaker to know which one is intended. Unless a system of dots was introduced, the misreading would continue. This problem was first recognized by the governor of Iraq, Ḫajjāj ibn Yusuf, who commissioned Nasr ibn 'Asim and Yahya ibn Ya'mar to solve it. Nasr and Yahya invented a system of dots to distinguish each of these letters and marked the Qur'an with this new system.[82] In the sciences of the Qur'an, the processes of marking the letters with dots is called *i'jam*. Zarqānī says:

> May God have mercy on these two scholars (Yahya ibn Ya'mar and Nasr ibn 'Asim), for they were successful in this endeavour (of adding dots to the Qur'an), and completed the addition of the dots for the first time. They conditioned upon themselves not to increase the number of dots of any letter above three. This system spread and became popular amongst the people after them, and it had a great impact in removing confusion and doubts concerning (the proper recitation of) the *Muṣḫāf*.[83]

---

79 Qur'ān: 9: 3.

80 Ibn Abī, Dāwud, *Masāḫif*, p. 144.

81 Ibn Nadīm, *al-Fihrist*, p. 60, Zarqānī, *Manāhil*, p. 408.

82 Ibn Abī Dāwud, *Masāḫif*, p. 141.

83 Zarqānī, *Manāhil*, 1/407.

To avoid confusion, different colours were used in the Qur'an to mark the letters with diacritical marks and dots. Scribes used black for the dots and red for the *tashkeel* and hundreds of copies of the *Muṣḫāf* from the first two centuries after *Hijrah* used this colour system. Some can still be viewed with red, yellow, green and sometimes blue ink.[84] This system prevailed for hundreds of years until the profound scholar Ḫalil ibn Ahmad (d. 791 A.H.) invented the modern system which we use today and settled this conflict forever.

It is narrated that some of the early scholars such as Ibn Mas'ud, an-Nakhāī (d. 96 A.H.), Qatāda (d. 117 A. H.) and others of the first two generations after the Prophet disapproved of the additions and prohibited their use. Others, however, such as Hasan al-Basrī (d. 110 A.H.) and Ibn Sīrin (d. 110 A.H.), did not see a problem with the addition of these dots.[85] When asked his opinion Imam Malik (d. 179 A.H.) replied:

> The people continued to ask me concerning the addition of dots in the Qur'an, so I said: As for the major *Muṣḫāf*, I don't think they should be dotted, nor should anything be added that is not in them. As for the minor *Muṣḫāf* - the ones that the children learn from- then I don't see any problem with it.[86]

Dānī reports:

> I happened to come across an old copy of the *Muṣḫāf*, written during the beginning of the Caliphate of Hishām ibn 'Abd al-Malik. Its date (of writing) was written on the last page: 'Written by Mughira ibn Mina, in Rajab, in the year 110 A.H. It had *tashkil*, the *hamzahs* ... and the dots (*nuqat*) were in red.[87]

Both these quotes show that, eventually, the addition of *tashkil* and *nuqat* were accepted as a part of the writing of the *Muṣḫāf*.

Over the next few centuries there were further developments such as adding the names of the *surah* and separating the verses using special symbols and numbers. Initially, verses were separated using three dots; after five verses the word *khams* (five) was written and after ten verses *'ashr* (ten) was written. Following this the numbering would begin again until the end of the *surah*. Soon afterwards, the word *khams* was abbreviated to the letter *khaa*, and the word *'ashr*

---

84 Ad-Dānī, *al-Muqnī Fi Rasmi Masāḫif al-Amsār*, p. 130.

85 Qadhi, *the Sciences of Qur'ān*, p. 143.

86 Ibn Abī Dāwud, *Masāḫif*, pp. 141–143.

87 Zarqānī, *Manāhil*, 1/410.

to the letter *'ayn*, both of which were written in the margin of the *Muṣḥāf*. Eventually, the verses were indicated by a circle at the end of each verse, and the sequential number of the verse was written in the circle, as it is presented today.[88]

Ḫalil b. Ahmad was the first to beautify and add today's *tashkeel* to the Qur'an. He also developed *sukun, shadda* and *hamza* which we use today. In the sixth century, Muhammad b. Tayfur al-Sajawandi (d. 560 A.H. / 1165 C.E.) put *wuquf* (stop marks) at the end of the verses or to denote the place where the meaning of the verse has been completed. These signs are called *'sajawand.'* Gustav Flugel (1841) (using Hafiz Uthman's script) introduced the verse numbers. *Muṣḥāf* were published in Kazan, Cairo, Tehran, and İstanbul and in 1925 King Fu'ad's standard edition was published under the supervision of Sheikh Muhammad Ali Khallaf al-Husayni.

Summary: Qur'anic Script

1. The 'Uthman *Muṣḥāf* was written in Kūfī with no demarcation marks which caused mistakes to be made in the recitation of non-native Arab speakers.
2. A demarcation system to indicate vowel sounds was necessary to protect the Qur'an from mistakes.
3. The first change, the addition of the diacritical marks; the *tashkeel* was introduced by Abu al-Aswad ad-Dualī on the order of 'Ali ibn Abī Tālib.
4. Later, the system of dots (*i'jam*) was introduced to clarify the letters. This was commissioned by the governor of Iraq, Ḫajjāj ibn Yusuf who commissioned Nasr ibn 'Asim and Yahya ibn Ya'mar to solve it.
5. Different colours were used for the marks to avoid confusion. Scribes used black for the dots and red for the *tashkil*. Some can still be viewed with red, yellow, green and sometimes blue ink.
6. Hundreds of years later, Ḫalil ibn Ahmad (d. 791 A.H.) invented the modern system which we use today.
7. Over the next few centuries there were further developments such as adding the names of the *surah* and separating the verses using special symbols and numbers.
8. Ḫalil b. Ahmad was the first to beautify and add today's *tashkil* to the Qur'an. He also developed *sukun, shadda* and *hamza* which we use today.

---

[88] Ad-Dānī, *al-Muqnī*, p. 130.

The Value of the Qur'an in Islamic Jurisprudence

The Qur'an is accepted by all Muslims as the primary source of Islamic law. It is obligatory to act according to the rulings in the Qur'an based on general consensus. If the rule for a case is clearly indicated in the Qur'an, it is not permissible to investigate any other source for an answer.

There are two periods of Qur'anic revelation. That which took place in Mecca during the first thirteen years of Prophethood which accounts for the majority of the verses. The rest was revealed after emigration to Medina (*Hijrah*) over a period of ten years. The former mainly deals with issues of belief, the oneness of God (*tawḥīd*), the afterlife, the necessity of Prophethood, arguments with the unbelievers and their invitation to Islam. The latterly revealed verses contain legal rules and guidance for the various aspects of Muslim life. This period saw the development of the nascent Islamic state and therefore the Qur'anic emphasis changed to values regulating the legal, social, political and economic life of the Muslims.

Knowledge of which verses where revealed in Mecca and which were revealed in Medina provides scholars with insight into the context and conditions at the time the verses were revealed. It is mostly relevant to the understanding of the abrogation (*naskh*) of verses in the Qur'an where the chronology of the revelation helps to differentiate the abrogating (*al-nāsikh*) from the abrogated (*al-mansūkh*) parts of the verses. According to the most preferred opinion a *surah* is considered to be Meccan (*Makkī*) if its revelation began in Mecca, even if it contains verses that were later revealed in Medina. Meccan verses are generally short and very eloquent. They are intense in their emotional appeal to the pagan Arabs, whereas the Medinan (*Madanī*) *surah* are more detailed and convey a sense of serenity that marks a different style in the revelation of the Qur'an.[89]

Summary: The Value of the Qur'an in Islamic Jurisprudence

1. The Qur'an is accepted by all Muslims as the primary source of Islamic law; if the rule for a case is clearly indicated in the Qur'an, it is not permissible to investigate any other source for an answer.
2. There are two periods of Qur'anic revelation; Meccan and Medinan. Meccan revelations mainly deal with issues of belief whereas Medinan revelations contain legal rules and guidance.

[89] Von Denffer, *'Ulūm al-Qur'ān*, p. 90.

3. Knowledge of where the verses were revealed provides scholars with valuable insight particularly into the abrogation (*naskh*) of verses.
4. A *surah* is considered Meccan if it's revelation began there, even if some of its verses were revealed later in Medina.

Characteristics of the Qur'an Regarding Islamic Rulings

As explained earlier, the Qur'an has been transmitted until the present day in its original unaltered form, without change to even one single word because the chain of transmission was *mutawātir* which provides definite knowledge. The Qur'an itself is definite and it is necessary for Muslims to accept every single verse. However, contained within the Qur'an are verses that are clear and definite and others that are unclear and open to interpretation as regards their legislative effect. Definite (*qat'ī*) evidence is precise and not open to other possible interpretation. Unclear or speculative (*ẕannī*) verses are open to variant interpretation. For example, the verses related to inheritance and penal rules are *qat'ī;*

> God commands you in (the matter of the division of the inheritance among) your children: for the male is the equivalent of the portion of two females...[90]

> The fornicatress and the fornicator—flog each of them with a hundred stripes...[91]

Verses that are specific (*khās*) are definite evidence because the meaning they contain is obvious, for example; quantitative rulings such as one half, one hundred, and eighty are definite and not open to interpretation. There is no dispute among the *mujtahid* in the understanding of this type of verse.

Speculative (*ẕannī*) verses become definite if they are explained by other verses. However, if there is no such explanation in the Qur'an or Sunnah and they remain unclear, they remain *ẕannī* and are open to interpretation. For example, the word '*quru*' in the verse: "*Divorced women shall keep themselves in waiting for three menstrual courses (quru) ...*"[92] has two possible meanings, purity after menstruation and the time of menstruation itself, therefore it is not *qat'ī* in legislation. In Arabic, it is used with both meanings and the verse does not make it clear which meaning is intended. Thus, both meanings are *ẕannī* and therefore,

---

[90] Qur'ān, 4: 11.
[91] Qur'ān, 24: 2.
[92] Qur'ān, 2: 228.

open to interpretation and *ijtihād.* After *ijtihād*, some *mujtahid* understood the word *quru* to mean the menstruation term while others understood it as the term of purity. Another example of a *ẕannī* text is the following verse;

> God does not take you to task for a slip (or blunder of speech) in your oaths, but He takes you to task for what you have concluded by solemn, deliberate oaths. The expiation (for breaking such oaths) is to feed ten destitute persons with the average of the food you serve to your families, or to clothe them, or to set free a slave. If anyone does not find (the means to do that), let him fast for three days. That is the expiation for your oaths when you have sworn (and broken them).[93]

In this verse it is clear that the expiation for breaking an oath is feeding ten destitute people, setting a slave free, or fasting for three days. Scholars however, differ in their opinion of the nature of the oath. Ḫanafī scholars hold that a vain oath is one that was sworn on circumstances assumed to be true that, in fact, turn out to be different; whereas, other scholars hold that it is an oath sworn without the intention of fulfilling it. Other differences have arisen between the scholars concerning the precise definition of what may be considered a deliberate oath. There is also disagreement as to whether the three days of fasting should be undertaken on three consecutive or non-consecutive days.

There are occasions where a Qur'anic ruling may possess at the same time a definitive and a speculative meaning, in which case each meaning will convey a ruling independent of the other. An example of this is the ruling on the ablution for Prayers.[94] The text is definitive on the requirement of wiping the head in ablution, but since it does not specify the precise area of the head to be wiped, it is speculative.[95]

Scholars agree that the specific (*khās*) of the Qur'an is definitive, but they are in dispute as to whether the general (*'āam*) is definitive or speculative. Ḫanafī scholars hold that the *'āam* is definitive and binding, whereas others maintain that the *'āam* by itself is speculative and open to specification. For example;

> Forbidden to you are your mothers and daughters, your sisters, your aunts paternal and maternal, your brothers' daughters, your sisters' daughters, your mothers who have given suck to you, your milk-sisters, your wives'

93 Qur'ān, 5: 89.
94 Qur'ān, 5: 6.
95 Kamali, *Principles of Islamic Jurisprudence*, p. 30.

mothers, your stepdaughters—who are your foster-children, born of your wives with whom you have consummated marriage...[96]

This verse is the expression of the general ruling (*'āam*) about who it is prohibited to marry including ones mother, daughter, sister, etc. However, they may include ones step-mother, grandmother, granddaughter, blood daughter, step-daughter, and even illegitimate daughters. All these meanings are included in the verse and are definite (*qat'ī*) in their ruling according to Ḫanafī scholars. Other scholars, however, consider them to be speculative evidences. Ḫanafī scholars hold their opinion because if *z̲annī* text can be explained by other verses in the Qur'an or by the Sunnah, they become *qat'ī* in meaning. There are examples where the general text might be speculative (*z̲annī*) on its own if the other explanations are disregarded. For example, in the following verse about trading and interest, any sale is lawful but any interest is unlawful: "*...God has made trading lawful, and interest unlawful...*"[97]

However, this general meaning is specified by the Sunnah which forbids certain trading mechanisms such as trading unripened fruit on a tree. Similarly, the expression 'any interest' is general and unclear, but the Sunnah specifies this ruling by mentioning six types of interest; through these explanations the verse becomes clear and definitive.

Some verses that are *qat'ī* in ruling and therefore not open to interpretation still contain some room for interpretation. For example; "*...The expiation (for breaking such oaths) is to feed ten destitute persons with the average of the food you serve to your families, or to clothe them, or to set free a slave...*"[98]

It is clear from this specific (*khās*) text that the expiation for breaking deliberate oaths is to feed ten poor people. The expression 'ten destitute persons' is clear and has one meaning. However, Ḫanafī scholars interpreted the verse to mean that either ten poor people could be fed, or one poor person could be fed ten times, both of which fulfil the requirement of expiation. This example shows that the scope of *ijtihād* is not always confined to the *'āam* but that even the *khās* and definitive rulings may require scholarly elaboration.[99]

Qur'anic legislation also contains the concepts of the absolute (*mutlaq*) and the qualified (*muqayyad*). An example of this is the two separate rulings on the

---

96 Qur'ān, 4: 23.

97 Qur'ān, 2: 275.

98 Qur'ān, 5: 89.

99 Kamali, *Principles of Islamic Jurisprudence*, p. 32.

subject of witnesses in the Qur'an; one is absolute and the other one is qualified in regard to the attributes of the witness. In the following verse, the witness is not qualified in any way, any witness can fulfil the requirement; therefore it is *mutlaq:*

> ...do take witnesses when you settle commercial transactions with one another ...[100]

The following verse qualifies that the witness in the divorce process must be Muslim;

> ...call upon two Muslim men of probity from among you as witnesses...[101]

Here, only Muslim witnesses can fulfil this requirement and therefore this is *muqayyad* (qualified). Scholars studied the verses and agreed that the qualified terms of the second verse must also be applied to the first case as well. However, Ḥanafī scholars differed in their opinion and they hold that both verses must be applied within their own context.

It is easy to observe that the Qur'an usually brings general principles in legislation but in some cases it provides specific details. Experience shows that every *mujtahid* who has resorted to the Qur'an in search of the solution to a problem has found in it a principle that has provided him with some guidance on the subject.[102]

"*We have neglected nothing in the Book*"[103]

The above verse is understood by scholars to mean that the Qur'an provides general principles in every field to enable *mujtahid* of all times to solve their problems. As a divine source that came from the eternal knowledge and contains the names, attributes and essential qualities of God, the Qur'an necessarily requires comprehensive explanation. The Sunnah provided some, but not all of this for Qur'anic legislation. It is impossible to discover every aspect contained within the Qur'an. However, the aspect related to the responsibility of the servants of God is clearly explained by the Prophet.

> O you who believe! Obey God and obey the Messenger, and those from among you who are invested with authority; and if you are to dispute among yourselves about anything, refer it to God and the Messenger, if

100 Qur'ān, 2: 282.
101 Qur'ān, 65: 2.
102 Shātibī, *Muwafaqaat*, vol. 3, p. 219.
103 Qur'ān, 6: 38.

indeed you believe in God and the Last Day. This is the best (for you) and fairest in the end.[104]

Scholars view this verse as evidence for the first four sources of Islamic jurisprudence; the Qur'an, Sunnah, *ijma'* (general consensus), and *qiyāṣ* (analogy). 'Obey God' refers to the Qur'an, 'Obey the Messenger' refers to the Sunnah of the noble Prophet, 'those of you who are in authority' refers the consensus of the *mujtahid* and the last part of the verse 'If you are to dispute among yourselves…' refers to *qiyāṣ*. This is because a dispute can only be referred to God and his Messenger by extending the rulings of the Qur'an and Sunnah to similar cases and this process is called *qiyāṣ* (analogy).

Even though the Qur'an contains specific injunctions on a number of topics it is related to the exposition and better understanding of its general principles.[105] The Qur'anic legislation on civil, economic, constitutional and international affairs is, on the whole, confined to an exposition of the general principles and objectives of the law. With regard to civil transactions, for example, the verses of the Qur'an on the fulfilment of contracts, the legality of sale, the prohibition of usury, respect for the property of others, the documentation of loans and other forms of deferred payments are all concerned with general principles.[106]

Summary: Characteristics of the Qur'an Regarding Islamic Rulings.

1. The Qur'an contains clear and definite verses and others that are unclear and open to interpretation.
2. Definite (*qat'ī*) evidence is precise and not open to other possible interpretation. Unclear or speculative (*ẕannī*) verses are open to variant interpretation.
3. Verses that are specific (*khās*) are definite evidence because the meaning they contain is obvious. There is no dispute among the *mujtahid* in understanding this type of verse and interpretation is not valid.
4. Speculative (*ẕannī*) verses become definite if they are explained by other verses. However, if there is no such explanation in the Qur'an or Sunnah and they remain unclear, they remain *ẕannī* and are open to interpretation.

[104] Qur'ān, 4: 59.

[105] Shātibī, *Muwafaqaat*, vol. 3, p. 217.

[106] Kamali, *Principles of Islamic Jurisprudence*, p. 36.

5. There are occasions where a Qur'anic ruling may at the same time possess a definitive and a speculative meaning, in which case each meaning will convey a ruling independent of the other.
6. Scholars agree that the specific (*khās*) of the Qur'an is definitive, but they are in dispute as to whether the general (*'āam*) is definitive or speculative.
7. Some verses that are *qat'ī* in ruling and therefore not open to interpretation still contain some room for interpretation.
8. Qur'anic legislation also contains the concepts of the absolute (*mutlaq*) and the qualified (*muqayyad*).
9. The Qur'an usually brings general principles in legislation but in some cases it provides specific details. Every *mujtahid* who has resorted to the Qur'an in search of the solution to a problem has found in it a principle that has provided him with some guidance.

The Style of the Qur'an in *Aḫkām Shar'iyya* (Legal Rules)

The commands and prohibitions in the Qur'an are expressed in a variety of forms and can be determined from the context and the words of the verse. It is necessary to examine the verse to see if the command raises obligatory duty (*wujub*), recommendation (*mandub*) or permissibility (*mubah*). There are various ways in which commands and prohibitions are expressed in the Qur'an; God may command something or praise the positive quality of something. He sometimes recommends something by promising a reward for the act. Definite language regarding the ruling infers obligation (*wujub*), otherwise the conduct is understood to be *mandub* (recommended). If an action is explained in the Qur'an as being permissible and a person is able to choose whether or not to perform it, this type of expression is understood as *mubah* (permissible) in ruling. The following verses are examples for these rulings and the associated forms of expression;

> ...Spend (in God's cause and for the needy) out of whatever We provide for you before death comes to any of you...[107]

> You will never be able to attain godliness and virtue until you spend of what you love (in God's cause). Whatever you spend, God has full knowledge of it.[108]

---

[107] Qur'ān, 63: 10.
[108] Qur'ān, 3: 92.

> This day (all) pure, wholesome things have been made lawful for you. And the food of those who were given the Book before is lawful for you, just as your food is lawful for them.[109]

Similarly, different forms of expression are used for the prohibition of actions, either through clear language or through defining the action as a cause for punishment. On occasion, in the Qur'an, God may curse the perpetrators of such act, liken it to an act of Satan, or declare the negative consequences of such an act. Similarly, the expressions 'unclean', 'sin' and 'deviation' are used in the Qur'an for prohibitions. The following verses demonstrate these rulings and their forms of expression in the Qur'an;

> ...you do not kill any soul, which God has made sacred and forbidden...[110]

> ...spend in God's cause (out of whatever you have) and do not ruin yourselves by your own hands[111]

> ...It is not virtue that you enter dwellings from the backs of them...[112]

> ...Those who hoard up gold and silver and do not spend it in God's cause (to exalt His cause and help the poor and needy): give them (O Messenger) the glad tidings of a painful punishment[113]

If the language used with regard to the prohibition is definite and clear the ruling is considered *haram* (forbidden). However, if it is open to interpretation and not definite, the ruling is *makruh* (disliked). It is necessary for the *mujtahid* to determine the precise value of such expressions in light of both the language of the text and the general objectives and principles of the Shari'ah.[114]

Summary: The Style of the Qur'an in *Aḥkām Shar'iyya* (Legal Rules)

1. The Qur'an contains various kinds of commands and prohibitions in the Qur'an through varying styles of expression.
2. *Wujub* is obligatory duty expressed though definite language.

---

[109] Qur'ān, 5: 5.
[110] Qur'ān, 6: 151.
[111] Qur'ān, 2: 195.
[112] Qur'ān, 2: 189.
[113] Qur'ān, 9: 34.
[114] Sha'bin, *Manhaj*, pp. 22–23.

3. *Mandub* are recommended actions that are expressed through clear language but which are not as definite as *wujub.*
4. *Mubah* is that which is permissible and expressed through language that suggests the action is allowed but the person has the choice of whether or not to do it.
5. Different forms of expression are used for the prohibition of actions, either through clear language or through defining the action as a cause for punishment.
6. *Haram* means forbidden and is expressed through definite and clear language.
7. *Makruh* is that which is disliked and is expressed through language that is not definite and is therefore, open to interpretation.
8. The *mujtahid* must determine the precise value of such expressions in light of both the language of the text and the general objectives and principles of the Shari'ah.

Ta'līl (Causation) in the Qur'an

Ta'līl literally means causation and the logical relationship between cause and effect. In Islamic jurisprudence, *ta'līl* is the effective cause of the rulings, the mentality and purpose behind them. The following words are used to explain the causation of rulings; *'illah* (the underlying reason), *ḫikmah* (wisdom) and *sabab* (the reason).

'Illah refers to the underlying reason; the specific reason underlying the ruling. The reason necessitates the ruling and vice versa. *Ḫikmah* is different to *'illah. Ḫikmah* explains some of the wisdom in the ruling but it is not the underlying reason for the ruling. *Sabab* (reason) is used in reference to devotional matters (*'ibadāt*) and shows the existence of duty. For example, time is *sabab* for the prescribed Prayers and each fixed time brings a new responsibility, but the real reason for the duty is the command of God. The Qur'an often justifies its rulings with verses that reference the benefits to be achieved from them. Such explanations are often designed to make the Qur'an easier to understand, for example;

> Tell the believing men that they should restrain their gaze (from looking at the women whom it is lawful for them to marry, and from others' private parts), and guard their private parts and chastity. This is what is purer for them. God is fully aware of all that they do.[115]

[115] Qur'ān, 24: 30.

Restraining the gaze from looking at women is justified as it obstructs the means to *zina* (adultery and fornication).

Scholars are in dispute about the nature of causation (*ta'līl*); whether it is the reason behind the rulings or whether it is just for ease of understanding the Qur'anic legislation. Ẕahirī scholars hold that causation is the speculative (*ẕannī*) work of a *mujtahid* and if the Qur'an (or Sunnah) do not provide causes for the rulings it is impossible to know them. If the cause is already provided in the text, there is no need to perform *ijtihād* to find it. However, if it is not provided by God through the Qur'anic text, the work of the *mujtahid* in this matter is only speculative. These scholars also maintain that the believer should surrender himself to the will of God by accepting the rulings without questioning them. Trying to understand the cause behind the rulings prevents one from submitting sincerely to the will of God. Additionally, the *mujtahid* may make a mistake in trying to uncover the cause. It may be possible that there are multiple reasons underlying the ruling, in which case, he cannot be sure what the correct one is.[116] The majority of the scholars hold that the rulings in Islam are to achieve certain objectives, and when these are recognized, it is not only permissible, but is a duty to make an effort to detect and use them. For this to happen, it is necessary to identify the cause of the rulings. It is the *mujtahids* duty to discover these in order to pursue the general objectives of the religion.[117]

Ta'līl has a significant place in *qiyāṣ* (analogical deduction). *'Illah* is an essential requirement of the analogy process. To be able to extend the application of an existing rule of Shari'ah to similar cases, the *mujtahid* must establish a common *'illah* between the original and the new case. If a common *'illah* cannot be identified in two apparently parallel cases, *qiyāṣ* cannot be applied.

Summary: *Ta'līl* (Causation) in the Qur'an

1. In Islamic jurisprudence, *ta'līl* is the effective cause of the rulings, the mentality and purpose behind them.
2. The causation of rulings is explained through *'illah* (the underlying reason), *ḫikmah* (wisdom) and *sabab* (the reason).
3. *'Illah* refers to the underlying reason; the specific reason underlying the ruling. The reason necessitates the ruling and vice versa. *Ḫikmah* explains some of the wisdom in the ruling but it is not the underlying reason for

[116] Ibn Ḫazm, *Iḫkām*, vol. 8, p. 76.

[117] Sābūnī, *Madkhal*, p. 75.

the ruling. *Sabab* (reason) is used in reference to devotional matters (*'ibadāt*) and shows the existence of duty.

4. Scholars dispute the nature of causation (*ta'līl*); whether it is the reason behind the rulings or whether it is just for ease of understanding the Qur'anic legislation.
5. Ẕahirī scholars hold that causation is the speculative (*ẕannī*) work of a *mujtahid* and if the Qur'an (or Sunnah) do not provide causes for the rulings it is impossible to know them.
6. The majority of the scholars hold that the rulings in Islam are to achieve certain objectives, and it is the *mujtahids* duty to discover these in order to pursue the general objectives of the religion.
7. *Ta'līl* has a significant place in *qiyāṣ* (analogical deduction). *'Illah* is an essential requirement of the analogy process.

I'jāz (Inimitability) of the Qur'an

The word '*i'jāz*' comes from 'a-j-z' which means to be incapable of, to be weak, to render powerless and to make dumb founded. The word '*mu'jizah*' which is derived from the same root means miracle. A miracle is an extraordinary event through which God enables his Prophets to prove their Prophethood, strengthen the believers' faith, and break the unbelievers' obstinacy.

Fethullah Gülen says the following words about *mu'jizah*;

> The universe operates according to God's fixed laws. In the absence of His laws and the uniform character of natural events, everything would be in continual flux. In such an environment, we would be unable to discover the Divine laws of nature or make any scientific progress. Although recent discoveries in atomic physics have shown that whatever exists is a wave in continuous motion, on the surface everything occurs according to classical or Newtonian principles. This has forced scientists to admit that they cannot state that anything will exist in the same state as it did even one second ago. Normally, life has its own laws according to which we behave. We need food and water to satisfy our hunger and thirst, and go to a doctor when we are sick. We use animals for labour, but cannot talk to them. Trees are fixed in their places, and neither they nor stones and mountains greet us. We conform to the laws of gravitation and repulsion, and do not attempt to rise into the sky without first making the relevant calculations. All of these and other laws make human life possible. However, since God has determined them, He is not bound by them. Therefore, He may sometimes annul a law or change the ordi-

> nary flow of events to allow a Prophet to perform what we call a miracle or to show that He can do whatever He wills at whatever time He desires.[118]

Whenever God sends a Prophet, He endows them with certain miracles and signs to prove their Prophethood. The miracles of Moses, Jesus and the other Prophets, peace be upon them, are well-known to all Muslims:

> We will make him Jesus a Messenger to the Children of Israel, (saying), I have come to you with a sign from your Lord, that I design for you out of clay, as It were, the figure of a bird, and breathe into it, and it becomes a bird by God's leave; and I heal him who was born blind, and the leper, and I bring the dead to life by God's leave. And I inform you of what you eat and what you store in your houses. Surely, therein is a sign for you, If you believe.[119]

The unbelievers in Mecca claimed that the Prophet was a liar who forged the Qur'an, a magician, and one possessed by *jinn* (supernatural beings). They even claimed that they could imitate the Qur'an:

> And when Our verses are recited to them, they say, 'We have heard this! If we wish, we can say something similar to it. These are nothing but stories of old.'[120]

Thereupon, God challenged them to fulfil this claim of theirs in three stages;

1) God, through the Qur'an, issued a challenge to the unbelievers to produce a book which is similar to the Qur'an:

> Say: If all of mankind and jinn gathered together to produce the like of the Qur'an, they could not produce it even if they help one another![121]

> Do they say, 'He has forged it!' Nay! (Rather) they do not believe! Let them, then, produce a book similar to it, if indeed they are truthful.[122]

2) The Qur'an challenged the unbelievers to bring 10 chapters similar to itself;

---

[118] Gülen, *Essentials of the Islamic Faith*, pp. 194–195.
[119] Qur'ān, 3: 49.
[120] Qur'ān, 8: 31
[121] Qur'ān, 17: 88.
[122] Qur'ān, 52: 33–34.

> Do they say, 'He (Muhammad) has forged it? Say: Bring then ten forged chapters similar to it, and call upon whomsoever you can, besides God, if you are truthful.[123]

3) The Qur'an challenged them to bring one chapter which is similar to any of its chapters;

> Do they say, 'He (Muhammad) has forged it!' Say: Bring then a one single chapter similar to it, and call upon whomsoever you can, besides God, if you are truthful.[124]

Said Nursi articulates the following regarding this challenge of Qur'an;

> The people of 'Arabia were mostly unlettered at that time, and therefore preserved their tribal pride, history, and proverbs in oral poetry. They attached great importance to eloquence, and so any meaningful, unique expression was memorized for its poetical form and eloquence and then handed down to posterity. Eloquence and fluency were therefore in such great demand that a tribe treated its eloquent literary figures as national heroes. Those intelligent people, who would govern a considerable portion of the world after Islam's advent, were more eloquent than other nations. Eloquence was so esteemed that two tribes would sometimes go to war over a saying of a literary figure and then be reconciled by the words of another. They even inscribed in gold the odes of seven poets and hung them on the wall of the Ka'ba. They were called the Seven Suspended Poems. At a time when eloquence was in such demand, the Qur'an of miraculous exposition was revealed. Just as God Almighty had endowed Moses and Jesus with the miracles most suitable to their times—the miracles of Staff and Bright Hand to Moses, and those of raising the dead and healing certain illnesses to Jesus—He made eloquence the most notable aspect of the Qur'an, the chief miracle of Prophet Muhammad, upon him be peace and blessings. When it was revealed, it challenged first the literary figures of the 'Arabian Peninsula: If you doubt what We have sent down on Our servant, produce a surah like it (2:23). It defeated their intellectual pretensions and humbled them by continuing: If you cannot, and you certainly cannot, fear the Fire, whose fuel is people and stones, prepared for unbelievers (2:24). Those self-conceited people could not dispute the Qur'an. Although this was an easy and safe course to obstruct and falsify its message, they chose to fight it with swords, the perilous and most difficult course. If those intelligent people, skilled in diplomacy, could have disputed the Qur'an, they would not have chosen the per-

---

[123] Qur'ān, 11: 13.

[124] Qur'ān, 10: 38

> ilous, difficult course and risked losing their property and lives. Since they could not argue with it verbally, they had to fight it with swords. There were two powerful reasons for trying to produce something like the Qur'an: its enemies strongly wished to dispute it to refute its claim of Revelation, and its friends had the desire to imitate it. The result was, and continues to be, innumerable books written in 'Arabic. All people, whether scholars or not, who read such books are forced to admit that they do not resemble the Qur'an. So, either the Qur'an is inferior—friend and foe admit that this is inconceivable —or superior to all of them. There are no other options.[125]

When the unbelievers asked for miracles from the Prophet, God revealed that the Qur'an itself is sufficient as a miracle;

> And they say, 'Why are not miracles sent down to him from his Lord?' Say: 'The signs are only with God, and I am only a plain warner.' Is it not a sufficient 'miracle' for them that We have sent down to you the Book which is recited to them? Verily, herein is a mercy and a reminder for a people who believe.[126]

The noble Prophet also indicated the status of the miracle of the Qur'an when he said;

> There has not been a single Prophet except that God gave him miracles because of which people believed in him. I have been given (as my miracle) the Revelation (i.e., the Qur'an) which God revealed to me. I hope, therefore, that I will have the largest number of followers on the Day of Judgement.[127]

Summary: *I'jāz* (Inimitability) of the Qur'an

1. The word '*i'jāz*' comes from '*a-j-z*' which means to be incapable of, to be weak, to render powerless and to make dumb founded.
2. The word '*mu'jizah*' which is derived from the same root means miracle: an extraordinary event through which God enables his Prophets to prove their Prophethood.
3. The Meccan polytheists claimed Prophet Muhammad, peace and blessings be upon him, was a liar who forged the Qur'an.

---

[125] Nursi, *The Words, the Twenty Fifth Word*, pp. 390–391.

[126] Qur'ān, 29: 50–51.

[127] Bukhari, *Sahīh, Holding fast to the Qur'ān and Sunnah*, hadith no: 379.

4. God challenged them in three stages to produce the like of the Qur'an which they were unable to do.
5. God indicated the Qur'an is sufficient as a miracle.
6. The Prophet also indicated the status of the Qur'an as a miracle.

Arguments for the Divine Authorship of the Qur'an

The Qur'an in its words, styles and meanings is completely unique; it did not imitate and cannot be imitated, because it is the direct word of God and above all other books. The Qur'an was revealed to the unlettered Prophet and presented an eternal challenge to humanity: *"If you are in doubt about what We have sent down to Our servant, then produce a chapter similar to it, if you are truthful."*[128] No one has ever met this challenge successfully.

Over a period of 23 years, the Qur'an was revealed, detailing the truths about God, metaphysics, religious beliefs, worship, prayer, law, morality, the afterlife, psychology, sociology, epistemology, history, scientific facts, and the principles of a happy life. It never contradicts itself, in fact, the Qur'an clearly declares that it contains no contradictions and is therefore the Word of God;

> Do they not contemplate the Qur'an (so that they may be convinced that it is from God)? Had it been from any other than God, they would surely have found in it much (incoherence or) inconsistency.[129]

As previously mentioned, pre-Islamic Arabia was renowned for the eloquence of its poets and orators who enjoyed the highest level of prestige in society. Regular poetry competitions saw the winning works written in gold and hung on the walls of the Ka'ba, the most sacred building in Mecca. The unlettered Prophet was never reported to have spoken even a few lines of poetry. However, the Qur'an he brought eventually forced all known experts to surrender to its superior eloquence. The Qur'an is a literary masterpiece that cannot be duplicated. Its style and eloquence, even its actual sentences, words, and letters form a miraculous harmony. With respect to rhythm, music, geometric proportions, mathematical measures, and repetition, each verse is in its exact place and is perfectly interwoven and interrelated with the others.[130]

Despite the high level of poetry, the vocabulary of the Arabic language was too primitive to adequately express metaphysical ideas, scientific, religious, or

---

[128] Qur'ān, 2: 23.

[129] Qur'ān, 4: 82.

[130] Gülen, *Essentials of Islamic Faith*, p. 224.

philosophical concepts. Using the words and expressions of a simple, desert people, Islam enriched the language and made it so complex it formed the basis of the most magnificent civilization, one that made many entirely original contributions to the scientific, religious, metaphysical, literary, economic, juridical, social, and political arenas.[131] How could an unlettered person launch a philological revolution that has no parallel in human history?

On a superficial analysis, the Qur'an reads like a basic text which can be understood by anyone. However, it is a very deep text with multiple layers of meaning which has illuminated many scientists in different fields who, through it, have been assisted in their studies and in their daily lives. Poets, musicians, and orators as well as sociologists, psychologists, scientists, economists, jurists and many more have benefitted from the Qur'an equally in their fields. In this sense, no other book can equal it.

We do not usually read a book more than three times without becoming bored and losing interest. The Qur'an on the other hand is read and re-read by Muslims and has been every day for the past fourteen centuries without losing its appeal. Muslims admit that the more they recite the Qur'an, the more they benefit from it; they never tire of its recitation, meaning, and content and it never loses any of its originality and freshness. As time passes, it breathes new truths and meanings into minds and souls, thereby increasing their activity and dynamism.

The Qur'an describes all our physical and spiritual aspects and contains principles to solve all social, economic, juridical, political, and administrative problems regardless of the time or place. Furthermore, it satisfies the mind and spirit simultaneously and guarantees happiness in both worlds.

The noble Prophet first experienced and practised the teachings of the Qur'an and then preached it to others. Thus, the perfect life outlined in the Qur'an was presented by the Prophet first; it designed his character and led his followers to the best human values. When the wife of the Prophet, A'isha was asked about his character, she said: 'don't you read the Qur'an? His character was the Qur'an.'

The Qur'an is universal and objective when dealing with particular issues and exact and precise when dealing with universal matters. When writing, most authors are influenced by their context and it is impossible to get rid of these influences in their writing. However, the Qur'an uses precise expressions even while describing the beginning of creation, the end of time, humanity's creation and the afterlife. Just as it sometimes draws universal conclusions from particular worldly

---

[131] Ibid.

events, it also goes from universal principles to particular events in history. [132] This typical Qur'anic style cannot be found in any human work.

The Qur'an is unique in its content. It not only encompasses many different scientific fields but also phrases them accurately. There is no other book which covers such a diverse array of fields without making contradictions. The Qur'an also contains the principles of all branches of knowledge, either in summary or in detail, and not one piece of this knowledge has ever been contradicted.

Scientific conclusions change constantly. What was true 50 years ago is disproved today. No author can claim that their book will remain true forever, but the Qur'an remains true and fresh. It continues, even now, to conquer new hearts and reveal its unlimited hidden treasures; to bloom like a heavenly rose with countless petals.

The Prophet himself is admonished in the Qur'an. This alone disproves his authorship. If he were its author, would he give such a noticeable place to the grave slander against his wife? His beloved uncle, Abu Tālib raised him from the age of eight and protected him for ten years after he declared his Prophethood. To the distress of the Prophet Abu Tālib never embraced Islam. In the Qur'an the noble Prophet was told; "*You guide not whom you love, but God guides whom He wills. He is best aware of those who are guided.*"[133] If he were the Qur'an's author, he could have claimed the conversion of Abu Tālib.

In the Qur'an there are many verses beginning, "*They ask you*" and continuing with "*Say (in answer*)." These were specifically revealed to answer questions asked by Muslims and non-Muslims, especially the Jews of Medina, about permissible or prohibited matters, the distribution of war booty, (astrological) mansions of the moon, the Judgment Day, Dhul-Qarnayn (an ancient believing king who made great conquests in Asia and Africa), the human spirit, and so on.[134] It is impossible for a person without an all-encompassing knowledge to answer such questions, however the answers of the Prophet satisfied everybody proving that he was taught by God, the All-Knowing.[135]

Jews and Christians at that time were very strong opponents of the Prophet and he was forced to fight the Jews of Medina several times and eventually to expel them. Despite this, the Qur'an mentions Prophet Moses, peace be upon him, about 50 times, and mentions Jesus, peace be upon him, many times but it men-

---

132 Gülen, *Essentials of Islamic Faith*, p. 226.

133 Qur'ān, 28: 56.

134 Gülen, Essentials of Islamic Faith, p. 227.

135 Ibid.

tions Prophet Muhammad's name only four times: Is it possible for a false prophet to mention the Prophets of his opponents so frequently? Or is it more likely that jealousy, prejudice, selfishness and other negative emotions were the reason for denying Prophet Muhammad's Prophethood?

Additionally, contained within the Qur'an are certain facts of creation that have only recently been established by modern scientific methods. How, except for Divine authorship, could the Qur'an be correct on matters of which the people listening to it had no idea?[136]

Summary: Arguments for the Divine Authorship of the Qur'an

1. The Qur'an is unique, does not imitate and cannot be imitated. No one has been able to respond to the challenge to imitate it with any success.
2. The Qur'an detailed the truth about many subjects and was revealed over 23 years without a single contradiction.
3. The Qur'an is of the highest form of eloquence in every aspect.
4. The Qur'an enriched the Arabic language enabling it to form the basis of a magnificent civilization.
5. The Qur'an is multi-layered in meaning and has illuminated people of all walks of life.
6. The Qur'an's appeal never fades; rather it becomes fresher and more original with each reading.
7. The Qur'an can be applied to all areas of life, public and private; it satisfies the mind and spirit simultaneously and guarantees happiness in both worlds.
8. The perfect life outlined in the Qur'an was presented by the noble Prophet first; it designed his character and led his followers to the best human values.
9. The Qur'an is universal and objective when dealing with particular issues and exact and precise when dealing with universal matters. This cannot be found in any human work.
10. The Qur'an is unique in its content. It not only contains many different scientific fields but also phrases them accurately. It contains the principles of all branches of knowledge, none of which has ever been contradicted.

[136] Ibid., p. 228.

11. In the Qur'an the Prophet is admonished and there are various verses that would have caused him personal distress, proving he could not have authored it.
12. The Qur'an could not have been written by someone without an all-encompassing knowledge to satisfactorily answer the questions of everyone. However the answers of the Prophet satisfied everybody.
13. The Qur'an mentioned Prophet Muhammad's enemies many times.
14. The Qur'an contains certain facts of creation that have only recently been established by modern scientific methods.

Asbāb an-Nuzūl (The Occasions of the Revelations)

There is a divine wisdom in the method of the verses of the Qur'an being revealed at specific times and locations. The verses fall into two categories with regards to whether or not we know the reasons behind their revelation. The majority of verses were revealed without relating to any occasion or reason but others were revealed as a result of, or to address, specific reasons and occasions. Similarly, some verses and *surah* of the Qur'an were revealed upon specific occasions or as answers to questions asked of the Prophet. These narrations of specific occasions are called *asbāb an-nuzūl.*

Asbāb an-nuzūl is the knowledge of the reasons for the revelation and the relationship between the revelation and the events that occurred during the 23 years of Prophet Muhammad's Prophethood.

There are three types of reason connected with the revelation of particular passages in the Qur'an:

1) Revelation in response to an event or a general situation.
2) Revelation in response to a particular question that has been asked by someone (a person, group, or even the Prophet himself).
3) Revelation upon an event which requires some explanation or warning.

The Benefits of Knowing the *Asbāb an-Nuzūl*

In the sciences of the Qur'an, it is very important to know the reasons behind the revelation and this brings many benefits:

> 1) To explain that the Qur'an is revealed by God. On many occasions the noble Prophet was asked questions and he would withhold his response until he was inspired with the revelation. Sometimes God informed the Prophet through the revelation about the true facts of the question/

questioner when the Prophet didn't know the real essence of the events he was being questioned upon.

'Abdullah ibn Mas'ud reports:

> While I was in the company of the Prophet on a farm, and he was reclining on a palm leaf stalk, some Jews passed by. Some of them said to the others: Ask him about the Spirit. Some of them said: What urges you to ask him about it. Others said: (Don't) lest he should give you a reply which you dislike, but they said, Ask him. So they asked him about the Spirit. The Prophet kept quiet and did not give them any answer. I knew that he was being divinely inspired so I stayed in my place. When the divine inspiration had been revealed,"[137] the Prophet recited the verse; "They ask you about the spirit. Say: "The spirit is of my Lord's Command, and of knowledge, you have been granted only a little.""[138]

2) We learn through *asbāb an-nuzūl* that God always supported the Prophet and defended him against the unbelievers. For example, on returning from an expedition to the Banī Mustaliq in the sixth year of the *Hijrah*, A'isha, who had accompanied the Messenger during that expedition, was inadvertently left behind when the Muslim army moved on from its camp. After spending several hours alone, she was found by Safwān ibn al-Mu'attal, one of the Emigrants who had participated in the Battle of Badr, whose duty it was to make sure that nothing and no one got left behind. A'isha got on his camel, and they re-joined the army at the next bivouac. This gave occasion to the enemies to raise a malicious scandal, which was led by 'Abdullah ibn Ubayy ibn Salul, the chief of the hypocrites in Medina. Upon this grave slander about A'isha, God revealed verses 24: 11–20 defending the Prophet and his wife against the hypocrites.

3) It is very important to know *asbāb an-nuzūl* to understand the original intent of the verses. For example;

> (The hills of) as-Safa and Marwa are among the emblems God has appointed (to represent Islam and the Muslim community). Hence, whoever does the Hajj (the Major Pilgrimage) to the House (of God, the Ka'ba) or the 'Umrah (the Minor Pilgrimage), there is no blame on him to run between them (and let them run after they go round the Ka'ba as an obligatory rite). And whoever does a good work voluntarily (such as additional going-round the Ka'ba and running between as-Safa and Marwa, and other

[137] Bukhari, *Kitāb al-Ilm*, 125.

[138] Qur'ān, 17: 85.

> kinds of good works), surely God is All-Responsive to thankfulness, All-Knowing.[139]

If one does not know the reason behind this revelation he may think that it is a sin to run between two hills Safa and Marwa, and wouldn't know whether this act is permissible. However, the ruling is that it is obligatory and one of the rituals of *Hajj*. The following report explains *asbāb an-nuzūl* behind this verse:

'Urwa reports:

> ...this divine inspiration was revealed concerning the Ansār who used to assume iḫrām (special attire for Hajj and 'Umrah) for worship ping an idol called 'Manāt' which they used to worship at a place called al-Mushallal before they embraced Islam. Whoever assumed iḫrām (for the idol), would consider it wrong to perform *tawaf* between Safa and Marwa. When they embraced Islam, they asked God's Messenger regarding it, saying, 'O God's Messenger! We used to refrain from *tawaf* between Safa and Marwa.' So God revealed: 'Verily; Safa and Marwa are among the symbols of God'..."[140]

4) We learn through *asbāb an-nuzūl* whether the meaning of a verse is specific or general. Sometimes a verse can be understood to be specific when it is not.

Ibn 'Abbas reports:

> Hilal ibn Umayya accused his wife before the Prophet of committing illegal sexual intercourse with Sharik ibn Sahma. The Prophet said, 'Produce a proof, or else you would get the legal punishment (by being lashed) on your back.' Hilal said, 'O God's Messenger! If anyone of us saw another man over his wife, would he go to search for a proof'? The Prophet went on saying, 'Produce a proof or else you would get the legal punishment (by being lashed) on your back.'[141]

The noble Prophet then recited the following verses:

> As for those who accuse their own wives of adultery but have no witnesses except themselves, such a person must testify four times swearing by God in each oath that he is indeed speaking the truth, and the fifth time, that God's curse be upon him if he is lying. But the punishment will be averted from the wife if she testifies four times by swearing by God in

[139] Qur'ān, 2: 158.

[140] Muslim, *Saḫīḫ, the Book of Hajj*, hadith no: 1278.

[141] Bukhari, *Saḫīḫ, the Book of Testimony*, hadith no: 2571.

> each oath that the man is surely telling a lie, and the fifth time, that the wrath of God be upon her if the man is speaking the truth.[142]

The other benefits of knowledge of *asbāb an-nuzūl* include:

5) It provides the immediate meaning of the verse. This allows the meaning to be seen within its original context and removes any misinterpretation concerning the meaning.

6) Understanding the wisdoms and reasons behind legal rulings. This in turn strengthens the faith of the believers and helps the unbelievers see the truth and come to the right path.

7) It assists in our understanding of the chronology of the revelation.

8) *Asbāb an-nuzūl* reports shed light on the historical socio-political situation at the time of the Prophet.

9) The reports identify the person and situation which prompted the revelation.

10) The reports provide the narrative context of the verses.

This information, supplied by *asbāb an-nuzūl* allows for the proper application and interpretation of the verses.

Summary: The Benefits of Knowing the *Asbāb an-Nuzūl*

1. To explain that the Qur'an is revealed by God. On many occasions the noble Prophet was asked questions and he would withhold his response until he was inspired with the revelation.
2. We learn through *asbāb an-nuzūl* that God always supported the Prophet and defended him against the unbelievers.
3. It is very important to know *asbāb an-nuzūl* to understand the original intent of the verses.
4. We learn through *asbāb an-nuzūl* whether the meaning of a verse is specific or general.
5. It provides that immediate meaning of the verse, allowing the meaning to be seen within its original context.
6. It helps with understanding the wisdoms and reasons behind legal rulings, strengthening the faith of the believers and helping the unbelievers see the truth.
7. It assists in our understanding of the chronology of the revelation.

[142] Qur'ān, 24: 6–9.

8. It sheds light on the historical socio-political situation at the time of the Prophet.
9. The reports identify the person and situation which prompted the revelation.
10. The reports provide the narrative context of the verses.
11. It allows for the proper application and interpretation of the verses.

Chapter Three

Sunnah

Sunnah

Introduction

The literal meaning of '*sunnah*' is: a path, customary practice, or an established course of conduct. Sunnah can be good or bad, it refers to someone's usual customs and modes of conduct. For example, the word '*sunnah*' in the following hadith is used in this meaning:

> He who introduced some good practice in Islam which was followed after him (by people) he would be assured of reward like one who followed it, without their rewards being diminished in any respect. And he who introduced some evil practice in Islam which had been followed subsequently (by others), he would be required to bear the burden like that of one who followed this (evil practice) without theirs being diminished in any respect.[143]

The word '*sunnah*' is used in the Qur'an to mean the established practice or course of conduct. The Qur'an uses different words to describe the noble Prophet, for example, in the following verse 'excellent example' is used instead of *sunnah*:

> Assuredly you have in God's Messenger an *excellent example* to follow for whoever looks forward to God and the Last Day, and remembers and mentions God much.[144]

The Qur'an also uses the word 'wisdom' (*ḥikmah*) as a source of guidance instead of *sunnah*:

> He it is Who has sent among the unlettered ones a Messenger of their own, reciting to them His Revelations, and purifying them, and instructing them in the Book and *the Wisdom*, whereas before that they were indeed lost in obvious error.[145]

---

[143] Muslim, *Saḥīḥ, Kitāb al-'Ilm*, hadith no: 6466.

[144] Qur'an 33: 21.

[145] Qur'an, 62: 2.

The Sunnah is the record of the Messenger's every act, word and confirmation. It serves as the second source of evidence for Islamic legislation. Depending on the Islamic science that is referring to it, this term has different terminological connotations. *Fiqh* scholars view Sunnah as including everything connected to the religious commandments reported from the Prophet. These are categorized as obligations, necessities and practices that are particular to, or encouraged by, the Prophet as recommended and desirable. To the scholars of *Uṣūl al-Fiqh*, Sunnah refers to a source of Islamic jurisprudence and a legal proof second only to the Qur'an. For the hadith scholars, it refers to everything that is narrated from the Prophet, his actions, sayings and whatever he has tacitly approved, as well as all the reports that describe his physical attributes and character.[146]

Islamic jurisprudence does not concern itself with the Prophet's personal affairs unless they touch upon the voluntary and purposed acts, whereby they should be dealt with under the relevant law. However, if they are just matters pertaining to the preferences and dislikes of the Prophet, which are not a basis for legislation, the jurists do not take them into account.

The word *sunnah* was used by both the noble Prophet and his Companions:

> When the Messenger of God intended to send Mu'adh ibn Jabal to the Yemen, he asked: How will you judge when the occasion of deciding a case arises? He replied: I shall judge in accordance with God's Book. He asked: (What will you do) if you do not find any guidance in God's Book? He replied: (I shall act) in accordance with the Sunnah of the Messenger of God. He asked: (What will you do) if you do not find any guidance in the Sunnah of the Messenger of God and in God's Book? He replied: I shall do my best to form an opinion and I shall spare no effort. The Messenger of God then patted him on the breast and said: Praise be to God Who has helped the messenger of the Messenger of God to find something which pleases the Messenger of God.[147]

The noble Prophet said; "I have left two sources with you. As long as you hold to them, you will not go the wrong way. They are the Book of God and the Sunnah of His Prophet."[148]

The Prophet ordered his Companions to obey his Sunnah absolutely. In conveying information to them he spoke clearly, so they could understand and memorize his words. He encouraged them to report his every word to future genera-

146 Siba'ī, *al-Sunnah*, p.47.

147 Tirmidhi, *Sunan, Aḫkām*, hadith no: 3.

148 Imam Mālik, *Muwatta, the Decree*, hadith no: 46.1.3.

tions and sometimes even urged them to write his words down. In turn, the Companions were fully attentive to his words and deeds and showed a great desire to mould their lives according to his, even down to the smallest details. Every word of his was regarded as a divine trust and they adhered to them as closely as possible, at the same time memorising, preserving and transmitting them.[149] Among the hadith collections made during the time of the Companions, three are very famous: *Al- Ṣaḫīfa al-Ṣādiqa* by 'Abd Allah ibn 'Amr ibn al-'As, *Al-Ṣaḫīfa al-Ṣaḫīha* by Hammam ibn Munabbih, and *Al-Majmu'* by Zayd ibn 'Ali ibn Husayn.

When it came to relating the hadiths, the Companions were extremely careful. A'isha and 'Abd Allah ibn 'Umar would relate hadiths word for word, not even changing a letter. Ibn Mas'ud and Abu al-Dardā' would tremble, as if feverish, when asked to report a hadith. It was on the order of Caliph 'Umar ibn 'Abd al-'Aziz (ruled 717–20 C.E.) that the orally preserved and transmitted traditions of the Prophet were recorded in writing. Such illustrious figures as Sa'id ibn al- Musayyib, Sha'bī, 'Alqama, Sufyan al-Thawrī, and Zuhrī pioneered this sacred task. They were followed by the greatest specialists, who were entirely focused on the accurate transmission of the hadiths. They also used meticulous critiquing systems to study the meaning and wording of the hadiths and their chain of narrators.[150]

Derived from the word *'haddatha'* (to inform), hadith literally means 'a tiding or information.' Over time, it assumed the meaning of every word, deed, and approval ascribed to Prophet Muhammad, peace and blessings be upon him. Another literal meaning of hadith is 'something that takes place within time' which clarifies why some of the finest scholars define hadith as that which is not divine, eternal, or without beginning in time, thus separating hadith from the Qur'an which has those attributes.

Sunnah is a broader concept than hadith which covers both the hadith (the narration of the conduct of the Prophet by his Companions) and the established practise of the Muslim community and, therefore, the example of the law that is deduced from the hadith. Hadith in this sense is the vehicle or the carrier of Sunnah. Scholars used these interchangeably. Sunnah used to be used widely before its literal meaning gave way to its juristic usage.[151]

The words *khabar* and *athar* are often used as substitutes for hadith. *Khabar* literally means news or report, and *athar*, trace or influence. Some scholars used hadith, *khabar* and *athar* synonymously, whereas others distinguished *khabar* from *athar*. These scholars use *khabar* and hadith interchangeably whereas *athar*

---

[149] Gülen, *The Messenger of God*, p. 314.

[150] Gülen, *the Messenger of God*, p. 315.

[151] Kamali, *Principles of Islamic Jurisprudence*, p. 49.

is used to mean the example of the Companions. Imam Mālik holds that *athar* represents the authentic Sunnah, because the Companions were in the best position to determine it. Sometimes the word *athar* is used to include the legal opinions of the Companions as it was their practise to discuss legal matters and sometimes reach agreement on them. Imam Shāfi'ī (d. 204 A.H. / 819 C.E.) however, did not accept this definition; instead, if he could not locate a hadith related to a legal issue he would search for the opinions of the Companions. If there were different opinions among the Companions, he preferred the opinion of the first four caliphs over the others, or whichever was in greater harmony with the Qur'an.[152]

Summary: Introduction

1. The literal meaning of 'Sunnah' is: a path, customary practice, or an established course of conduct. It can be good or bad. It refers to someone's usual customs and modes of conduct.
2. The word 'Sunnah' is used in the Qur'an to mean the established practice or course of conduct. Words like 'excellent example' and 'wisdom' are also used to refer followers to the practises of the noble Prophet.
3. The Sunnah is the record of the Messenger's every act, word and confirmation. It serves as the second source of evidence for Islamic legislation.
4. *Fiqh* scholars view Sunnah as including everything connected to the religious commandments reported from the Prophet.
5. *Uṣūl al-fiqh* scholars view Sunnah as a source of Islamic jurisprudence and a legal proof second only to the Qur'an.
6. Hadith scholars view it as everything that is narrated from and about the Prophet.
7. The Prophet ordered his Companions to obey his Sunnah absolutely and encouraged them to memorize his words and record them.
8. Famous collections of hadith from the Companions are *Al- Ṣaḫīfa al-Ṣādiqa* by 'Abd Allah ibn 'Amr ibn al-'As, *Al-Ṣaḫīfa al- Ṣaḫīha* by Hammam ibn Munabbih, and *Al-Majmu'* by Zayd ibn 'Ali ibn Husayn.
9. Caliph 'Umar ibn 'Abd al-'Aziz (ruled 717–20 C.E.) ordered that the orally preserved and transmitted traditions of the Prophet were recorded in writing.
10. Derived from the word '*haddatha*' (to inform), hadith literally means 'a tiding or information.'

[152] Imam Shāfi, *Ar-Risāla*, pp. 128–130.

11. Sunnah is a broader concept than hadith which covers both the hadith (the narration of the conduct of the Prophet by his Companions) and the established practise of the Muslim community.
12. The words *khabar* (news/report) and *athar* (trace/influence) are often used as substitutes for hadith. Scholars varied in their use of these words.

Proof-Value of Sunnah in Legislation

Sunnah is the second source of Islamic jurisprudence. It holds the same weight as the Qur'an in its rulings regarding legal issues relevant to the liable Muslims.[153] The Qur'an itself commands absolute obedience to the Messengers, for they have been sent to guide people to truth in every sphere of their lives. Similarly, God also commanded us to obey Prophet Muhammad, peace and blessings be upon him; *"O you who believe! Obey God and His Messenger, and do not turn away from him when you are hearing (from him God's Revelations)."*[154] This verse conveys that Muslims must not turn away from the Messenger. Therefore, disobeying, belittling, or criticizing the Sunnah amounts to heresy or even apostasy:

> O you who believe! Obey God and obey the Messenger, and those from among you who are invested with authority; and if you are to dispute among yourselves about anything, refer it to God and the Messenger, if indeed you believe in God and the Last Day. This is the best (for you) and fairest in the end.[155]

The verse stresses obedience to God and his Messenger. The repetition of 'obey' in the imperative tense indicates that the Messenger is authorized to command or forbid, and that Muslims must heed what he says. The noble Prophet comes above others in authority concerning his right to be obeyed.[156]

> Obey God and His Messenger, and do not dispute with one another, or else you may lose heart and your power and energy desert you; and remain steadfast. Surely, God is with those who remain steadfast.[157]

The source of Muslim strength and unity lies in submission to God and His Messenger. The Messenger established the Sunnah by being a living embodiment of the Qur'an, giving his community the perfect example to follow for guar-

---

153 Shawkānī, *Irshād*, p. 33.
154 Qur'an, 8: 20.
155 Qur'an, 4: 59.
156 Gülen, *The Messenger of God*, p. 318.
157 Qur'an, 8: 46.

anteed success in this life and the afterlife. Based on this, we can say that the Sunnah is more comprehensive than the Qur'an and is indispensable for leading an upright life in Islamic terms.[158]

> Say (to them, O Messenger): "If you indeed love God, then follow me, so that God will love you and forgive you your sins." God is All- Forgiving, All-Compassionate.[159]

The only valid way for Muslims to show their love for God is to obey Him, obey His Messenger and follow the Sunnah of the Messenger.

> But no! By your Lord, they do not (truly) believe unless they make you the judge regarding any dispute between them, and then find not the least vexation within themselves over what you have decided, and surrender in full submission.[160]

In one narration, a woman said to 'Abdullah ibn Mas'ud:

> I have heard that you call down God's curse upon women who tattoo their bodies, pluck their facial hair, force their teeth apart in order to look more beautiful, and who change the creation of God"[161] Ibn Mas'ud answered: "All of this is found in the Qur'an." The woman objected: "I swear by God that I have read the entire Qur'an, but I couldn't find anything related to this matter." Ibn Mas'ud told her: "Our Prophet called God's curse upon women who wear wigs, who join somebody's hair to theirs, and who have tattoos on their bodies. Haven't you read:[162] 'Whatever the Messenger brings you, adopt it; whatever he forbids you, refrain from it.'[163]

The way of the Prophet is the way of God; therefore, as the Sunnah is the way of the noble Prophet, those who reject it are, in essence rejecting (and disobeying) God. The Prophet stated; "Whoever obeys me, obeys God. Whoever disobeys me disobeys God."[164]

---

158 Gülen, *The Messenger of God*, p. 319.

159 Qur'an, 3: 31.

160 Qur'an, 4: 65.

161 This covers such cosmetic surgery procedures as changing the shape of the nose or lips, inserting breast implants, or somehow altering other bodily features through cosmetic surgery to look more beautiful. Such operations are allowed only when medically necessary, as in the case of severe burns or deformity.

162 Muslim, *Saḫīḫ, Libās*, hadith no: 120.

163 Qur'an, 59: 7.

164 Bukhari, *Saḫīḫ, Aḫkām*, hadith no: 1

On another occasion the Prophet emphasized the importance of his Sunnah with the following statement; "My nation will enter Paradise, except those who rebel." When asked who these rebels were, the Prophet answered: "Whoever obeys me will enter Paradise; whoever disobeys me rebels."[165]

The words of the noble Prophet are evidence upon anyone who has heard them. Since we have received them through the verbal and written reports of narrators, it is important that we can determine their authenticity.[166] Proof of the authenticity of the narrations may be definitive (*qat'ī*), or it may amount to preferable conjecture (*al-ẕannī*); in either case, the Sunnah commands the obedience of all liable Muslims. All the rulings of the Prophet, especially those which correspond with the Qur'an and corroborate its contents, constitute binding law.[167]

In the Islamic sciences Sunnah is classified by scholars according to its different aspects and representations of different values. According to one classification, it is divided into three categories: verbal, practical, and based on approval.

Summary: Proof-Value of Sunnah in Legislation

1. Sunnah is the second source of Islamic jurisprudence; it holds the same weight as the Qur'an. Disobeying, belittling, or criticizing the Sunnah amounts to heresy or even apostasy.
2. The Sunnah is more comprehensive than the Qur'an and is indispensable for leading an upright life in Islamic terms. It was embodied by the living example of the Prophet.
3. The Sunnah commands the obedience of all liable Muslims. All the rulings of the noble Prophet, especially those which correspond with the Qur'an and corroborate its contents, constitute binding law.
4. In the Islamic sciences Sunnah is classified by scholars according to its different aspects and representations of different values.

The Verbal Sunnah

The verbal Sunnah consists of the Messenger's words, which provide a basis for many religious commandments. There were occasions where the Prophet would utter specific words which constituted the basis of Islamic jurisprudence. The following hadiths are examples for this category of Sunnah:

---

[165] Bukhari, *Saḫīḫ, 'I'tisām,* hadith no: 2.
[166] Ghazali, *Muṣtaṣfā*, vol. I, p. 83.
[167] Kamali, *Principles of Islamic Jurisprudence*, p. 52.

"No bequest to the heir."[168] Practically, this means that as heirs will naturally inherit the bulk of the estate, it is not permissible to bequeath extra wealth to them.

"Don't harm (others), and don't return harm for harm."[169] This is a commandment to avoid engaging in negative and damaging behaviour, including retaliation, towards others.

"A tithe will be given (out of crops grown in fields) watered by rain or rivers; but a twentieth (out of those grown in fields) watered by people (irrigation or watering)."[170] This stipulates the amount of *zakat* (charity) that is to be given from crops depending on their method of watering.

"A sea is that of which the water is clean and the dead animals are lawful to eat."[171] The Prophet gave this response to a question on whether ablution was permissible with seawater. These words provided the basis for many other rulings.

The Practical Sunnah

The daily practises of the noble Prophet served to explain the rulings of the Qur'an to the Muslim community. The revelation usually imparted general rules and principles, but the inspiration the Prophet received from God and through angel Gabriel, enabled him to practice the fine detail of these rulings. For example, the Qur'an enjoins Prayer and pilgrimage on liable Muslims without giving the detail as to how they should be performed. The Prophet led the Prayers of the Companions five times a day and ordered them to pray as he prayed.[172] His whole life was a unique exposition of the Qur'an to be followed by all Muslims.

The Sunnah Based on His Approval

This category encompasses the occasions when the Prophet heard the words or saw the actions of his Companions and gave his tacit approval by neither approving nor rejecting them. The Prophet had the divine mission of guiding people to the truth which entailed correcting wrong beliefs, actions, characters and customs and he would have rejected any practises that were not in line with this mission. Therefore, if he did not reject the words or acts of the people even though

[168] Ibn Majah, *Sunan, Wasaya*, hadith no: 6

[169] Ahmad ibn Hanbal, *Musnad*, vol. 1, hadith no: 313.

[170] Bukhari, *Saḥīḥ, Zakat*, hadith no: 55.

[171] Abu Dāwud, *Sunan, Tahara*, hadith no: 41; Tirmidhi, *Sunan, Tahara*, hadith no: 52.

[172] Bukhari, *Saḥīḥ, Salah*, hadith no: 70.

he had knowledge of them, he advertently indicated his approval and also the permissibility of them.

When the Prophet saw something agreeable in his Companions, he gave his approval either explicitly or by keeping silent. For example:

1) Two Companions travelling in the desert could not find enough water for ablution before praying, and so used sand (*tayammum*). Before the Prayer time had passed, they found water. One of the Companions performed ablution and repeated the Prayer, and the other did not. When they asked the Prophet about this incident, he told the one who had not repeated the Prayer: "You acted in accordance with the Sunnah." Then, he turned to the other one and said: "For you, there is double the reward."[173]
2) The noble Prophet ordered a march upon Banī Qurayza immediately after the Battle of the Trench. He said: "Hurry up! We will perform the Afternoon Prayer there." Some Companions who concluded that they should hasten and pray over there set off without delay. Others understood that they were to hasten to the Banī Qurayza's territory only, and that they could pray before departing. The Prophet approved of both interpretations.[174]
3) During a military expedition, 'Amr ibn 'As led the Prayer with sand ablution for the Companions whilst in state of major impurity—*junub*. When he returned to Medina, he informed the Prophet about it. He explained; "I feared for my life from the cold and God says in Qur'an 'don't kill yourselves, as God is most merciful to you.'" The Prophet listened to the argument and did not say anything.[175]

A different way of categorising the Sunnah is to divide it into legal and non-legal. Non-legal Sunnah consists mainly of the personal habits of the Prophet such as the manner in which he ate, slept, dressed and other activities which do not constitute part of the Shari'ah. Additionally, Sunnah which involves specialized or technical knowledge such as medicine, commerce and agriculture, are outside of the Prophetic mission and are therefore not part of the Shari'ah. This is also the same for the acts and sayings of the Prophet that relate to particular circumstances such as the strategy of war, including such devices to mislead the enemy forces, the timing of an attack and siege withdrawal. These are also considered situational and are not a part of the Shari'ah.[176]

---

[173] Dārimī, *Sunan, Tahara*, hadith no: 65; Abu Dāwud, *Sunan, Tahara*, hadith no: 126.
[174] Dārimī, *Sunan, Maghāzī*, hadith no: 30.
[175] Abu Dāwud, *Sunan, Tahara*, hadith no: 334.
[176] Kamali, *Principles of Islamic Jurisprudence*, p. 53.

There are also certain matters which are specific only to the noble Prophet and do not constitute law for all Muslims. For example, polygamy, marriage without a dowry, prohibition of remarriage for the widows of the Prophet, fasting successively (*sawm al-wisal*) are restricted to the Prophet only.

Some of the Prophet's Sunnah fall in between the two categories of legal and non-legal as they combine the characteristics of both, making it difficult to determine whether an act was strictly personal or was intended to set an example for others to follow. For example, the Prophet kept his beard at a certain length and trimmed his moustache. Some scholars hold this was a practice of the Arabs designed to prevent resemblance to other people whereas others maintain that it is an example for believers to follow.

Summary: The Sunnah Based on His Approval

1. This is when the noble Prophet heard the words or saw the actions of his Companions and gave his tacit approval by neither approving nor rejecting them.
2. When the Prophet saw something agreeable in his Companions, he gave his approval either explicitly or by keeping silent.
3. Sunnah can be categorised as legal and non-legal.
4. Non-legal Sunnah are: the personal habits of the Prophet which are not part of the Shari'ah; matters specific only to the Prophet rather than to all Muslims.
5. Other Sunnah fall in-between legal and non-legal such as beard length.

The Role of Sunnah in Legislation

The Sunnah has two main functions: First, it enjoins and prohibits, lays down the principles related to establishing all religious obligations and necessities, and determines what is lawful or unlawful. The second function of the Sunnah is that it interprets the Qur'an.

> Guide us to the Straight Path, The Path of those whom You have favored, not of those who have incurred (Your) wrath (punishment and condemnation), nor of those who are astray.[177]

[177] Qur'an, 1: 6–7.

To explain who was intended in this verse the Prophet explained; "Those who incurred God's wrath are the Jews who have gone astray, and the misguided are the Christians who have gone astray."[178]

The following verse is another example which is explained by the Sunnah:

> Those who have believed and not obscured their belief with any wrongdoing, they are the ones for whom there is true security, and they are rightly guided.[179]

On the revelation of this verse, the Companions were fearful and asked the noble Prophet fearfully; "Is there one among us who has never done wrong?" The Prophet explained; "It's not as you think. It's as Luqman said to his son: '*Don't associate any partners with God; surely, associating partners with God is a grave wrongdoing*.'"[180]

In addition to interpreting the Qur'an's ambiguities, the Sunnah gives the details on subjects only briefly mentioned in the text. One example of this is the order in the Qur'an for Muslims to pray. It is through the Sunnah of the Messenger that the Muslim community learned the detail of the obligatory Prayers; the conditions, all obligatory, necessary, and commendable acts that validate it; and all that invalidates it. He told his followers; "Pray as you have seen me praying."[181]

The purpose of the Sunnah is also to make specific that which is mentioned generally in the Qur'an. For example, when the Prophet's daughter Fatima went to Abu Bakr, the first Caliph, and asked for her inheritance, Abu Bakr replied: "I heard the Messenger say: 'The community of the Prophets does not leave anything to be inherited. What we leave is for charity.'"[182] In this hadith, Sunnah excludes the Prophets and their children from the laws of inheritance.

The Prophet specified the general rules regarding inheritance in the hadith; "The killer (of his testator) would be deprived from the inheritance."[183] God commands in the Qur'an:

---

178 Tirmidhi, *Sunan, Tafsir al-Qur'an*, hadith no: 2. The Qur'ān forbids us to follow the ways of those who have incurred God's wrath (punishment and condemnation), and those who are astray. Whoever commits the sins or crimes which incur God's wrath, for instance, are included in "*those who have incurred (Your) wrath.*"

179 Qur'an, 6: 82.

180 Bukhari, *Saḫīḫ, Tafsir*, hadith no: 31.

181 Bukhari, *Saḫīḫ, Adhan*, hadith no: 604.

182 Bukhari, *Saḫīḫ, 'I'tisām*, hadith no: 5.

183 Tirmidhi, *Sunan, Farāiḏ*, hadith no: 17.

> For the thief, male or female: cut off their hands as a recompense for what they have earned, and an exemplary deterrent punishment from God. God is All-Glorious with irresistible might, All-Wise.[184]

This verse is *'āam* (general) and ambiguous for various reasons because it is not clear whether the punishment is to be applied to every thief or just to those who steal goods of a certain value. The Sunnah specified (*takhsis*) this general rule and explained its conditions. It was particularly pertinent during 'Umar's caliphate, when there was a period of famine; he did not apply this punishment for thieves due to the extenuating circumstances.

In the Qur'an, trade is made permissible by the general statement; "*...Do not consume one another's wealth in wrongful ways, except it be dealing by mutual agreement (trade)...*"[185] This was specified by the noble Prophet in the report; "Don't sell fruits until their amount is definite in the tree [so that the amount to be given as alms can be determined]."[186]

There are rulings that originate directly from the Sunnah, that are not mentioned at all in the Qur'an. For example, the prohibition regarding simultaneous marriage to the maternal and paternal aunt of one's wife, the grandmother's entitlement to a share in inheritance, and the punishment for the fornication of married people.[187]

Imam Shāfi'ī explains briefly the role of Sunnah in legislation as follows:

> First is the Sunnah which prescribes the like of what God has revealed in His Book; next is the Sunnah which explains the general principles of the Qur'an and clarifies the will of God; and last is the Sunnah where the Messenger of God has ruled on matters on which nothing can be found in the Book of God.[188]

The legal Sunnah may be divided into three types: the acts, words and approvals of the Prophet as Messenger of God, head of state and judge.

Summary: The Role of Sunnah in Legislation

1. The Sunnah has two main functions: to lay down the law and to interpret the Qur'an.

---

[184] Qur'an, 5: 38.
[185] Qur'an, 4: 29.
[186] Bukhari, *Sahīh, Buyu*, hadith no: 82.
[187] Kamali, *Principles of Islamic Jurisprudence*, p. 63.
[188] Imam Shāfi, *Risāla*, pp. 52–53.

2. In addition to interpreting the Qur'an's ambiguities, the Sunnah gives the details on subjects only briefly mentioned in the text.
3. The purpose of the Sunnah is also to make specific that which is mentioned generally in the Qur'an.
4. There are rulings that originate directly from the Sunnah, that are not mentioned at all in the Qur'an.
5. The legal Sunnah may be divided into three types: the acts, words and approvals of the Prophet as Messenger of God, head of state and judge.

The Prophet as a Messenger of God

The noble Prophet not only established rules that were complementary to Qur'anic legislation, but also on areas where the Qur'an was silent. In this category, the Sunnah may consist of a clarification of the ambiguous (*mujmal*) parts of the Qur'an, or specifying and qualifying its general (*'āam*) and absolute (*mutlaq*) verses. It also covers the principles of religion; in particular devotional matters (*ibadāt*) and rules expounding the lawful and the unlawful. It constitutes general legislation whose validity is not restricted to the limitations of time and circumstance. All commands and prohibitions that are imposed by the Sunnah are also binding on every Muslim.[189]

The Prophet as a Ruler

This Sunnah originated from the Prophet in his capacity as the Head of State. For example, the distribution and spending of public funds, decisions pertaining to military strategy and war, the appointment of state officials, the distribution of war booty, and the signing of treaties, etc., do not constitute general legislation. These matters do not bind individuals directly and do not entitle them to act on their own initiative without the express permission of the lawful authority.[190] The following hadith is an example for this type of Sunnah; "Whoever kills a warrior [in battle] may take his belongings."[191]

The Prophet as a Judge

Disputes usually consist of two parts; the claims and evidence in a case and the resulting judgment. The claims and evidence are situational and do not consti-

---

[189] Kamali, *Principles of Islamic Jurisprudence*, p. 54.
[190] Shaltut, *Al-Islam*, p. 513.
[191] Abu Dāwud, *Sunan, Jihad*, hadith no: 758.

tute general law whereas the judgment lays down general law. Since the Prophet himself acted in a judicial capacity, the rules that he has enacted must be implemented by the office of the judge.[192]

To distinguish the legal from non-legal Sunnah, it is necessary for the *mujtahid* to ascertain the original purpose of, and context in which, a particular Sunnah ruling has been issued, and whether it was designed to establish a general rule of law.[193]

The noble Prophet said; "Whoever reclaims barren land becomes its owner."[194] This hadith caused a dispute among scholars as to whether the Prophet uttered this ruling in his capacity as Messenger or the head of state. If he issued it in his capacity as a Messenger the ruling would be binding on all Muslims and would not necessitate legal permission. However, if it was issued as head of state it would imply that anyone who wished to reclaim barren land must obtain the permission of the ruler first. The ruler must then grant the citizen the right to reclaim the barren land. The majority of jurists have adopted the first view whereas Ḥanafī scholars hold the second.

The Differences between the Qur'an and Sunnah

Even though the Qur'an and Sunnah came from the same divine origin, there are some differences between them regarding their transmission and revelation type. Both are sources of Islamic law and both were taught by God to the Prophet; nevertheless, there are some significant differences between them:

1) Transmission reliability: Sunnah has been classified as *mutawātir*, *mashhūr*, and *āḥād* (explained below). The Qur'an as whole has been transmitted to us via *mutawātir* reports.

2) Definite and speculative ruling types: *Mutawātir* Sunnah is *qat'ī* (definite) for the rulings but the other types of Sunnah are *ẕannī* (speculative). The whole Qur'an is *qat'ī* (definitive). In the Ḥanafī school, the category of *mashhūr* Sunnah are close to *mutawātir* in regards to their transmission and therefore are also *qat'ī* (definitive) for legal rulings. Other schools however consider them to be *ẕannī*. *Āḥād* Sunnah are *ẕannī*, but are still used as evidence by the imams of all four schools. Even though, by way of transmission, Sunnah may sometimes be considered *ẕannī*, the indication for the ruling might be precise and definite. For

192 Shawkānī, Irshād, p. 36.

193 Kamali, *Principles of Islamic Jurisprudence*, p. 57.

194 Abu Dāwud, *Sunan, Tribute, Spoils, and Rulership,* hadith no: 3067.

example, the following report is an *āḥād* hadith but its meaning is definite; "There is one sheep *zakat* for each five camels up until twenty-four camels..."[195] In this hadith the numbers one, five and 24 are definite and not open to interpretation, however this report was transmitted as *āḥād*. Sometimes *āḥād* reports might be *ẕannī* in both meaning and transmission. For instance, the following report was understood differently by the imams of the four schools; "There is no Prayer for a person who does not recite Fatiha."[196] Some *mujtahids* understood this hadith to indicate that omitting the recitation of Fatiha in the Prayers invalidates them. However, Ḥanafī scholars understood the hadith to relate to perfecting the Prayer. They held that even though it is necessary (*wājib* not *fard*) to recite *surah* Fatiha, it is not a pillar of the Prayer. Due the discrepancy between reports, the evidence is not definite; rather it is open to interpretation. Consequently, the Prayer without the recitation of Fatiha is valid.

3) All of the verses of the Qur'an were recorded in writing during the lifetime of the Prophet, however, neither the Sunnah nor the hadiths of the Prophet were not. In fact, the noble Prophet warned his community against writing down any of his words except the Qur'an. He only allowed some Companions to write his own words, but mostly the Companions memorised the Sunnah and reported them to others from their memories.

4) If the Companions did not understand a verse of the Qur'an, they would ask the Prophet for clarification, whereas there are no such incidences of this happening for the Sunnah.

5) Unlike the Qur'an, it is permissible to transmit the Sunnah in meaning not in exact words. Most of the Sunnah is transmitted in meaning whereas the whole Qur'an is transmitted in its exact wording as *mutawātir*.

6) Scholars dispute over the Sunnah with regard to both transmission and meaning, whereas the *mujtahids* only dispute regarding the meaning of the Qur'an.

7) The Sunnah is the second source in Islamic jurisprudence after the Qur'an and if there is a conflict between them the Qur'an is preferred. A practical consequence of this order of priority may be seen in the Ḥanafī distinction between *fard* and *wājib*. The former is founded in the definitive authority of the Qur'an, whereas the latter is founded in the definitive Sunnah, but is one degree weaker because of a possible doubt in its transmission and accuracy of content.[197]

---

195 Nasaī, *Sunan, Zakat,* hadith no: 5.

196 Tirmidhi, *Sunan, Mawaqīt as-Salah,* hadith no: 69.

197 Kamali, *Principles of Islamic Jurisprudence*, p. 60.

Summary: The Differences between Qur'an and Sunnah

1. The Qur'an and Sunnah are different in their transmission and revelation type.
2. Both are sources of Islamic law and both were taught by God to the noble Prophet
3. Transmission reliability: Sunnah has been classified as *mutawātir*, *mashhūr*, and *āḥād*. The Qur'an as whole has been transmitted to us via *mutawātir* reports.
4. Definite and speculative ruling types: *Mutawātir* Sunnah is *qat'ī* (definite) for the rulings but the other types of Sunnah are *ẕannī* (speculative). The whole Qur'an is *qat'ī* (definitive).
5. All verses of the Qur'an were recorded in writing during the lifetime of the Prophet; however the Sunnah and the hadiths of the Prophet were not.
6. The Prophet frequently explained verses of the Qur'an but this didn't occur with the Sunnah.
7. Unlike the Qur'an, it is permissible to transmit the Sunnah in meaning not in exact words.
8. Scholars dispute over the Sunnah with regard to both transmission and meaning, whereas the *mujtahids* only dispute regarding the meaning of the Qur'an.
9. The Sunnah is the second source in Islamic jurisprudence after the Qur'an and if there is a conflict between them the Qur'an is preferred.

Forgery in the Hadith

There are many instances of forgery in the history of hadith literature and books called *al-Mawdu'at* were written to specifically address this. These books contained fake hadiths and explain the reasons behind their fabrication. It is not clear as to when forgery in hadith literature began; one opinion is that it started in the time of Caliph 'Uthmān whereas another holds that it started around the end of Çaliph Ali's rule when the political dispute arose with Mu'awiya. This was a period where serious differences arose in the Muslim community and sectarian movements such as Kharijites and the Shi'ah emerged. Fabricated hadith were used by different groups to defend their political beliefs using the Qur'an and Sunnah. They also tried to refute the views of opposing sects by using these sources. When they couldn't find any supporting arguments for their views in the Qur'an and Sunnah, they fabricated some hadiths.[198] Other reasons for forgery in hadith literature include:

1) To credit or discredit some leading political figures with exaggerated claims. Sunni scholars hold that the followers of Shi'ah forged some hadith to credit 'Ali, such as; "Ali is my brother, executor and successor. Listen to him and obey him.' There are numerous fabricated hadiths condemning Mu'awiya, because the Muslims were unhappy with his reign, including; 'When you see Mu'awiya on my pulpit, kill him.' The followers of Mu'awiya also fabricated some hadith to credit their leader, for instance; 'The trusted ones are three: I (the Prophet), Gabriel and Mu'awiya.'[199]

2) One group of unbelievers used fabricated hadith to discredit Islam in the eyes of its followers in order to get revenge. For example; 'Eggplants are cure for every illness', and 'beholding a good-looking face is a form of worship.' They fabricated around 14,000 hadiths in many cases changing rules to their opposite. For example, if something is mentioned as permissible in an authentic hadith they changed it to forbidden in their forgeries.

3) Racial, tribal and linguistic fanaticism also contributed to hadith forgery, for example; 'Whenever God was angry, He sent down the revelation in Arabic, but when contented, He chose Persian for this purpose.'

4) Professional story-tellers and preachers were not afraid of fabricating hadith. They aimed to gain attention of people and raise their emotions by forging hadith and to this purpose they made up stories and attributed them to the Prophet. It is reported that once a story-teller cited an hadith to audiences in the mosque on the authority of Ahmad ibn Hanbal and Yahya ibn Ma'in: 'Whoever says 'There is no god but God', God will reward him, for each word uttered, with a bird in Paradise, who has a beak of gold and feathers of pearls.' At the end of his sermon, the speaker was confronted by Ahmad ibn Hanbal and Yahya ibn Ma'in who were present on the occasion and told the speaker that they had never related any hadith of this kind. But the speaker told them; 'There are many hadith scholars named Ahmad ibn Hanbal and Yahya ibn Ma'in, you are not the only ones. I heard that you are idiots but I didn't think that much.'[200]

---

[198] Shabir Ahmad, *Authority of hadith*, p. 51.

[199] Shabir, *Authority of hadith*, p. 81.

[200] Azami, *Studies*, p. 69.

5) Differences between the juristic and belief schools caused some fanatic followers to fabricate hadiths in support of their particular sect's views, such as; 'Whoever raises his hands during the performance of Prayer, his Prayer is invalid.'

6) The religious enthusiasm of some individuals led them to carelessly attribute hadiths to the noble Prophet. For instance, Nuh ibn Maryam fabricated some hadiths to praise the Qur'an and the virtues of its *surahs*. Later on he explained this forgery and defended himself saying that people were turning away from the Qur'an.[201]

Summary: Forgery in the Hadith

1. The many instances of forgery in the history of hadith literature are addressed in books called *al-Mawdu'at* which contain the fake hadiths and explanation behind their existence.
2. Fabricated hadith were used by different groups to defend their political beliefs using the Qur'an and Sunnah.

   Other reasons for forgery in hadith:
3. To credit or discredit some leading political figures with exaggerated claims.
4. One group of unbelievers used fabricated hadith to discredit Islam in the eyes of its followers in order to get revenge.
5. Racial, tribal and linguistic fanaticism also contributed to hadith forgery.
6. Professional story-tellers and preachers aimed to gain attention of people and raise their emotions by forging hadith.
7. Differences between the juristic and belief schools caused some fanatic followers to fabricate hadiths in support of their particular sect's views.
8. The religious enthusiasm of some individuals led them to carelessly attribute hadiths to the Prophet.

Classification of Hadith in regard to Chain of Transmission

The hadiths are classified as *muttasil* (continuous) and *ghayr muttasil* (discontinued) regarding their chain of transmission. The *muttasil* hadith has a complete chain of transmission from the last narrator all the way back to the Prophet, whereas the chain of transmission of *ghayr muttasil* hadith contains a deficiency. The

[201] Sibā'ī, *Sunnah*, pp. 86–87.

majority of scholars agree that two types of hadiths are *muttasil*; *mutawātir* and *āḥād*. Ḥanafī scholars add *mashhūr* to their classification.

Muttasil (The Continuous) Hadith

This section deals with the *muttasil* hadith giving more details about the three different classifications.

a) *Mutawātir* Hadith

The literal meaning of *mutawātir* is 'continuously repeated' and in hadith literature it means a report by a large number of people from the generations of the Companions, *Tabi'in* and *Atba' at-Tabi'in* that is related in such a way as to prevent the possibility of their agreement to perpetuate a lie. The large number of the narrators, their diversity of residence and their known reliability makes the possibility of fabrication inconceivable.[202] For a hadith to be able to be considered *mutawātir* it is necessary that it was narrated by a large number of people from the three generations immediately succeeding the noble Prophet. Without this level of authenticity it isn't possible for a hadith to be considered *mutawātir*. The number of transmitters of the hadith is not specified; the criterion is that the number must be large enough to verify the impossibility of such a number either unwittingly or agreeing to perpetuate a lie. The following are the conditions for a report to be classified *mutawātir*:

1) A large number of people (such as to preclude their agreement in spreading falsehood) from the first three generations of Muslims (the Companions, *Tabi'in* and *Atba' at-Tabi'in*) must narrate the report. If this condition is missing in any of the three generations, the hadith cannot be accepted as *mutawātir*.
2) The reporters must base their report on sense perception; it should not be mere assumption. The report must also be based on certain knowledge, not mere speculation.
3) The reporters must be upright persons. They must neither be unbelievers nor commit major sins.
4) The reporters should not be biased in their cause and should not be associated with one another through political or sectarian movements.

---

[202] Shawkānī, *Irshād*, p. 46

All of these conditions must be met from the origin to the end of the report's transmission.[203]

There are two types of *mutawātir* reports; literal and meaning. Reports with exactly the same wording in each transmission are known as literal (*lafẕī*) *mutawātir*. Reports with different wording but the same meaning are known as *mutawātir* in meaning (*ma'nawī*). The following hadith is an example of a literal *mutawātir* hadith:

> The reward of deeds depends upon the intentions and every person will get the reward according to what he has intended. So whoever emigrated for worldly benefits or for a woman to marry, his emigration was for what he emigrated for.[204]

An example of *ma'nawī mutawātir* is the raising of the hands when making dua. There are hundreds of reports which state in different ways that the Prophet raised his hands when he made dua. *Ma'nawī mutawātir* hadiths contain a lot of information about the Sunnah practises in *ibadāt* (worship); for example, the details of how to perform ablution and the rituals of *Hajj* have been transmitted to us through this type of hadith.

The majority of scholars agree that the value of the evidence from the *mutawātir* hadiths is equivalent to that of the Qur'an. Universal continuous testimony produces certainty and the knowledge that it creates is equivalent to knowledge that is acquired through sense-perception.[205]

b) *The Mashhūr* (Well-Known) Hadith

Mashhūr hadith are those that were originally transmitted by a small number of people, maybe one, two or more Companions directly from the Prophet or from another Companion and have later become well known and transmitted by a large number of people.[206] The condition for these hadiths is that they should have become well-known during the first or second generation following the death of the Prophet and not later.[207]

Ḫanafī scholars hold that *mashhūr* hadiths convey definite knowledge albeit with a lesser degree of certainty than *mutawātir* hadiths. Other scholars do not

---

203 Kamali, *Principles of Islamic Jurisprudence*, p. 70.
204 Bukhari, *Saḫīḫ, Revelation*, hadith no: 1.
205 Kamali, *Principles of Islamic Jurisprudence*, p. 71.
206 Abu Zahrah, *Uṣūl*, p. 84
207 Shawkānī, *Irshād*, p. 49

acknowledge this category of hadith but consider them to be part of the *āḫād* hadith, conveying only speculative knowledge for the rulings in Islamic jurisprudence. According to Ḫanafī scholars, actions based on *mashhūr* hadith are obligatory but denying them is not disbelief.[208]

The only difference between the *mutawātir* and *mashhūr* hadiths is the number of people reporting them in the first three generations of Muslims. The *mutawātir* are transmitted by a large number of narrators in each generation, whereas the *mashhūr* are transmitted by only one or two people from the Companions' generation with the number of transmitters increasing after this. For Ḫanafī scholars, the *mashhūr* hadith can specify the general ruling (*āam*) or qualify the absolute (*mutlaq*) expression of the Qur'an. The following hadiths are *mashhūr* and specified the Qur'an:

"The killer (of his testator) would be deprived from the inheritance."[209] This hadith specified the verse; "God commands you in (the matter of the division of the inheritance among) your children..."[210]

"No woman shall be married simultaneously with her paternal or maternal aunt."[211] This *mashhūr* hadith restricted the ruling of the verse; *"And (also forbidden to you are) all married women..."*[212] The list of prohibitions outlined in this verse does not include simultaneous marriage with the maternal or paternal aunt of one's wife. However, this meaning is provided by the related hadith.

c) *Āḫād* (Solitary) Hadith

From the perspective of transmission, the *āḫād* hadith are lower in value than the *mutawātir* and *mashhūr.* The number of narrators of these hadiths is much lower, maybe a single person or odd individuals from the time of the noble Prophet. Most of the Sunnah has been transmitted to us through this type of report.

As *āḫād* hadiths convey only speculative knowledge (*ẕannī*), they are not accepted for matters of belief. Most jurists agree that *āḫād* hadith create a rule of law if related by a reliable narrator and if the content of the hadith cannot be rejected.[213] For the four Sunni schools, acting upon these hadiths is obligatory even if they fail to produce definite knowledge. Thus, in practical legal matters,

---

208 Abu Zahrah, *Uṣūl*, p. 84

209 Tirmidhi, *Sunan, Farāiḏ*, hadith no: 17.

210 Qur'an, 4: 11.

211 Dārimī, *Sunan, Kitāb al-Farāiḏ*, hadith no: 384.

212 Qur'an, 4: 24.

213 Āmidī, *Iḫkām*, vol. 1, p. 161.

speculative knowledge is sufficient as a basis of obligation if it meets the following conditions:

1) The narrator is mentally healthy, mature and not insane.
2) The narrator is Muslim. Reports cannot be accepted from unbelievers.
3) The narrator must be trustworthy (*'adl*). Scholars vary in their definitions of what constitutes a trustworthy person, however, the minimum requirement is that the person has not committed a major sin and does not persist in committing minor ones. Ḫanafī scholars agree that one who has not committed a major sin is trustworthy, but their character must also be known as this verifies whether they can be considered trustworthy. All of the Companions of the Prophet are considered trustworthy by default, because the Qur'an praises them on many occasions.
4) It is necessary for the narrator of *āḫād* hadith to possess a healthy memory (*ḏabt*) for his report to be trusted; his report is not acceptable if he is known to have made frequent mistakes. This can be evaluated by how well he listens to, comprehends the meaning of, and accurately preserves the hadith.[214]
5) The narrator must not be implicated in any form of distortion in either the textual contents of a hadith or in its chain of transmitters.[215] Distortion means changing or adding to the words of the Prophet to convey a different meaning and mislead the listener. Distortion in the chain of transmitters is to tamper with the names and identity of narrators.[216]
6) The narrator must listen to the hadith from the source directly. The content must not contradict the Qur'an or the authentic Sunnah.

If these conditions are fulfilled, then *āḫād* hadith are accepted by Abū Ḫanīfa, Shāfi'ī and Ahmad ibn Hanbal. Abū Ḫanīfa added one more condition to the above criteria; the narrator must not contradict his reports. For example, the following *āḫād* hadith was not accepted by Abū Ḫanīfa because the narrator did not act upon it himself; "When a dog licks a dish, wash it seven times, one of which must be with clean sand."[217] This hadith is reported by Abu Hurayra; however he did not act upon this hadith himself and therefore the Ḫanafī School ruled that washing the dish three times is sufficient.

---

[214] Shawkānī, *Irshād*, p. 52.
[215] Kamali, *Principles of Islamic Jurisprudence*, p. 75.
[216] Shawkānī, *Irshād*, p. 55.
[217] Muslim, *Saḫīḫ*, hadith no: 119.

For Ḫanafī scholars to accept *āḫād* hadith, the subject matter should not refer to something that occurs frequently, or that which is necessary knowledge for all liable Muslims, otherwise this would have been reported by many people, not just a single person. If the report relates to something like this and is only transmitted by one person it is not accepted by Ḫanafī scholars. For example, they did not rule based on the report; "The Prophet would raise his hands when he was bowing and rising from bowing."[218] Their reasoning was that many people prayed with the Prophet many times and this action would have been reported by them, not just one narrator. Also, being related to the Prayers, this action would have been obligatory for all Muslims and would have been transmitted by them through many channels.

There is one further condition that must be met for Ḫanafī scholars to accept *āḫād* hadith: if a solitary hadith is reported by a non-*fāqih* (jurist) narrator it should not contradict *qiyāṣ* (analogy) and the principles of Islam. If it contradicts *qiyāṣ* and Islamic principles and it is not transmitted by *fāqih* narrator such as Abu Bakr, 'Umar, 'Uthman and 'Ali, it should not be accepted. However if the report came through *fāqih* narrators, the Ḫanafī scholars accept it even if it contradicts *qiyāṣ*. The following *āḫād* hadith is not used as a basis for ruling in the Ḫanafī School because the last condition is missing;

> Do not retain milk in the udders of a she camel or goat so as to exaggerate its yield. Anyone who buys a such camel has the choice, for three days after having milked it, either to keep it, or to return it with a quantity [i.e. a sa'] of dates.[219]

Abū Ḫanīfa explains the reason for not accepting this hadith: the quantity of dates may not be equal in value to the amount of milk the buyer has consumed. Hence, if the buyer wishes to return the beast, he must return it with the cost of milk which was in its udders at the time of purchase, not with a fixed quantity of dates.[220]

All the four Imams of jurisprudence have considered *āḫād* hadith to be authoritative in principle, and none reject them unless there is evidence to suggest a weakness in their attribution to the Prophet, or which may contradict other pieces of evidence that are more authoritative in their view.

---

218 Bukhari, *Saḫīḫ, Adhan*, hadith no: 83.

219 Muslim, *Saḫīḫ*, hadith no: 928.

220 Kamali, *Principles of Islamic Jurisprudence*, p. 77.

Summary: *Muttasil* (the Continuous) Hadith

1. Three types of *muttasil* hadiths; *mutawātir, mashhūr* and *āḫād.*

Mutawātir

2. The literal meaning of *mutawātir* is ‘continuously repeated.
3. In hadith literature it means a report by a large number of people from the generations of the Companions, *Tabi’in* and *Atba’ at-Tabi’in* that is related in such a way as to prevent the possibility of their agreement to perpetuate a lie.
4. Conditions: A large number of people from the first three generations of Muslims must narrate the report; they must base their report on sense perception and it must be sound knowledge; they must be trustworthy and unbiased.
5. There are two types of *mutawātir* reports; literal (*lafẕī*) reports which are narrated with the exact same words by all narrators, and meaning (*ma’nawī*) reports related using varied words but each conveying the same meaning.
6. *Mutawātir* reports hold the same weight as the Qur’an when used as evidence.

***Mashhūr* (Well-Known) Hadith**

7. *Mashhūr* hadith were original transmitted by few Companions but became well known within the next two generations.
8. For Ḫanafī scholars the *mashhūr* hadiths convey definite knowledge, although with a lesser degree of certainty than the *mutawātir* hadiths. Other scholars do not acknowledge this category of hadith but consider them to be part of the *āḫād* hadith.

***Āḫād* (Solitary) Hadith**

9. *Āḫād* hadith are lower in value than the *mutawātir* and *mashhūr* as regards transmission as they are narrated by a single person or odd numbers.
10. Most of the Sunnah has been transmitted to us through this type of report.
11. As *āḫād* hadiths convey only speculative knowledge (*ẕannī*), they are not accepted for matters of belief.
12. Most jurists agree that *āḫād hadith* creates a rule of law if it is related by a reliable narrator and the content of the hadith cannot be rejected: the narrator must be mentally healthy, mature, Muslim and trustworthy.
13. The narrator must have a healthy memory.
14. The narrator must not be implicated in any form of distortion in either the textual contents of a hadith or in its chain of transmitters.

15. The narrator must listen to the hadith from the source directly and its content must not contradict the Qur'an or the authentic Sunnah.
16. For Abū Ḫanīfa the narrator must also not contradict his reports.
17. For Ḫanafī scholars to accept *āḫād* hadith the subject matter should not refer to something that occurs frequently or something that it is necessary for all liable Muslims to know; otherwise this would have been reported by many people.
18. For Ḫanafī scholars if a solitary hadith is reported by a non-*fāqih* (jurist) narrator it should not contradict *qiyāṣ* (analogy) and the principles of Islam.

Ghayr Muttasil (The Discontinued) Hadith

Ghayr muttasil hadith is those which have a break in their chain of transmission, and therefore, the chain does not go all the way back to the Prophet. There are three types of *ghayr muttasil*: *mursal, mu'ḏal* and *munqati.'*

a) *Mursal* Hadith

These hadiths have been transmitted by a Successor (*tabi'in*) and attributed directly to the noble Prophet without mentioning the Companion who narrated it. The Ḫanafī scholars defined *mursal* as a hadith that a reliable narrator has attributed to the Prophet while omitting a part of its chain of transmitters.[221] Since the identity of the missing narrator is not known, it is possible that he may or may not have been a trustworthy person; therefore scholars generally do not rely on this type of hadith.[222]

Mursal hadith transmitted by prominent Successors such as Said b. al-Musayyib, al-Zuhrī, 'Alqama, etc. are accepted if they meet the following conditions:[223]

1) The *mursal* hadith is supported by another more reliable hadith.
2) The *mursal* hadith is supported by another *mursal* hadith which is used as evidence by scholars.
3) The *mursal* hadith does not contradict the authentic hadiths.
4) It is accepted and used as evidence by the scholars.
5) The narrator of the *mursal* hadith is not known to be a weak or doubtful narrator.

The majority of scholars hold that acting upon *mursal* hadith is not obligatory.

---

[221] Kamali, *Principles of Islamic Jurisprudence*, p. 80.
[222] Abu Zahrah, *Uṣūl*, p.86.
[223] Shawkānī, *Irshād*, p. 64

b) *Munqati'* Hadith

Munqati' hadith are those whose chain of narrators has a single missing link somewhere in the middle. They are neither reliable nor used as evidence in Islamic law.

c) *Mu'ḏal* Hadith

Mu'ḏal hadith are those in which two consecutive links are missing in the chain of its narrators. They are also not reliable and are not used as evidence in Islamic law.

SUMMARY: *GHAYR MUTTASIL* (THE DISCONTINUED) HADITH

1. These hadith have a break in their chain of transmission. There are three types of *ghayr muttasil*: *mursal, mu'ḏal* and *munqati.'*

   ***Mursal* Hadith**
2. Transmitted by a Successor (*tabi'in*) and attributed directly to the noble Prophet without mentioning the Companion who narrated it.
3. Since the identity of the missing narrator is not known, it is possible that he may or may not have been a trustworthy person; therefore scholars generally do not rely on this type of hadith.
4. *Mursal* hadith transmitted by prominent Successors are accepted if they meet certain conditions.
5. The majority of scholars hold that acting upon *mursal* hadith is not obligatory.

   ***Munqati'* Hadith**
6. *Munqati'* hadith have a single missing link somewhere in the middle. They are neither reliable nor used as evidence in Islamic law.

   ***Mu'ḏal* Hadith**
7. *Mu'ḏal* hadith have two consecutive links are missing in the chain of its narrators. They are also not reliable and are not used as evidence in Islamic law.

Saḫīḫ, Ḫasan and *Da'īf*

Scholars have classified the hadith into three further categories based on the reliability of the narrators: *saḫīḫ, ḫasan* and *da'īf.* The levels of reliability for hadith narrators in descending order are:

1) The Companions (accepted to be trustworthy by default)
2) *Thiqāt dābitūn* (emphasized trustworthy)

3) *Thiqāt* (trustworthy)
4) *Ṣadūq* (truthful)
5) *Ṣadūq yahim* (truthful but committing errors)
6) *Maqbūl* (accepted) there is no proof to the effect that his report is unreliable
7) *Majhūl* (unknown)
8) *Fussāq* (sinners)

Hadith are classified as *saḫīḫ* (authentic) when all of the narrators in the chain belong to the first three categories. If one belongs to a different category then the value of the hadith changes to either *ḫasan* or *da'īf*.

Ḫasan hadith differ from *saḫīḫ* in that its narrators can include people from the fourth to the sixth categories. Weak, or *da'īf* hadith are those whose narrators do not possess the qualifications required for *saḫīḫ* or *ḫasan*. They are classified as weak owing to a weakness that exists in the chain of narrators or in the textual contents.[224]

The general rule for classifying hadith is according to the weakest element in its chain of narrators. Just one weak element results in weakening the ranking of the hadith. If one of the narrators is suspected of lying whereas all the rest are classified as trustworthy (*Thiqāt*), and the hadith is not known through other channels, it is graded as weak.[225]

Summary: *Saḫīḫ*, *Ḫasan* and *Da'īf*

1. Categories of hadith based on the reliability of the narrators: *saḫīḫ*, *ḫasan* and *da'īf*.
2. The levels of reliability for hadith narrators have been defined as above.
3. Hadith are classified as *saḫīḫ* (authentic) when all of the narrators in the chain belong to the first three categories.
4. *Ḫasan* hadith can include people from the fourth to the sixth categories.
5. *Da'īf* hadith are those whose narrators do not possess the qualifications required for *saḫīḫ* or *ḫasan*. They have a weakness that exists in the chain of narrators or in the textual contents.
6. The general rule for classifying hadith is according to the weakest element in its chain of narrators.

[224] Kamali, *Principles of Islamic Jurisprudence*, p. 82.
[225] Kamali, p. 83.

CHAPTER FOUR

Ijma' (General Consensus)

Ijma' (General Consensus)

Introduction

The literal meaning of *ijma'* is consensus, intention, absolute decision and agreement.[226] In the Qur'an, it is used in the verse; "*So, coming together, decide upon your course of action.*"[227] In the following hadith of the noble Prophet the word *ijma'* is used to mean intention or absolute decision; "There is no fasting for a person who does not intend (*ijma'*) it before the dawn."[228]

In Islamic jurisprudence, *ijma'* is the general consensus on a religious matter by the Muslim *mujtahids* who were practising within the same time frame after the death of the Prophet. According to the scholars of *Uṣūl al-Fiqh* the following conditions must be met for *ijma'* to be actualized:

1) A certain number of *mujtahids* must reach a general consensus. People who are not *mujtahid* are not qualified to make *ijtihād* so their views do not affect the general consensus. As a result, if there are no *mujtahids* in a particular time frame, *ijma'* cannot be achieved. However if there are some *mujtahids* (regardless of their numbers) and they achieve a general consensus on a religious matter, *ijma'* is valid and accepted. There are differing views as to how many *mujtahid* are necessary to make *ijma.'* Some scholars hold that the number should be the same as that which is required for the *mutawātir* hadith whilst others maintain that three *mujtahids* are sufficient for *ijma.'* There is a dispute as to whether the consensus of two *mujtahids* is sufficient where they are the only *mujtahids* of their time. If there is only one *mujtahid* in a specific time frame, his views are not considered *ijma'*, because no opportunity for discussion of the matter would have existed.

2) General consensus is necessary. All the *mujtahids* living during the same time frame must agree on the issue of *ijma.'* According to the scholars of *Uṣūl al-Fiqh,* if even one of the *mujtahids* holds a different opinion from the majority view, *ijma'*

---

[226] 'Abdulaziz al-Bukhari, *Kashfu'l Asrār*, vol. 3, p. 946.

[227] Qur'an, 10: 71.

[228] Tirmidhi, *Sunan, Sawm*, hadith no: 3.

cannot be achieved because the dissenting opinions do not show which side holds the truth. For *ijma'* to occur there must be complete unanimity of opinion of all scholars. In such a case, some scholars accept the opinions of the majority as evidence but not as *ijma.'*[229]

3) The *mujtahids* must be Muslims. The consensus of non-Muslim nations or people of other scriptures are not accepted as *ijma.'* The reason behind this condition is that the followers of Prophet Muhammad, peace and blessings be upon him, cannot agree on a mistake. In other words, the Muslims are protected from the consensus on error (*'Ismah*). This is a quality specific to this *ummah* (Muslim community) which other belief groups do not possess.

4) *Ijma'* must happen after the death of the Prophet. Whilst the Prophet was alive, there was no place for *ijma'* because he was the sole authority on religious matters. If the Prophet consulted his Companions on a matter and they all agreed it is categorised as a Sunnah, not *ijma.'* However, if the Prophet does not accept their agreement then it cannot be considered as Sunnah either.

5) The subject of *ijma'* must be to do with a case of legal ruling such as *wajib, haram, mubah,* etc.; the consensus on a grammatical issue or on a principle of logic is not considered *ijma.'*

Ijma' is one of the good qualities of the Muslim community and cannot be undertaken by a layman but only by *mujtahids* who are experts in Islamic disciplines. They evaluate the issues based on the sources of Islamic law and reach a general consensus at the end of their *ijtihād.*[230]

The agreement of ordinary people on a matter and the general consensus on a matter which contradicts the evidences of the Qur'an and Sunnah are not considered *ijma.'* Moreover, if God established the rules through the sources of Islamic law, there is no place for *ijma',*[231] just as there is no *ijma'* on topics which are obvious and well-known by everyone such as, 'The world is created.' Topics such as the existence and oneness of God, the notion of revelation and Prophethood are excluded from the arena of *ijma.'* If it is only possible to have knowledge of a topic via direct information from God, this topic is also outside the scope of *ijma.'* Such topics include the characteristics of the afterlife, the signs of the end of this world, Paradise, Hell, the divine bridge, etc.[232]

---

229 Āmidī, *Iḥkām*, vol. 1, p. 140.

230 Gülen, *Kendi Dünyamıza Doğru*, pp. 95–96.

231 Ibid.

232 Ibid.

Summary: Introduction

1. The literal meaning of *ijma'* is consensus, intention, absolute decision and agreement.
2. In Islamic jurisprudence, *ijma'* is the general consensus on a religious matter by the Muslim *mujtahids* who were practising within the same time frame after the death of the noble Prophet. The following conditions must be met for *ijma'* to be actualized:
3. A certain number of *mujtahids* must reach a general consensus.
4. The *mujtahids* must be Muslims.
5. *Ijma'* must happen after the death of the Prophet.
6. The subject of *ijma'* must be to do with a case of legal ruling such as *wājib, haram, mubah,* etc.
7. Rules established through the sources of Islamic law are not suitable for *ijma.'*
8. Topics such as the existence and oneness of God, the notion of revelation and Prophethood are excluded from the arena of *ijma.'*

The Types of *Ijma'*

Ijma' is defined in two categories: *ṣarīh* (clear) and *sukūtī* (tacit).

a) *Ṣarīh Ijma'*

Ṣarīh ijma' can be defined as the clear consensus on a religious matter of all the *mujtahids* who lived during the same time period. Each *mujtahid* explains his view clearly and, at the end, there is a general consensus. There are different methods of achieving this type of *ijma'*: for example, the *mujtahids* of the time congregate and examine the case whose ruling is to be determined. If, at the end of the *ijtihād* process, they reach a unanimous agreement and phrase it clearly, this consensus is named *ṣarīh ijma.'* A second example for this type of *ijma'* is when a *mujtahid* explains his view about a case which appears during in his time and all other contemporary *mujtahids* explain the same view on the matter; the result of the process is *ṣarīh ijma.*

b) *Sukūtī (tacit) Ijma'*

Sukūtī (tacit) ijma' occurs when a couple of *mujtahids* explain their views on a case and the other contemporary *mujtahids* remain silent on the issue neither affirming nor negating it when ordinarily they would give their opinion about it. The conditions that need to be fulfilled for this type of *ijma'* are:

1) The silence of the *mujtahids* about the case must not indicate a positive or negative opinion. If a positive opinion is expressed this is classed as *ṣarīh ijma'* not *sukūtī ijma.'* However, if a negative view is expressed on this matter, *ijma'* cannot be achieved.

2) Sufficient time to consider and evaluate the case is required. The *mujtahids* should have enough time, which varies according to the issue and the *mujtahid,* to investigate the case and make *ijtihād*. If they then choose to remain silent this is considered *sukūtī ijma.'*

3) The case must be suitable for *ijtihād*. This requires that there is no definite evidence for the case. Where speculative (*ẕannī*) evidence exists in a case, it is necessary for the *mujtahids* to investigate and present their own opinions. However, if definite evidence exists, there is no place for *ijtihād.* If definite evidence for a case exists and some *mujtahids* present views contradicting this evidence regardless of the silence of other *mujtahids*, it is not considered *sukūtī ijma.'* The silence of other *mujtahids* on this matter indicates their rejection of the opinion since it contradicts the definitive evidence.

SUMMARY: THE TYPES OF *IJMA'*

1. *Ijma'* is defined in two categories: *ṣarīh* (clear) and *sukūtī* (tacit).
2. *Ṣarīh ijma'* can be defined as the clear consensus on a religious matter of all the *mujtahids* who lived during the same time period. They can meet in a group and discuss the matter and agree a consensus, or one scholar can give his view and then the others comment on it afterwards.
3. *Sukūtī (tacit) ijma'* occurs when a couple of *mujtahids* explain their views on a case and the other contemporary *mujtahids* remain silent. There are conditions for this type of *ijma.'*
4. The silence of the *mujtahids* about the case must not indicate a positive or negative opinion.
5. Sufficient time to consider and evaluate the case is required.
6. The case must be suitable for *ijtihād*.

The Proof Value of *Ijma'*

The two types of *ijma'*; *ṣarīh and sukūtī*, are sources of Islamic jurisprudence with different rulings. The majority of scholars hold that *ṣarīh ijma'* is evidence and one of the sources for extracting the rules of Islamic law. If *ṣarīh ijma'* occurs on a religious matter and it is known by Muslims, it is obligatory to obey it. Acting against it, making new *ijtihād* on the same issue, or disputing it is *haram* (forbidden). Mutazalite scholar Naẕẕām, the sect of Kharijites and Shi'ah do not accept *ijma'* as evidence and have tried to support their view with arguments from the Qur'an and Sunnah.

The majority of scholars accept *ṣarīh ijma'* evidence and cite the following verses to support their view:

> While whoever cuts himself off from the Messenger after the guidance (to what is truest and best in thought, belief, and conduct) has become clear to him, and follows a way other than that of the believers (for whom it is impossible to agree unanimously on a way that leads to error), We leave him (to himself) on the way he has turned to, and land him in Hell to roast there: how evil a destination to arrive at![233]

This verse informs us that following a different way other than the way of the believers will lead people to Hell; therefore, this is the wrong way and the only true path is that of the believers. The Muslim *mujtahids* agreed on this issue by general consensus, therefore it is obligatory to obey the ruling and acting against it is *haram*.

> O you who believe! Obey God and obey the Messenger, and those from among you who are invested with authority; and if you are to dispute among yourselves about anything, refer it to God and the Messenger, if indeed you believe in God and the Last Day. This is the best (for you) and fairest in the end.[234]

In this verse the believers are commanded to obey God, His Messenger and the rulers among them (*ulu al-amr*). God does not command obedience to errant rulers, so they must be free from error which is achieved by making decisions after consulting the *mujtahids*.[235]

> (O Community of Muhammad!) You are the best community ever brought forth for (the good of) humankind, enjoining and actively promoting what is right and good and forbidding and trying to prevent the evil, and (this you do because) you believe in God.[236]

---

[233] Qur'an, 4: 115.

[234] Qur'an, 4: 59.

[235] Rāzī, *Tafsīr*, vol. 3, p. 243.

[236] Qur'an, 3: 110.

The Muslims community is distinguished by God from all other nations. If the Muslim community agreed on error, God would not praise them as in the above verse.

> We have made you a middle way community that you may be witnesses for the people (as to the ways they follow), and that the (noblest) Messenger may be a witness for you...[237]

The expression 'a middle way' connotes justice, balance and the best pattern for human kind; demonstrating that the agreement of the Muslims is just and right. Being a witness requires being just and acting righteously in all matters and, since God described the believers as witnesses, their decisions and agreement are the just and righteous evidence for the ruling.

Many hadiths support the notion of *ijma'*:

a) "My community shall never agree upon an error"[238]

b) "God will not let my community agree upon an error"[239]

c) "I beseeched Almighty God not to bring my community to the point of agreeing on error and He granted me this"[240]

d) "Whatever the Muslims hold to be good is good in the eyes of God"[241]

There are many more hadiths addressing this issue and they are reported by trustworthy narrators. Even though they are not *mutawātir* hadith, they are nevertheless considered *mutawātir* from their meaning since they all emphasize the same point. *Ma'nawī mutawātir* hadiths (*mutawātir* by meaning) produce definite knowledge about a subject in the same way *mutawātir* reports do. For this reason, based on the previous verses and hadiths, the majority of scholars accept *ijma'* evidence and place it after Sunnah in the order of sources of Islamic law.

Summary: The Proof Value of *Ijma'*

1. The two types of *ijma'*; *ṣarīh and sukūtī*, are sources of Islamic jurisprudence with different rulings.
2. The majority of scholars hold that *ṣarīh ijma'* is evidence and one of the sources for extracting the rules of Islamic law.

---

[237] Qur'an, 2: 143

[238] Tirmidhi, *Sunan, Fitan*, hadith no: 8.

[239] Abu Dāwud, *Sunan, Fitan*, hadith no: 1.

[240] Abu Dāwud, *Sunan, Fitan*, hadith no: 4552.

[241] Ahmed ibn Hanbal, *Musnad*, and vol. 1, hadith no: 379.

3. Mutazalite scholar Nazẕām, the sect of Kharijites and Shi'ah do not accept *ijma'* as evidence and have tried to support their view with the arguments from the Qur'an and Sunnah.
4. Verses in the Qur'an and many hadiths reported by trustworthy narrators support the notion of *ijma.'* Based on the verses and hadiths, the majority of the scholars accept *ijma'* evidence and place it after Sunnah in the order of sources of Islamic law.

The Arguments of the Scholars Who do not Accept *Ijma'* Evidence

Nazẕām (d. 845 C.E.), a prominent Mutazalite theologian, holds that whilst God commanded human beings to obey Him and His Messenger in the verse 4:59, He did not command the Muslims to obey the *mujtahids*. Nazẕām holds that the solution to disputes should be arrived at by referring to God and His Messenger as indicated in the above verse; i.e. referring to the Qur'an and the Sunnah. Nazẕām argues that God did not command the Muslims to return the dispute to the *mujtahids* whose consensus is not proof and should not be accepted as evidence in Islamic law. Scholars who accept *ijma'* evidence refute Nazẕām's claim using the same verse as evidence: God says; *"If you are to dispute among yourselves about anything, refer it to God and the Messenger."*[242] The issue is disputed between the majority of scholars and Nazẕām. The authorities to consider in this dispute are the Qur'an and Sunnah and the dispute should be remedied by considering the judgements contained within them. When applying the Sunnah, we find many proofs which demonstrate *ijma'* evidence at play, therefore by accepting *ijma'* evidence we are in fact acting according to the Qur'an and the Sunnah which implies any rejection of *ijma'* evidence as being contrary to the their guidance.

Another argument used by scholars who reject *ijma'* is based on the following hadith:

> When the Messenger of God intended to send Mu'adh ibn Jabal to the Yemen, he asked: How will you judge when the occasion of deciding a case arises? He replied: I shall judge in accordance with God's Book. He asked: (What will you do) if you do not find any guidance in God's Book? He replied: (I shall act) in accordance with the Sunnah of the Messenger of God. He asked: (What will you do) if you do not find any guidance in the Sunnah of the Messenger of God and in God's Book? He replied: I shall do my best to form an opinion and I shall spare no effort. The

---

[242] Qur'an 4: 59.

> Messenger of God then patted him on the breast and said: Praise be to God Who has helped the Messenger of the Messenger of God to find something which pleases the Messenger of God.[243]

On this occasion, the Prophet accepted the methodology of Mu'adh but *ijma'* did not take place within this conversation. The scholars argue that if *ijma'* was important evidence for judgment in the rulings, the Prophet would not approve the statement of Mu'adh without mentioning it. However, this argument does not stand up to reason; Mu'adh mentioned sources available at his time and, as *ijma'* cannot occur during the Prophet's lifetime, it was not mentioned by him. Therefore, the arguments against *ijma'* are flawed and the majority of scholars are correct in accepting it as a source of evidence. The preferred view is the opinion of the majority of the scholars and consequently *ijma'* is evidence in Islamic law.

However, some scholars who accept *ṣarīh ijma'* evidence do not accept *sukūtī ijma'* and some do not even name it *ijma.'* They hold that it is possible for *mujtahids* to remain silent on the case of *sukūtī ijma'* for different reasons, not necessarily because they accept it. For instance, they might be silent because they have not reached a conclusion about the case yet, or they may be afraid of bad consequences if they explain their view. Their silence may also be interpreted as respect for more qualified *mujtahids* whom they do not want to publicly oppose if their own personal view is different. Their view is that there are many more possible reasons for the silence of the *mujtahids* and it cannot be automatically accepted as tacit approval. Therefore, without real consensus, *ijma'* cannot materialize, because the essence of *ijma'* is genuine consensus.

The majority of scholars of *uṣūl,* including Ḫanafī scholars, hold the opposing view and accept *sukūtī ijma'* as evidence with some holding that it is evidence like *ṣarīh ijma.'* Ḫanafī scholars hold that the arguments which prove *ṣarīh ijma'* as being evidence also prove *sukūtī ijma'*; the proofs do not discriminate between *ṣarīh* and *sukūtī ijma.'* Ḫanafī scholar Karkhī and Shāfi'ī scholar Āmidī hold that *sukūtī ijma'* is speculative evidence (*ẕannī*) and accept it as such. This view seems acceptable as the silence of other *mujtahids* could be for many reasons and doesn't necessarily demonstrate their approval for the view of the spoken *mujtahids.* As such, *sukūtī ijma'* cannot be definite evidence. Their silence is more likely to indicate positive approval as Muslims generally express their views openly; however, it is possible that it could indicate disapproval.

---

[243] Abu Dāwud, *Sunan, Kitāb Al-'Aqdiya*, hadith no: 3585.

On examination, we can see that the early scholars expressed their views even at the risk of incurring severe punishments. They did not refrain from telling the truth regardless who the addressee might be. An example is when 'Umar decided to apply the punishment for fornication to the pregnant woman after her guilt was proven; Mu'adh disagreed with the decision and expressed his disapproval publicly. Mu'adh told 'Umar, 'Even though God gave you the permission to apply the punishment for the adulterer He didn't allow you to punish the baby in the womb of the mother.' Thereupon 'Umar said, 'If Mu'adh was not present 'Umar would have perished.'[244]

On another occasion, during the Friday sermon 'Umar asked the Muslims to reduce the amount of dowry and also said 'Do not ask for an excessive dowry, if I find out that you took more than four hundred dirhams, the excess will be taken to the treasury.' Thereupon a woman stood up and rejected his decision by reciting the following verse; '*But if you still decide to dispense with a wife and marry another and you have given the former (even so much as amounts to) a treasure, do not take back anything thereof...*'[245] She stated that 'God gave us this right; because in the verse God says '*You have given the former a treasure*' it means it is permissible to ask for an excessive dowry. She said, 'Is 'Umar preventing our right?' After listening to the argument presented by this woman 'Umar said, 'The woman knew the truth but 'Umar did not.'[246]

Summary: The Arguments of the Scholars Who do not Accept *Ijma'* Evidence

1. Naẕẕām holds that God did not command the Muslims to obey the *mujtahids* and that the solution to disputes should be arrived at by referring to God and His Messenger.
2. This issue is disputed between the majority of scholars and Naẕẕām and the Qur'an and Sunnah should be examined for the answer.
3. There are many proofs in the Sunnah which demonstrate *ijma'* evidence at play.
4. Another argument used by scholars who reject *ijma'* is based on the hadith about a conversation between the Prophet and Mu'adh about judging cases. The Prophet accepted the methodology of Mu'adh but *ijma'* was

[244] Sarakhsī, *Mabsūt*, vol. 4, p. 343.
[245] Qur'an, 4: 20.
[246] Sarakhsī, *Mabsūt*, vol. 4, pp. 344–345.

not mentioned. But as *ijma'* only became possible after the Prophet's death, this is not a reasonable argument.

5. However, some of the scholars who accept *ṣarīh ijma'* evidence do not accept *sukūtī ijma'* and view that it is possible that the *mujtahids* remain silent on the case of *sukūtī ijma'* for different reasons other than tacit approval.
6. On the other side, the majority of scholars of *uṣūl,* including Ḫanafī scholars, accepted *sukūtī ijma'* evidence and some hold that it is evidence like *ṣarīh ijma.'* Their view is that scholars always spoke their view if they opposed a judgement; therefore, their silence is most reasonably positive approval. Examples support this view.

Feasibility of *Ijma'*

There are different views about the feasibility of *ijma'* and whether or not it actually occurred. The majority of scholars hold that it is both possible and did occur whilst Naẕẕām and Shi'ah scholars hold that it is impossible and never happened. Their arguments for this are as follows:

1) According to the definition of *ijma'* all the *mujtahids* who are alive at the same time must unanimously agree on the ruling of the case. If even one *mujtahid* disagrees with the view of majority, *ijma'* cannot occur. To recognise whether *ijma'* occurred or not, it is necessary to know the following two points;

a) All the *mujtahids* at the time of *ijma'* must be known, because the occurrence of *ijma'* is dependent on the consensus of all of them.

b) The view of every single *mujtahid* about the case of *ijma'* must be known. As the criteria for who qualifies as *mujtahid,* are not clear, the first condition cannot be met and consequently as a result of this, the second condition cannot be fulfilled. Additionally, the *mujtahids* are spread out living in different cities so it is not feasible to bring them together in the same place and learn their views at the same time.

2) *Ijma'* must rely on a report or evidence which can either be definite (*qat'ī*) or speculative (*ẕannī*). Rulings resulting from definite evidence are clear and there is no need for *ijma.'* If the evidence is speculative, it is impossible for *mujtahids* to reach the same conclusion on this evidence because they are many in number and each has a different character, knowledge and ability to comprehend the sources of Islamic law. From the viewpoint of logic, it is almost impossible for them to reach the same conclusion based on speculative evidence. Moreover,

there are many different evidences for extracting the rulings from the sources of Islamic law and they are not all known to all *mujtahids*.

The arguments of those who advocate the feasibility of *ijma'* are based on the evidence that *ijma'* occurred at the time of Companions and thereafter. For example, the following cases indicate the existence of *ijma'*;

1) A grandmother has a one-sixth share of the inheritance.
2) Merchandise goods cannot be sold before receiving them from the seller.
3) If a Muslim woman gets married to an unbelieving man, their marriage is invalid.
4) *Nikāḫ* (the marriage contract) without allocating a dowry is valid.
5) The son's son is excluded from the inheritance when there is a son.
6) Land in the conquered territories may not be distributed to the conquerors.

The majority of scholars hold that *ijma'* is feasible and occurred in the history of Islam and use the above examples to support their view. Instead of answering in detail the claims of the scholars who reject *ijma'* they address them briefly as being claims which are against reality. This method is not right and cannot be justified as good character requires accepting the truth in discussion if the opposite side proves their claim.

We will now examine the arguments of the opposite side. Firstly, the existence of evidence is not an obstacle for the work of *ijma.'* Even if there is evidence, it is not necessarily known by all people, they sometimes need to be reminded of its existence. The case of 'Umar delivering the sermon on Friday is a good example because a woman used a Qur'anic verse to argue against the view of 'Umar and consequently he admitted, 'A woman knew but 'Umar knew not.' 'Umar had made *ijtihād* without taking the verse into consideration regarding the reduction of the value dowry for the marriage. However, when a woman reminded him of the verse which contradicted his decision, 'Umar changed his decision. This demonstrates that in cases where there is definite evidence, it may not be known, or remembered, by Muslims. This refutes the argument of the opposite side who state that, 'If the evidence is definite the Muslims usually know it and the ruling is clear and there is no place for *ijma'* for this case.'

A similar incident occurred when the noble Prophet died. The Qur'an clearly states that; "*Muhammad is but a Messenger, and Messengers passed away before him. If, then, he dies or is killed, will you turn back on your heels?...*"[247]

[247] Qur'an, 3: 144.

The Prophet's death was initially not accepted by some of the Companions, particularly 'Umar. Aisha reports:

> Abu Bakr came from his house at Sunh on a horse. He dismounted and entered the mosque, but did not speak to the people till he entered upon Aisha and went straight to God's Messenger who was covered with a kind of Yemenite cloth. He then uncovered the Prophet's face and bowed over him and kissed him and wept, saying, 'Let my father and mother be sacrificed for you. By God, God will never cause you to die twice. As for the death which was written for you, has come upon you.' Abu Bakr went out while 'Umar ibn Al-Khattāb was talking to the people. Abu Bakr said, 'Sit down, O 'Umar!' But 'Umar refused to sit down. So the people came to Abu Bakr and left 'Umar. Abu Bakr said, 'To proceed, if anyone amongst you used to worship Muhammad, then Muhammad is dead, but if (anyone of) you used to worship God, then God is alive and shall never die. God said in the Qur'an; 'Muhammad is no more than a Messenger and indeed (many) Messengers have passed away before him...' By God, it was as if the people never knew that God had revealed this verse before till Abu Bakr recited it and all the people received it from him, and I heard everybody reciting it (then). 'Umar said, 'By God, when I heard Abu Bakr reciting it, my legs could not support me and I fell down at the very moment of hearing him reciting it, declaring that the Prophet had died.'[248]

If there is definite evidence on a matter and *ijma'* occurs on the same matter this is not a worthless effort as the opposite side claim. Indeed, *ijma'* strengthens the meaning of the evidence and provides precedence for future scholars eliminating the need for them to investigate the ruling about the case. The process of *ijma'* in a case supported by definite evidence is beneficial and useful rather than of no value.

We will now examine the case where *ijma'* relies on speculative evidence such as *khabar wāḫid* and *qiyāṣ*. In reality, it is not difficult for scholars to reach a general consensus based on speculative evidence as some of these are very clear in regards to rulings. For example, in the case of not reselling merchandise goods before they have been received the evidence is *khabar wāḫid*; however the *mujtahids* reached a general consensus on this issue. The hadith for this case is; "Whoever buys an item of food does not sell it before receiving it."[249]

The last argument of the opposite side is; 'There are no clear criteria to know who is a *mujtahid* and who is not and as a result we cannot know the views of

---

[248] Bukhari, *Saḫīḫ, Al-Maghāzī*, hadith no: 733.

[249] Bukhari, *Saḫīḫ, Buyu*, hadith no: 54.

all the *mujtahids.'* This argument has strong grounds and warrants discussion. If we look at the time periods after the Prophet died we can see that this objection is not always true. There are two time periods in this regard; a) the time of Abū Bakr and 'Umar, b) from the time of 'Uthman until the end of the *mujtahids'* time.

In the first period, it was easy to know who the *mujtahids* were and what their views were, because there were few of them and they mostly resided in Medina. In order to be able to consult with the Companions and knowledgeable Muslims, 'Umar didn't allow them to leave Medina. He could easily learn their views, and the view of those outside Medina, when he needed to. Therefore, it is mere assumption to claim the impossibility of knowing who all the *mujtahids* were and what their views were. Abū Bakr and 'Umar never rejected the opinions of *mujtahids*, especially when they reached a general consensus which proves the feasibility of *ijma.'*

Summary: Feasibility of *Ijma'*

1. The majority of scholars hold that *ijma'* is both possible and did occur.
2. Nazẕām and Shi'ah scholars hold that *ijma'* is impossible and never happened because: a) it was impossible for all *mujtahids* to have been known for consensus to happen and b) it would be impossible to know all of their views if it was impossible to know who they all were and c) if definite evidence is available *ijma'* isn't necessary and it would be impossible for all *mujtahids* to agree on speculative evidence as they would all have different views based on their characters, knowledge of the evidences and experience.
3. The arguments of those who advocate the feasibility of *ijma'* are based on the evidence that *ijma'* occurred at the time of Companions and thereafter by giving examples (see above). They do not answer the claims of the scholars who reject *ijma'* in detail.
4. In the case of definite evidence being available, it is possible that either it is not known by all people or they need to be reminded of it, as we see in the case of 'Umar delivering his sermon about dowry and the case where 'Umar initially didn't accept the death of the Prophet. *Ijma'* in the light of definite evidence strengthens the meaning of the evidence and is useful for future scholars.
5. *Ijma'* regarding speculative evidence does not make it difficult for scholars to reach a general consensus as some of these are very clear in regards to rulings like the example of reselling goods.

6. The argument about knowing who the *mujtahid* are is not a valid objection as in the first period after the Prophet's death the scholars were few and were located in the same area so their views could easily be obtained.

Sanad (Basis) of *Ijma'*

The basis of *ijma'* refers to the evidence which the *mujtahids* rely on when they reach a general consensus on the ruling of a case. The majority proponent holds that the evidence must have a basis (*sanad*) otherwise it would lead *mujtahids* to make *ijtihād* based on mere assumptions posing the risk of new religious innovations after the death of the Prophet.

The scholars are in agreement that *ijma'* may be based on the Qur'an or the Sunnah. The following verse is an example for the *ijma'* based on the Qur'an; "*Forbidden to you (O believing men) are your mothers (including stepmothers and grandmothers)*..."[250] The scholars reached a general consensus on the ruling that grandmothers are also forbidden for marriage based on this verse, because the expression 'mother' means a root and implies direct or indirect connection; therefore, grandmothers are included in this expression because family members are connected to them.

The following hadith is an example for the *ijma'* based on the Sunnah; "Whoever buys an item of food, he does not sell it before receiving it."[251] Based on this hadith, the scholars reached a general consensus on the ruling that it is forbidden to sell edible goods before receiving them in person.

There is, however, disagreement as to whether *ijma'* can be based on a ruling from secondary evidence such as *qiyāṣ* or *istiḫsān*. Some scholars hold that *qiyāṣ* cannot be a base for *ijma'* because *ijma'* itself is definite evidence, however *qiyāṣ* is speculative evidence and definite evidence cannot be built on speculative evidence.

On the other hand, some scholars maintain that secondary sources such as *qiyāṣ* can be the basis for *ijma'* and it has already occurred. This is the view of the majority and the preferred one, because *qiyāṣ* is one of the sources for extracting the rulings in Islamic law and as such it can be the basis for *ijma.'* We can find supporting evidence in the practice of the Companions. For example;

1) The noble Prophet died before assigning his successor. At first, the Companions disagreed on who would rule but they reached a general consensus on

---

[250] Qur'an, 4: 23.

[251] Bukhari, *Saḫīḫ, Buyu*, hadith no: 54.

Abū Bakr's leadership. To reach this decision they used analogy (*qiyāṣ*). When the Prophet was sick, he assigned Abū Bakr to lead the Prayers for the Muslims. Some of the Companions analogized the case of being imam in the Prayers to the case of leadership and the other Companions agreed with this analogy. They preferred Abū Bakr for the Caliphate of the Muslims based on general consensus. The basis for this *ijma'* was *qiyāṣ*.

2) A father is invested with the guardianship of the person and property of his child until they reach maturity. By *ijma'* this right is also given to the grandfather regarding his grandchild. This ruling of *ijma`* is founded upon an analogy between the father and grandfather.

3) The punishment for drinking alcohol is fixed at eighty lashes. This ruling was the result of *ijma'* occurred based on *qiyāṣ*. Ali ibn Abī Tālib made an analogy between drinking alcohol and slanderous accusation. Since drunkenness can lead to slanderous accusation and the prescribed penalty for the slander is eighty lashes, by way of analogy, it is also assigned for the drinking of alcohol.

The scholars who accept *qiyāṣ* as a basis for *ijma'* also accept *maslaḫah* (considering the benefits of the public) as grounds for *ijma.'* They bring the following examples as evidence for their view;

1) During the life of the noble Prophet it was impossible to collect the whole Qur'an together into one single book, because the revelation continued until his death. In the reign of Abū Bakr many reasons conspired to make this collation a necessity. After the death of the Prophet, Abū Bakr was selected as the caliph of the Muslims. Some Arab tribes tried to benefit from this change and disobeyed him. One of the reasons for the riots against his rule was the presence of fake Prophets who declared their Prophethood and renounced obedience to Abū Bakr. One of these fake Prophets was Musaylama. Abū Bakr sent an army to destroy Musaylama and his followers and in the following battle in 633 C.E. many *hafiz* (those who have memorised the entire Qur'an by heart) were martyred. 'Umar's comment on this was; 'The Companions of the Prophet died in the battle of Yamama as if they were butterflies falling into the fire.' Historical sources put the losses at around 10,200 Muslims, 500 or 700 of whom were *qurra* (someone who knows the Qur'an by heart). It was a very dangerous result for the Muslims, not only for the loss of so many Muslims but with respect to the preservation of the Qur'an which had not yet been brought together as one single book. The first Companion to perceive this danger was 'Umar. He recognized that if any more *qurra* were lost it would harm the completeness of the Qur'an, because it was still in

different pieces amongst the scribes and in the memories of *qurra*. 'Umar went to Abū Bakr and openly expressed his fears and concerns. He offered to collect the whole Qur'an into one single book. Abū Bakr was hesitant at first, he thought that Muslims would become complacent and neglect memorising the Qur'an. Also, the Prophet hadn't collated the Qur'an, so how come he could do something that the Prophet hadn't done. However, after a short time he accepted the offer[252] because it was necessary for the greater benefit of the public (*maslaḫah*).

2) At the time of Caliph 'Umar the lands of Jerusalem and Iraq were conquered by Muslims. Due to this expansion, some Companions such as 'Abdurrahman ibn 'Awf and 'Ammār ibn Yāsir asked 'Umar to distribute the conquered lands among the soldiers as was the practise in the time of the Prophet. Some other Companions such as 'Umar, 'Uthman, Ali and Mu'adh ibn Jabal held the view that the conquered lands shouldn't be distributed amongst the soldiers, rather they should be used for the following purposes;

a) As the common property of all Muslims.
b) The lands should be left to their original owners (before they were conquered) and tax collected from them.
c) The revenue collected from the tax should be used for the payment of judges, officers, soldiers, widows, orphans and the needy.

These Companions believed that this would be better for the public because all Muslims would benefit from the conquered lands and they could continue to do so over the next generations. 'Umar deflected the opposing views by demonstrating the strain it would have on future generations. He held that if the lands remained in the possession of soldiers they would be inherited by their sons and their prodigy and as the ruler he did not believe this was just. After a lengthy dispute his view was accepted by the majority of the Companions. This example shows the basis for *ijma'* is the notion of *maslaḫah* (considering the public benefit).

The proof value for *ijma'* based on consideration of *maslaḫah* is not eternal and unchangeable. As long as public benefit is achieved through this *ijma'* it is valid and acceptable. However, if it loses its value and *maslaḫah* cannot be provided through it, it is not binding and new *ijtihād* can be made. For these reasons *mujtahids* gave rulings later which were contrary to this type of *ijma'*, because their main concern was the public benefit not the *ijma'* itself.

---

[252] Bukhari, *Saḫīḫ, Fadāil al-Qur'an*, hadith no: 3; Zāhid al-Kawtharī, *Maqālāt al- Kawtharī*, p. 9; Ibn Ḫajar, *Fatḫ al-Bari*, vol. 9, p. 13.

Summary: *Sanad* (Basis) of *Ijma`*

1. The basis of *ijma'* refers to the evidence which the *mujtahids* rely on when they reach a general consensus on the ruling of a case which is necessary to avoid innovations in the religion.
2. The scholars are in agreement that *ijma'* may be based on the Qur'an or the Sunnah.
3. There is disagreement as to whether *ijma'* can be based on a ruling from secondary evidence such as *qiyāṣ* or *istiḥsān*. Some scholars hold that *qiyāṣ* cannot be a base for *ijma'* because *ijma'* itself is definite evidence but *qiyāṣ* is not and definite evidence cannot be built on speculative evidence.
4. Other scholars maintain that secondary sources such as *qiyāṣ* can be the basis for *ijma'* and it has already occurred. This is the view of the majority and the preferred one, because *qiyāṣ* is one of the sources for extracting the rulings in Islamic law and as such it can be the basis for *ijma.'* Evidence from the practice of the Companions supports this view.
5. The scholars who accept *qiyāṣ* as a basis for *ijma'* also accept *maslaḫah* (considering the benefits of the public) as grounds for *ijma'* and use evidence to support their claim such as the collation of the Qur'an in Abu Bakr's time and the distribution of lands issue in 'Umar's reign.
6. The proof value for *ijma'* based on consideration of *maslaḫah* is not eternal and unchangeable. Only as long as public benefit is achieved through this *ijma'* it is valid and acceptable.

Transmission of *Ijma'*

Ijma' is divided into two types; 'attained' and 'reported.' The first is established with the direct participation of the *mujtahid* without the mediation of reporters or transmitters. The *mujtahid* thus gains direct knowledge of the opinions of other *mujtahids* when they all reach a consensus on a ruling. Reported *ijma'* is established by means of reports which may either be solitary (*āḫād*) or definite (*mutawātir*). In the case of transmission of *mutawātir,* there is no problem of proof. However, there is disagreement regarding *ijma'* which is reported by way of solitary reports.[253] Some scholars hold that it is not accepted as evidence, because *ijma'* is decisive proof whereas *āḫād* reports are speculative evidence and therefore cannot form the basis of *ijma.'*

[253] Kamali, *Principles of Islamic Jurisprudence*, p. 175.

A number of scholars hold that *ijma'* can be actualised through solitary reports; however, they all agree that anything which is proved by means of a solitary report is speculative proof even if it is definitive with regards to its content.[254] *Ijma'* through *mutawātir* reports occurred during the lifetime of the Companions. For this reason, scholars disputed whether *ijma'* occurred after this as most scholars maintain that transmission through solitary reports is speculative evidence only.[255] This issue was discussed in detail earlier along with the arguments and evidence.

[254] Āmidī, *Iḥkām*, vol. 1, p. 281.
[255] Abū Zahrah, *Uṣūl*, pp.167–68.

Chapter Five

Qiyas (Analogy)

Qiyas (Analogy)

Introduction

The literal meaning of *qiyāṣ* is to measure something with something else; to compare something to another; to judge something and make two things equal. When we say 'I measured the fabric with a meter' the word 'measure' has the equitant meaning of the verb '*qā-sa*' which is used as a physical measurement. When we compare two things or make them equal, it can be related to either physical or rational things. For example, comparing two different people from different perspectives and finding similarities between them. This comparison process is expressed with the word '*qiyāṣ*' in Arabic.

In *Uṣūl al-Fiqh*, jurists define *qiyāṣ* as: the assignment of the *ḫukm* (rule) of an existing case found in the texts of the Qur'an, Sunnah or *ijma'* to a new case whose *ḫukm* is not found in these sources, on the basis of a common underlying attribute called the "*illah* of the *ḫukm*."[256]

Qiyāṣ demonstrates the universal and eternal characteristics of the Qur'an and Sunnah by containing the element of the underlying cause for the rulings. In this way, *qiyāṣ* is constantly able to provide infinite solutions for contemporary cases by relying on the Qur'an and Sunnah. Reliance on the Qur'an and Sunnah means that one will always be fruitful in finding a solution to his problems. Whilst the Qur'an and Sunnah do not cover all the solutions for every single case, they have universal and eternal principles which can be utilized as a source for a constant *ijtihād* process. In this sense, *qiyāṣ* is an instrument of Islamic law which provides infinite solutions for the *mujtahids*.[257]

The use of analogy is resorted to only if the solution to a new case cannot be found in the Qur'an, the Sunnah or a definite *ijma*`. It would be futile to attempt to solve a case by *qiyāṣ* if the new case was already addressed within the first three sources of Islamic law. If however, the new case is not covered by the primary

---

[256] Bazdawī, *Uṣūl al-Bazdawī*, vol.3, p.395.

[257] Gülen, *Ruhumuzun Heykelini Dikerken*, vol. 2, p. 97.

sources of Islamic law it is then permissible to benefit from the application of analogical reasoning.

Qiyāṣ has four elements:

1) *Asl*: the case (set of facts) that is mentioned in the primary sources with its *ḫukm* (ruling). This is also called the *magīs 'alayh* (the case upon which analogy has been constructed).
2) *Ḫukm al-asl*: the *ḫukm* (the ruling) of the case that is mentioned in the sources; the rule to be passed on.
3) *'Illah*: the underlying cause of the *ḫukm*, which is determined by the jurist.
4) *Far'i*: the new case for which the *ḫukm* has not been explicitly mentioned and which needs a *ḫukm*.

Qiyāṣ is achieved by following specific steps. First, it is necessary for the *mujtahid* to find the ruling of a similar case in the Qur'an, Sunnah or *ijma.'* The second step includes the *mujtahid* analysing the case to discover the underlying reason for which the ruling was given. When the *mujtahid* meets a new case which is not mentioned in the Qur'an, Sunnah or *ijma'*, he investigates it, tries to understand the nature of it and compares it to similar cases which are mentioned in the primary sources. If the original and the new cases share a common underlying reason he can apply the ruling of the original case to the new case. At the end of this process, the two cases become equal with regard to the ruling and the final product is *qiyāṣ* (analogy).

The following examples explain the process of *qiyāṣ*:

1) The prohibition of alcohol in the Qur'an:

> O you who believe! Intoxicants, games of chance, sacrifices to (anything serving the function of) idols (and at places consecrated for offerings to other than God), and (the pagan practice of) divination by arrows (and similar practices) are a loathsome evil of Satan's doing; so turn wholly away from it so that you may prosper (in both worlds). Satan only seeks to provoke enmity and hatred among you by means of intoxicants and games of chance, and to bar you from the remembrance of God and from Prayer. So, then, will you abstain?[258]

The Qur'an prohibited *khamr* (wine), an intoxicating liquor made from grape juice. However, this prohibition did not include other intoxicating liquors such as whiskey and beer. Even if the word *khamr*, in its literal meaning, does not

[258] Qur'an 5: 90–91.

cover other types of intoxicating liquor, the *ḥukm* of the word can be extended to them through *qiyāṣ* (analogy).

The underlying cause or reason (*'illah*) for which *khamr* has been prohibited is intoxication, because it causes enmity and hatred among the Muslims by making them drunk and removing their sobriety in judgment. The jurists used this reason as a basis for examining other liquors. If they found the same cause, intoxication, in other liquors they extended the *ḥukm* of *khamr*, which is prohibition, to the other intoxicating liquors.

2) In the hadith, the noble Prophet said; "The killer (of his testator) would be deprived from the inheritance."[259] This hadith introduced the ruling that if one kills his relatives to gain an inheritance before its natural time he cannot be heir to his victim's estate and cannot benefit from their inheritance as a punishment for his crime. The ruling for this case is the prohibition of the killer from the inheritance. The underlying cause for this ruling is killing close relatives in order to gain inheritance before its proper time. The punishment accorded is the opposite of the killer's aim which is depriving him of the inheritance. By *qiyāṣ*, this rule is extended to cover bequests meaning that a killer cannot benefit from the will of his victim. In both cases the underlying cause is the same; attempting to achieve a legal right before its proper time by killing the benefactor. In this *qiyāṣ* process the *asl* (original case) is 'The killer shall not inherit' and the *far'i* (new case) is that of the bequest. Killing close relatives or the one who bequests in order to obtain the legal right of the inheritance or bequest before its proper time is the underlying cause for the ruling. The application of *qiyāṣ* (analogy) to discover the rule for the new case, extended the application of the ruling to the new case, therefore the punishment for both is depriving the killer from their legal inheritance or bequest. The rule for the original case is passed on to the new case through *qiyāṣ*.

3) In the hadith the Prophet said:

> Muslims (the believers) are brothers. It is not permissible for a man to make an offer of marriage to a woman who is already offered to another man unless the latter permits it or has totally abandoned his offer.[260]

This hadith prohibits a man making an offer of marriage to a woman when there is already an offer of marriage outstanding by another and it is unknown whether she accepted it or he gave up on it. The underlying cause (*'illah*) for this

---

[259] Tirmidhi, *Sunan, Farāiḏ*, hadith no: 17.

[260] Bukhari, *Saḫīḫ, Nikāḫ*, hadith no: 45.

ruling (prohibition) is clear that it will cause enmity, hatred and disconnection between Muslims and will be harmful for the community. The Prophet prohibited this to prevent conflicts, disunity and enmity amongst them. In the new case, there is a question as to whether it is permissible for a Muslim to make an offer to someone who rents his house when he has already received another offer from a Muslim. The Qur'an and Sunnah do not contain a ruling on this matter, however, on investigation we can see that this case is similar to the case covering marriage offers. If someone makes an offer to rent a property when there is an outstanding offer existing, there is the potential for disunity and enmity in the Muslim community. Since the underlying cause (*'illah*) of the original case is similar to the new case, the ruling can be applied to the new case too. As such, it is not permissible to make an offer to someone who is looking for tenants for his rental property where he already received an offer from another Muslim tenant.

4) On one particular occasion the noble Prophet said; "When you are three, two must not secretly speak between them, because it will upset your brother."[261] This hadith prohibits two Muslims from speaking secretly when there are three of them together. This hadith itself explains the reason behind this rule as such an act will upset the third person. The logical reasoning is that the third person may think the others don't trust him or that they are keeping secrets from him which can both break his heart and destroy the brotherhood between them. The consequence of such an act is disunity amongst the Muslim community and can weaken the trust between them. We can apply this to a new case where people speak different languages. There are three people but two of them speak in a language they know that the third one does not have knowledge of. The rule for this new case is not mentioned in the Qur'an or Sunnah, however as the first case is very similar we can apply the same rule to it through *qiyāṣ*. In this analogy, two people speaking secretly amongst themselves is the original case (*asl*), speaking in a language that the third party does not understand is the new case (*far'i*) and upsetting the third person causing disunity amongst Muslims is the underlying (*'illah*) cause for the rule. The rule (*ḫukm*) for both cases is the prohibition of such acts.

The *mujtahids* who resort to *qiyāṣ* utilize the wisdom in the rules of Shari'ah and follow certain objectives which are in harmony with reason. A rational approach to the discovery and identification of the objectives and intentions of

---

[261] Ibn Majah, *Sunan, Adab,* hadith no: 50.

God necessitates recourse to human intellect and judgment in the evaluation of the rulings.[262]

Summary: Introduction

1. The literal meaning of *qiyāṣ* is to measure something with something else; to compare something to another; to judge something and make two things equal.
2. In *Uṣūl al-Fiqh*, jurists define *qiyāṣ* as: the assignment of the *ḥukm* (rule) of an existing case found in the texts of the Qur'an, Sunnah or *ijma'* to a new case whose *ḥukm* is not found in these sources, on the basis of a common underlying attribute called the "*'illah* of the *ḥukm*."[263]
3. *Qiyāṣ* is constantly able to provide infinite solutions for contemporary cases by relying on the Qur'an and Sunnah which contain universal and eternal principles which can be utilized as a source for a constant *ijtihād* processes.
4. The use of analogy is resorted to only if the solution to a new case cannot be found in the Qur'an, the Sunnah or a definite *ijma`*.
5. There are four elements of *qiyāṣ*: *asl,* the case mentioned in the primary sources with its ruling; *ḥukm al-asl,* the ruling to be passed on to the new case; *'illah,* the underlying cause of the *ḥukm* and; *far'i*: the new case for which the *ḥukm* has not been explicitly mentioned and which needs a *ḥukm*.
6. *Qiyāṣ* is achieved by a) the *mujtahid* finds the ruling of a similar case in the Qur'an, Sunnah or *ijma';* b) the *mujtahid* analyses the case to discover the underlying reason for which the ruling was given; c) when the *mujtahid* meets a new case which is not mentioned in the primary sources he investigates and compares it to similar cases which are mentioned in them; d) if the original and the new cases share a common underlying reason he can apply the ruling of the original case to the new case making them equal in ruling.

The Proof Value of *Qiyāṣ*

The majority of scholars hold that *qiyāṣ* is evidence in Islamic jurisprudence and is utilized to deduce the rules for new cases from their sources. Naẕẕām, the

[262] Kamali, *Principles of Islamic Jurisprudence*, p. 181.
[263] Bazdawī, *Uṣūl al-Bazdawī*, vol.3, p.395.

Mutazalite scholar and the scholars of the Ẕahirī School, Ahmad ibn Hanbal and Shi'ah Muslims do not accept *qiyāṣ* evidence. Both of the conflicting sides use evidence to support their views.

The Arguments of the Majority

The majority of the scholars rely on the Qur'an, Sunnah, *ijma'* and also logical arguments to justify their view for the permissibility of *qiyāṣ* as evidence.

Evidence from the Qur'an includes many verses, for example:

> He it is Who drove out those who disbelieve from among the People of the Book from their (fortified) homes as the first instance of gathering (them for punishment and banishing from the heartland of Islam). You did not think that they would go forth (so easily), just as they thought that their strongholds would protect them against God. But (the will of) God came upon them from where they had not reckoned (it could come): He cast dread into their hearts. And so they were wrecking their homes by their own hands, as well as by the hands of the believers. Learn a lesson, then, O people of insight.[264]

The part of this verse which supports their argument is the line; 'Learn a lesson, then, O people of insight.' The verse informs us about the tribe Banī Nadr, their denial of the Prophet and their attempts to harm the Muslims. God punished them and made their traps in vain. After that God says, 'Learn a lesson, then, O people of insight.' The verse reminds Muslims to consider the events of that time, the punishment that the Banī Nadr tribe incurred, the reason for the punishment and the underlying cause for their eventual ruin. God asks Muslims to ponder over these events, discover the effective cause for their punishment and prevent it amongst themselves. He warns them that a similar result would occur to them as they are also human beings so, in similar cases, the same rule would apply. These explanations show that effects are bound to their causes. If causes are present, consequently the effects are also present. The logic behind the application of analogical reasoning (*qiyāṣ*) is the same; it is no different to the reasoning that takes place in this verse, therefore the application of *qiyāṣ* binds the ruling to its underlying cause. As such, where a new case has the same cause, it also binds these cases to the same ruling.

Evidence from the Sunnah;

---

264 Qur'an, 59: 2.

1) We know that when the noble Prophet was asked questions about the rulings on different cases, he did not answer directly but instead explained them through analogical reasoning. He would answer the questioner with a question similar to the one asked and whose answer was known by them. When the questioner responded to this, the Prophet would explain to him that this was similar to the matter they had queried and, therefore, the same rule applies to them both. This indicates that the application of *qiyāṣ* was used by the Prophet himself, for example:

> Once a man came to the Prophet and told him; 'My father converted to Islam at a very late stage of his life. He cannot travel mounted on an animal, but the duty of *Hajj* is obligatory upon him. Can I go to *Hajj* and perform it behalf on him?' The Prophet asked him, 'Are you the oldest of his sons?' he answered affirmatively. This time the Prophet asked him again, 'What do you think if your father has debt and you pay it, is it counted as payment of the debt of your father?' the man said, 'yes.' Thereupon the Prophet said; 'similarly you can perform the *Hajj* on behalf of your father.'"[265]

This gives a clear example that the Prophet did not answer the question directly; rather he helped the questioner come to a conclusion using analogical reasoning. The Prophet did this by asking him about a case which has same underlying cause as the case in question. In this way, he taught the questioner how to apply his reason and understand the cause of the case he was asking about. This is simply the application of analogy and supports the proof value of *qiyāṣ*.

On another occasion 'Umar went to the noble Prophet and said; 'I made a big mistake today. I kissed my wife while I was fasting (does it nullify fasting?)! The Prophet told him 'What do you think if you rinse your mouth with water while you are fasting?' 'Umar said, 'There is no harm in it.' Thereupon the Prophet said, 'Why then are you so upset? (Similarly it does not nullify fasting).'[266] In this example again the Prophet did not answer the question directly but helped 'Umar to understand the effective cause of what does and doesn't nullify the fast through the application of analogical reasoning. This is the meaning of *qiyāṣ* and its application by the Prophet is a supporting argument for it.

2) The following hadith is also used as supporting evidence for the use of *qiyāṣ* as evidence.

---

[265] Muslim, *Saḫīḫ, Kitāb al-Hajj*, hadith no: 3090.

[266] Abu Dāwud, *Sunan, Kitāb al-Sawm*, hadith no: 2379.

> When the Messenger of God intended to send Mu'adh ibn Jabal to the Yemen, he asked: How will you judge when the occasion of deciding a case arises? He replied: I shall judge in accordance with God's Book. He asked: (What will you do) if you do not find any guidance in God's Book? He replied: (I shall act) in accordance with the Sunnah of the Messenger of God. He asked: (What will you do) if you do not find any guidance in the Sunnah of the Messenger of God and in God's Book? He replied: I shall do my best to form an opinion and I shall spare no effort. The Messenger of God then patted him on the breast and said: Praise be to God Who has helped the messenger of the Messenger of God to find something which pleases the Messenger of God.[267]

From this conversation we can understand that the process of *ijtihād* is permissible when investigating the rulings for new cases and *qiyāṣ* is one of its ways, because it is the application of analogical reasoning.

Supporting evidence from *ijma'*:

There are many reports which indicate that the Companions used *qiyāṣ* to solve their problems and find rulings for new cases. These reports are at the level of *ma'nawī mutawātir* and show that the Companions accepted *qiyāṣ* evidence in Islamic jurisprudence. There are no reports suggesting that there were any disputes between the Companions regarding using *qiyāṣ* evidence for deducing rulings. Some examples of this category include;

The first Caliph, Abu Bakr, used *qiyāṣ* about fathers and grandfathers regarding their entitlement to inheritance. Similarly, 'Umar ibn al-Khattāb ordered Abu Musa al-Ash'arī to determine the similarities for purposes of analogy.[268] The Companions pledged their allegiance to Abu Bakr as Caliph of the Muslims after the Prophet passed away on the strength of the analogy that 'Umar used *qiyāṣ* between two forms of leadership: 'Umar asked the Companions, 'Will you not be satisfied, with regards to worldly affairs, with the man with whom the Prophet was satisfied with regards to religious affairs?' They agreed with 'Umar on the basis of *qiyāṣ*.[269] On another occasion, the Companions reached a general consensus on the ruling for the punishment for consuming alcohol based on analogy made by 'Ali ibn Abī Tālib. He reasoned by way of analogy that the penalty of false accusation should be applied to the wine drinker; 'When a person gets drunk, he lies and when he lies, he accuses falsely.'[270]

---

[267] Abu Dāwud, *Sunan, Kitāb Al-'Aqdiya*, hadith no: 3585.

[268] Abu Zahrah, *Uṣūl*, p. 177.

[269] Ibn Ḫazm, *Iḫkām*, vol. 7, p. 160.

[270] Shawkānī, *Irshād*, p. 223.

Evidence using logic:

Scholars who hold the view that *qiyāṣ* is evidence in Islamic jurisprudence use logical arguments to justify their view. God sent Islam as the final religion to teach and suffice humankind until the Judgment Day; therefore, it stands to reason that Islam must necessarily contain the solutions to all problems that will occur until the end of days. It is obvious that the Qur'an and Sunnah related to rulings (*aḫkām*) are limited and cannot cover each individual case; the revelation has ended and therefore cannot address new issues. However, humankind does and will continue to face new unlimited problems that need solving and the limited solutions in the primary sources cannot address these; therefore, a new source is needed to solve them. One of the possible sources is identifying the effective causes for the establishment of the rulings in the Qur'an and Sunnah and applying them to similar cases through analogy. As a result, *qiyāṣ* can be applied broadly and can be a solution for many new cases, because it is the assignment of the *ḫukm* (ruling) of an existing case found in the texts of the Qur'an, Sunnah or *ijma'* to a new case whose *ḫukm* is not found in these sources on the basis of a common underlying attribute. This ensures both the dynamism of Islamic jurisprudence and its ability to meet the needs of Muslims until the end of time. It can also be applied in every place and every time period. If we do not accept *qiyāṣ* evidence, it will freeze Islamic jurisprudence and it will no longer be able to fulfil the demands to resolve unlimited problems. This is not fitting for the universal religion of Islam.

Summary: The Arguments of the Majority

1. The majority of the scholars rely on the Qur'an, Sunnah, *ijma'* and also logical arguments to justify their view for the permissibility of *qiyāṣ* as evidence.
2. Evidence from the Qur'an includes many verses used to support their view including that about the Banī Nadr tribe.
3. Evidence from the Sunnah shows that when the noble Prophet was asked questions about the rulings on different cases, he did not answer directly but instead explained them through analogical reasoning, answering the questioner with a question similar to the one asked and whose answer was known by them. This indicates that the application of *qiyāṣ* was used by the Prophet himself.
4. Supporting evidence from *ijma'* are reports indicating that the Companions used *qiyāṣ* to solve their problems and find rulings for new cases.

These reports are at the level of *ma'nawī mutawātir* and show that the Companions accepted *qiyāṣ* evidence in Islamic jurisprudence.

5. Evidence using logic include arguments such as Islam is the final religion and must teach and suffice humankind until the Judgment Day, therefore, it stands to reason that Islam must necessarily contain the solutions to all problems that will occur until the end of days. If we do not accept *qiyāṣ* evidence, it will freeze Islamic jurisprudence and it will no longer be able to fulfil the demands to resolve unlimited problems.

The Arguments against *Qiyāṣ*

Scholars such as Naẕẕām who do not accept the use of *qiyāṣ* as evidence support their view with the following arguments:

1) In the Qur'an, God warns Muslims against speculation (*ẕann*) in numerous places, for instance;

> "Most of them follow only conjecture. Surely conjecture can never substitute for anything of the truth. God surely has full knowledge of all that they do"[271]

"O you who believe! Avoid much speculation, for some speculation is grave sin (liable to God's punishment)..."[272]

Qiyāṣ is a type of speculation. When determining the underlying cause for the ruling, there is a heavy reliance on speculation rather than definite knowledge which, according to the Qur'an, is not permissible and therefore, cannot be evidence in Islamic jurisprudence. This argument is refuted by highlighting that the warning in the Qur'an addresses matters of belief and faith on which speculation is not permissible. However, speculation is a necessary tool and logical reasoning in the process of *ijtihād* and *qiyāṣ* as well as in understanding the text of the Qur'an and Sunnah. Speculation on the rulings pertaining to practices is permissible and speculative evidence (*ẕannī*) is sufficient for making rulings. As we discussed earlier, most of the Sunnah was transmitted as *khabar wāḫid* which is speculative evidence from the view point of transmission. If we deny *qiyāṣ* because it is speculative evidence, we will necessarily end up denying most of the Sunnah. This is unacceptable and as a result, *qiyāṣ* is considered evidence.

2) Some reports state that the Companions condemned *qiyāṣ;* for example, when Abū Bakr asked about a ruling not mentioned clearly in the Qur'an, he was

[271] Qur'an, 10: 36.
[272] Qur'an, 49: 12.

so afraid he stated; "If I interpret the Qur'an according to my personal view I would perish." There are other reports that tackle the issue in the same manner. However, all of the reports which condemn *qiyāṣ* are weak compared to those supporting its use and cannot be preferred over the stronger supporting reports. Moreover, there is a consensus of the Companions accepting *qiyāṣ* evidence and other reports cannot be used against this.

3) The rules of Islamic jurisprudence are explained in the form of commands and prohibitions. Additionally, there are also 'recommended' (*mandub*) and 'disliked' (*makruh*) categories, which can be studied under *mubah* (permissible). If there is a matter on which the text is not clear it would fall under the category of permissibility. Commands and prohibitions are outlined clearly in the Qur'an, the Sunnah, or *ijma'*, and cannot be determined in any other way. There is thus no room for *qiyāṣ* in the determination of the rulings.[273]

This can be counter argued with the fact that in most cases, neither the Qur'an nor the Sunnah clearly identify whether something is *halal* or *haram*, obligatory or recommended, permissible or disliked. Generally, the scholars analyze the verses and using *ijtihād* they determine the ruling. In most cases, the rules of Islamic law are explained by *mujtahids* therefore, it is both necessary and permissible to extract new rulings for new cases and one of the tools to do this is *qiyāṣ*.

4) It is possible that *qiyāṣ* may cause disunity, conflicts and disputes among the Muslims. In the process of *qiyāṣ* it is necessary to identify the underlying cause of the ruling and then to investigate whether the same cause exists in the new case. All these works are speculative and may cause conflicts among the Muslims which would displease God, as mentioned in the Qur'an:

> And obey God and His Messenger, and do not dispute with one another, or else you may lose heart and your power and energy desert you; and remain steadfast. Surely, God is with those who remain steadfast[274]

This argument is counteracted by understanding that the disputes and disagreements prohibited in the verse are related to the matters of creed, the essentials of Islam and obedience to the noble Prophet. The meaning of this verse is not related to discussions of practical rules; the verse explains that these people are separated in matters of belief as opposed to those related to practical rules. The disagreements on the basis of *qiyāṣ* are not matters of faith or the essentials of Islam; rather they are the views of different *mujtahids* on the details (*furu'*) of

---

[273] Ibn Ḥazm, *Iḥkām*, vol. 8, p. 3.

[274] Qur'an, 8: 46.

Islamic jurisprudence. This type of dispute does not cause disunity among Muslims, indeed this is the mercy of God and a blessing of Islam, because it provides ease for Muslims in the variety of views of the *mujtahids*. Evidentially, the arguments for *qiyāṣ* as a source of Islamic jurisprudence are sound and preferable.

Summary: The Arguments against *Qiyāṣ*

1. Some scholars do not accept the use of *qiyāṣ* as evidence and support their view with specific arguments.
2. The Qur'an warns Muslims against speculation (*ẕann*) in numerous places and, when determining the underlying cause of a ruling, *qiyāṣ* relies heavily on speculation rather than definite knowledge, therefore it is not permissible. The counter to this argument is that only matters of faith cannot use speculation but in practical matters, it is a necessity. If we deny *qiyāṣ* because it is speculative evidence, we will necessarily end up denying most of the Sunnah.
3. Some reports state that the Companions condemned *qiyāṣ* but they are weak compared with those supporting its use. Moreover, there is a consensus of the Companions accepting *qiyāṣ* evidence and other reports cannot be used against this.
4. Commands and prohibitions are outlined clearly in the Qur'an, the Sunnah or *ijma'*, and cannot be determined in any other way. There is thus no room for *qiyāṣ* in the determination of the rulings. However, the counter to this is that in most cases, the Qur'an and Sunnah do not clearly identify the commands and prohibitions and it is left to the *mujtahids* to explain the rules. *Qiyāṣ* is just one of the necessary and permissible tools they use when extracting the new rulings for new cases.
5. It is possible that *qiyāṣ* may cause disunity, conflicts and disputes among the Muslims which is prohibited in the Qur'an. This argument is counteracted by understanding that the disputes and disagreements prohibited in the verse are related to the matters of creed, the essentials of Islam and obedience to the Prophet.
6. Evidentially, the arguments for *qiyāṣ* as a source of Islamic jurisprudence are sound and preferable.

The Conditions of *Qiyāṣ*

There are some conditions that need to be present before *qiyāṣ* can be made. As previously mentioned, *qiyāṣ* has four essential elements; *asl* (the original case), *far'i* (the new case), *'illah* (the underlying cause) and *ḫukm* (the ruling). Each of these elements has conditions pertaining to the occurrence of *qiyāṣ* which are explained in detail below.

The conditions related to *asl*;

Asl refers to the source, such as the Qur'an or the Sunnah and to the ruling which is mentioned in them. There are two conditions pertaining to *asl*;

a) The particular ruling of an original case must be found in the Qur'an and Sunnah. There is a dispute if it is found in *ijma.'* According to some scholars, *ijma'* cannot constitute a valid base for *qiyāṣ* because *ijma'* does not always explain its own justification. In the absence of such information, it is difficult to make *qiyāṣ*, because it is applied based on effective cause. *'Illah* also can be used in its original case but cannot be the basis for a new case. A particular example highlighting this interplay is in the Qur'an's ruling regarding *khamr* (wine produced from grapes). In the original case, *khamr* is forbidden. The ruling for whiskey is not mentioned here but through analogy it is also forbidden due the underlying cause for the ruling being the same as that of the original case. However, the ruling for whiskey cannot be used for another case by the process of *qiyāṣ*. According to the majority of scholars it is not permissible for one *qiyāṣ* to constitute the original case of another *qiyāṣ*.

b) The *asl* must have an underlying cause which can be understood by the *mujtahids*. If the effective cause for a ruling in the text of the Qur'an and Sunnah is secret and there is no way of discovering it, this case cannot be used as *asl* in the process of *qiyāṣ* to find a ruling for a new case. Since *qiyāṣ* is the application of a ruling between two cases which have the same underlying cause (*'illah*), if the underlying cause is unknown, *qiyāṣ* cannot be applied. For this reason *qiyāṣ* cannot be used in the matters of *ibadāt* (worship), because the effective cause is the command of God. In other words, God does not explain why He commanded Muslims to carry out such devotional duties (*ibadāt*); only God knows the real reason behind them. Regardless, Muslims must perform these acts of worship even if they do not understand the effective cause underlying them. As it is impossible to identify the *'illah* in devotional matters it is impossible to make *qiyāṣ* between similar cases. The five Daily Prayers, *zakat*, *Hajj* and its rituals, etc. are devotional matters (*ibadāt*) and the underlying cause for them is known only by God, therefore they cannot be used in *qiyāṣ*.

If *mujtahids* know the effective cause for the ruling of a case, it can be used in *qiyāṣ* for similar cases. God sometimes explained very clearly the reason behind a ruling and *mujtahids* were able to understand it and apply it to similar cases through *qiyāṣ*. In other situations, the effective cause is not mentioned clearly and it is the duty of the *mujtahid* to determine the *'illah* in those cases in light of the general principles of Islam.

The conditions related to *far'i* (a new case);

Far'i is a new case whose rulings are not mentioned in the primary sources of Islamic jurisprudence but are investigated through the application of *qiyāṣ*. The *far'i* must have the following conditions;

1) *Far'i* must be equal to the *asl* from the aspect of *'illah*. If it is not the case, *qiyāṣ* cannot be applied. In other words, the effective cause of both cases must have similarities for the ruling to be made. If *qiyāṣ* is applied without this condition being met it is called *qiyāṣ ma' al-farq* (analogy with difference). For instance; "*Test the orphans well until they reach the age of marriage. Then, if you find them to be mature of mind, hand over to them their properties...*"[275] According to this verse and what is similar a woman who has reached puberty is entitled to run her own business. Ḫanafī scholars hold that similarly a woman who reached puberty can make her own marriage contract. Through the use of *qiyāṣ* they analogised business transactions and marriage contracts and reached the conclusion that a mature woman is entitled to make her own marriage contract without obtaining permission from her legal guardians. The other scholars disagreed with the Ḫanafī view and said there is no equal or similar underlying cause in both cases, thus they named this, *qiyāṣ ma' al-farq* (analogy with difference).[276]

2) The application of *qiyāṣ* must not result in a solution which is against the rulings of the Qur'an, Sunnah or *ijma.'* In other words, if the result of *qiyāṣ* contradicts one of the rulings in the primary sources of Islamic jurisprudence, it is neither valid nor acceptable. For example, in the Qur'an the compensation for mistakenly killing a believer is freeing a Muslim slave.[277] To compensate the crime, it is necessary to free a Muslim slave, otherwise the compensation is not fulfilled according to the Qur'anic verse. If this ruling is also applied through *qiyāṣ* as compensation for the case of a false oath it is not valid, because the Qur'an does not specify the nature (i.e. Muslim) of the slave for the compensation of false oath. It is clearly stated in the Qur'an and *qiyāṣ* cannot overrule it; "*The expiation (for breaking such oaths) is to feed ten destitute persons with the average of the food you*

275 Qur'an, 4: 6.

276 Zakiy ad-Din Sha'ban, *Uṣūl*, p. 134.

277 Qur'an, 4: 92.

serve to your families, or to clothe them, or to set free a slave"[278] Since such a *qiyāṣ* is against the clear ruling of the Qur'an, it is not valid.

3) The new case must not be covered by the text or *ijma'*; if it does exist already in the primary sources there is no need for the application of *qiyāṣ*.[279]

The conditions related to *'illah*;

Literally, *'illah* means the situation which causes change when it is present. Sickness is also named *'illah*, because it changes the state of health of the sufferer. In Islamic jurisprudence, it has three meanings;

a) It is the underlying cause which is suitable for the ruling. For example, a person travelling during Ramadan is permitted to not observe the fast until their travelling is finished. The underlying cause for this is hardship and difficulty; if difficulty is present, easiness comes after it and this is a suitable reason for this ruling.
b) It is the purpose of the ruling, or the benefit which is obtained by the ruling. For example, trade is made permissible, because people need each other and meet their needs through business transactions; this is the *'illah* for making trade lawful.
c) It is a clear and consistent attribute which is a suitable cause for regulating a ruling. For example, the *'illah* for not observing fasting in Ramadan is travel, because travel is a clear and easily understood attribute, not affected by people, time or places and which usually includes the possibility of difficulty and hardship.

According to the scholars of *Uṣūl al-Fiqh, 'illah* is an attribute of the original case which is consistent and clear and has a proper association with the ruling of the case.[280] Some scholars stipulated conditions for the *'illah*, including;

1) It must be a consistent attribute which can be used for all cases regardless of time, persons, place or circumstances.
2) It must be clear and understood by the *mujtahids*. If it is secret or hidden, it cannot be the basis for the application of *ijtihād.*
3) It must be a proper attribute which has a reasonable relationship with the ruling. Islam aids people to achieve benefits and protects them from any type of harm. All the rulings in Islamic law are established within this wis-

[278] Qur'an, 5: 89.
[279] Kamali, *Principles of Islamic Jurisprudence*, p. 188.
[280] Abu Zahrah, *Uṣūl*, p. 188.

dom. For example, consuming alcohol is prohibited because it harms people and society.

4) It must be applicable to other cases. If it is a unique case or belongs to a certain person, time or place; it cannot be basis for the application of *qiyāṣ*.

The conditions related to the original ruling (*ḫukm*) in the application of *qiyāṣ*;

1) The ruling for the original case must be present because without it, *qiyāṣ* cannot be applied.
2) The ruling must not be abrogated for it cannot be the basis for *qiyāṣ*.
3) The underlying cause of the ruling must be able to be understood by the *mujtahids*. In devotional matters the underlying cause is only known by God and therefore it is not permissible for *qiyāṣ* to be applied in these cases.
4) The ruling must not be restricted to a person, place or time. For instance, there are many rulings which are related to the noble Prophet alone, such as rulings about his marriages.
5) The ruling must not belong to exceptional cases (*rukhṣah*) such as, not fasting during Ramadan if one travels.

SUMMARY: THE CONDITIONS OF *QIYĀṢ*

1. *Qiyāṣ* can only be made if certain conditions are met to do with its four essential elements; *asl* (the original case), *far'i* (the new case), *'illah* (the underlying cause) and *ḫukm* (the ruling).
2. The conditions related to *asl*: the particular ruling of an original case must be found in the Qur'an and Sunnah. There is a dispute if it is found in *ijma'*; the *asl* must have an underlying cause which can be understood by the *mujtahids*.
3. The conditions related to *far'i* (a new case): *far'i* must be equal to the *asl* from the aspect of *'illah*. *Qiyāṣ* applied without this condition being met is called *qiyāṣ ma' al-farq* (analogy with difference); the application of *qiyāṣ* must not result in a solution which is against the rulings of the Qur'an, Sunnah or *ijma'*; The new case must not be covered by the primary sources or *ijma.'*
4. In Islamic jurisprudence, *'illah* has three meanings; it is the underlying cause which is suitable for the ruling; it is the purpose of the ruling or the benefit which is obtained by the ruling; it is a clear and consistent attribute which is a suitable cause for regulating a ruling.
5. Some scholars stipulated conditions for the *'illah*, including: It must be a consistent attribute; It must be clear and understood by the *mujtahids*;

it must be a proper attribute which has a reasonable relationship with the ruling; it must be applicable to other cases.

6. The conditions related to the original ruling (*ḫukm*) in the application of *qiyāṣ*: the ruling for the original case must be present; the ruling must not be abrogated later on; the underlying cause of the ruling must be able to be understood; the ruling must not be restricted to a person, place or time; the ruling must not belong to exceptional cases (*rukhṣah*).

Determining the *'Illah*

The *'illah* for the ruling is sometimes clearly stated in the primary sources of Islamic law and there is no dispute among the scholars over it. However, sometimes it is not clear and there is a need to investigate and find the proper *'illah* for the ruling. There are different methods to achieve this, the three most important of which are explained below:

1) Investigating the *'illah* in the text of the Qur'an and Sunnah;

If the text of the Qur'an or Sunnah indicates an attribute as an *'illah* of one ruling, we understand that such an attribute is the *'illah* of that ruling. This is the *'illah* which is explained by the text of the Qur'an and Sunnah. Sometimes it is clearly stated and at other times it is only implied. The clearly stated *'illah* can be understood from the expression itself or through the words which are specifically used to explain the causes for the ruling. The following verse is an example of this type of *'illah*;

> It is because of this that We ordained for (all humankind, but particularly for) the Children of Israel: He who kills a soul unless it be (in legal punishment) for murder or for causing disorder and corruption on the earth will be as if he had killed all humankind; and he who saves a life will be as if he had saved the lives of all humankind...[281]

The expression 'It is because of this that We ordained' explains that the prohibition of killing innocent people resulted from the killing of one of Adam's sons by his brother. In other words, since killing innocent people is very serious crime and prohibited for the Children of Israel, it is also prohibited for you.

The Prophet said; "I used to prohibit the storing of the meat of sacrificial animals because of the poor people who came to Medina, but now you can eat and

[281] Qur'an, 5: 32.

store it."[282] In this hadith the words 'because of' indicate the *'illah* of the ruling. In other words, the Prophet explained the underlying cause (*'illah*) for the prohibition of storing the meat of sacrificial animals as being the presence of poor people in Medina at that time.

On another occasion, the noble Prophet said; "Asking permission (before entering someone's house) is ruled to prevent seeing (what is forbidden to see, i.e. the private parts of the women)."[283] This hadith explains the *'illah* of the ruling which is stated in the following verse: "*O you who believe! Do not enter dwellings other than your own until you have ascertained the permission of their residents and have greeted them with peace.*"[284]

In this verse God commands Muslims to ask permission before entering the dwellings of other people but He does not explain the reason behind this command. However, the Prophet explained the underlying cause for this command as being the possibility of seeing the private parts of women or men.

> What God has bestowed on His Messenger as gains of war from the peoples of the townships: (one-fifth of) it belongs to God, and to the Messenger, and his near kinsfolk, and orphans, and the destitute, and the wayfarer (lacking means to sustain a journey), so that it should not become a fortune circulating among the rich among you.[285]

In this verse God explained the underlying cause for distributing the war booty among the allocated recipients such as orphans, the destitute and the wayfarer. He indicated 'It should not become a fortune circulating among the rich among you.' In other words, God ordered the distribution of war booty among the proper recipients so that it would not just benefit the rich which was common practice during the time of ignorance (*jahiliyyah*).

The leftovers of a cat are deemed pure because the Prophet said in the hadith; "They are like the household walking in your houses."[286] The *'illah* for this ruling is that it is very difficult to be protected against them and if this ease is not provided for Muslims it will cause them hardship.

Sometimes the *'illah* is not clearly stated in the text of the Qur'an or Sunnah but is implied within the text. In such cases, there is an indication that such an attri-

---

282 Muslim, *Sahīh*, *Adāhī*, hadith no: 37.

283 Bukhari, *Sahīh*, *Istizan*, hadith no: 1.

284 Qur'an, 24: 27.

285 Qur'an, 59: 7.

286 Abu Dāwud, *Sunan*, *Tahāra*, hadith no: 38.

bute may be the underlying cause but it is not clear and definite. *Mujtahids* then investigate the text, examine the nature of the evidence and determine the proper attribute as the *'illah* of the ruling. For example; "*And for the thief, male or female: cut off their hands as a recompense for what they have earned, and an exemplary deterrent punishment from God.*"[287]

In this verse, the punishment of cutting off the hands is connected to the crime of theft with the Arabic particle '*la*.' Thus, the crime of stealing is the underlying cause for the punishment of cutting off the hands, because it is mentioned immediately after the crime.

The noble Prophet said; "A judge does not give a ruling when he is angry."[288] In this hadith, judgment is prohibited when anger accompanies it. It implies that the underlying cause for postponing judgment is the anger which distracts the mind and negatively affects the ruling capacity of the judge. Here, a connection is made between erroneous decisions and judging in the state of anger. A judge cannot be objective in a state of anger and therefore he is prohibited from using his authority to judge whilst in this state.

2) Investigating the *'illah* in *ijma'*

If *mujtahids*, at any time and collectively, accept an attribute as the underlying cause for a ruling, this attribute becomes the *'illah* for such a ruling based on general consensus (*ijma'*). For example, why do parents have the right of execution of their minor children's property and possessions? The answer to this question is because they are minor and not yet mature enough to take care of their own property. There is an *ijma'* on this attribute.

There is also *ijma'* on the ruling that a judge should not give a ruling when he is angry. This is the same in cases where a judge is upset or afraid; he cannot pass judgement because of a situation which negatively affects the mind. As a result, it can be stated that if a judge is in a state where he cannot judge healthily and is likely to err in his judgment, it is not permissible for him to judge.

The designation of a proper attribute as the *'illah* must demonstrate a connection between the proper attribute and the benefit which God aims to provide His servants through a specific ruling. This is discoverable where there is an indication in the text of the Qur'an and Sunnah; otherwise this methodology is not applicable. For instance, the parents or guardians of minor children are expected to look after their property as it actualizes the benefit and also prevents harm.

[287] Qur'an 5: 38.

[288] Bukhari, *Saḫīḫ, Aḫkām*, hadith no: 13.

Summary: Determining the *'Illah*

1. The *'illah* for the ruling is sometimes clearly stated in the primary sources but sometimes it is not clear and needs to be investigated using various methods.
2. Investigating the *'illah* in the text of the Qur'an and Sunnah whether it is clear or implied in the expression.
3. Investigating the *'illah* in *ijma'*: If *mujtahids*, at any time and collectively, accept an attribute as the underlying cause for a ruling, this attribute becomes the *'illah* for such a ruling based on general consensus (*ijma'*).
4. The designation of a proper attribute as the *'illah* must demonstrate a connection between the proper attribute and the benefit which God aims to provide His servants through a specific ruling and can only be discovered through the Qur'an or Sunnah.

The Categories of a Proper Attribute

A proper attribute is classified into three categories based on whether it is accepted by God, the Lawgiver or not;

1) The proper attribute which is accepted by the Lawgiver. This is a proper attribute for which there is evidence for its acceptance by God. If God has given a ruling based on an attribute which is understood by the *mujtahids* as the underlying cause for such a ruling, it is permissible to make *qiyāṣ* on the basis of it. Some scholars have named this attribute as the affective proper attribute (*al-munasabah al-muaththira*). For instance God says; "*Test the orphans well until they reach the age of marriage. Then, if you find them to be mature of mind, hand over to them their property...*"[289]

As we discussed earlier, the property of minors is to be taken care of by their legal guardians. This verse clearly shows that God has taken age into consideration, as He mentions both the age of marriage and testing them to see if they are mature of mind. Therefore, age is a proper attribute which is accepted by God.

2) The proper attribute which is not accepted by the Lawgiver. This is an attribute which is not accepted by God as an effective cause because there is no evidence in the Qur'an or Sunnah. It is not permissible to determine the *'illah* based on this attribute. This attribute is named the rejected attribute (*munasa-*

[289] Qur'an, 4: 6.

bah mulqah) by the *mujtahids*. A particular example which demonstrates this type of rejected *'illah* is the case of the king of Andalusia. One of the kings of Andalusia broke his fast in Ramadan without a valid excuse. A student of Imam Mālik, Yahya al-Laysi issued a fatwa (legal ruling) for this case declaring that he must fast two months successively as compensation for his offense. The Maliki School rules that a person has three options of compensation for breaking the fast without a valid excuse; a) fasting b) freeing a slave c) feeding the destitute. The reason behind the fatwa for the King of Andalusia was explained by Laysi. He states that the main objective for compensation is to deter the person who violates the rules of Islam. The deterrent punishment for the king was determined as fasting for two months because, being a king with vast wealth, the other options would be very easy for him and would not act as a deterrent. This form of logical reasoning is sound; however as there is no indication in the text of the Qur'an and Sunnah to justify this opinion. It is rejected and cannot be the basis of determining the underlying cause for the ruling.

3) The proper attribute which is controversial among the *mujtahids*. This will be covered under the subject *masālih mursala* (public benefits).

Determining the *'illah* through finding the proper attribute is the most important methodology of them all. This is the essential category for determining the *'illah*, because when we examine the examples of *qiyāṣ* we can see that most of them are determined through finding the proper attribute for the underlying cause. Only on a few occasions is the *'illah* determined by the text of the Qur'an and Sunnah or *ijma.'* The methodology for determining the *'illah* for the application of *qiyāṣ* is the main cause of disputes among the *mujtahids*. Generally, *mujtahids* are in agreement on a ruling but they may have disagreements on the proper attribute of the underlying cause (*'illah*) and may vary in their choice of what constitutes the proper attribute.

Takhrīj al-Manāt

Takhrīj al-manāt is defined in *Uṣūl al-Fiqh* as identifying the proper attribute of the underlying cause for the ruling which is mentioned in the text of the Qur'an, Sunnah or in *ijma.'* In other words, *mujtahids* work to discover the *'illah* through examining the attributes of the ruling and find one of them to be the real reason for it. For example, it is ruled that if one spouse converts to Islam and the other remains non-Muslim the marriage contract is over. The underlying cause for this ruling is not mentioned in the text of the Qur'an or Sunnah. *Mujtahids* investigated this case and tried to find the *'illah* for this ruling. If the *'illah* is found to be either that a woman converted to Islam or a man remained non-Muslim and as a result of his research he accepts one of them as the *'illah* it is known as *takhrīj al-manāt.*

Tanqīh al-Manāt

When the *'illah* is neither stated nor alluded to in the text, the only way to identify it is through *ijtihād*. The jurist thus takes into consideration the attributes of the original case, and only that attribute which is considered to be proper (*munasib*) is identified as the *'illah*.[290] The scholars of *Uṣūl al-Fiqh* define *tanqīh al-manāt* as the process of *ijtihād* to identify the *'illah* by purifying the possible attributes and finding from amongst them the one which can be the basis for the ruling. *Tanqīh al-manāt* suggests that a ruling may have more than one attribute and it is not clear which one is the underlying cause. The *mujtahid* tries to identify the proper attribute which can be the cause for the ruling. The following case is an example for this type of *'illah* identification;

> A man came to the Prophet and said, 'I have been ruined for I have had sexual relations with my wife in Ramadan (while I was fasting).' The Prophet said (to him), 'free a slave.' The man said, 'I cannot afford that.' The Prophet said, '(Then) fast for two successive months continuously.' The man said, 'I cannot do that.' The Prophet said, '(Then) feed sixty poor persons.' The man said, 'I have nothing (to feed them with).' Then a big basket full of dates was brought to the Prophet. The Prophet said, 'Where is the questioner? Go and give this in charity.' The man said, '(Shall I give this in charity) to a poorer person than I? By God, there is no family in between these two mountains (of Medina) who are poorer than us.' The Prophet then smiled till his premolar teeth became visible, and said, 'Then (feed) your (family with it).'[291]

This hadith indicates that a man who breaks his Ramadan fast by having sexual intercourse with his wife has to compensate for his offense. This hadith also shows the underlying cause for the compensation of this offense. When *mujtahids* examine this case they can find some attributes which cannot be considered the proper *'illah*. For example, the offender is a Bedouin or the offence was committed with his wife. The *mujtahid* purifies this attributes, because they cannot be the proper cause for the ruling. In the end, he discovers that the underlying cause for this compensation is the act of sexual intercourse whilst fasting in Rama-

290 Kamali, *Principles of Islamic Jurisprudence*, p. 194.

291 Bukhari, *Saḥīḥ, Adab*, hadith no: 110.

dan. In *Uṣūl al-Fiqh* this form of *ijtihād* is called *tanqīh al-manāt*. The difference between *takhrīj al-manāt* and *tanqīh al-manāt* is that in the former the *mujtahid* is dealing with a situation where the *'illah* is not identified whereas in the latter, more than one cause has been identified. The *mujtahid's* task is to find the proper *'illah*.[292]

Taḫqīq al-Manāt

If an *'illah* for a different case has been identified, whether by the text of the Qur'an, Sunnah or by *ijma'*, the *mujtahid* investigates whether the same *'illah* also exists in different cases. In other words, this process is determining the presence of the same *'illah* in individual cases. For example, God forbade *khamr* (wine) because it is an intoxicant and makes people drunk. The underlying cause for the prohibition of *khamr* is the attribute of intoxication. *Mujtahids* investigate different cases to see if the same *'illah* is present in them. This form of *ijtihād* is called *taḫqīq al-manāt* in *Uṣūl al-Fiqh*. The task of the *mujtahid* is to discover if the same *'illah* exists in different cases, and if it does, he applies the same ruling to them.

Summary: The Categories of a Proper Attribute

1. A proper attribute is classified into three categories based on whether or not it is accepted by God the Lawgiver;
2. The proper attribute which is accepted by the Lawgiver is a proper attribute for which there is evidence for its acceptance by God. Some scholars have named this attribute as the affective proper attribute (*al-munasabah al-muaththira*).
3. The proper attribute which is not accepted by the Lawgiver because there is no evidence in the Qur'an or Sunnah. It is not permissible to determine the *'illah* based on this attribute. This attribute is named the rejected attribute (*munasabah mulqah*) by the *mujtahids*.
4. The proper attribute which is controversial among the *mujtahids*.
5. Determining the *'illah* through finding the proper attribute for it is the most important methodology because when we examine the examples of *qiyāṣ* we can see that most of them are determined through finding the proper attribute for the underlying cause and is the main source of dispute between the *mujtahids*.
6. *Takhrīj al-Manāt:* is identifying the proper attribute of the underlying cause for the ruling which is mentioned in the text of the Qur'an, Sunnah

[292] Ghazali, *Muṣtaṣfā*, vol. 2, p. 55.

or in *ijma.'* In other words, *mujtahids* work to discover the *'illah* through examining the attributes of the ruling and find one of them to be the real reason for it.

7. *Tanqīh al-Manāt: Uṣūl al-Fiqh* defines *tanqīh al-manāt* as the process of *ijtihād* to identify the *'illah* by purifying the possible attributes and finding from amongst them the one which can be the basis for the ruling.
8. *Taḫqīq al-Manāt:* is if an *'illah* for a different case has been identified, whether by the text of the Qur'an, Sunnah or by *ijma'*, the *mujtahid* investigates whether the same *'illah* also exists in different cases.

Chapter Six

Istiḫsān (Juristic Preference), *Qawli Saḫābah* (the Statement of the Companions) and Revealed Law Preceding the *Shari'ah* of Islam

Istiḫsān (Juristic Preference), *Qawli Saḫābah* (The Statement of the Companions) and Revealed Law Preceding the *Shari'ah* of Islam

Istiḫsān (Juristic Preference)

Introduction to *Istiḫsān* (Jurist's Preference)

Istiḫsān literally means to like or to be liked and view positively or deem something good. *Istiḫsān* in Islamic law, and fairness in Western law, are both inspired by the principle of fairness and conscience. Both authorise departure from the rule of positive law when its enforcement leads to unfair results. The main difference between them is, however, to be sought in the overall reliance of equity in the concept of natural law, and of *istiḫsān* in the underlying values and principles of the Shari'ah.[293] *Istiḫsān* does not aim to establish an independent authority beyond Islamic jurisprudence; it is an integral part of it.[294] Many scholars, including Abū Ḥanīfa, accepted it as evidence in Islamic law. Some scholars who did not accept *istiḫsān* evidence employed the same principles in their *Uṣūl al-Fiqh* but using different terminological names.[295]

In its juristic sense, *istiḫsān* is the method of exercising personal opinion in order to avoid any rigidity and unfairness that might result from the literal enforcement of the existing law. Juristic preference is a fitting description of *istiḫsān*, as it involves setting aside an established analogy in favour of an alternative ruling which serves the ideals of justice and public interest in a better way.[296]

Before delving into the proof value of *istiḫsān* it is important to clarify the following concepts;

---

293 Kamali, *Principles of Islamic Jurisprudence*, p. 217.

294 Makdisi, *Legal Logic*, p. 90.

295 Gülen, *Kendi Dünyamıza Doğru*, p. 98.

296 Kamali, ibid, p. 218.

a) The meanings of *qiyāṣ* as used by jurists and how it differs when considered alongside *asl.*
b) The meanings of *asl* (the original case).
c) The reasons why some jurists utilized *istiḫsān* in their *ijtihāds*, whilst others criticized it severely.

SUMMARY: INTRODUCTION TO *ISTIḪSĀN* (JURIST'S PREFERENCE)

1. *Istiḫsān* in Islamic law, and fairness in Western law, are both inspired by the principle of fairness and conscience.
2. *Istiḫsān* does not aim to establish an independent authority beyond Islamic jurisprudence; it is an integral part of it.
3. In its juristic sense, *istiḫsān* is the method of exercising personal opinion in order to avoid any rigidity and unfairness that might result from the literal enforcement of the existing law.
4. Before delving into the proof value of *istiḫsān* it is important to clarify the following concepts of *qiyāṣ*, *asl* and the reasons why some jurists utilized *istiḫsān* in their *ijtihāds*, whilst others criticized it severely.

The Terminological Meanings of *Qiyāṣ*

The concept of *qiyāṣ* has different meanings in the cases which are used;

1) In *Uṣūl al-Fiqh* it is used to extend the ruling of the original case to a new case because of a common *'illah* (underlying reason or effective cause) between them. The word *qiyāṣ* is mostly used in this concept.

2) *Qiyāṣ* can be used to mean the general religious rule (*āam shar'ī naṣṣ*). For example, the punishment for married people who commit adultery is stoning (*rajm*), but this is against the general rule (*qiyāṣ*) about the punishment for adultery indicated in the verse; "*The fornicatress and the fornicator—flog each of them with a hundred stripes...*"[297] The expression here is general and includes both married and single people. However, married people are excluded from this general statement and their punishment is stoning instead of the hundred lashes. Many authentic reports prove that in Prophet Muhammad's time, the punishment of stoning was applied to married people who committed adultery. Due to this evidence, an exemption is made from the general rule for married people. This example demonstrates why Abū Ḫanīfa developed the notion of *istiḫsān* meaning 'exemp-

[297] Qur'an, 24: 2.

tion from the general rule.' Since the punishment of stoning for the married adulterers is against *qiyāṣ* (the general ruling), it is labelled *istiḫsān* by Abū Ḫanīfa.

3) Sometimes jurists use *qiyāṣ* to mean a well-established or well-known general principle in Islamic law. An example of this is Abū Ḫanīfa's reported statement that if there was no hadith about a case in which a person breaks his fasting forgetfully he would make *ijtihād* according to *qiyāṣ*. Here the concept of *qiyāṣ* is used to mean general principle and is referring to a principle that is well-known by the jurists; 'If a pillar of something is absent it becomes void.' The pillar of fasting is refraining from eating, drinking and sexual relationships from dawn to the evening. According to the principle, if the pillar of fasting is removed forgetfully or deliberately the fast becomes void. However, a hadith from the Prophet states that if a person eats or drinks forgetfully, it does not break their fast. With this evidence, Abū Ḫanīfa issued a fatwa against *qiyāṣ* (a well-established general principle) and forwent the general principle using *istiḫsān*. This is an example of *istiḫsān* which is used against the *qiyāṣ* by abandoning a well-established general principle in favour of a hadith.

Summary: The Terminological Meanings of *Qiyāṣ*

1. In *Uṣūl al-Fiqh* it is used to extend the ruling of the original case to a new case because of a common *'illah*.
2. It is used to mean the general religious rule (*āam shar'ī naṣṣ*).
3. Sometimes *qiyāṣ* is used to mean a well-established general principle in Islamic law or well-known principle by the jurists.

The Terminological Meanings of *Asl*

Asl literally means a foundation that other things are built up on. In juristic terminology, it has a few different meanings;

a) Shar'ī evidence; for example, when the jurists say 'The *asl* for this ruling is the Qur'an', the meaning of *asl* is the religious evidence upon which such rulings rely. *Asl* is also used in the same way for the Sunnah, *ijma'* and other sources of Islamic law.

b) A well-established general principle in Islamic jurisprudence; for example, 'The *asl* for the command is that it indicates the obligation of its subject. In this example, *asl* means a well-established principle in Islamic jurisprudence.

c) The preferred one; for example, 'If the literal and metaphoric meanings of something contradict each other in a case, the *asl* (the preferred) is the literal meaning.' In this statement the *asl* is used to mean the preferred one.

d) The original case in the process of *qiyāṣ*; for example, wine (*khamr*) is the original case because it is mentioned in the Qur'an, and whiskey is the new case (*far'i*). The ruling for the new case is unknown since it is not mentioned in the primary sources.

Summary: The Terminological Meanings of *Asl*

1. *Asl* literally means a foundation that other things are built up on. In juristic terminology, it has a few different meanings.
2. Shar'ī evidence.
3. A well-established general principle in Islamic jurisprudence.
4. The preferred one.
5. The original case in the process of *qiyāṣ.*

The Reason for the Dispute over *Istiḫsān*

All jurists, except those from the Ẕahirī School, issued fatwas (legal rulings) according to *istiḫsān* but not necessary using that particular term. Some of them even harshly criticized the scholars who used *istiḫsān* in their *ijtihāds*. One of the possible explanations for this criticism is that they did not fully understand the reasoning of Abū Ḫanīfa in his usage of *istiḫsān*. Ḫanafī jurists used *istiḫsān* for extracting rulings in many cases as if it were one of the independent sources of Islamic law and generally used it alongside *qiyāṣ*. For example, 'The ruling for this case is such according to *qiyāṣ* and such according to *istiḫsān*', or '*qiyāṣ* would result in such ruling but we used *istiḫsān* and gave such ruling.' These types of expressions can often be seen in Ḫanafī *fiqh* books.

Despite being used frequently in their *ijtihāds*, the early Ḫanafī jurists did not report the definition of *istiḫsān*. Similarly, the meaning of *qiyāṣ* which is used as the opposite of *istiḫsān* was also not reported by them. As we explained earlier, *qiyāṣ* is used with different meanings by the Ḫanafī jurists and this ambiguity led to disputes and severe criticism from other scholars. They assumed that Ḫanafī jurists made *ijtihāds* based on their personal opinions without applying to the sources of Islamic law. For example, Imam Shāfi'ī holds that using *istiḫsān* is innovation in the religion.

When the jurists of the Ḫanafī School became aware of this severe criticism they began to explain the meaning of *istiḫsān*, the logic behind it and the reasons for using it in their *ijtihāds*. Moreover, they refuted the accusation that Imam Abū Ḫanīfa issued fatwas based on his personal opinions. They were able to prove not only that Abū Ḫanīfa used the evidence with which the other imams agreed but also that the other imams used the notion of *istiḥsān* without naming it in their *ijtihāds*. This dispute arose because there was not a single definition of *istiḥsān* commonly agreed amongst the jurists.

Summary: The Reason for the Dispute over *Istiḥsān*

1. All jurists, except those from the Ẕahirī School, issued fatwas (legal rulings) according to *istiḥsān* but not necessary using that particular term.
2. Some scholars harshly criticized the scholars who used *istiḥsān* in their *ijtihāds*.
3. Ḥanafī jurists used *istiḥsān* for extracting rulings and generally used it alongside *qiyāṣ* but the early Ḥanafī jurists did not report the definition of *istiḥsān*.
4. Other scholars assumed that Ḥanafī jurists made *ijtihāds* based on their personal opinions.
5. Ḥanafī scholars proved not only that Abū Ḥanīfa used the evidence with which the other imams agreed but also that the other imams used the notion of *istiḥsān* without naming it in their *ijtihāds*.

The Definition of *Istiḥsān*

There are many different definitions for *istiḥsān* and it is very difficult to include all of them in one single definition. However, one inclusive definition could be the following based on the practical usage of *istiḥsān* by Ḥanafī jurists: *Istiḥsān* is a juristic preference when a *mujtahid*, using his personal opinion, abandons the ruling which he gave for similar cases because of the existence of a verse or a hadith or *ijma'* or *'urf* (custom) or *maslaḥah* (public benefit) and gives a different ruling for the case at hand. This definition will be explored further.

Sometimes one case might be in the scope of a general statement (*āam*) or in the scope of a general principle which is adopted by the jurists or the legal schools. On the other hand, for the same case, evidence might exist in the sources of Islamic law (the Qur'an, Sunnah, *ijma'* etc.) that opposes the general statement or principle requiring an opposing ruling. If a *mujtahid* uses his personal opinion in the favour of the exceptional evidence and gives a ruling accordingly, abandoning the general ruling which is applied for similar cases, he is considered to have applied *istiḥsān* in this case. The resulting ruling achieved through this method is called a *mustaḥsan* ruling established in opposition to *qiyāṣ*. The meaning of opposition is that it is excluded from the general ruling, i.e. it is the exception to the rule otherwise founded in *qiyāṣ*.

Sometimes one case may not be in the scope of *naṣṣ* (the Qur'an, Sunnah and *ijma'*) and a *mujtahid* uses *istiḫsān* to find the ruling for this case. However, in this process he encounters two possible options; one of them is open or clear (*ẕāhir* or *jalī*) *qiyāṣ*. Clear *qiyāṣ* is the case that is the subject of *istiḫsān*. It is similar to the case which has a ruling within the sources of Islamic law because in both cases the effective cause is similar and the relationship between them can be established through this common *'illah* (effective cause). Another option is unclear (*khafī*) *qiyāṣ*. The effective cause or similarity between the two cases cannot be seen unlike the case of clear *qiyāṣ*. However, a *mujtahid* comes to the conclusion that the result based on unclear *qiyāṣ* is better with regard to both fairness and the benefit of the people. This is defined as *istiḫsān* which is opposite to clear *qiyāṣ*. Both Ḫanafī and Maliki scholars' use of *istiḫsān* mostly pertains to the latter definition.

When we examine the cases of *istiḫsān* we discover that the *mujtahid* either abandons the general ruling because of the existence of special evidence or that there are two options of *qiyāṣ* available to the *mujtahid*; one is clear and another is unclear *qiyāṣ*. In this situation, the *mujtahid* prefers the unclear *qiyāṣ* because it offers a means of avoiding hardship and it is harmonious with the higher objectives of Islamic law.

The Ḫanafī jurist al-Sarakhsī, defines *istiḫsān* as a method of seeking easiness in legal rulings. In other words, it is a departure from *qiyāṣ* in favour of a ruling which removes hardship and brings ease.[298] Indeed, removing hardship from the Muslims is one of the high objectives of Islamic law. The Qur'anic verse; "*God wills ease for you, and He does not will hardship for you*..."[299] constituted this high objective. Similarly, the noble Prophet encouraged Muslims to bring ease in the religion; "The best of your religion is that which brings ease to the people."[300]

Ibn Taymiyyah defines *istiḫsān* as departing from one ruling (*ḫukm*) for another which is considered better, on the basis of the Qur'an, Sunnah, or general consensus.[301] For ibn al-'Arabi, *istiḫsān* is making an exception from what is required by the general rule because its application would result in deviation from the higher objectives of Islamic law.[302] Abu Zahra holds that *istiḫsān* is juristic pref-

---

[298] Sarakhsī, *Mabsūt*, vol.10, p. 145.

[299] Qur'an, 2: 185.

[300] Ahmad ibn Hanbal, *Musnad*, vol.5, p. 22.

[301] Ibn Taymiyyah, *Mas'alah al-Istiḫsān*, p. 446.

[302] Ibn al-'Arabi, *Aḫkām al-Qur'an*, vol.2, p. 57.

erence which abandons *qiyāṣ* for a reason that necessitates such departure and aims to sustain a higher objective of Islamic law.[303]

Istiḫsān is a form of legal opinion which gives preference to the *mujtahid* from amongst the possible solutions for a particular problem. Imam Malik holds that *istiḫsān* represents nine-tenths of the knowledge. The notion of *maslaḫah* is also included in this statement.

Summary: The Definition of *Istiḫsān*

1. *Istiḫsān* is a juristic preference when a *mujtahid*, using his personal opinion, abandons the ruling for a case which he gave for similar cases because of the existence of a verse or a hadith or *ijma'* or *'urf* (custom) or *maslaḫah* (public benefit) and gives a different ruling for the case at hand.
2. When we examine the cases of *istiḫsān* we discover that the *mujtahid* either abandons the general ruling because of the existence of special evidence or that there are two options of *qiyāṣ* available to the *mujtahid*; one is clear and another is unclear *qiyāṣ*. In this situation, the *mujtahid* prefers the unclear *qiyāṣ* because it offers a means of avoiding hardship and it is harmonious with the higher objectives of the Islamic law.
3. The Ḫanafī jurist al-Sarakhsī, defines *istiḫsān* as a method of seeking easiness in legal rulings.
4. Ibn Taymiyyah defines *istiḫsān* as departing from one ruling (*ḫukm*) for another which is considered better, on the basis of the Qur'an, Sunnah, or general consensus.
5. *Istiḫsān* is a form of legal opinion which gives preference to the *mujtahid* from amongst the possible solutions for a particular problem.

The Different Types of *Istiḫsān*

As we explained earlier, a *mujtahid* using his personal opinion abandons a ruling he has given for similar cases because of the existence of a verse, a hadith, *ijma'*, *'urf* (custom) or *maslaḫah* (public benefit) and gives a different ruling for the case in question. All these reasons are the foundations of making a ruling using *istiḫsān*. There are six types of *istiḫsān* all of which are elaborated below:

1) *Istiḫsān* because of the existence of *naṣṣ* in that specific matter.
2) *Istiḫsān* because of *ijma.'*
3) *Istiḫsān* because of necessity.

[303] Abu Zahrah, *Uṣūl*, p. 207.

4) *Istiḫsān* because of unclear *qiyāṣ.*
5) *Istiḫsān* because of *'urf* (custom).
6) *Istiḫsān* because of *maslaḫah.*

Istiḫsān because of *Naṣṣ*

This refers to a specific case which is excluded from the general rule or well-established principle due to the existence of another *naṣṣ* evidence. Any exceptions which God as Lawgiver makes also fall into this category. The following examples demonstrate this type of *istiḫsān.*

1) The contract of *salam*[304] is an example of *istiḫsān* because of *naṣṣ. Salam* is a contract whereby one sells something by describing it in detail and receives cash under the proviso that the goods will be delivered in the future. In this type of business transaction, the trader sells something before he actually owns it. There are two *naṣṣ* (evidence from the Qur'an and Sunnah) pertaining to this type of business; the first of them prohibits this type of business in general and makes the *salam* contract void. The noble Prophet told Hakim ibn Hizam, 'Do not sell something which you don't own.'[305] The second *naṣṣ* permits this type of business and validates the *salam* contract. When the Prophet came to Medina he discovered that the people of Medina were making contracts on their fruit crops for cash but the fruit itself would be given in one or two years. Thereupon the Prophet said; "If you sell something by making a *salam* contract you'd better make it according to the fixed amount, fixed scale and fixed time."[306] Because of this *naṣṣ,* jurists departed from the general ruling and issued fatwa making the *salam* contract valid. Ḫanafī scholars said that the *salam* contract is contrary to *qiyāṣ* but it is permissible from the view point of *istiḫsān*. The evidence shows that the ruling for *salam* is a departure from the general ruling because of the existence of a specific *naṣṣ* referencing that contract type. As such, Ḫanafī scholars departed from *qiyāṣ* instead of departing from *naṣṣ* and they meant by this expression the hadith which prohibits selling something before actually owning it.

2) There are two contradicting hadiths about the ruling for eating and drinking out of forgetfulness while fasting. According to one narration, the result is that the fast becomes void. The evidence for this ruling is the general principle 'If one of the pillars of something is absent it becomes void.' Abstaining from eating, drinking and sexual relationships are the pillars of fasting and if any of them is

[304] Selling unripen fruits for the cash money.
[305] Abu Dāwud, *Sunan, Buyu,* hadith no: 70.
[306] Abu Dāwud, *Sunan, Buyu,* hadith no: 57.

missing it invalidates the fast. These pillars of fasting are deemed to be removed even if they are done out of forgetfulness. To the contrary, there is another *naṣṣ* which opposes this ruling. The noble Prophet said; "If a fasting person eats and drinks forgetfully he completes his fasting, for sure God made him eat and drink."[307] When Ḫanafī scholars issued a fatwa according to this specific evidence they said that even though the ruling for eating and drinking forgetfully while fasting is opposite to *qiyāṣ,* nevertheless it does not invalidate fasting from the view point of *istiẖsān*. In this example, *qiyāṣ* indicates the general ruling that eating and drinking while fasting (even if done through forgetfulness) invalidates the fast. Abū Ḫanīfa acknowledged this saying that if this specific hadith didn't exist he would have ruled on the issue according to *qiyāṣ*; i.e. he would have issued a fatwa ruling that eating and drinking invalidate the fast regardless of whether it was intentional or through forgetfulness. However, due to the hadith evidence opposing *qiyāṣ*, he used *istiẖsān* and made an exemption from the general ruling.

SUMMARY: *ISTIẖSĀN* BECAUSE OF *NAṢṢ*

1. This is a specific case which is excluded from the general rule or well-established principle on this type of case due to the existence of another *naṣṣ* such as a verse or a hadith.
2. The contract of *salam* is an example of *istiẖsān* because of *naṣṣ*. Because of this *naṣṣ,* jurists departed from the general ruling and issued fatwa making the *salam* contract valid. The evidence shows that the ruling for *salam* is a departure from the general ruling because of the existence of a specific *naṣṣ* referencing that contract type.
3. There are two contradicting hadiths about the ruling for eating and drinking out of forgetfulness while fasting. In this example, *qiyāṣ* means eating and drinking while fasting (even through forgetfulness) invalidates the fast because this is the general ruling. However, the existence of the hadith evidence opposing the *qiyāṣ* meant *istiẖsān* was used and resulted in an exemption from the general ruling.

Istiẖsān because of *Ijma'*

This type of *istiẖsān* occurs when the *mujtahid* issues a fatwa for a case that is different than the fatwas of similar cases and other scholars either confirm it or do not reject it. This type of ruling is known as *istiẖsān* because of *ijma.'* For exam-

[307] Bukhari, *Saẖīẖ, Oaths and Vows,* hadith no: 662.

ple, the contract agreed between manufacturers and customers is deemed *istiḫsān* in this category. According to this contract, the manufacturer accepts to make products for a certain amount of money for his customer. This contract is void from the viewpoint of general principles which are well-established in the subject of business, because the goods, the subject of business, are not ready and present at the time the contract is agreed. It is not permissible to make a contract on items that are not produced yet. However, Muslims were making this type of contract from the early days of Islam and jurists did not oppose this practise.

Ḫanafī jurists hold that this type of contract is opposite to *qiyāṣ* but permissible from the view point of *istiḫsān*. The rulings of these contracts are excluded from the general rules of business transactions. In this example, *qiyāṣ* refers to the general rule for business transactions that 'It is not permissible to make a contract on something which physically does not exist.' Nevertheless, the Ḫanafī jurists issued a fatwa against this general ruling because of the *ijma'* evidence available on this matter.

Summary: *Istiḫsān* Because of *Ijma'*

1. This type of *istiḫsān* occurs when the *mujtahid* issues a fatwa for a case that is different than the fatwas of similar cases and other scholars either confirm it or do not reject it. This type of ruling is known as *istiḫsān* because of *ijma.'*
2. In the example of a business contract between a supplier and customer, *qiyāṣ* refers to the general rule for business transactions that 'It is not permissible to make a contract on something which physically does not exist.' Nevertheless, the Ḫanafī jurists issued a fatwa against this general ruling because of the *ijma'* evidence available on this matter.

Istiḫsān because of Necessity

This type of *istiḫsān* occurs when the jurist encounters two opposing situations; the general rule and the strong need which opposes this rule. The main purpose of *istiḫsān* is to consider the needs of people and remove any excessive burden that may arise from applying the usual ruling, therefore meeting the needs of the people is necessary. For example:

1) It is required to clean the water of wells and pools from filth and what has fallen into them. According to the well-established rule, pools and wells cannot be cleaned even if the water in them is partially or totally emptied. If just some of the water is emptied, the rest cannot be deemed pure because the filth is in

every part of it. If all the water is emptied the filth on the wall and floor will pollute the fresh water again. However, this general principle will bring hardship and difficulty for the Muslims if it is applied without taking the need of the people into consideration. For this reason, jurists issued a fatwa in this case to benefit the people and bring ease to them. They ruled based on *istiḫsān* that if some of the water or the water that is visibly filthy is emptied then the rest of the water is deemed pure.[308] The scholars agree that although the fatwa is against *qiyāṣ*, it is true for *istiḫsān*. The meaning of *istiḫsān* in this example is departing from the general rule regarding the cleaning of wells and pools because of the needs of the people. The *qiyāṣ* which is deemed to be opposite to this *istiḫsān* is the general rule for the cleaning of the dirty wells and pools; that is that the water can never be deemed pure even if the water is emptied completely. However, *istiḫsān* removes the hardship associated, by providing a fatwa ruling that emptying some water but not all of the water suffices in purifying the water from filth.

2) Cleaning the leftover water used by predatory birds such as falcons, eagles, etc. Predatory birds feed off carcasses and therefore, their beaks become filthy. Is it also possible that whilst drinking, their saliva can contaminate the water. The ruling for their saliva is the same as the ruling for their meat; it is considered filthy and unlawful. As a result, the logical fatwa about leftover water should be that it is deemed filthy as in the case of predatory animals. However, there is a difference between predatory birds and predatory land animals, in that the birds usually approach the water from the sky making it difficult to protect the water from them. People living in the desert or rural areas often encounter this problem. Whilst considering the ruling Ḫanafī scholars took their needs into consideration. They departed from the general rule and issued a different fatwa for the leftover water of predatory birds deeming it pure based on *istiḫsān*. The meaning of *istiḫsān* in this example is departing from the general rule due to necessity, the result being that the leftover water of predatory birds is deemed pure for the benefit of the people. The meaning of *qiyāṣ* which is opposite to *istiḫsān* in this case is the *qiyāṣ* in *Uṣūl al-Fiqh* (the assignment of the *ḫukm* of an existing case found in the texts of the Qur'an, Sunnah or *ijma'* to a new case whose *ḫukm* is not found in these sources on the basis of a common underlying attribute called the *'illah* of the *ḫukm*). The cases of the leftover water of predatory land animals and the predatory birds share a common *'illah* therefore it would seem logical for

[308] Al-Marghinanī, *al-Hidayah*, p. 67.

the ruling on both to be the same. However, Ḫanafī jurists departed from this *qiyāṣ* for the benefit of the people by applying principles of *istiḫsān.*

Summary: *Istiḫsān* Because of Necessity

1. This type of *istiḫsān* occurs when the jurist encounters two opposing situations; the general rule and the strong need which opposes this rule.
2. The main purpose of *istiḫsān* is to consider the needs of people and remove any excessive burden that may arise from applying the usual ruling, therefore meeting the needs of the people is necessary.
3. The examples are cleaning the water of wells and pool from filth and cleaning the leftover water used by predatory birds such as falcons, eagles, etc.

Istiḫsān because of *Khafī* (Unclear) *Qiyāṣ*

In this type of *istiḫsān,* the jurist encounters two types of *qiyāṣ* available for the solution; one is clear *qiyāṣ* and another is unclear *qiyāṣ*. However, the two types of *qiyāṣ* contradict one another and the jurist must choose just one for his *ijtihād.* The following are examples of this type of *istiḫsān.*

1) In the view of Ḫanafī jurists, a legal guardian (*wali*) has some rights over the property of minors or the mentally ill, including using the property or goods to make a deposit on a contract. However, a legal guardian may not use the property of minors for his own benefit, such as paying his own debts. Still, there are some legal situations that seem to interplay between these two practices. One of these situations is hypothecating the property of minors to someone to ensure a loan and taking it back when the debt is repaid. This practice is similar to both making a deposit and paying a debt. In the case of leaving property with someone else, depositing and hypothecating are similar as in both cases the legal guardian leaves the minor's property in the hands of someone else which is lawful practice. However, if the legal guardian then cannot repay his debt the property of the minor will be sold and used to pay the debt. This then makes the case similar to the case of paying his own debt with the wealth of the minor, which is unlawful. For this reason there are two types of *qiyāṣ* for this case. In the first type, hypothec is analogized to deposit and the result is that the legal guardian has the authority to deposit the property or wealth of the minor and also he has the right to hypothecate it. In the second type of *qiyāṣ*, hypothec is analogized to debt payment and in this case the legal guardian neither has the right to pay his own debt with the wealth of the minor nor to hypothecate it. There is a question around which

of the two cases is clear *qiyāṣ* and which one is *istiḫsān* (unclear *qiyāṣ*). Abu Ḫanīfa's opinion is that hypothec and deposit are similar to each other and this is clear *qiyāṣ*; as a result, it is permissible for the legal guardian to hypothecate the property or wealth of minors for his/her own benefit. According to the unclear *qiyāṣ*, hypothec and debt payment are similar to each other. In this case, the unclear *qiyāṣ* is preferred over the clear *qiyāṣ* and is an example of *istiḫsān* departing from clear *qiyāṣ* in the favour of the unclear *qiyāṣ*. The reason for this ruling is because it is more suitable for the benefit of the people. In this example the unclear *qiyāṣ* is *istiḫsān*.

2) Another example for this type of *istiḫsān* is leftover water from predatory birds which, as we discussed earlier, it is deemed clean from the view point of *istiḫsān*. There are two types of *qiyāṣ* (clear and unclear) possible for this case. According to the clear *qiyāṣ* option, the leftover water of predatory birds is analogized to the leftover water of predatory land animals such as lions or wolves because the meat of both types of animals is unlawful and their leftovers have the same ruling as their meat. The saliva and the meat are connected to each other because the saliva occurs in the meat of the animal, therefore if the meat is unlawful, the saliva is also unlawful. Because of this analogy (clear *qiyāṣ*), the ruling for the leftover water of predatory birds is deemed to be filthy and unclean. However, there is another *qiyāṣ* option available for this case and that is unclear (*khafī*) *qiyāṣ*. The relationship between the two cases is hidden at first but when deeply considered it can be seen by the jurist that there is a strong relationship between them. Choosing this unclear (*khafī*) *qiyāṣ* is in the best interest of the people and it is named unclear *qiyāṣ* for this reason. According to the unclear *qiyāṣ* option, the leftover water of predatory birds is analogized to the leftovers of humans. These birds drink the water with their beaks which are just clean bones. Their saliva does not mix in the water and does not contaminate it. According to this *qiyāṣ*, in the same way that humans do not contaminate water by drinking it, predatory birds do not make water impure by drinking from it with their beaks. Therefore, the leftover water from predatory birds is deemed to be clean and pure. The second option is preferred as it considers the needs of the people.

Summary: *Istiḫsān* Because of Unclear (*Khafī*) *Qiyāṣ*

1. In this type of *istiḫsān* the jurist encounters two types of *qiyāṣ* available for the solution; one is clear *qiyāṣ* and another is unclear *qiyāṣ*. However, the two types of *qiyāṣ* contradict one another and it is up to the jurist to choose one of them for his *ijtihād*.

2. The examples for this are the rights of the legal guardian over the property of minors or the mentally ill, specifically using the property or goods to make a deposit on a contract. The other example is water leftover from predatory birds for which there is clear and unclear *qiyāṣ*.

Istiḫsān because of *'Urf*

Istiḫsān might be used for a situation where people make something a custom which is opposite to *qiyāṣ* or opposite to one of the established general rulings. Ḫanafī *fiqh* books contain many examples for this type of *istiḫsān,* some of which are detailed below.

1) Ḫanafī jurists hold that every condition which is adopted by *'urf* (custom) for business contracts is valid. This is a result of *istiḫsān* based on *'urf* which is against *qiyāṣ* and the established general rulings. The general ruling on this matter is indicated in the hadith; "The Messenger of God prohibited the business transactions that are restricted with the conditions"[309] which outlines that setting conditions for purchase or sales transactions is forbidden. *Istiḫsān* opposes this well-established general ruling, because it is more suitable for the benefit of Muslims. According to *istiḫsān*, if there is a custom (*'urf*) in which conditions are placed on business transactions it is acceptable.
2) According to the general rule, if one makes over his wealth to a charitable foundation it is valid forever. The expression 'forever' limits the type of wealth that can be donated to a charitable foundation, making it unlawful to donate moveable wealth which will naturally be consumed or depleted over time. The expression 'forever' in this ruling is not practical. Imam Muhammad ruled against *qiyāṣ* and the general ruling and said that books and similar items can be donated to charitable foundations because, despite not remaining forever, it is *'urf* (custom) and very common among the people. He took the *'urf* into consideration and issued a fatwa accordingly as a result of *istiḫsān*.

Summary: *Istiḫsān* Because of *'Urf*

1. *Istiḫsān* might be used for a situation where people make something a custom which is opposite to *qiyāṣ* or opposite to one of the established general rulings.

[309] Zaylaī, *Nasb al-Rāye*, vol.4, p. 17–18.

2. The first example is that according to Ḫanafī jurists every condition which is adopted by *'urf* (custom) for business contracts is valid.
3. The second example is the condition of donating moveable assets to charitable foundations.

Istiḫsān because of *Maslaḫah*

If the notion of *maslaḫah* (considering the benefit of public) necessitates giving a fatwa for a case by making an exception from the general *naṣṣ* or from the general ruling, it is called *istiḫsān* because of *maslaḫah*. The following examples demonstrate this.

1) According to a well-established rule in the Ḫanafī School an agricultural partnership ends when one of the partners dies in the same way as ruled for the rental contract. However, in some cases, this general rule is not applied; exceptions are made by taking the notion of *maslaḫah* into consideration. For example; in the case of a partnership between a landlord and a labourer, if the landlord dies before the crop has ripened or is harvested the partnership continues even though it is against *qiyāṣ* and the general rule. The notion of *maslaḫah* as the basis of *istiḫsān* here is to protect the benefit of the partners and to prevent harm. If the ruling was based on the general rule, the labourer would have worked in vain if the crop had not yet been harvested. For the benefit of the partnership it is necessary to wait until the crop is harvested and distributed between the partners before ending the contract.

2) According to the well-established rule it is forbidden for the progeny of the noble Prophet (the Banī Hashim tribe) to receive *zakat*. The evidence for this ruling is the following hadith; "*Zakat* is not permissible for Muhammad and his progeny."[310] In another hadith, the Prophet explained that for them there is a share from the war booty.[311] However, Abū Ḫanīfa and Imam Malik in their time issued a fatwa making it permissible to give *zakat* to the people from the progeny of the Prophet as a result of *istiḫsān*. This *istiḫsān* is based on the notion of *maslaḫah* even though it is against the hadith and the general rule. The reason for this fatwa was that during the time of Abu Ḫanīfa and Imam Malik the rulers were not giving the Banī Hashim their due rights from the war booty. To protect their benefit and prevent them from harm they made it permissible for them to receive *zakat*.

---

[310] Muslim, *Saḫīḫ, Zakat,* hadith no: 168.

[311] Zaylaī, *Nasb al-Rāye,* vol.2, p. 404.

3) According to an established rule, a trustee is not responsible for indemnifying the damage of the goods he is entrusted with, even if it occurs as a result of his own mistake. According to this rule, tailors and those similar do not compensate the goods in their stores if they are damaged accidentally. However, Imam Abū Yusuf and Muhammad issued a fatwa with the opposite ruling making it the responsibility of these people to indemnify the goods entrusted to them. In the Prophet's time Muslims were trustworthy and protected the property of others, however, over time this changed with people becoming less trustworthy and therefore the ruling was changed accordingly. Application of the general ruling would result in harm to people at the hands of reckless trustees. Therefore, the notion of *maslaḫah* necessitated this fatwa even though it was against the general rule.

These six categories demonstrate the most important types of *istiḫsān*. *Qiyāṣ* opposing *istiḫsān* is not the only type known in *Uṣūl al-Fiqh*, Ḫanafī jurists also used it in various other concepts.

Summary: *Istiḫsān* Because of *Maslaḫah*

1. If the notion of *maslaḫah* (considering the benefit of public) necessitates giving a fatwa for a case by making an exception from the general *naṣṣ* or from the general ruling, it is called *istiḫsān* because of *maslaḫah*.
2. The first example is to do with the ruling that an agricultural partnership ends when one of the partners dies. The notion of *maslaḫah* which is the basis of *istiḫsān* in this example is that it is necessary to protect the benefit of the partners and to prevent something that will harm them. It is necessary to wait until the crop is harvested and distributed between the partners before ending the contract.
3. The second example is the rule that it is forbidden for the progeny of the noble Prophet (the Banī Hashim tribe) to receive *zakat*. In the time of Abu Ḫanīfa and Imam Malik, the rulers were not giving the Banī Hashim their due rights from the war booty so to protect their benefit they issued a fatwa making it permissible for them to receive *zakat*. This *istiḫsān* is based on the notion of *maslaḫah* even though it is against the hadith and the general rule.
4. The third example is of the trustee not indemnifying the damage of the trust if it occurs as a result of his own mistake, because he is not responsible for indemnifying this type of damage. However, Imam Abū Yusuf and

Muhammad issued a fatwa that gave the opposite ruling making it the responsibility of these people to indemnify the goods entrusted to them because it was common amongst them to deceive the Muslims and betray their trusts. Therefore, the notion of *maslaḫah* necessitated this fatwa even though it was against the general rule.

The Proof Value of *Istiḫsān*

Istiḫsān is one of the types of evidence in Ḫanafī *fiqh* and is included in the *uṣūl al fiqh* books. The meaning and functions of *istiḫsān* are accepted by all scholars despite arguments to the contrary, the only difference being how they refer to the process. When examining the other schools' *fiqh* books there are many examples of *istiḫsān*. For example, Imam Malik accepts *istiḫsān* and used it in his *ijtihāds* under the name of *maslaḫah*.

Although Imam Shāfi'ī takes a rigid stance on *istiḫsān* and criticized it severely he himself used it in his *ijtihāds* in some cases. An example is related from Āmidī who reported from Imam Shāfi'ī; 'Once when the punishment for the thief was being applied, the thief extended his left hand and the punishment was applied to this left hand.' This practice is against the hadith and *qiyāṣ*. Imam Shāfi'ī said that according to *qiyāṣ* the punishment must also be applied to the right hand, however, as a result of *istiḫsān* he issued a fatwa opposing the *qiyāṣ*.[312] Similarly, Imam Shāfi'ī issued a fatwa based on *istiḫsān* making it permissible to take a bath in a bathhouse without agreeing a time and price at the beginning. He also issued a fatwa based on *istiḫsān* making it permissible to sell water without setting a quantity and price because it would be insensitive to the prevailing *'urf* (custom) to do so. He took the *'urf* into consideration and did not set rigid rules on this issue. These are just a few of many examples of *istiḫsān* because of *'urf* which can be found in Shāfi'ī *fiqh* books.

Ḫanafī jurists support their view with the following verses and use them to extract the foundations and different uses of *istiḫsān*;

> Who, when they hear speech, follow the best of it [*ahsanahu*]. Those are the ones whom God has guided, and those are the ones who are people of discernment[313]

[312] Āmidī, *Iḫkām*, vol.3, p. 138.
[313] Qur'an, 39: 18.

> Follow in the best [*ahsan*] way possible what has been sent down to you from your Lord...[314]

The Qur'an indicates a better course of conduct from the ordinary. For example, punishing the wrong-doer is the normal course enjoined by Islamic law however, forgiveness may at times be preferable (*ahsan*) and thus represents the higher course of conduct.[315]

There are two hadiths which are used by Ḫanafī jurists to support their view about *istiḫsān*; The noble Prophet said; "What the Muslims accept to be good is good in the sight of God."[316] On another occasion the Prophet said; "No harm shall be done to one, nor anyone harm others."[317] Both hadiths use the word '*istiḫsān*' which for Ḫanafī jurists is proof of the notion of *istiḫsān*.

We can conclude that all the scholars accepted *istiḫsān* and used it in their *fiqh*. Imam Shāfi'ī only opposed it if it was conducted on the basis of mere opinion without relying on any principles or objectives of Islamic law. If *istiḫsān* is conducted based on the principles and higher objectives of Islamic jurisprudence it is valid and accepted. The Maliki jurist al-Shātibī maintains that *istiḫsān* does not mean following one's personal whims; rather, it is an indication that the jurists have deeper understanding of the aims of Islamic law. In the case where the strict application of *qiyāṣ* to a new problem leads to the loss of the public benefit and a negative result, jurists must prefer *istiḫsān*.[318]

When solving problems, the Companions first applied the Qur'an and the Sunnah but if they could not find answers there, they used their personal *ijtihād* in accordance with the general principles and higher objectives of Islamic law. *Istiḫsān* is essentially a form of *ijtihād* which offers better solutions for new problems. *Istiḫsān* results from understanding the spirit of Islam and using it in a broad sense to resolve new problems and to bring fairness and ease to Muslims.

Summary: The Proof Value of *Istiḫsān*

1. *Istiḫsān* is one of the types of evidence of Ḫanafī *fiqh* and is included in their *uṣūl al fiqh* books.
2. Despite claims to the contrary, other schools accepted and used *istiḫsān* in their *fiqh* and many examples can be found in their *fiqh* books.

---

[314] Qur'an, 39: 55.
[315] Kamali, *Principles of Islamic Jurisprudence*, p. 221.
[316] Shātibī, *I'tisām*, vol.2, p. 319.
[317] Ibn Majah, *Sunan*, vol. 2, hadith no: 784.
[318] Shātibī, *Muwafaqaat*, vol.4, p. 206.

3. Although Imam Shāfi'ī takes a rigid stance on *istiḫsān* and criticized it severely he himself used it in his *ijtihāds* in some cases.
4. Ḫanafī jurists support their view with Qur'anic verses and hadiths and use them to extract the foundations and different uses of *istiḫsān*.
5. All scholars accepted *istiḫsān* and used it in their *fiqh*. Imam Shāfi'ī only opposed it if it was conducted on the basis of mere opinion without relying on any principles or objectives of Islamic law.
6. If *istiḫsān* is conducted based on the principles and higher objectives of Islamic jurisprudence it is valid and accepted.
7. When solving problems, the Companions first applied to the Qur'an and the Sunnah but if they could not find answers there, they used their personal *ijtihād* in accordance with the general principles and higher objectives of Islamic law.

Comparing *Istiḫsān* with *Maslaḫah*

Istiḫsān differs from *maslaḫah*; in order to determine a question based on *istiḫsān* it is necessary to find an existing case that is similar to the new case and its general ruling. Then, based on evidence, *istiḫsān* makes an exception from this general ruling and an opposite fatwa is issued. *Maslaḫah* is when there is no existing case similar to the new case for which the fatwa is sought. Therefore, the fatwa for the new case is given directly based *maslaḫah* rather than given differently to an existing case.

Qawli Saḫābah (The Statement of the Companions)

Introduction

Saḫābah literally means a Companion. It is defined by the scholars of *Uṣūl al-Fiqh* as; a person who lived at the same time as the noble Prophet, who saw him, believed in him, was with him for a long time and died as a Muslim. For example, the four Caliphs, the wives of the Prophet, Abdullah ibn Mas'ud, Zayd ibn Thabit, etc. were the Companions, because they were together with the Prophet for a long time and witnessed his acts, words and approvals. Moreover, they adopted the same moral values as him and had an in-depth understanding of the essentials of Islam. Some defined Companion as a person who saw the Prophet, believed in him and died as a Muslim. There is no minimum time required for companionship with the Prophet in order to be considered a Companion in this definition.

Thus, the majority holds that there were more than a hundred thousand Companions when the Prophet passed away.

A number of the Companions were distinguished as *fāqih* (expert in Islamic law) from amongst the others and would issue fatwa for the problems they faced after the death of the noble Prophet. They were well-versed in the Qur'an and Sunnah and also knew the methodology for extracting the rules for new cases from the sources of Islamic jurisprudence. Following the death of the Prophet, these Companions undertook the task of issuing fatwa and making *ijtihāds* to solve the problems of the Muslims. Their legal rulings and opinions have been transmitted to us via the scholars of the early generations but are not collected into a single book, rather they are scattered in hadith books and the books of legal schools.

Uṣūl scholars have discussed the statements of the Companions and debated their value in Islamic law, resulting in various views on the subject which are summarized below.

The Proof Value of the Statement of the Companions

The rulings for the cases mentioned by the Companions of which it would be impossible for them to have knowledge by logic or reasoning are considered evidence and binding according to the majority of scholars. It is most likely that they heard or witnessed this directly from the noble Prophet and therefore could be deemed to be Sunnah. As we discussed earlier, Sunnah is evidence according to all scholars. For example, Ḥanafī scholars use the following statements of the Companions as evidence in their legal school; the minimum menstruation period is three days according to 'Abdullah ibn Mas'ud and the maximum pregnancy time is two years based on the statement of 'A'isha. These topics cannot be known through logic, so it is most likely that those Companions heard them from the Prophet and therefore Ḥanafī scholars accept these types of statements as evidence.

Another example is a report that 'Ali ibn Abī Tālib prayed six *rak'ah* one night and prostrated six times in every *rak'ah*. The method of Prayer was taught by the Prophet and strictly followed by the Companions. In such matters there is no room for logical reasoning and Imam Shāfi'ī indicated this saying that if he could be certain of the report's authenticity he would have ruled accordingly because the performance of such acts (six prostrations in every *rak'ah*) would have been based on seeing the Prophet doing it himself.[319]

[319] Sharif Jalal al-Mahalli, *Jam al-Jawāmī'*, vol. 2, p. 36.

Scholars agree that the consensus of all the Companions is binding proof and it is not permissible to disagree with that consensus; however, they vary in their opinion of whether the statement of a single Companion should also be recognised as proof, and whether it should be given precedence over other evidence. [320] We appreciate that the Companions had many points of difference in different cases and the point for discussion here is whether or not the statement of the Companions is binding for the generations after them. There are two main views about the statements of the Companions which are explained below.

The first view is that the statement of the Companions is not evidence in Islamic law. Scholars with this view argue that a Companion can be deemed as the same as any *mujtahid*. It is possible for *mujtahids* to make mistakes in their *ijtihāds;* therefore, the statement of the Companions cannot be evidence or a source of Islamic law for the *mujtahids.*

The second view is that the statement of the Companions is evidence and binding for *mujtahids* if they are unable to find the solution in the Qur'an, Sunnah or *ijma.'* This is the view of Imam Malik, one of the two views of Imam Shāfi'ī, one of the two views of Imam Ahmad b. Hanbal and of some Ḥanafī jurists.[321] They assert that even though it is possible for the Companions to make mistakes in their *ijtihāds*, most of the time they are correct because they were educated in the classroom of the noble Prophet. The Companions were well-versed in the language of the Qur'an and had a detailed knowledge of the objectives of Islam. Additionally, as first hand witnesses of the Prophet's life they knew the occasions behind the revelation and the reasons for the occurrence of the Sunnah. As such, they differed from the *mujtahids* who came after them and their statements are superior to other *ijtihāds* and constitute binding proof for all the *mujtahids.*

The Critique of These Two Views

Even though the statement of the Companions in legal matters is a positive contribution for *mujtahids*, it cannot prevent them from making their own *ijtihāds* on those cases. *Mujtahids* may accept their view or make their own *ijtihāds* on them. There are two supporting arguments for this critique;

1) For something to be accepted as evidence in Islamic law it must be proven. There is no definite evidence to support the view that the Companions' statements are binding, therefore this is not permissible.

---

320 Kamali, *Principles of Islamic Jurisprudence*, p. 210.

321 Kamali, ibid, p. 212.

Some *Tabi'in* (the Successors, the generation following the Companions) scholars disagreed with the views of the Companions in some cases and their views were not rejected or corrected by the Companions. If the statement of the Companions were binding for all *mujtahids* it would not be permissible for the *Tabi'in* scholars to dispute their statements. This occurred on many occasions; for example: one day 'Ali saw a Jew carrying some armour and claimed that it was his. The Jew refuted the claim and the matter was brought before a judge. The judge, Qādi Shurayh, a *Tabi'in mujtahid* requested that 'Ali bring two witnesses to prove his claim. The witnesses were 'Ali's slave and his son Ḫasan who both testified in favour of 'Ali. However, Qādi Shurayh refused to accept the testimony of 'Ali's son despite being told by 'Ali that a son can be a witness for his father. Qādi Shurayh did not accept this view and handed over the armour to the Jew. Following the verdict, the Jew reported that the ruler of the believers ('Ali) lost a case in front of a judge that he himself had appointed. Furthermore, he accepted and respected the decision. In fact, 'Ali's claim was correct and the armour was his. Following this, the Jew converted to Islam and remained with 'Ali until he was martyred in one of the wars. This example is a clear and strong argument for this critique; the statement of the Companions in legal matters is a positive contribution for *mujtahids* but it is not binding and cannot prevent them from making *ijtihāds* in those cases.

Summary: The Statement of the Companions (*Qawli Saḫābah*)

1) *Saḫābah* is a person who lived at the same time as the noble Prophet, who saw him, believed in him, was with him for a long time and died as a Muslim.
2) A number of *Saḫābah* were distinguished as *fāqih* and issued fatwa for the problems they faced after the death of the Prophet which have been transmitted via the scholars of the early generations and are scattered in hadith books and the books of legal schools.
3) *Uṣūl* scholars have discussed the statements of the Companions and debated their value as evidence in Islamic law.
4) The ruling for the cases mentioned by the Companions of which it would be impossible for them to have knowledge by logic or reasoning are considered evidence and binding according to the majority of scholars.
5) Scholars vary in their opinion of whether the statement of a single Companion should also be recognised as proof, and whether it should be given precedence over other evidence.

6) The first view is that the statement of the Companions is not evidence in Islamic law.
7) The second view is that the statement of the Companions is evidence and binding for *mujtahids* if they are unable to find the solution in the Qur'an, Sunnah or *ijma.'*
8) Even though the statement of the Companions in legal matters is a positive contribution for *mujtahids*, it cannot prevent them from making their own *ijtihāds* on those cases. To be able to accept something as evidence in Islamic law it is necessary for it to be proven. However, there is no definite evidence supporting the view that the statement of the Companions is binding. Some *Tabi'in* scholars disagreed with the views of the Companions in some cases and their views were not rejected or corrected by the Companions.

Shar'u Man Qablanā (The Laws Preceding Islam)

Introduction

Shar'u man qablanā means the laws preceding the Shari'ah of Islam. From the earliest days of humankind, God has sent Messengers to all people, the most renowned of whom are those such as Ibrahim, Moses and Jesus, peace be upon them. Through revelations He established and regulated laws. Islamic scholars have debated whether the previous revelations are a source of Islamic law and whether their rulings are also binding for Muslims. What is the place of the laws preceding Islamic Shari'ah?

The Classifications of Previous Laws

The laws given to previous nations can be classified according to two main categories with regards to Islamic law. The first category relates to laws which are not mentioned in the Qur'an or Sunnah. There is a general consensus that these types of regulations and rulings are not binding on Muslims. The second category relates to the laws which are mentioned in them; these are divided further into three key areas:

1) The rulings and regulations which are abrogated in Islamic law. These are the rulings where there is evidence which clearly states that the previous rulings are abrogated by the Qur'an or Sunnah. Muslim scholars have an agreement on that this type of previous law is not valid and it is not binding for the Muslims. For instance;

> Say (O Messenger): "I do not find in what has been revealed to me anything made unlawful to one who would eat except it be carrion or blood outpoured (not that which is left in the veins of such organs as the liver and spleen), or the flesh of swine, which is loathsome and unclean, or that which is profane having been slaughtered in the name of other than God (or without pronouncing God's Name over it). Yet whoever is constrained by dire necessity (to eat thereof) provided he does not covet nor exceed (the bounds of the necessity): (no sin shall be on him). Your Lord is indeed All-Forgiving, All-Compassionate[322]

> And for those who are Jews We have made unlawful all beasts with claws, and of oxen and sheep We have made unlawful for them their fat, save that which is in their backs or entrails, or that which is mixed with the bone. Thus did We recompense them for their continuous rebellion. And We are indeed true (in all Our decrees and deeds)[323]

The first verse explains what is forbidden for Muslims and the second explains what is forbidden for Jews. The regulations on the Jews were given as a punishment for their continuous rebellion and it is obvious that these restrictions are intended for the Jews only; therefore, they are not valid in Islamic law, because the Qur'an abrogated them. Another example for this type of previous law is the following hadith of the noble Prophet; "...The booty has been made *halal* (lawful) for me yet it was not lawful for anyone else before me..."[324] War booty is what is gained from the enemy and collected after wars and it was forbidden for every nation before Islam. The previous ruling is abrogated in Islamic law resulting in war booty being permissible for Muslims.

2) The previous rulings which are also valid and binding for the Muslims. This group constitutes the previous rulings for which there is evidence in the Shari'ah of Islam that they are also binding for Muslims. For example;

> O you who believe! Prescribed for you is the Fast, as it was prescribed for those before you, so that you may deserve God's protection (against the temptations of your carnal soul) and attain piety[325]

This verse clearly states that fasting was prescribed for previous nations and is also a prescribed pillar for Muslims.

---

[322] Qur'an, 6: 145.
[323] Qur'an, 6: 146.
[324] Bukhari, *Sahīh, Tayammum*, hadith no: 331.
[325] Qur'an, 2: 183.

Another example of this type of previous law is the hadith of the Prophet; "Sacrifice an animal because it is the Sunnah of your ancestor Ibrahim."[326] The act of sacrificing an animal was performed by Ibrahim and according to this hadith it is also commanded to Muslims.

3) The previous rulings which are mentioned in the Qur'an or in the Sunnah without any indication of whether they are valid for Muslims or without evidence of whether or not they were abrogated.

> And We prescribed for them in it (concerning murder): A life for a life, and an eye for an eye, and a nose for a nose, and an ear for an ear, and a tooth for a tooth, and a (like) retaliation for all wounds (the exact retaliation of which is possible). But whoever remits (the retaliation), it will be an act of expiation for him. Whoever does not judge by what God has sent down, those are indeed wrongdoers[327]

This verse informs us about one of the rulings of the Torah. This ruling was binding for the Jewish community but it is not clear if it is also binding for Muslims. The text is not clear and definite in regards to Islamic law.

Another example is the verse; "*And inform them that the water is to be shared between her and them; each sharer will be present by the water when it is their turn to drink.*"[328] This verse was related to Prophet Salih, peace be upon him, when he had a problem with his followers. The verse tells how water was being distributed between the followers of Prophet Salih, peace be upon him. The miracle camel was allocated for each side in turn. The verse does not indicate whether the ruling is valid for Muslims and the Prophet didn't mention whether this ruling was binding or abrogated in Islamic law.

This category of laws is the subject of dispute amongst jurists. The sound view in this discussion is that these rulings are also valid for Muslims and this is supported by the following evidence; the noble Prophet said, "If you forget or sleep and cannot perform the Prayer in its fixed time, make it up when you remember." After this statement the Prophet recited the following verse as evidence for this ruling; "*Establish the Prayer in conformity with its conditions for remembrance of Me.*"[329] In this verse, God is speaking to Moses, peace be upon him, but Prophet Muhammad, peace and blessings be upon him, used it as evidence that his fol-

[326] Ibn Majah, *Sunan, Aḏāhī*, hadith no: 3.
[327] Qur'an, 5: 45.
[328] Qur'an, 54: 28.
[329] Qur'an, 20: 14.

lowers must perform the Prayers when they remember. Therefore, the previous laws mentioned in the Qur'an and Sunnah are accepted as evidence in Islamic law. God mentioned them in the Qur'an and even though they are neither clear nor definite, their presence implies that they are also valid for Muslims.

When we evaluate *shar'u man qablanā* we can see that it is not an independent source of Islamic law, rather it is a part of the Qur'an and Sunnah. As we mentioned earlier, *shar'u man qablanā* can be used as evidence if the laws are mentioned in the Qur'an and Sunnah without being identifiably rejected or abrogated. As such, *shar'u man qablanā* is a consideration to be made under the Qur'an and Sunnah as sources of Islamic law.

Summary: *Shar'u Man Qablanā* (The Laws Preceding Islam)

1) *Shar'u man qablanā* means the laws preceding the Shari'ah of Islam.
2) Islamic scholars discussed whether they are considered a source of Islamic law.
3) The laws given to previous nations are classified into two categories: a) laws not mentioned in the Qur'an or Sunnah on which there is a general consensus that they are not binding on Muslims; b) laws mentioned in the sources of Islamic jurisprudence which are divided into three key areas.
4) The rulings and regulations which are abrogated in Islamic law. These are the rulings where there is evidence which clearly states that the previous rulings are abrogated by the Qur'an or Sunnah.
5) The previous rulings which are also valid and binding for Muslims. This group constitutes the previous rulings for which there is evidence in the Shari'ah of Islam that they are also binding for Muslims.
6) The previous rulings which are mentioned in the Qur'an or in the Sunnah without any indication of whether they are valid for Muslims or without evidence of whether or not they were abrogated.
7) This category of laws is the subject of dispute amongst jurists. The sound view in this discussion is that these rulings are also valid for Muslims.
8) When we evaluate *shar'u man qablanā* we can see that it is not an independent source of Islamic law, rather it is a part of the Qur'an and Sunnah. As such, *shar'u man qablanā* is a consideration to be made under the Qur'an and Sunnah as sources of Islamic law.

Chapter Seven

'Urf (Custom) and *Maslaḫah Mursala* (Consideration of Public Interest)

'Urf (Custom) and *Maslaḫah Mursala* (Consideration of Public Interest)

'Urf (Custom)

Introduction

'Urf is an Arabic word derived from the root *'a-ra-fa'* which means 'to know.' *'Urf* means something that is known. The juristic definition is: the collective practice of a large group of people which has been adopted and made a custom, or, a word or words which have gained a special meaning to the extent that when they are used the other meanings are excluded and only the special meaning is understood. *'Urf* is a custom that is accepted and practised by the people even though it is not regulated. It is not against reason, sense or nature or the principles of Islam.[330] *'Urf* (custom) is not the same as *'ādah* (habit). *'Urf* is specifically good customs or practices whereas *'ādah* can refer to either good or bad habits.[331] The *ādah* can result from imitation and following the ancestors blindly.[332] The Qur'an criticized the Meccan pagans for this kind of practice:

> When it is said to them (who follow in the footsteps of Satan), "Follow what God has sent down," they respond: "No, but we follow that (the traditions, customs, beliefs, and practices) which we found our forefathers in." What, even if their forefathers had no understanding of anything, and were not rightly guided?[333]

As the definition shows, *'urf* can be linguistic (*qawlī*), practical (*amalī*), general or specific. Each of these categories can be further classified into two from the view point of validity (*saḫīḫ*) or invalidity (*fāsid*). *'Amalī 'urf* (practical customs) are the deeds and practices which later became the customs of the people. For example, the words giving and receiving were used by the people to mean busi-

[330] Gülen, *Kendi Dünyamıza Doğru*, p. 102.
[331] Ibid.
[332] Ibid.
[333] Qur'an, 2: 170.

ness transactions. Similarly, *mahr muajjal* is used to mean the women who will receive their dowry following a delay and *mahr mu'ajjal* is used to mean those women who receive their dowry immediately before consummating the marriage. Another example of *'amalī 'urf* is, using the public bath without assigning either the amount of water to be used or the duration of time to be spent there.

The linguistic (*qawlī*) *'urf* is when people give a specific meaning to a word whose literal meaning is different. The specific meaning becomes the linguistic (*qawlī*) custom. Examples include using the Arabic word '*walad*' (child) to mean only son, not daughter and also '*dabba*' (living being) which is used to indicate animals which have four legs.

'Urf differs from *ijma'* in that it is the general consensus of the public whereas *ijma'* is the general consensus of the *mujtahids*. Also, with *ijma'* it is necessary for all the *mujtahids* to agree on a fatwa but with *'urf* there is no such condition, rather it refers to the practice of the majority of both the general public and scholars.

'Amalī and *qawlī 'urf*, can be general or specific. General (*āam*) *'urf* refers to customs and practices which have been adopted by the majority of people who are living during the same time period. An example of *āam 'amalī 'urf* (a general practical custom) is the practice of making exceptions from contracts. An example of *āam qawlī 'urf* (a general linguistic custom) is the usage of the word '*haram*' to mean divorce (*talaq*). Specific customs are the habits belonging to specific locations, groups or cities. For example, in Iraq, the Arabic word '*dabba*' is used to mean horse and is an example of a specific linguistic *'urf*. Again, in Iraq, the accounts book of a business is used as evidence to prove customer debts and is an example of a specific practical *'urf*.

'Urf is classified into two further categories: *saḫīḫ* (valid) and *fāsid* (invalid) according to the general principles of Islamic law. *Saḫīḫ 'urf* is a custom of the people which does not change a *halal* (lawful) action into a *haram* (unlawful) action or a *haram* action into a *halal* action. Two examples of *saḫīḫ 'urf* are; a deposit for a business contract and a woman refusing to go to her husband. These customs are not against the general principles of Islamic jurisprudence and they do not change *halal* into *haram* or *haram* into *halal*.

'Urf fāsid is a custom of the people which changes one *halal* into *haram* or one *haram* into *halal* thereby rendering it invalid. Examples of this are, consuming interest or performing interest-based bank transactions; men and women being together in a wedding and celebrating it in improper ways such as danc-

ing, etc.; offering alcohol in banquets and abandoning the Prayers in such gatherings.

Summary: Introduction

1. *'Urf* is derived from the root *'a-ra-fa'* which means 'to know.' *'Urf* means something that is known.
2. In Islamic law it means a collective practice of a large group of people which has been adopted and made a custom, or, a word or words which have gained a special meaning to the extent that when they are used the other meanings are excluded and only the special meaning is understood.
3. *'Urf* can be linguistic (*qawlī*), practical (*amalī*), general or specific and each category can contain valid (*sahīh*) or invalid (*fāsid*) *'urf.*
4. *'Amalī 'urf* (practical customs) are the deeds and practices which later became the customs of the people.
5. Linguistic (*qawlī*) *'urf* is when the people give a specific meaning to words whose literal meanings are different. The specific meaning becomes the linguistic (*qawlī*) custom.
6. *'Amalī* and *qawlī 'urf,* can be general or specific. General (*āam*) *'urf* is the customs and practices which are adopted by the majority of people who are living during one time. Specific customs are the habits belonging to specific locations, groups or cities.
7. *'Urf* is classified into two further categories: *sahīh* (valid) and *fāsid* (invalid) according to the general principles of Islamic law.
8. *Sahīh 'urf* is a custom of people which does not change one *halal* (lawful action) into *haram* (unlawful action) or one *haram* into *halal.*
9. *'Urf fāsid* is a custom of the people which changes one *halal* into *haram* or one *haram* into *halal* thereby rendering it invalid.

Proof Value of *'Urf*

The majority of scholars agree that if the *'urf* is against the general principles and objectives of Islam it is not valid, and it is even necessary to end such customs. For example, consuming alcohol, all forms of gambling, usury transactions, placing candles in cemeteries, etc. are against the values of Islam. However deeply ingrained they have become these customs are not valid and should be ended in Muslim communities. They are against the spirit of Islamic law which has certain prohibitions to protect the values such as religion, life, property, etc. If a custom removes any of these values or harms them in any way they are rejected.

Conversely, if the *'urf* is not against any general principle or objective of Islam, it is valid and can be used as the basis to extract rulings for new cases. In general, issuing fatwa based on *'urf* is done using the application of *maslaḫah mursala*. It can be done by restricting the general rules or making exceptions from them. Sometimes *qiyāṣ* may find in favour of *'urf* and the fatwa may be ruled based on custom.[334]

Scholars who accept *'urf* evidence use some Qur'anic verses to support their view[335]; "*Adopt the way of forbearance and tolerance, and enjoin what is good and right, and withdraw from the ignorant ones.*"[336] In this verse the Arabic word *'urf* is used to mean what's good and right. Another argument is the hadith of the Prophet; "What the Muslims accept to be good is good in the sight of God as well."[337] Some scholars used this hadith as an argument for *ijma'* but not for *'urf*.[338]

The ultimate goal of Islamic law is to provide justice for the citizens, to promote their welfare and to protect them from harm. It would cause unnecessary hardship if the *mujtahids* disregarded the customs of sound intellectual people that were not against the general principles of Islam. Therefore, it is permissible for these customs to be used as a source for *ijtihāds* regarding business transactions, political and social regulations, judgment systems and the moral values of the public. Islam did not abolish all the customs of the pre-Islamic time, rather it removed some and kept some with new regulations.[339] Examples of the customs that remained are; the payment of blood money in case of an accidental killing (100 camels), the business transactions, the lease, the contracts, etc. The customs that were ruled against by God, the Lawgiver were those that were harmful, such as usury, gambling, burying daughters alive and depriving women of the right to an inheritance.

Scholars from different schools accepted the valid *'urf* and used them in their *ijtihāds* as evidence using expressions such as, 'The custom is strong' and 'If something is accepted by the '*urf* it is deemed as if it is accepted by *shar'ī* evidence.'[340] *Fiqh* books contain many examples of fatwa which were given based on *'urf*, some of which are detailed below;

---

334 Shātibī, *Muwafaqaat*, vol.2, pp. 279–288.

335 Qarafi, *Furuq*, vol.3, p.179.

336 Qur'an, 7: 199.

337 Shātibī, *I'tisām*, vol.2, p. 319.

338 Āmidī, *Iḫkām*, vol.3, p.112.

339 Abdul Rahim, *Jurisprudence*, p. 137.

340 *The Mejelle* (Tyser's trans.) (Art. 36).

1) The contract which makes an exception from the general rule. According to the general rule, this type of contract is not valid as it is a contract made over non-existent goods. However, even though it is against the general rule of business transactions, it is accepted by the general *'urf* due to necessity and the general custom of the people. The majority of jurists deem this custom valid and base their *ijtihāds* on this *'urf*.

2) Selling the fruits of the crop before they have ripened. Imam Malik and some other jurists deemed this transaction permissible based on the prevailing *'urf*. According to the general rule, selling the fruit before it is ripe is like selling non-existent goods and, therefore, is not permissible. However, due to the existence of the general custom the jurists including the Ḩanafī jurists Hulwanī and Muhammad Abū Fadl issued a positive fatwa on this issue making it permissible for the people of that time. Abū Fadl said, 'I took the custom of people into consideration and I made *istiḩsān* on this issue. The public adopted this transaction (selling the unripened fruits) for the grapes as their custom; there is a clear *'urf* in this matter. Rejecting this custom and giving the fatwa against it would cause great harm to the public.'[341]

3) Abū Ḩanīfa and his two disciples hold that the conditions in contracts which are the customs of people are valid even if they are not included in the contract or they do not fit the meaning of them. The presence of the specific *'urf* in this matter is sufficient for this fatwa. This fatwa is against the general ruling initiated by the Prophet prohibiting the transaction by indicating some conditions. However, the *'urf* restricted this general rule and these transactions were excluded from the scope of this general rule.

4) Imam Muhammad issued a fatwa that moveable goods can be given to charitable associations as *waqf* (charity) in the same way as immoveable goods, because it is the custom (*'urf*) to do so. This fatwa opposes the general rule that *waqf* is permanent and therefore moveable goods cannot be given as *waqf* because they cannot remain forever.

Summary: Proof Value of *'Urf*

1. The majority of scholars agree that if the *'urf* is against the general principles and objectives of Islam it is not valid, and it is even necessary to end such customs.

---

[341] Ibn 'Ābidīn, *Majma al-Rasāil*, vol.2, p. 104.

2. If the *'urf* is not against any general principle or objective of Islam, it is valid and can be the basis used to extract rulings for new cases.
3. In general, issuing fatwa based on *'urf* is done using the application of *maslaḫah mursala*. It can be done by restricting the general rules or making exceptions from them or sometimes *qiyāṣ* may find in favour of *'urf* and the fatwa may be ruled based on custom.
4. Scholars who accept *'urf* evidence use Qur'anic verses to support their view.
5. Scholars from different schools accepted the valid *'urf* and used them in their *ijtihād. Fiqh* books contain many examples of fatwa which were given based on *'urf,* such as; the contract which makes an exception from the general rule; selling the fruits of the crop before they have ripened; conditions in contracts which are the customs of people; donating moveable goods to charitable associations.

The Conditions for the Validity of *'Urf*

Certain conditions must be met for *'urf saḫīḫ* (valid customs) to be accepted and used as the basis for *ijtihāds*;

1) The *'urf* must not be against any general principle or objective of Islam. If this is not the case, the *'urf* is rejected and it is not valid to use it as a basis for *ijtihād*. Examples of this are the Bedouin practice of depriving female heirs from inheritance, or the practice of usury and gambling.[342]

2) The *'urf* must be a permanent custom of the people and adopted by the majority. The practice of a few individuals or of some of the people within community is not sufficient to constitute *'urf.* Effect is only given to a custom which regularly occurs.[343]

3) The *'urf* must be practised at the time a transaction is concluded and must continue afterward. This condition is particularly important for the interpretation of contracts, because they can be understood in light of the custom that prevailed at the time they were made.[344]

4) The *'urf* must not be contrary to the clear stipulation of an agreement. If people make a contract which states some clear conditions against the *'urf* or by acting differently to the *'urf,* the *'urf* is not taken into consideration. For exam-

[342] Badran, *Uṣūl*, p. 121.

[343] *Mejelle*, art 14.

[344] Sābūnī, *Madkhal*, p. 143

ple, if a custom exists by which the transit expenses are the responsibility of the customer but the customer and seller make a contract stating the opposite, the contract is valid and the *'urf* is not taken into consideration.[345]

'Urf facilitates a better understanding of the general expressions in the Qur'an and Sunnah. For example, the Qur'an states; "*...Call upon two men of probity from among you as witnesses, and establish the testimony for God...*"[346] In this verse, probity is stipulated for the persons who will testify. According to the jurists, probity is a characteristic which protects the person from immoral acts; therefore, any immoral acts remove this characteristic from the person. However, immoral acts can be relative and changeable depending on the time and place. For example, according to Shātibī, if men walk on the streets without covering their head it is against piety and therefore it removes the quality of probity. However, the same is not true in Western countries and thus, it does not remove this quality.

Summary: The Conditions for the Validity of *'Urf*

1. Certain conditions must be met for *'urf saẖīẖ* (valid customs) to be accepted and used as the basis for *ijtihāds*;
2. The *'urf* must not be against any general principle or objective of Islam.
3. The *'urf* must be a permanent custom of the people and adopted by the majority.
4. The *'urf* must be practised at the time a transaction is concluded and must continue afterward.
5. The *'urf* must not be contrary to the clear stipulation of an agreement.
6. *'Urf* facilitates a better understanding of the general expressions in the Qur'an and Sunnah.

Changes in the Rulings by Changing *'Urf*

According to Islamic law, if an *'urf* changes, the rulings that have been issued based on that *'urf* must also change accordingly. If there is a change in the root (*asl*), the change in the branches (*far'*) is inescapable. For this reason, jurists, even from within the same schools, issued different fatwas for the same cases because the *'urf* on which the previous fatwas were based had changed over time. The jurists referred to these as 'differences in time' but not differences in evidence or proof. Some examples include;

[345] 'Izz ibn Abd as-Salam, *al-Qawā'id*, vol.2, p. 178.
[346] Qur'an, 65: 2.

1) Abū Ḫanīfa held that in cases other than those related to legal punishments (*hadd* and *qiṣaṣ*), two decent witnesses are sufficient and there is no need to investigate to make sure they are really upright. This is based on the saying of the Prophet; "The Muslims are deemed upright in testimony of each other."[347] This *ḫukm* (ruling) was suitable in Abū Ḫanīfa's time because the people were honest and trustworthy. Over time, this changed and the level of dishonesty amongst people increased. Abū Ḫanīfa's pupils, Abū Yusuf and Muhammad, concluded that accepting Muslims as being upright in general was not sufficient and it was necessary to investigate their character. They issued this fatwa to ensure justice was provided and to remove the potential for harm. This change occurred because the *'urf* in Abū Yusuf and Muhammad's time was different to the *'urf* in Abū Ḫanīfa's time.

2) Abū Ḫanīfa holds that it is only permissible for rulers to execute orders[348] through compulsion (*ikrah*). He ruled according to the custom of his time. However, Abū Yusuf and Muhammad issued a different fatwa ruling that orders can be executed by any oppressors or tyrants, not just by rulers because in their time it became possible for any wrong doers to force people to do things against their will. They took this into consideration and issued their fatwa accordingly.

3) In the Ḫanafī School, it is generally agreed that one cannot accept money for teaching the Qur'an because it is considered to be an act of obedience to God and a form of worship. At the time this fatwa was issued the Qur'an teachers' needs were being met by the government (*bayt al-mal*). However, as time passed the situation changed and teachers experienced hardship due to the time they allocated to teach the Qur'an. They were not able to take care of their families and meet their needs. They were unable to abandon giving instruction in the Qur'an due to the risk of people forgetting it, so the *mujtahids* of this time issued a fatwa making it permissible for them to receive payment for teaching the Qur'an. This ruling also extended to payment for calling the *adhan* and for leading the Prayers in the *masjids*.

4) The Ḫanafī School has a well-established rule stipulating that when buying a house it is sufficient to just see the outside and some of its rooms. If a person buys a house without seeing it, he has the right to annul the contract after seeing it. However, if he has already viewed the house, (the exterior and some rooms), it is not permissible for him to annul the contract even if he views other rooms and no longer wishes to buy the property. Later jurists issued a new fatwa which

---

[347] Zaylaī, *Nasb al-Raya*, vol.4, p.81.

[348] This is a reason for many rulings in Islamic Law and it brings easiness for many cases.

took a change of *'urf* into consideration. They stipulated that the buyer has the right to see every room of the house; otherwise he has the right to annul the contract. At the time the first fatwa was issued, houses were built in the same style and it was sufficient to see a few rooms to gain a good idea of the structure of the house. However, later, houses were built in varying styles and it was necessary to see all the rooms to understand the structure of the house.

We can see in this form of examples that *'urf* constitutes one of the more dynamic and universal aspects of Islamic law and is a very fertile source when extracting the rulings for new cases. *'Urf* is considered to be evidence by Islamic jurists because it is a source which ensures the needs of Muslims from different times and places are met.

Summary: Changes in the Rulings by Changing *'Urf*

1. According to Islamic law, if an *'urf* changes, the rulings that have been issued based on that *'urf* must also change accordingly.
2. Examples include: the rulings on the investigation of the characters of witnesses; the rulings on who can effect compulsory actions; the rulings on payment for teaching the Qur'an; the rulings on viewing property before purchase.
3. The examples show that *'urf* is a dynamic and universal aspect of Islamic law and important when extracting the rulings for new cases.
4. *'Urf* is considered to be evidence by Islamic jurists because it is a source which ensures the needs of Muslims from different times and places are met.

Maslaḫah Mursala (Considerations of Public Interest)

Introduction

Maslaḫah is applied by the *mujtahids* in cases where *qiyāṣ* or *ijtihād* are used.[349] The principle of *maslaḫah* promotes the welfare of human beings and protects them from harm.[350] The following points help to gain a more comprehensive understanding of this principle. In general, rulings are made based on a set of valid conditions, attributes or reasons. This is known by jurists as the proper benefits

---

[349] Gülen, *Kendi Dünyamıza Doğru*, p. 98.
[350] Ibid.

of rulings. These benefits can be classified into three groups based on what is deemed valid or invalid by God, the Lawgiver.

1) The first group, *maslaḫah mu'tabara* (valid public benefit), constitutes benefits which are determined by the Lawgiver and supported by evidence in Islamic law. Jurists who accept *qiyāṣ* evidence hold that these benefits can be used as the basis for rulings in Islamic law. This category contains every benefit which Islamic law aims to actualize such as protecting the life, the mind and property. Examples of the benefits that fall into this category include: the prohibition of alcohol, the aim of which is to protect the mind. Violating this prohibition carries certain punishments. Killing has been prohibited to protect human life and committing this crime incurs specific punishments. Theft and robbery are prohibited to protect the property of people and punishments are assigned for those who violate this prohibition. The *qiyāṣ* on these cases takes into account public benefits resulting from the prohibitions. The reasoning behind *qiyāṣ* comprehends the benefits which the Lawgiver aims to actualize through the rulings of Islamic law. New cases that are not included in the text of the Qur'an or Sunnah can be analogized (*qiyāṣ*) to those within the sources, based on a common benefit, and can inherit the ruling of the original case. For example, the Lawgiver aims to protect the mind from harmful things and for this purpose He prohibited alcohol and set a punishment for its violation. When the *mujtahid* investigates the ruling for alcohol he discovers the underlying benefit in it. He is then able, through the application of *qiyāṣ,* to apply the same ruling for other substances which harm the mind.

The valid *maslaḫah* are classified into three categories; *ḏaruriyyāt* (the essentials), *ḫājiyyāt* (the necessaries to complete the essentials) and *taḫsiniyyāt* (embellishments).[351] The *ḏaruriyyāt* are the essentials of human life such as religion, life, intellect, lineage and property. These values are not only to be accepted but also be protected against any kind of violation. The *ḫājiyyāt* (the necessaries to complete the essentials) are the supplementary considerations that support the five essential values. Their aim is to bring ease and remove hardship from the lives of Muslims. Examples in this category are: permission for the sick and travellers not to observe the Ramadan fast. The aim of rulings regarding matters related to worship is to bring ease (*rukhṣah*), they are considered *ḫājiyyāt.*[352] The *taḫsiniyyāt* (embellishments) rulings improve the life of Muslims and help them to attain their goals. Examples for this category include; being in a constant

---

[351] Shātibī, *Muwafaqaat,* vol.2, pp. 3–5.

[352] Ibid., p. 5.

state of cleanliness, moral virtues, preventing lavishness, and being moderate in the enforcement of penalties.[353]

2) The second group is the benefits which are neither valid nor accepted based on evidences. In *Uṣūl al-Fiqh* they are known as *maslaḫah mulga* (rejected or invalid benefits). Jurists agree that this type of benefit cannot be used as the basis for rulings. An important point to note is that God, the Lawgiver who established the Law based on wisdom, does not disregard any benefit unless the acceptance of it cancels a higher benefit. This conclusion can be reached when the rejected benefits are examined. The following are a few of the many examples for *maslaḫah mulga*. The first example is that the prohibition of polygamy would be beneficial both for individuals and society as it would prevent hatred, enmity and quarrels between wives and the destruction of family ties. However, these benefits were disregarded by the Lawgiver as the greater benefit of polygamy is the provision of justice for wives. This ruling contains many valid benefits including; the continuation of the generations, prevention of fornication amongst those who cannot control their carnal desires and a reduction in the occurrence of adultery. It also addresses the imbalance of numbers between men and women (particularly after wars), and the social problems caused by having many single women. The second example is that surrendering to the enemy without fighting would be beneficial as it would prevent the loss of many lives or being captured as prisoners of war. Additionally, this action would prevent the loss of property. However, the Lawgiver disregarded all these benefits and commanded the Muslims to fight against their enemies to protect their lands, honour, and dignity and freedom.

3) The third group covers benefits which may or may not be valid because there is no supporting evidence making it clear. Jurists refer to this group as *maslaḫah mursala* meaning that the validity of these benefits is determined through *ijtihād.*

Summary: Introduction

1. *Maslaḫah* is applied by the *mujtahids* in cases where *qiyāṣ* or *ijtihād* are used.
2. The principle of *maslaḫah* promotes the welfare of human beings and protects them from that which would bring harm to them.

353 Kamali, *Principles of Islamic Jurisprudence*, p. 239.

3. Rulings are made based on a set of valid conditions, attributes or reasons (the proper benefits) which are classified into three groups based on what is deemed valid or invalid by God, the Lawgiver.
4. The first group, *maslaḫah mu'tabara* (valid public benefit), constitutes benefits which are determined by the Lawgiver and supported by evidence in Islamic law. Jurists who accept *qiyāṣ* evidence hold that these benefits can be used as the basis for rulings in Islamic law. This category contains every benefit which Islamic law aims to actualize such as protecting the life, the mind and property.
5. The valid *maslaḫah* are classified into three categories; *ḏaruriyyāt* (the essentials), *ḫājiyyāt* (the necessaries to complete the essentials) and *taḫsiniyyāt* (embellishments).
6. The *ḏaruriyyāt* are the things that people's lives depend on such as religion, life, intellect, lineage and property.
7. The *ḫājiyyāt* (the necessaries to complete the essentials) are the supplementary considerations that support the five essential values. Their aim is to bring ease and remove hardship from the lives of Muslims.
8. The *taḫsiniyyāt* (embellishments) rulings improve the life of Muslims and help them to attain their goals.
9. The second group is the benefits which are neither valid nor accepted based on evidences. In *Uṣūl al-Fiqh* they are known as *maslaḫah mulga* (rejected or invalid benefits). Jurists agree that these types of benefits cannot be used as the basis for making the rulings.
10. The third group is the benefits for which it is unknown whether they are deemed valid or invalid by God, the Lawgiver because there is no supporting evidence. Jurists refer to this group as *maslaḫah mursala* which means the validity of these benefits is determined through *ijtihād.*

The Definition of *Maslaḫah Mursala*

Maslaḫah mursala is defined as something which is of benefit to the public and which a ruling can be based on as long as it provides benefit and prevents harm, but there is no indication from the Lawgiver on whether it is valid. In other words, *maslaḫah mursala* refers to the things which are of general public benefit but they are not mentioned in the primary sources of Islamic law and there is no evidence about their validity or otherwise.[354] For al-Ghazali, *maslaḫah* is the considerations

[354] Khallaf, *'Ilm*, p. 84.

which provide benefit for the public or prevent them from harm in a way that is harmonious with the objectives of Islamic law.[355]

The definition outlines that *maslaḫah mursala* can be applied in situations where the ruling has not already been explained by the Lawgiver and there are no ṣimilar cases in the Qur'an, Sunnah or *'ijma* with which to make *qiyāṣ* (analogy). Alongside these two negative conditions one positive condition is also necessary for *maslaḫah mursala* to be applied; the benefit for the public has to have a proper attribute that is suitable to be the reason for the ruling and that a fatwa can be based on. If the *mujtahid* unearths this type of benefit (*maslaḫah*) in a case which he meets he can issue a fatwa based on it. Examples that fall into this category include; the issuance of currency, the establishment of prisons and the tax imposed on agricultural lands in the conquered lands. These were initiated by the Companions even though there was no textual evidence to support these practices.[356]

SUMMARY: THE DEFINITION OF *MASLAḪAH MURSALA*

1. *Maslaḫah mursala* is defined as something which is of benefit to the public and which a ruling can be based on as long as it provides benefit and prevents harm, but there is no indication from God about whether it is valid.
2. *Maslaḫah mursala* can be applied in situations where the ruling has not already been explained by the Lawgiver and there are no similar cases in the Qur'an, Sunnah or *'ijma* with which to make *qiyāṣ* (analogy).
3. The benefit for the public has to have a proper attribute that is suitable to be the reason for the ruling and that a fatwa can be based on.

The Proof Value of *Maslaḫah Mursala*

The majority of jurists hold that *maslaḫah mursala* can be used as evidence in Islamic law and that it is necessary for *mujtahids* to take this evidence into consideration when extracting the rulings for new cases. Each of the four imams accept *maslaḫah mursala* and in many cases established fatwa based on this notion. Some scholars claim that *maslaḫah mursala* is accepted only by Mālikī jurists but there is clear evidence in the *fiqh* books of the other three schools that they also used it in their *ijtihāds*. If a *mujtahid* does not find an explicit ruling in the Qur'an or Sunnah and the *maslaḫah* is identified, it is his responsibility to take the neces-

[355] Ghazali, *Muṣtaṣfā*, vol.1, pp. 139–140.
[356] Khallaf, *'Ilm*, p. 84.

sary steps to secure it. This is because God's purpose in revealing the Shari'ah was to promote the welfare of people and to prevent corruption on earth.[357]

Some jurists such as Ẕahirī, Āmidī, Ibn Hājib and some Shāfi'ī scholars reject *maslaḫah mursala* evidence. They hold that *maslaḫah mursala* can neither be the basis for *ijtihād* nor for rulings. Both the proponents and the opponents of *maslaḫah mursala* use arguments to support their views. These will be considered later.

The Conditions for the Application of *Maslaḫah Mursala*

Before mentioning the arguments on both sides, it is important to note that jurists who accept *maslaḫah mursala* evidence applied strict conditions for its use. If any condition was missing, they did not use it. The most important conditions for using *maslaḫah mursala* are the following:

1) The *maslaḫah* for a case should not be invalidated by any *shar'ī* evidence. If there is such evidence available, it is not permissible to act based on *maslaḫah*.[358] For example, even though surrendering to the enemy without fighting has some benefits, the *mujtahids* cannot base their *ijtihād* on these benefits because there is evidence which invalidated them. This evidence consists of commandments in the Qur'an and Sunnah regarding the protection of land, honour, property and religion.

2) The *maslaḫah* must be present and not assumed. In other words, the ruling cannot be given based on imagined benefits but must be based on definite *maslaḫah* that prevent harm. Before ruling, a *mujtahid* must first establish *maslaḫah* (benefit for the public); it is not permissible for him to rule based on his personal opinion and assumed benefits. For example, taking the authority for divorce from husbands and giving it exclusively to judges is *maslaḫah* based on imaginary benefits.[359]

3) The *maslaḫah* must be general, i.e. it must provide benefit and prevent harm for the majority of people, not just a specific few. If this is not the case, it is not permissible to issue fatwa based on it. For example, a fatwa cannot be issued to provide benefit to rulers only.[360]

4) The *maslaḫah* must be rational and deemed acceptable by people of sound intellect.[361] In other words, the jurist accepts the *maslaḫah* because it provides

---

[357] Kamali, *Principles of Islamic Jurisprudence*, p. 236.

[358] Abu Zahrah, *Uṣūl*, p. 219

[359] Khallaf, *'Ilm*, p. 86.

[360] Badran, *Uṣūl*, p. 214.

[361] Shātibī, *I'tisām*, vol.2, pp. 307–314.

benefits or protections for the people which can be justified by logic. Shātibī holds that despite the different views of jurists on *maslaḫah mursala* they can be classified into four groups;[362]

a) If the *maslaḫah* does not depend on valid evidence it is rejected, however if it depends on evidence it turns into *qiyāṣ*.
b) If the *maslaḫah* is suitable according to the purposes of Shari'ah and is not opposed to any *shar'ī* evidence, it is valid and accepted.
c) If the *maslaḫah* does not completely fit in with the objectives of Islamic law but it is near to them, the *maslaḫah* is valid and accepted even if it does not rely on evidence.
d) If the *maslaḫah* relies on bare necessity it is also valid and accepted.

Summary: The Conditions for the Application of *Maslaḫah Mursala*

1. Jurists who accept *maslaḫah mursala* evidence applied strict conditions for its use, all of which had to be present for its use.
2. The *maslaḫah* for a case should not be invalidated by any *shar'ī* evidence.
3. The *maslaḫah* must be present and not assumed.
4. The *maslaḫah* must be general, i.e. it must provide benefit and prevent harm for the majority of people, not just a specific few.
5. The *maslaḫah* must be rational and deemed acceptable by people of sound intellect.
6. Shātibī holds that despite the different views of jurists on *maslaḫah mursala* they can be classified into four groups detailed above.

The Arguments of the Proponents

Jurists who accept *maslaḫah mursala* evidence support their views with the following:

1) When the noble Prophet sent Mu'adh to Yemen the following conversation took place between them;

> How will you judge when the occasion of deciding a case arises? Mu'adh replied: I shall judge in accordance with God's Book. He asked: (What will you do) if you do not find any guidance in God's Book? He replied: (I shall act) in accordance with the Sunnah of the Messenger of God. He asked: (What will you do) if you do not find any guidance in the Sunnah of the

[362] Ibid., p. 305.

> Messenger of God and in God's Book? He replied: I shall do my best to form an opinion and I shall spare no effort (ijtihād). The Messenger of God then patted him on the breast and said: Praise be to God Who has helped the messenger of to find something which pleases him.[363]

The Prophet confirmed Mu'adh's answer when he said he would make *ijtihād* if he could not find the answer in the Qur'an or in Sunnah. *Ijtihād* is when personal opinion is used; it can be practised using *qiyāṣ* or by considering the objectives of Islamic law and the underlying reason of a ruling. Similarly, in *maslaḫah mursala,* the *mujtahids* understand the purpose of the ruling and the objectives of Islamic jurisprudence and give a ruling based on these. The mission of both *maslaḫah mursala* and Islamic law is to actualize the public benefit.

2) The Companions frequently issued fatwa based on the notion of *maslaḫah* and never rejected this method, therefore we can consider they had an *ijma'* (consensus) on the *maslaḫah* and on its validity. Some examples of fatwa the Companions issued based on *maslaḫah* are;

a) The first collection of the Qur'an into a single volume did not take place until the time of Caliph Abū Bakr and was carried out due to the suggestion of 'Umar. There is no evidence in the Qur'an or Sunnah about this collection; rather it was initiated based on the notion of *maslaḫah.* Abū Bakr expressed his hesitation in doing something the Prophet himself didn't do, however 'Umar held that there would be a great benefit for Islam and Muslims in this collection. Abū Bakr accepted this view and ordered Zayd ibn Thabit to collect the Qur'an.[364]

b) When Abū Bakr felt his death was imminent he nominated 'Umar for the Caliphate. This was done based on the notion of *maslaḫah.* There is no evidence in the Qur'an or Sunnah for this decision as the noble Prophet did not indicate who should rule after him. However, it was greatly in to the benefit of the public to clarify who would rule the Muslims after the death of Abū Bakr. This would prevent disputes and disagreements between Muslims. Abū Bakr had the foresight to anticipate this danger and therefore prevented harm coming to the Muslims by nominating 'Umar as Caliph after him.[365]

c) As Caliph, rather than distributing conquered lands amongst the soldiers as war booty, 'Umar instead ruled that they should remain with their pre-

---

[363] Abu Dāwud, *Sunan, Kitāb Al-Aqdiya,* hadith no: 3585.

[364] Shātibī, *I'tisām*, vol.2, p. 287.

[365] Khallaf, *'Ilm*, p. 86.

vious owners but be taxed. This ruling was based on *maslaḫah* as the tax would be a continuous revenue stream for the Muslims. 'Umar reasoned that if the land was distributed amongst the soldiers, later generations could find themselves rich or poor based on the financial position of their predecessors. However, by allocating a tax to the original landowners, all Muslims for generations to come would benefit from it. At first, this idea was the source of dispute amongst the Companions, however, they later understood the *maslaḫah* (public benefit) and accepted the fatwa.

d) During the Caliphate of 'Umar, a case was brought to him of a man who had married a woman who had not completed the full duration of the waiting period between her marriages. 'Umar ruled that the man could not ever marry her as a deterrent for the Muslims against committing this act. This ruling took into consideration the general public benefit (*maslaḫah mursala*).

e) Caliph 'Uthman ordered scribes to write the official Qur'an and send copies of it to the main Islamic capital cities. By doing this he aimed to settle conflicts among the Muslims which had arisen due to the various readings of the Qur'an, and thereby unite them under one official copy. At the same time, he ordered the Muslims to burn their personal *Muṣḫāfs* (the Qur'an copies) as they were the main cause of dispute amongst the Muslims. This fatwa was issued based on the notion of *maslaḫah*. Caliph 'Uthman addressed the need to settle all disagreements surrounding the various readings of the Qur'an as a consideration for the benefit of the public (*maslaḫah mursala*) and ruled accordingly.

f) When the population of Medina increased, Caliph 'Uthman ruled that a second *adhan* should be called for the Friday Prayer. This ruling was based on the notion of *maslaḫah* to give the residents time to make their ablution and other preparations between the first and second calling of the *adhan*. This *adhan* is still being called today when the time of Friday Prayer arrives. Prior to this, the *adhan* was called just once and some people would miss the Prayer which was performed immediately after it. Caliph 'Uthman aimed to inform people about the time of the Friday Prayer, especially those who worked in the markets, to prevent them from missing it. As such, this fatwa was issued based on *maslaḫah mursala*.

g) During the caliphate of 'Uthman, just before dying, a man divorced his wife to deprive her of her rightful inheritance. In this case, 'Uthman ruled that the wife should benefit from the inheritance despite the divorce as the man's action was to harm the wife which is against the meaning of marriage. This ruling which was made based on the notion of *maslaḥah* was made to prevent harm and deter others from doing the same thing.

h) The fourth Caliph, 'Ali, ruled that craftsmen and traders should be responsible for the loss of goods that were placed in their custody. He based his ruling on the reasoning that it would benefit the public to ensure that craftsmen take greater care to protect people's property.[366]

3) Islamic law ultimately aims to secure the welfare of the Muslims by promoting their benefit or protecting them from harm. It is a well-known fact that when times and conditions change the benefits of the public (the *maslaḥah*) also change accordingly and new principles for the public benefit surface.[367] Since what constitutes the public benefit changes according to time, prevailing conditions and the place, it is impossible to limit them and address them all at one specific time. A *mujtahid* must take into consideration the legal rights of the public when they are significantly different to the rights of previous nations or it will cause harm to the new generation. The Qur'an states; *"He has chosen you and has not laid any hardship on you in the Religion"*[368] and *"God wills ease for you, and He does not will hardship for you."*[369] A'isha reports; "Whenever the Prophet was left between two options he always preferred the easier one as long as it was not a sin."[370] These verses and the hadith clearly indicate that hardship and difficulty must be removed from the path of Muslims.

Islamic law is dynamic and renews itself when times and conditions change. When issuing fatwa, it is necessary to consider new public benefits and this can only be done by finding solutions to new problems based on the notion of *maslaḥah*; failure to do this would result in Islamic law stagnating and eventually being rendered redundant. Islamic jurisprudence is sufficient for all cases and issues regardless of their time and conditions. One of the high objectives of Islamic law which is used as a basis for the *ijtihāds* is to facilitate the benefit of the public and prevent harm from being done to them. Neglecting this duty and disregarding what is in the public benefit when extracting rulings for new cases is against the spirit of the *Shari'ah*.

---

[366] Abu Zahrah, *Uṣūl*, p. 223.

[367] Shātibī, *Muwafaqaat*, vol.2, pp. 2–3.

[368] Qur'an, 22: 78.

[369] Qur'an, 2: 185.

[370] Bukhari, *Saḥīḥ, Adab*, hadith no: 80.

Summary: The Arguments of the Proponents

1. Jurists who accept *maslaḫah mursala* evidence support their views with: the hadith about the conversation between the noble Prophet and Mu'adh; the fact that the Companions issued fatwa based on the notion of *maslaḫah* of which there are many examples.
2. Islamic law is dynamic and renews itself when times and conditions change.
3. When issuing fatwa, it is necessary to consider new public benefits and this can only be done by finding solutions to new problems based on the notion of *maslaḫah.*
4. Islamic law would stagnate and become redundant if the notion of *maslaḫah* was not considered when making rulings.

The Arguments of the Opponents

The scholars who reject *maslaḫah mursala* support their view with the following three arguments:

1) The Lawgiver, who is wise in every command, accepts that some benefits are valid and some are invalid. *Maslaḫah mursala* sits between these two groups and is speculative regarding which group it belongs to. It is possible that it could belong to either of them and therefore falls into the category of speculative evidence, on which it is not permissible to rule. If a fatwa is ruled based on *maslaḫah mursala*, it indicates that the *mujtahids* prefer one of the possible two sides regarding the benefit be it valid or invalid and abandons the other possible option. It is not permissible to prefer one side without presenting a valid justification.

The rebuttal for this argument is that in Islamic law, most rulings are speculative with very few being definite. Scholars who accept *maslaḫah mursala* do not indicate that the preference is definite but that, in taking into consideration the public benefit, the ruling seems more in line with the main principles and objectives of Islamic jurisprudence. During *ijtihād*, *mujtahids* endeavour to uncover the truth based on their personal opinions and similarly, *maslaḫah mursala* does the same as it is also a type of *ijtihād*. Another point is that *maslaḫah mursala* does not mean preferring one of two options without a valid reason, rather the jurists compare both options and rule in favour of that which is more suitably aligned with the objectives of Islamic law. Therefore, it is inaccurate to suggest that these fatwa are issued based on personal desire or without valid reasoning. The *mujtahids* examine the valid and invalid benefits provided by the Lawgiver and compare the *maslaḫah mursala* with them. They then prefer one option over the other based on the benefit it affords the public. Lastly, the opponents own argument can be used against them. It is valid to point out that it is not permissible to prefer one of two speculative options without there being a valid reason for the preference. The *maslaḫah mursala* may either belong to a valid or invalid benefit according to the Lawgiver. Stating that the *maslaḫah mursala* is rejected and belongs to the side of the invalid benefit is making a negative preference without a valid reason which is (as previously stated) not permissible.

2) The second argument of the opponents is that when the *maslaḫah mursala* holds the position of accepted evidence in Islamic law, it will open the door for layman and those not capable of making *ijtihād* to do so based on the notion of *maslaḫah*. They would start giving fatwa according to their own benefits and consequently they would damage Islamic jurisprudence greatly.[371] It is not permissible to cause this damage.

This argument is easily rebutted when we consider the definition of *maslaḫah mursala. Maslaḫah mursala* means a benefit (whose validity cannot be confirmed in the primary sources) upon which a ruling can be made which both provides an advantage for the public and prevents them from harm. It is extremely difficult to make *ijtihād* about the *maslaḫah mursala* if there is no *shar'ī* evidence. *Ijtihād* can only be performed by scholars who have reached a certain level in their profession. Only those *mujtahids* who can extract the rulings from their sources can understand the principles underlying *maslaḫah mursala* and whether they are in conformity with the principles and objectives of Islamic jurisprudence. If this wasn't the case, every benefit could potentially be accepted as *maslaḫah* even if it has no truth value. However, this is not possible as the scholars who accept *maslaḫah mursala* attach conditions to validate its use; if any of these conditions are missing they omit such *maslaḫah* from consideration.

3) The third argument of the opponents is that the *maslaḫah* are changeable according to time, the prevailing conditions and the place. When a new situation arises, the new *maslaḫah* would appear as parallel to them. If the *maslaḫah mursala* are accepted as evidence in Islamic law, any change of time, condition or place will result in a change to the rulings. This is against the reality that Islamic jurisprudence is universal and sufficient for all times, places and conditions.

This argument is weaker than the previous two. It is the concept of *maslaḫah* that gives Islamic law its unique dynamism and universality because its rulings can be revised making it relevant to the time, conditions and places. This quality

371 Ghazali, *Muṣtaṣfā*, vol.1, p. 294.

increases the value of Islamic law. On the other hand, there is never any change to rulings about devotional matters or those in the Qur'an and Sunnah; change only occurs in cases which are open to *ijtihād* and interpretation. When the *mujtahids* examine all the evidences in the Qur'an, Sunnah and *ijma'* they deduce the objectives of *Shari'ah* and understand the purposes behind these rulings. This enables them to apply the general principles and objectives of Islamic law in every time and place. If the *maslaḫah* can be justified based on these unchanging principles, the *mujtahids* accept it and rule accordingly. In other words, even though primary evidence is not available for every new case, the *mujtahids* can evaluate them according to the general principles and objectives of Islamic law. Where they believe a public benefit can be afforded and a potential harm can be prevented through the notion of *maslaḫah*, they apply a fatwa accordingly.

In conclusion, it is evident that although some oppose the use of *maslaḫah*, the arguments of the proponents are stronger and more valid. The *maslaḫah* approach is aligned with the way of the Companions which is a predominant reason why jurists from different times have accepted *maslaḫah mursala* and used it in their *ijtihāds*. Rejection of *maslaḫah mursala* is against the spirit of Islamic law and would result in its stagnation and redundancy.

Maslaḫah mursala is one of the important sources of Islamic law. Scholars who are expert in the Islamic disciplines and who examine *Uṣūl al-Fiqh* carefully benefit from this source and are able to use it to solve every contemporary problem that Muslims face. The *mujtahids* who comprehend the spirit and objectives of Islamic law are able to solve new problems and meet the needs of the public based on the notion of *maslaḫah* even if they cannot find evidence in the Qur'an, Sunnah, *ijma'* and *qiyāṣ*. The following are some of the cases that were justified by the principle of *maslaḫah mursala*: it is permissible for the government to set a tax upon the rich citizens when it is necessary; if wealthy people have multiple residences when there are homeless people, the government can force the wealthy to give their extra homes to the poor; it is permissible for the government to assign fitting salaries for labourers if the employers abuse this matter. These are just a few of the many cases which express the importance of *maslaḫah mursala* in regards to providing benefit to the public and preventing them from harm. In reality, all the imams accepted *maslaḫah mursala* but they may have referred to it with different terminology.[372] The Companions also used this principle in their *ijtihāds* which we have seen in some of the examples mentioned above.

---

[372] Al-Karafi, *Sharh Tanqīh al-Fuṣūl*, pp. 199–244.

Summary: The Arguments of the Opponents

1. Opponents of *maslaḫah mursala* put forward three arguments to support their view, each of which can be rebutted.
2. *Maslaḫah mursala* is speculative as it isn't clear whether it is invalid or valid, therefore it isn't permissible to rule based on it. It is not permissible for jurists to prefer one side without presenting a valid justification.
3. The rebuttal for this argument is that in Islamic law most rulings are speculative with very few being definite but are given taking into account the main principles and objectives of Islamic jurisprudence.
4. When the *maslaḫah mursala* holds the position of accepted evidence in Islamic law, it will open the door for layman and those not capable of making *ijtihād* to do so based on the notion of *maslaḫah*.
5. This argument is easily rebutted as it is extremely difficult to make *ijtihād* about the *maslaḫah mursala* if there is no *shar'ī* evidence. *Ijtihād* can only be performed by scholars who have reached a certain level in their profession and they apply strict conditions for its use.
6. The *maslaḫah* are changeable according to time, the prevailing conditions and the place. This is against the reality that Islamic jurisprudence is universal and sufficient for all times, places and conditions.
7. In fact, Islamic law can only remain dynamic and universal if it rules according to *maslaḫah*. This quality increases the value of Islamic law and makes it applicable to every time, condition and place. On the other hand, there is never any change to rulings about devotional matters or those in the Qur'an and Sunnah; change only occurs in cases which are open to *ijtihād* and interpretation.
8. The *maslaḫah* approach is aligned with the way of the Companions and is a predominant reason why jurists who lived in different times have accepted *maslaḫah mursala* and used it in their *ijtihāds*.
9. The *mujtahids* who comprehend the spirit and objectives of Islamic law are able to solve new problems and meet the needs of the public based on the notion of *maslaḫah* even if they cannot find evidence in the Qur'an, Sunnah, *ijma'* and *qiyāṣ*.

Comparing *Maslaḫah Mursala* with *Qiyāṣ* and *Istiḫsān*

Scholars who investigate *maslaḫah mursala* and *qiyāṣ* in detail discover that not only do they have some similarities but they also have differences. The two similarities between them are:

a) They are applied when no evidence exists for a case in the Qur'an, Sunnah or *ijma.'*
b) The ruling or fatwa is given based on a proper attribute (*munasib wasif*) which is deemed suitable to be the effective cause (*'illah*) for the ruling.

There are two differences between *maslaḫah mursala* and *qiyāṣ*:

a) When a ruling is given for a new case based on *qiyāṣ*, there exists a similar case in the Qur'an, Sunnah or *ijma.'* When *maslaḫah mursala* is considered, there is no similar case available in those sources to extend the ruling.
b) In *qiyāṣ* there is *shar'ī* evidence supporting the notion of *maslaḫah* (benefit) on which the ruling is based but for *maslaḫah mursala* there is no evidence making it clear if the *maslaḫah* is valid or invalid in the eyes of the Lawgiver.

Istiḫsān operates differently to *maslaḫah*. In order to utilize *istiḫsān* the new case and the general ruling provided by former similar cases are necessary. Based on evidence, *istiḫsān* makes an exception to the general ruling and gives the opposite fatwa for the new case to benefit the public. For *maslaḫah*, there are no similar cases; the fatwa is issued based on *maslaḫah* alone. In other words, the fatwa for the case is not opposing that of a similar case. Rather in *maslaḫah* the fatwa is given directly based on the notion of *maslaḫah*.

Summary: Comparing *Maslaḫah Mursala* with *Qiyāṣ* and *Istiḫsān*

1. *Maslaḫah mursala* and *qiyāṣ* have two similarities and two differences.
2. Similarities: they are applied when no evidence exists for a case in the Qur'an, Sunnah or *ijma'*; the ruling or fatwa is given based on a proper attribute (*munasib wasif*) which is deemed suitable to be the effective cause (*'illah*) for the ruling.
3. Differences: When a ruling is given for a new case based on *qiyāṣ*, there exists a similar case in the Qur'an, Sunnah or *ijma.'* When *maslaḫah mursala* is considered when ruling, there is no similar case available in those sources; *Qiyāṣ* has supporting *shar'ī* evidence for the notion of *maslaḫah* (benefit) on which the ruling is based but for *maslaḫah mursala* there is no evidence making it clear if the *maslaḫah* is valid or invalid.
4. *Istiḫsān* operates differently to *maslaḫah*. In order to utilize *istiḫsān* the new case and the general ruling provided by former similar cases are necessary. For *maslaḫah*, there are no similar cases; the fatwa is issued based on *maslaḫah* alone.

Chapter Eight

Istiṣḥāb and *Sadd Dharā'ī*

Istiṣḫāb and *Sadd Dharā'ī*

Istiṣḫāb (Presumption of Continuity)

Introduction

Istiṣḫāb (presumption of continuity) is derived from the Arabic word *'ṣa'ḫu'ba'* which means to be together and not to leave. *Uṣūl* scholars define it as the facts or rules, proven in the past which remain without change if there is no evidence against them.[373] In other words, the facts or the rulings from the past remain the same in the present time because no new evidence has been presented which indicates they should change. *Istiṣḫāb* is another rational proof for extracting the rulings for new cases when there is no supporting evidence for them in the primary and secondary sources of Islamic law. *Istiṣḫāb* is related with both the presumption of facts and the previous rules, therefore, the permissibility or prohibition of certain things is presumed to continue in the same way as previously for there is no evidence indicating otherwise.[374] This means that if there is a ruling in Islamic law with a prohibition or an indication of permissibility, it is presumed to continue until the contrary is proven. However, the majority of jurists agree that if there is no such ruling available, the default fatwa is permissibility (*ibaha*); this is a general principle of Islamic jurisprudence regarding a matter that is deemed beneficial and free from harm.[375]

Istiṣḫāb (presumption of continuity) is accepted by the Shāfi'ī, Hanbalī and Ẕahirī schools. The Ḫanafī and Mālikī schools do not deem it a proof in its own right; they hold that proving the existence of a fact in the past does not mean it continued until the present time. The facts or cases of the present time require a proof to establish the rulings for them.[376]

If there is any doubt that a case or its facts exist, it remains the same in the present time as it was proved in the past; the same ruling continues based on

---

[373] Āmidī, *Iḫkām*, vol.4, 127.
[374] Khallaf, *'Ilm*, p. 92.
[375] Shawkānī, *Irshād*, p. 237.
[376] Abu Zahrah, *Uṣūl*, p. 234.

the notion of *istiṣḥāb* (presumption of continuity). Similarly if there is any doubt about the non-existence of a case or its facts and this is still the case in the present time, the ruling is given based the principle of *istiṣḥāb*; it is a presumed continuation of the negative ruling.

An example for *istiṣḥāb* is in the buying of goods. If a person buys something on condition that it is free from any defect but after the purchase detects a defect, the buyer is able to dispute this with the seller regardless whether the defect was present at the time of the sale or occurred afterwards. The default fact for the case is that the goods were presumed to be free of any defect, so it is not possible to request the seller to prove this was the case. The burden of proof rests on the buyer who must prove the defect existed when he bought the goods.

A second example is the case of purchasing a hunting dog on condition of it being trained as a hunter. If a person purchases a dog on this condition but finds the dog cannot hunt and returns it to the seller, it is the duty of the seller to prove the dog can hunt. This is because the natural state of the dog is not that of a hunter. It takes training for a dog to acquire this state.[377] The seller must prove the dog has been trained in the event of a dispute. The notion of *istiṣḥāb* applies in this case because the natural state of the dog is not that of a hunter. This natural state is changed over time through training and this must be proved by the seller. If this has not occurred, then it is presumed that the natural state of the dog has continued, therefore the rulings or the facts from the past are presumed to remain the same in the present; i.e. that the dog is not a trained hunter.

Summary: Introduction

1. *Uṣūl* scholars define *istiṣḥāb* (presumption of continuity) as the facts or rules, proven in the past which remain without change if there is no evidence against them.
2. *Istiṣḥāb* is another rational proof for extracting the rulings for new cases when there is no supporting evidence for them in the primary and secondary sources of Islamic law.
3. *Istiṣḥāb* is accepted by the Shāfi'i, Hanbalī and Ẕahirī schools. The Ḫanafī and Mālikī schools do not deem it a proof in its own right.
4. If there is any doubt that a case or its facts exist, it remains the same in the present time as it was proved in the past; the same ruling continues based on the notion of *istiṣḥāb* (presumption of continuity).

---

[377] Badran, *Uṣūl*, p. 218.

5. If there is any doubt about the non-existence of a case or its facts and this is still the case in the present time, the ruling is given based the principle of *istiṣẖāb.*
6. Examples include buying goods which later show a defect and purchasing a hunting dog which later shows no skill in hunting.

The Types of *Istiṣẖāb*

Istiṣẖāb is classified into the following three categories:

1) *Ibaha Asliyya*; means the continuity of permissibility for things or actions because there is no evidence against them, therefore they are presumed to be permissible. In other words, to do something or to use something is permissible if there is no proof to change this default fatwa. This rational proof is named *ibaha asliyya*. Most scholars agree that the default fatwa for the beneficial things for human beings is permissibility if there is no textual proof to state otherwise in the Qur'an, Sunnah or *ijma.'* There is a lot of evidence supporting this view including the following verses:

> It is He Who (prepared the earth for your life before He gave you life, and) created all that is in the world for you[378]

> He has also made of service to you whatever is in the heavens and whatever is on the earth, all is from Him (a gift of His Grace)[379]

The above verses indicate that the earth and everything in it has been created for the benefit of human beings. Therefore it is permissible for them to utilise the earth's resources to their advantage unless it has been specifically prohibited.[380] Any view contrary to this would render the verses meaningless. If it was forbidden to benefit from the earth's resources it would be forbidden by Lawgiver. When faced with a new problem, jurists investigate the primary sources (the Qur'an, Sunnah or *ijma'*) for an answer, or they try to find the solution based on *qiyāṣ* or *maslaẖah*. If they are unsuccessful they give fatwa based on *ibaha asliyya*; that the default ruling for the new cases is permissibility on condition there is no evidence to the contrary. Some jurists phrase this differently but they all usually validate ruling based on this type of *istiṣẖāb*.

---

378 Qur'an, 2: 29.

379 Qur'an, 45: 13.

380 Badran, *Uṣūl*, p. 219.

2) *Baraat Asliyya* (the principle of original freedom from liability); human beings are presumed to be innocent as long as there is no proof against them. In other words, the default fatwa when people are accused of something without conclusive evidence is that they are innocent.[381] In Islamic law, people are not held responsible for any religious or secular duties unless there is evidence proving otherwise. In the absence of such proof they are presumed to be innocent, as shown in the following examples.

If a person claims that he lent money to someone but cannot prove this claim, the ruling is given in favour of the accused. He is presumed to be innocent and is accepted to be free of debt. According to the general rule of *istiṣḥāb baraat asliyya,* people are innocent and free of any charges if the claim against them cannot be proved.[382]

If a person harms the property of another resulting in a dispute about the amount of damage caused, the person who caused the damage is given preference over the owner of the damaged property if he cannot prove his claim. The rule of *istiṣḥāb* holds that in the case where the owner's claim of damage exceeds that which the liable person is willing to accept, they are not responsible unless the claim if proved with evidence.

3) *Istiṣḥāb al Wasf*; if a ruling is given based on a reason, and that reason continues to exist there is a presumption of continuity for that ruling. In other words, if the reason for a past ruling still exists in the present, it is presumed that the ruling remains the same providing the contrary is not proven. The right of property, the contract of marriage, etc. fall under this category of *istiṣḥāb* as the following examples illustrate.

If a person's right of property through inheritance or purchase is proven, this ownership is presumed to continue no matter how much time passes if the contrary is not proved.

A marriage established on a valid marriage contract is presumed to continue indefinitely as long as there is no proof to show that the marriage contract has finished. Similarly, a person with a proven debt is only released from it when it is proven that he has paid it. Until then, the debt is presumed to continue.

After taking ablution, if a person is in doubt about whether it is still valid, the ablution continues as long as none of the actions occurs which would nullify it. In short, if a ruling is given based on certain reasons, the ruling is presumed

[381] Abu Zahrah, *Uṣūl*, p. 236.

[382] Shawkānī, *Irshād*, p. 237.

to remain valid if the reasons continue to be present and the contrary is not proven. Jurists accept this type of *istiṣḥāb* as valid and use it in extracting the rulings for new cases.

Summary: The Types of *Istiṣḥāb*

1. *Ibaha Asliyya*; means the continuity of permissibility for things or actions because there is no evidence against them, therefore they are presumed to be permissible.
2. Most scholars agree that the default fatwa for the beneficial things for human beings is permissibility if there is no textual proof to state otherwise in the Qur'an, Sunnah or *ijma.'*
3. *Baraat Asliyya* (the principle of original freedom from liability); human beings are presumed to be innocent as long as there is no proof against them.
4. *Istiṣḥāb al Wasf*; if a ruling is given based on a reason, and that reason continues to exist there is a presumption of continuity for that ruling.

The Proof Value of *Istiṣḥāb*

On examination it is clear that none of the varieties of *istiṣḥāb* produce new rulings or fatwa; they presume continuity of previous rulings or fatwa. In this regard, scholars accept *istiṣḥāb* as rational evidence for the continuation of rulings but not as evidence for producing new rulings.

Istiṣḥāb is only applied once the jurists have examined the primary and secondary sources for new cases. If there is a proof in any of these sources, the jurists base their fatwa on them. However, where there is no evidence, they apply *istiṣḥāb* in its different varieties. As such, *istiṣḥāb* is the last source of recourse for the *mujtahids*.[383]

The Principles of *Istiṣḥāb*

The following principles have been extracted by jurists based on *istiṣḥāb*:

1) The acceptance of something as it is where there is no evidence against it is a general principle of Islamic law. For example, jurists agreed that a missing person who was alive at the time he went missing is presumed alive until otherwise proven. His rights as a living person with regard to property, inheritance, etc. remain the same and, as a result, his wealth cannot be distributed among

[383] Shawkānī, *Irshād*, p. 208.

his legal heirs, his wife cannot remarry and his deposit cannot be taken from the trustee. The legal reasoning for this is that he was known to be alive before he disappeared and the attribute of life is presumed to remain as long as the contrary cannot be proven. However, in the event of the death of one of his relatives, he cannot benefit from their inheritance, but his share is separated and protected until he returns alive. The right of inheritance is actualised for legal heirs who are known to be alive. As the missing person is only presumed to be alive, he cannot benefit from the inheritance until he returns alive.

2) Everything is lawful by default if there is no evidence to contradict this. According to this principle, all business contracts are valid if there is no evidence rendering them invalid.

3) Definite knowledge is not invalidated by a later doubt.[384] The following cases are solved based on this principle:

a) If a person is certain he took ablution but is in doubt as to whether it has been invalidated, the fatwa is given in the favour of validity of his ablution.

b) If a person eats the pre-dawn meal before the Ramadan fast[385] but has a doubt about whether he ate during the prohibited time, he does not make up the fast for that day. This is because he is certain that he started the meal during the permitted time, but is in doubt as to whether he crossed into the prohibited time. In this case, he acts according to his definite knowledge and disregards the doubt. However, if he is certain that he ate during the prohibited time, he is liable to make up the fast for that day.

Istiṣḥāb is a last resort for jurists in finding solutions for new cases. It brings ease to their *ijtihād* by enabling them to solve cases more swiftly and easily. This source clearly indicates that Islam is a religion of easiness which aims to promote the welfare of the people and remove the hardships from them.

Summary: The Principles of *Istiṣḥāb*

1. The acceptance of something as it is where there is no evidence against it is a general principle of Islamic law. For example, jurists agreed that a missing person who was alive at the time he went missing is presumed alive until otherwise proven and keeps the same rights.

---

384 *Mejelle*, article 4 and 5.

385 The prohibition of eating and drinking starts with the dawn for the fasting person.

2. Everything is lawful by default if there is no evidence to contradict this. According to this principle, all business contracts are valid if there is no evidence rendering them invalid.
3. Definite knowledge is not invalidated by a later doubt.
4. *Istiṣḫāb* is a last resort for jurists in finding solutions for new cases. It brings ease to their *ijtihād* by enabling them to solve cases more swiftly and easily.

Sadd al-Dharā'ī (Blocking the Means)

Introduction

Sadd al-dharā'ī is derived from two Arabic words; *sadd* meaning blocking and *dharā'ī* (the plural of *dharia*) meaning ways, means and reasons. *Dharia* is a way or reason which leads to a specific end or result. The juristic definition of *sadd al-dharā'ī* is blocking the means which would lead to bad or evil results. The opposite meaning of *sadd al-dharā'ī* is *fatḫ al- dharā'ī* which means opening the means which leads to a good result. However this concept is not used by jurists. If the means or reasons do not lead to evil results, rather they lead to good and beneficial, they are not blocked or prevented.

Al-dharā'ī is the means for the *halal* (permissible) or *haram* (prohibited). It is the means which lead to the results, therefore, if a means leads to a *haram* then it is also *haram*; if it leads to *mubah* then it is also *mubah* and so on. An example of this is fornication which is *haram,* therefore the means which lead to fornication are also *haram.* Men are prohibited from looking at the private parts of the women. It is *haram* as it leads to the act of fornication.

Both the means and the end may be beneficial or harmful, physical or moral, visible or invisible. It is not necessary for the means and the end to be present simultaneously.[386] For example, meeting privately with members of the opposite sex is unlawful because it may be a means (*dharia*) to fornication whether or not it actually leads to it. Men and women are naturally inclined towards each other and this desire has been regulated in Islam through the act of marriage. Islam also regulates against fornication and the means which lead to it because it is harmful. *Sadd al-dharā'ī'* blocks that which is harmful before it has a chance to occur, even if the harmful action is not inevitable.

[386] Hashim Kamali, *Principles of Islamic Jurisprudence*, p. 269.

Summary: *Sadd al-Dharā'ī* (Blocking the Means)

1. The juristic definition of *sadd al-dharā'ī* is blocking the means which would lead to bad or evil results.
2. *Al-dharā'ī* is the means for the *halal* (permissible) or *haram* (prohibited). It is the means which lead to the results; therefore, if a means leads to a *haram* then it is also *haram.*
3. Both the means and the end may be beneficial or harmful, physical or moral, visible or invisible. It is not necessary for the means and the end to be present simultaneously.

Proof Value of *Sadd Dharā'ī*

According to the nature of their issue, legal rulings (*ahkām*) can be classified into two groups; the purposes (*maqāsid*) and the means (*dharā'ī*). The purposes consist of actions which are either beneficial or harmful; the means are the actions which lead to them. Legally, the means are similar to the purposes; therefore, if an act leads to something which is *haram*, legally it is also *haram* and if an act leads to something which is *halal*, its legal value is *halal.* There are various levels according to which the means are judged. If they serve the most significant purposes of Islamic law such as the five essential values (life, religion, property, progeny and intellect) they have the highest legal value and similarly if they lead to the most harmful results they hold the most serious legal value. The means which fall in between the most beneficial and the most harmful have their legal value attributed accordingly.[387]

The most important point in *sadd al-dharā'ī* (blocking the means) is the results. Acts are subjected to particular legal rules according to their results, regardless of the intention of the doer. If the means serve that which is beneficial, they are valid and accepted, however, if they serve that which is harmful, they are prohibited. The result, rather than the intention of the doer, is the most significant criteria in judging whether a means should be blocked or not. An act may be praised or blamed based on its result, for this reason God said:

> And do not (O believers) revile the things or beings that they have, apart from God, deified and invoke, lest (if you do so) they attempt to revile God out of spite, and in ignorance.[388]

---

[387] Qarafi, *Tanqīh al-Fuṣūl*, p. 200.

[388] Qur'an, 6: 108.

This verse prohibits insulting other people's deities in case they then revile God out of spite and ignorance.[389] In another verse, God prohibited the use of the Arabic word *ra'ina* (please attend to us) as it had been used by the Jews to insult the Prophet:

> O you who believe! Do not say (in your relationship and conversations with God's Messenger,) *ra'ina* (please attend to us), but say, *unzurna* (favour us with your attention), and pay heed to him.[390]

God blocked the means (the usage of the word) to prevent the insults. These verses clearly indicate that the notion of *sadd dharā'ī* (blocking the means) is taken into consideration by God; therefore, it is a valid source when extracting new rules in Islamic law.

There are many incidents in the Sunnah which demonstrate that the notion of *sadd dharā'ī* was accepted and rulings issued accordingly by the Prophet;

1) Despite the turmoil caused by the hypocrites in the wars, the noble Prophet did not order for them to be killed. This prevented outsiders claiming that the Prophet killed his own friends, a slander that would cause great harm to Islam.[391] The Prophet recognized this potentially harmful result and blocked the means to it.

2) The Prophet prohibited debtors from giving gifts to their lenders to block the means of usury and interest.[392]

3) During the wars, the punishment of amputation for thieves was suspended to prevent the criminals joining the enemy out of hardship. This would potentially harm the Muslim army so commanders were ordered not to apply this type of penal law in wartime.

4) Black market trading was prohibited by the Prophet; "A person who is profiteering is a sinner"[393] to avoid an artificial increase in the price of goods and a lack of availability. The means to this potential harm was blocked. On the other hand he praised those who brought their goods to the markets; "The provision of those people who bring their goods to the markets is increased and blessed."[394] This hadith falls under *fatḥ al- dharā'ī;* opening the means which lead to a beneficial result.

---

389 Abu Zahrah, *Uṣūl*, p. 228.
390 Qur'an, 2: 104.
391 Bukhari, *Saḥīḥ, Manāqib*, hadith no: 8.
392 Ibn Majah, *Sunan, Ṣadaqa*, hadith no: 2432.
393 Muslim, *Saḥīḥ, Musaqaat*, hadith no; 129.
394 Ibn Majah, *Sunan, Tijarah*, hadith no: 6.

5) The noble Prophet said:

> It is one of the greatest sins for man to curse his parents." The people asked him, 'O God's Messenger! How does a man curse his parents?' The Prophet said, "The man abuses the father of another man and the latter abuses the father of the former and abuses his mother.[395]

Cursing the parents of someone is phrased as cursing one's own parents for eventually it causes this harmful result. Therefore, this harm is prevented by blocking the means to it.

The examples clearly demonstrate that the results of actions are taken into consideration by God. Qarafi holds that in the same way that blocking the means to that which is harmful is obligatory, opening the means to that which is beneficial is also obligatory.[396] The last hadith supports this view. God has permitted and prohibited forms of conduct in accordance with the benefit or harm that they lead to. When a particular act or form of conduct brings about a result which is contrary to the objectives of the Lawgiver, it must be prohibited.[397]

Summary: Proof Value of *Sadd al-Dharā'ī*

1. Legal rulings (*ahkām*) can be classified into two groups; the purposes (*maqāsid*) and the means (*dharā'ī*).
2. Legally, the means are similar to the purposes.
3. If they serve the most significant purposes of Islamic law such as the five essential values (life, religion, property, progeny and the mind) they have the highest legal value and similarly if they lead to the most harmful results they hold the most serious legal value.
4. The result, rather than the intention of the doer, is the most significant criteria in judging whether a means should be blocked or not.
5. Many incidents in the Sunnah demonstrate that the notion of *sadd dharā'ī* was accepted and rulings issued accordingly by the noble Prophet.

The Classification of the Acts

The acts can be classified into four categories based on their results;

1) Acts which always result in harm. For example, if a deep pit is dug on a public way or at the entrance to someone's house, it can cause harm to those who don't know about it as they will fall into it. Therefore, this act is prohibited.[398]

---

[395] Bukhari, *Sahīh, Adab*, hadith no: 4.
[396] Qarafi, *Tanqīh al-Fuṣūl*, p. 200.
[397] Shātibī, *Muwafaqaat*, vol.4, p.194.
[398] Abu Zahrah, *Uṣūl*, p. 228.

2) Acts which rarely lead to harm. For example, selling food which usually doesn't harm anyone but sometimes may harm a few. This act is permissible as the benefits outweigh the harm. The general rule regarding this type of act or transaction is permissibility; no one can be blocked from them based on a possibility that it may lead to harm.[399] People performing such acts cannot be deemed guilty as they wish to get the benefit and the occurrence of a harmful result is rare.[400]

3) Acts which are most likely to lead to a harmful result and this is the predominant view (*al-ẕann al ghālib*). In these cases, the predominant view is accepted as definite knowledge because it is necessary to be cautious against means which mostly lead to harm according to the notion of *sadd al-dharā'ī*. For example, selling weapons during wartime or selling grapes to a wine maker.[401]

4) Acts which often lead to something harmful although it isn't certain or even probable that this will always be the case. For example, contracts such as *salam*[402] that can be a means to interest or usury. In this contract, the buyer may want to buy unripened fruit below its real saleable price and may mean usury or interest by this act. In other words, even though it is not certain or the predominant view, this type of contract often leads to something harmful. This type of act is disputed by jurists. Abu Ḫanīfa and Shāfi'ī hold that these acts are permissible, because the possibility of harm is not dominant to prohibit such acts. On the other hand, Imam Malik and Ahmad hold that these acts are prohibited because they are more cautious about harm possibly resulting from these contracts. Their view is that the permissibility and the high possibility of a harmful result are mixed. In cases like this, preventing harm is preferred when issuing fatwa as this is superior to the notion of providing benefit.

Despite minor disputes between scholars as to the application of *sadd al-dharā'ī*, the examples show that the majority of scholars accept its application in Islamic law.

Summary: The Classification of the Acts

1. Acts which always result in harm.
2. Acts which rarely lead to harm.
3. Acts which are most likely to lead to a harmful result and this is the predominant view (*al-ẕann al ghālib*).

---

[399] Ibid., p. 230.

[400] Shātibī, *Muwafaqaat*, vol.2, p. 249.

[401] Ibid., p. 359.

[402] Selling the unripen fruits by agreeing on certain conditions.

4. Acts which often lead to something harmful but it isn't certain or even probable that this will always be the case. Abu Ḫanīfa and Shāfi'ī hold that these acts are permissible, because the possibility of harm is not dominant to prohibit such acts. On the other hand, Imam Malik and Ahmad hold that these acts are prohibited because they are more cautious about harm possibly resulting from these contracts.
5. The majority of scholars accept the application of *sadd al-dharā'ī* in Islamic law.

Aḫkām Shar'ī (Value of Islamic Law)

Introduction

This section covers the legal rules which are extracted from the sources of Islamic law and the value assigned to them. In order to do this the legal rules, the types of legal rule, their values and the liable people are defined.

God is the ultimate authority who issues the rules, commands and prohibitions. He is also referred to as the Lawgiver in this book. Scholars have analysed and thoroughly debated the definition of the law. Mutazalite scholars believe that the law can be discovered by intellect alone; Sunni scholars hold that the law is only derived from the divine revelation and the Prophets whereas Māturidī scholars are of the opinion that legal rulings are known by intellect but this alone is not enough to issue a law therefore revelation is also needed.[403] This topic falls under *Kalām* (theology) rather than *Uṣūl al-Fiqh* and isn't covered here.

Ḫukm (The Law) and Its Types

The Arabic word *ḫukm* (pl. *aḫkām*) literally means a command. In Islamic law the definition of *ḫukm* is: a communication from God related to the acts of the liable human beings through a demand, option and a declaration.[404]

The *ḫukm* is a ruling of Islamic law. The study of *ḫukm-u shar'ī* (religious ruling) covers the nature of the rulings and the legal obligations they necessitate. There are three elements which effectuate the *ḫukm*.

1) The true source from which the *ḫukm* originates. The original source for Islamic law is God.

---

[403] Shawkānī, *Irshād al-Fuhūl*, pp. 7–9.

[404] Sadr al-Shari'ah, *al- Tawḫīd*, vol.1, p. 28.

2) The act on which the *ḥukm* operates (*wajib, mandub, haram, makruh* and *mubah*).

3) The liable person (*mukallaf*) for whose conduct the *ḥukm* is stipulated.[405]

God the Lawgiver is the ultimate source of Islamic law and liable human beings are the subjects bearing responsibility for practising this law. Accordingly, the law (*ḥukm*) is a religious attribute which operates on the practice of the liable person. *Uṣūl* scholars ascribe the law to God and His attributes from the view of point His name *Ḥākim* (Judge). The role of the jurist in Islam is to explain the laws of God, and the consequences of practising them in terms of rewards and punishments, to the liable people. There are some differences in the understanding of the law between the different juristic schools of *Uṣūl* and *Fiqh*. These will be looked at after the main two categories of law are explained.

Uṣūl scholars classify the law in two categories: 1) *Aḥkām Taklifiyya* (Defining Law) and 2) *Aḥkām Wad'iyya* (Declaratory Law).

Aḥkām taklifiyya (defining law) is defined by the scholars of *Uṣūl* as a communication from the Lawgiver concerning the conduct of the liable person which consists of a command, a prohibition or permissibility. In Islamic law a liable person is one who is Muslim, has attained puberty and has a sound intellect. The Arabic word *taklif* means offering responsibility to the liable person and the category *aḥkām taklifiyya* deals with the laws of conduct for liable people. Commands are binding and require absolute practice; they are referred to as '*wujub*' (obligatory) whereas recommended acts are named *nadb* (recommended). Prohibitions are binding and require absolute abstention; they are referred to as *haram*, whereas those prohibitions which are open to interpretation are named *makruh* (disliked). Acts which are permissible but are neither binding nor recommended are open to the choice of the liable person; these are called *mubah* (permissible).

Aḥkām wad'iyya (declaratory law) is defined by *Uṣūl* scholars as a communication from the Lawgiver which legislates something as a cause (*sabab*), a condition (*shart*) or an obstacle (*māni'*) for a ruling. In other words, if the Lawgiver connects a legal ruling to a cause, a condition or an obstacle it is called *aḥkām wad'iyya*. One attribute can be the cause, condition or obstacle for a legal ruling and without the existence of this the ruling cannot be known. They exist to enable human beings to know the values of the legal rulings, whether they are *wajib*, *haram* or *mubah*. If the Lawgiver did not provide such information, it would be impossible for human beings to extract the value of the laws. Similarly, people

---

[405] Imran Ahsan Khan Nyazee, *Islamic Jurisprudence*, pp. 45- 46.

cannot know whether an attribute is a cause, condition or obstacle for a legal ruling without such information. Scholars examine the primary sources of Islamic law, the Qur'an, Sunnah and *ijma'*, to understand the nature of the communication and deduce the principles and methodology (*Uṣūl al-Fiqh*). They use these as guidance for their determination and for this reason, the Qur'an, Sunnah and *ijma'* are called religious evidences (*adillah shar'iyya*).

An example of *aḫkām taklifiyya* (defining law) is the communication about the five Daily Prayers and *zakat* (obligatory charity). The Lawgiver prescribed these using definite expressions in the Qur'an; "*Establish the Prayer, and pay the Prescribed Purifying Alms (the Zakat)*...."[406] Since the evidence is definite (*dalil qat'ī*) the performance of these duties is *wajib* (obligatory) upon those liable and this law falls under the category of *aḫkām taklifiyya* (defining law). Another example in this category is the prohibition by God of the act of fornication which is *haram*. This law was communicated in the verse; "*Do not draw near to any unlawful sexual intercourse; surely it is a shameful, indecent thing, and an evil way.*"[407] The ruling about adultery (*zina*) is in the category of *aḫkām taklifiyya* and the previous verse is a piece of definite evidence establishing it.

An example for the category *aḫkām wad'iyya* (declaratory law) can be seen in the timing of the obligatory Prayers. The movement of the sun from its zenith at midday was prescribed by the Lawgiver as the cause (*sabab*) for the obligation of the Noon Prayer upon those liable. Jurists used evidence to extract the meaning determining the time segment of the Noon Prayer. At this time the Prayer becomes obligatory on the liable people. They must perform it within this time segment. The following verse was revealed by God to inform them about this ruling: "*Establish the Prayer in conformity with its conditions, from the declining of the sun to the darkness of the night*...."[408] In this verse, God assigned the declining of the sun as a sign or a cause (*sabab*) for the obligation of Prayer. This is evidence for the law which falls under the category *aḫkām wad'iyya.* A similar example for this category is the sighting of the moon in Ramadan being a cause (*sabab*) for the obligation of fasting upon the liable people. God also made the sighting of the moon at the beginning of the month of Shawwal a cause (*sabab*) for ending the fast and for the obligation of paying *fitr* (breaking the fast) charity. The evidence for this ruling is the words of the Prophet, inspired by God: "When you

---

406 Qur'an, 2: 43.

407 Qur'an, 17: 32.

408 Qur'an, 17: 78.

sight the moon (at the beginning of the month of Ramadan) you start fasting and when you sight it again (at the beginning of Shawwal) finish it."[409]

A further example for the category *aḫkām wad'iyya* is the condition (*shart*) of purification for the validity of the Prayers, informed to the liable people by the Prophet: "God does not accept Prayer without purification."[410] Purification is established as a condition for the Prayers by this hadith and it is in the category of *aḫkām wad'iyya.*

An example of an obstacle (*māni'*) in the category of *aḫkām wad'iyya* is shown with the law on inheritance. The Lawgiver made the act of killing an obstacle for the inheritance and this was informed to the liable people by the noble Prophet: "A man who murders another cannot inherit from him."[411]

There are two essential differences between *aḫkām taklifiyya* (defining law) and *aḫkām wad'iyya* (declaratory law). The first difference is that scholars understand that anything termed *aḫkām taklifiyya* (defining law) clearly defines whether a liable person must act, abstain from or is permitted to do something. This is not the case with *aḫkām wad'iyya*; laws in this category have an attribute which has been defined as a cause (*sabab*), a condition (*shart*) or an obstacle (*māni'*) by the Lawgiver.

The second difference is that liable people are able to be responsible for all the laws in the category *aḫkām taklifiyya,* such as performing the Prayers, giving *zakat,* etc. One of the principles of Islạmic law is that people cannot be responsible for acts that exceed their power and capacity. If they have a choice (*mubah*) as to whether or not to perform an act, it is implied that they have the power to do it. However, in the case of *aḫkām wad'iyya* (declaratory law) some of the laws are within a liable person's capacity whilst others are not. For example, the act of stealing was prescribed as the cause (*sabab*) for the punishment of amputation of the hands. A liable person has the power to avoid such a cause by not stealing. On the other hand, it is the movement of the sun which indicated the set times for the Daily Prayers and this is beyond the liable person's capacity to change.

An example for a condition (*shart*) within the power of the liable person is that of purification for the validity of the Prayers without which the Prayer is invalid. The liable person has the power and capacity to fulfil this condition. Contrary to this, the condition for becoming responsible for religious duties is the onset

---

[409] Nasaī, *Sunan, Siyam,* hadith no: 8.

[410] Ibn Majah, *Sunan, Tahāra,* hadith no: 2.

[411] Tirmidhi, *Sunan,* hadith no: 3048.

of puberty. It is not within the power of people to change this as they cannot change their nature or stop the onset of adulthood in order to avoid responsibility.

An example of an obstacle (*māni'*) that is within the power of liable people to avoid is the disinheritance from one who has been murdered. The act of murder is an obstacle for inheritance and is it possible for liable people to avoid this obstacle because it is within their power to not commit murder. On the other hand, the menstruation period and postnatal bleeding are obstacles to fulfilling certain obligations of worship such as performing the Daily Prayers and fasting. It is not within the power of a liable person to change these.

Summary: *Ḫukm* (The Law) and Its Types

1. *Ḫukm* (a ruling of law) is: a communication from God related to the acts of the liable human beings through a demand, option and a declaration.
2. There are three elements which effectuate the *ḫukm*: the true source from which the *ḫukm* originates; the act on which the *ḫukm* operates (*wajib, mandub, haram, makruh* and *mubah*); the liable person (*mukallaf*) for whose conduct the *ḫukm* is stipulated.
3. The role of the jurist in Islam is to explain the laws of God to the liable people and the consequences of practising this law in terms of rewards and punishments which reflects God's attitudes towards these actions.
4. *Uṣūl* scholars classify the law in two categories:
5. *Aḫkām taklifiyya* (defining law) is defined by the scholars of *Uṣūl* as a communication from the Lawgiver concerning the conduct of the liable person which consists of a command, a prohibition or permissibility. Examples include the communication about the five Daily Prayers and *zakat* (obligatory charity).
6. *Aḫkām wad'iyya* (declaratory law) is defined by *Uṣūl* scholars as a communication from the Lawgiver which legislates something as a cause (*sabab*), a condition (*shart*) or an obstacle (*māni'*) for a ruling. An example is the timing of the obligatory Prayers.
7. *Aḫkām taklifiyya* and *aḫkām wad'iyya* differ in two main ways: 1) anything termed *aḫkām taklifiyya* clearly defines whether a liable person must act, abstain from or is permitted to do something but this is not the case with *aḫkām wad'iyya*; 2) liable people are able to be responsible for all the laws in the category *aḫkām taklifiyya,* but, in the case of *aḫkām wad'iyya* some of the laws are within a liable person's capacity whilst others are not.

The Pillars of Islamic Law

Islamic law consists of three essential pillars: 1. *Ḥākim* (the Lawgiver), the authority by which the law is issued. 2. the subject matter of the law (*maḥkūm fīh*) and 3.the addressees which are liable persons (*maḥkūm 'alayh*). Each of these pillars is explained separately.

Ḥākim (The Lawgiver)

The ultimate source of Islamic law, whether by means of direct revelation (the Qur'an and Sunnah) or through *ijtihād*, is God alone and there is a general consensus on this matter. The following verse is evidence for this statement:

> ... (In the absolute sense) judgment and authority rest with none but God alone. He always relates the truth, and He is the best judge between truth and falsehood.[412]

The scholars hold different views over the methodology and principles used to gain the knowledge of the purpose of God and His injunctions. They dispute over whether the law and its objectives can be known by the intellect or whether religion is necessary. There are three different views related to this in the science of *Kalām* [413] but this is beyond the scope of *Uṣūl al-Fiqh*. Law and justice in the Muslim community must derive their validity and substance from the principles and values that the Lawgiver has sanctioned.[414] The unbelievers refused the revelation because it offered new laws and a new lifestyle. It was very difficult for them to abandon their customs and adopt the new belief and regulations. For this reason, the human intellect is not accepted as an independent source of Islamic law in its own right; even the Prophet did not establish the law in his human capacity free from divine revelation (the Qur'an) or divine inspiration (the Sunnah).[415]

Imam Māturidī holds that good and evil regarding the conduct of the liable person can be recognized by the human intellect but it does not mean God's purpose is always identical with the intellect, therefore the best conduct and the most proper way of life is known through divine guidance.[416] This is the strongest of all the views and is the one adopted by Ḥanafī scholars.

412 Qur'an 6: 57.

413 Taftazani, *Talwīḥ*, vol.1, p.172.

414 Kamali, *Islamic Jurisprudence*, p. 296.

415 Abu Zahrah, *Uṣūl*, p. 54.

416 Ibid., p. 56.

Summary: *Ḫākim* (the Lawgiver)

1. There is a general consensus that the ultimate source of Islamic law is God alone.
2. Scholars hold different views over the methodology and principles used to gain the knowledge of the purpose of God and His injunctions.
3. Law and justice in the Muslim community must derive their validity and substance from the principles and values that the Lawgiver has sanctioned.
4. Human intellect is not accepted as an independent source of Islamic law in its own right because God's purpose is not always identical with the intellect's ideas of good and evil.

Maḫkūm Fīh **(The Subject-Matter of the Law)**

Maḫkūm fīh is used by *uṣūl* scholars to mean the content or subject matter of the law and indicates the acts, rights and obligations of the liable persons. There are two categories of law (*ḫukm*) as mentioned previously: *aḫkām wad'iyya* and *taklifiyya. Aḫkām taklifiyya* is those communications from the Lawgiver in the form of demands, prohibitions or permissibility, regarding the conduct of liable people. *Aḫkām wad'iyya* is those rules communicated by the Lawgiver related to the conduct of liable people, in the form of *sabab, shart* or *māni.'*

In Islamic law, a liable person cannot be held responsible for an act if it does not meet the following two conditions:

The first condition is that the duty must be known by the liable person because the meaning of liability is carrying out the duty as demanded.[417] The duty can only be fulfilled if the person has the necessary information. For example, the duty of *zakat* cannot be performed without having information about the *nisab* value, *zakat* categories, their rates, performance time and so on. Liable people living in Muslim countries are deemed to be knowledgeable and have easy access to this information. Those living in foreign countries are supposed to search and learn about these duties.

The second condition is that the law must be applicable by the liable person. In other words, the duty must be within his capability. There is no law in Islam which is beyond the capacity of the liable persons.

God declared in the Qur'an;

[417] Shawkānī, *Irshād*, p. 11.

> ...God burdens no soul except within its capacity...[418]

> ...God does not charge a soul with a duty except in what He has (already) granted it (of capacity to discharge that duty). God will bring about, after hardship, ease.[419]

Humankind is given responsibility as a trial for those liable. If the duty is beyond their capacity the trial becomes meaningless. Therefore, the responsibilities offered by the Lawgiver are within the capacity of the liable people. However, the natural impulses which are beyond the capacity of humans such as hunger, thirst, positive and negative emotions are not within the scope of this responsibility. These are not subject to free will but can be controlled and used in the right direction. For example, when Ibrahim, the son of the noble Prophet was in his last moments the Prophet started shedding tears. Upon this, 'Sa'd ibn 'Ubāda said, 'O God's Messenger, even you are weeping!' He said, 'O Sa'd, this is the mercy of God.' Then he wept more and said, 'The eyes are shedding tears and the heart is grieved, but we will not say except what pleases our Lord. O Ibrahim! Indeed we are grieved by your separation.'[420]

The duties of a liable person certainly contain some hardship and difficulty but nothing that is outside his capacity. For example, the Prophet told one of the Companions to avoid anger. Removing the feeling of anger is beyond human capacity but controlling it and not doing something forbidden with this feeling is within the capacity of human kind. We can see this is a test from God. Although it is difficult to control the feeling of anger it is within the capacity of a liable person and this gives meaning to the test. God declared in the Qur'an:

> Those who avoid the major sins and indecent, shameful deeds (which are indeed to be counted among major sins), and when they become angry, even then they forgive (rather than retaliate in kind).[421]

The Lawgiver made some exemptions (*rukhṣah*) to the initial rules (*'azimah*) to remove the hardship and difficulty from people. For this reason, the noble Prophet said: "God loves to see that His exemptions are taken advantage of, just as He hates to see the commission of a sin."[422] The liable person is required to

---

[418] Qur'an 2: 286.
[419] Qur'an 65: 7.
[420] Bukhari, *Saḫīḫ, Janaiz*, hadith no: 32–33.
[421] Qur'an 42: 37.
[422] Ibn Hanbal, *Musnad*, vol.2, no: 108.

carry out their duties according to their capability. The Prophet said: "Fulfil your duties to the extent of your ability."[423]

The difficulty which is within the scope of human capacity can be divided into two categories:

The first type of difficulty includes acts that can be continuously performed but are not contrary to the meaning of responsibility; there is some hardship involved in these acts. If the act is very easy it is not considered to be responsibility. The Arabic word *taklif* (offering responsibility) is derived from the root *kulfah* that is load and burden. For this reason, being responsible is synonymous with being loaded with some kind of burden and difficulty. The duties which the Lawgiver demanded contain some hardship but they are within the capacity of the liable person.

The second type of difficulty includes acts that when performed continuously will lead to evil results and negligence of some essential duties. For example, continuous fasting and staying up all night for night vigil would lead to great difficulty and can result in the negligence of essentials duties.

There are four categories of rights pertaining to the subject matter of the law:[424] The rights of God; the rights of human beings; the rights of both God and human beings, where the rights of God are predominant and; the rights of both but where the rights of human beings are predominant.

1) The rights of God.

God does not need people's worship but it is beneficial to them and these rights are called the rights of God. The community rights are also named as the rights of God due to its importance. Indeed, the rights of the public are different to the rights of the individual and are the duty of the governors. The scholars of *uṣūl* classified the rights of God into the following categories;

a) Devotional rules (*ibadāt*) are the exclusive right of God. These include the five Daily Prayers, fasting, *Hajj, zakat,* etc.
b) Rights which consist of both devotional and financial acts. This includes giving *ṣadaqa* (charity) at the end of Ramadan.
c) Rights of financial acts which have a devotional element but the financial purpose predominates. This includes acts such as giving a tithe for the agricultural products of the earth.

---

[423] Muslim, *Saḥīḥ, Vows,* no: 378.
[424] Khallaf, *'Ilm,* p. 128.

d) Rights which consist of financial liability and the legal punishments to fulfil these rights such as imposing a land tax in the conquered territories.

e) Penal law such as punishment for fornication, theft, murder and false testimony. These rulings are established for the benefit of the public to protect their rights.

f) Limited penal law such as depriving a murderer from the inheritance of his victim.

g) Punishments in the nature of *ibadāt* such as compensation for certain offences. This includes freeing a slave, feeding the poor or fasting as compensation.

h) Community rights such as sharing the spoils of war.

2) The rights of the servants.

The second type is the rights of the servants. These are individual rights which aim to provide benefit and prevent harm. This type of right can be fulfilled by individuals or be given up by them. An example is the right to compensation for a loss.

3) The rights of God and the servants (where the rights of God are predominant).

The third type is the rights of both the servant and God but God's rights are greater. An example is the punishment for someone who slanders a chaste woman. In this case, there are two options; the first is to punish the offender and protect the honour of the woman. The second is to forgive the offender and not apply the punishment. However, the portion of woman is greater in this right and it is called the right of God, because preventing the wrongdoing to the women and punishing the wrongdoers is superior.

4) The rights of God and the servants (where the rights of the servants are predominant).

The fourth type is the rights of God and the servants but in which the portion of the servant is greater. An example of this is intentional murder. In this case, the right of retaliation is given to the relatives of the victim. They can either forgive the murderer or request the application of the death penalty. Providing security is the right of God, but retaliation is the right of the servant and in the case of murder, the rights of the servant are greater.

Summary: *Maḥkūm Fīh* (The Subject-Matter of the Law)

1. *Maḥkūm fīh* is used by *uṣūl* scholars to mean the content or subject matter of the law and indicates the acts, rights and obligations of the liable persons.

2. There are two categories of law (*ḫukm*) as mentioned previously: *aḫkām wad'iyya* and *taklifiyya*.
3. In Islamic law, a liable person cannot be held responsible for an act if it does not meet the following two conditions: the duty must be known by the liable person; and the law must be applicable by the liable person.
4. The duties of a liable person certainly contain some hardship and difficulty but nothing that is outside his capacity.
5. The Lawgiver made some exemptions (*rukhṣah*) to the initial rules (*'aẕimah*) to remove the hardship and difficulty from people.
6. The difficulty which is within the scope of human capacity can be divided into two categories: acts that can be continuously performed but are not contrary to the meaning of responsibility; acts that when performed continuously will lead to evil results and negligence of some essential duties.
7. There are four categories of rights pertaining to the subject matter of the law:
8. The Rights of God: including devotional rules, devotional and financial acts, financial acts with a devotional element, rights which consist of financial liability and the legal punishments to fulfil these rights, penal law, limited penal law, punishments in the nature of worship and community rights.
9. The rights of the servants: individual rights which provide benefit and prevent harm.
10. The rights of God and the servants (where the rights of God are predominant).
11. The rights of God and the servants (where the rights of the servants are predominant).

Maḫkūm 'Alayh (The Addressee of the Law)

Maḫkūm alayh is defined as the person to whom the ruling is addressed. This section deals with their legal capacity. Legal capacity (*ahliyah*) means the capacity to qualify a person as able to acquire rights and bear obligations. It relates to their power to conduct actions and transactions that are able to produce their legal effects.[425] It means a person is capable of receiving a legislative injunction and they are therefore responsible under legal rules. Legal capacity in Islamic law consists of two kinds: the capacity of acquiring rights; and the capacity of executing rights.[426]

---

[425] Bazdawī, *Kashf al-Asrār an Uṣūl,* vol.4, p. 335.

[426] 'Abdur Rahim, *Jurisprudence*, p. 217

The condition for a person to be able to acquire rights and bear obligations is that of being alive. Therefore, this applies to every living human being regardless of sex, colour, race, age, creed, mental and physical ability or disability. Accordingly, the mentally ill, foetuses, minors and foolish people, whether they are sick or in good health, possess legal capacity by virtue of their dignity as human beings.[427]

For a person to be able to execute their rights there are certain conditions that must be met: They must be Muslim, have reached maturity and be of sound mental and physical health. The absence of any of these conditions results in the person not being liable under Islamic law. Only a person who understands his acts and words is competent to conclude a contract, discharge an obligation, or be punished for violating the law.[428]

Maturity (the onset of puberty) has been assigned by the Lawgiver as the beginning of personal responsibility. This is a quality that is changeable according to time, condition and place but it is something which can be established by factual evidence. The most important criterion however is the intellectual capacity of the individual. Therefore, if a person is not of sound and healthy mind, they are not held responsible for religious duties. The noble Prophet said: "The pen is raised from three persons: the one who is asleep until he wakes, the child until he attains puberty, and the insane person until he regains sanity."[429]

There are three possible scenarios for judging legal capacity. The first is being free from any legal capacity due to being a child or being insane. The second is someone with partial legal capacity such as a discerning child (*mumayyiz*) between the age of seven and puberty. These individuals are not endowed with full legal capacity because they cannot fully comprehend the legal responsibilities and their consequences. The third scenario is a person who has reached puberty and is considered to be mature. At this point they are fully endowed with legal capacity and become responsible for the performance of their religious duties. They are also responsible for the consequences of legal acts.

Summary: *Maḫkūm 'Alayh* (the Addressee of the Law)

1. *Maḫkūm 'alayh* is defined as the person to whom the rule is addressed.
2. Legal capacity (*ahliyah*) means the capacity to qualify a person as able to acquire rights and bear obligations.

[427] Khallaf, *'Ilm*, p. 136.
[428] Kamali, *Islamic Jurisprudence*, p. 305.
[429] Tabrizi, *Mishkat*, vol.2, p. 980.

3. The condition for a person to be able to acquire rights and bear obligations is that of being alive.
4. For a person to be able to execute their rights they must be Muslim, have reached maturity and be of sound mental and physical health.
5. The absence of any of these conditions results in the person not being liable under Islamic law.
6. There are three possible scenarios for judging legal capacity; being free from legal responsibility, being partially responsible and full legal capacity.

Chapter Nine

Aḫkām Shar'ī
(Value of Islamic Law)

Aẖkām Shar'ī (Value of Islamic Law)

Aẖkām Taklifiyya (Defining Law)

As previously mentioned, *aẖkām taklifiyya* consists of laws prescribed by the Lawgiver concerning the conduct of liable people. This can be in the form of commands, prohibitions or things deemed permissible. The sections below explain the five categories of *aẖkām taklifiyya*: *wajib, mandub, haram, makruh* and *mubah*.

Wajib, Fard (The Obligatory)

Wajib and *farḏ* are the same in *Uṣūl al-Fiqh* but different in *Fiqh*. They both convey a binding demand regarding conduct. Duty that is raised from a definite source or evidence with respect to both the authenticity of its transmission and its interpretation is named *wajib* (obligatory) by the majority of *Uṣūl* scholars and *farḏ* by Ḫanafī scholars. Denying *farḏ* (*wajib* in *Uṣūl al-Fiqh*) is disbelief (*kufr*). The Ḫanafī School defines *wajib* as a duty that is raised from speculative evidence (*ẕannī dalil*). This makes it slightly weaker in its demand than *farḏ* which based on definite evidence. Additionally, the speculative evidence (*ẕannī dalil*) is open to interpretation. Denying *wajib* is not disbelief but *fisq* (corruption). A consequence of the distinction between *farḏ* and *wajib* is that when a *farḏ* act is neglected the whole act is nullified. An example of this is the omission of the standing or the recitation of the Qur'an during the obligatory Prayers results in the whole Prayer being nullified. However, if a *wajib* act is omitted during the Prayer it remains valid though deficient.

The majority of *Uṣūl* scholars hold that *wajib* conveys a binding command because the duty arises from definite evidence with respect to both its transmission and its meaning. Certain punishments have been assigned by the Lawgiver for omitting these duties and this indicates their absolute binding nature upon those liable to perform them. For example, the Daily Prayers, *Hajj*, and fulfilling the conditions of contracts are all binding commands issued by God and each brings a certain punishment if it is not fulfilled.

Wajib acts are absolutely binding and it is necessary to perform them. Those who perform these duties will be rewarded and saved from punishment. Denying *wajib* (*fard̲* in the Ḥanafī School) is disbelief because these commands are based on definitive evidence.

Wajib commands have been categorised into two types based on time conditions: *mutlaq wajib* (duty unrestricted by time) and *muqayyad wajib* (duty with time restrictions). *Mutlaq wajib* is a duty which is binding, the liable person must fulfil it, but there is no time restriction as to when it should be performed. An example is that usually when someone makes an oath to do something but cannot fulfil it, they must compensate for the offence. However, if the compensation has no time specification, they can make the compensation at any time during their life.

Muqayyad wajib is a duty which has a specific time frame assigned by the Lawgiver. The duty has a specific beginning and end time and the liable person must fulfil the duty within this time period by observing all its preconditions and pillars. If the *wajib* act is fulfilled in this manner it is called *edā* (performing the *wajib* in its allocated time). However, if the liable person is unable to perform the duty during its set time but makes it up later is known as *qada* (make-up). For example, performing the *Fajr* Prayer before sunrise is *edā* whereas performing it after the sunrise it is *qada*. Similarly performing the *Z̲uhr* Prayer in its fixed time is *edā* but performing it at other times is *qada*.

Muqayyad wajib has been further divided into three categories according to the length of the performance time.

The first category of *muqayyad wajib* is *muwassa'* (extended) which means the time set for the performance of the *wajib* sufficient not only for this *wajib* but also leaves time for the performance of other *wajib* that is in the same category of worship. For example, the fixed times for the five Daily Prayers are *muwassa' wajib* because the time is sufficient for the performance of both the Prayer assigned for that time and other optional or make-up Prayers.

The second category of *muqayyad wajib* is *mudayyaq* (limited) that is when the time set *wajib* duty is sufficient only for the performance of this *wajib* alone and does not allow for performing any other *wajib* in the same category of worship. For example, only the Ramadan fast can be observed by liable people during the month of Ramadan. Optional and make-up fasts are not permissible during this month. The set time only allows for the performance of the Ramadan fast.

The third category of *muqayyad wajib* is *dhush-shabahayn* (similar to the two sides) which is similar to both *muwassa'* and *mudayyaq wajib* from different aspects. The rituals of the *Hajj* are an example for this. The set time for *Hajj ibadah* (worship) is the well-known months. During these months only one obligatory *Hajj* can be performed and from this aspect it is similar to *mudayyaq wajib*. On the other hand, there are some rituals of *Hajj* such as *tawaf* and *sa'y* that can be performed any day during these months and for this reason, it is similar to *muwassa' wajib*.

In practice, duties that fall under the category of *muwassa' wajib* must be performed with a specific intention as of other rituals that are in the same category of worship can also be performed during the same time frame. Therefore, before performing this type of *wajib* it is necessary to specify the intention to separate it from other similar rituals such as optional or make-up. For example, in the time of *Fajr* Prayer if a person intends to perform it as *Fajr* Prayer it is accepted as intended. However, if the person makes his/her intention for the performance of other *wajib* or optional Prayers, the Prayer is accepted as such and the person remains responsible for performing the *Fajr* Prayer.

Conversely, *mudayyaq wajib* does not require a specific intention for there is no possibility for performing other similar acts of worship during the specified time. For example, if a person makes the intention to observe optional fasting during the month of Ramadan, his intention is counted as an intention for the obligatory fasting, because this *wajib* does not allow the performance of other types of fasting in the assigned time.

The intention for *dhush-shabahayn wajib* is different. If a person makes a general intention for performing *Hajj* without specifying whether it is obligatory or optional, his *Hajj* is accepted as an obligatory and the responsibility for *Hajj* is fulfilled. However, if a person intends to perform optional *Hajj* and has not already performed obligatory *Hajj* in his lifetime, the *Hajj* is accepted as optional and the liability of the obligatory one remains upon him.

Wajib acts have also been classified into two categories according to their amount; *muhaddad* (specific amount) and *ghayr muhaddad* (unspecific amount). *Muhaddad wajib* are duties which have been assigned with a specified amount, for example, the five Daily Prayers and the amount for *zakat*. These duties have to be carried out are soon as they become obligatory upon the liable persons and the responsibility remains for them until they have been performed according to their amounts and conditions. *Ghayr muhaddad* (unspecific amount) *wajib* are the duties which have not been quantified with an amount. They include such things as spending in the way of God, helping the poor and hospitality for the guests. Rather than amount, the most important criteria for *ghayr muhaddad wajib* is meeting the needs of the people. As these needs vary according to changes in time and place an amount has not been specified for this type of *wajib*.

Wajib duties are again divided into two categories from the viewpoint of the liable person upon which the ruling operates; *'aynī* (personal) and *kifaī* (communal) *wajib*. *'Aynī wajib* covers the duties which every liable person must fulfil. Each liable person must individually perform these duties and performance by one person does not remove the responsibility from the other. The five Daily Prayers, fasting, *zakat* and *Hajj* are *'aynī wajib*.

Kifaī wajib is the communal duties that have been assigned by the Lawgiver to the community rather than to every liable person. The duty must be undertaken by the community but does not necessarily include every liable person. Examples include the duty of judgment and fatwa, struggling in the way of God, the task of testimony, promoting good and prohibiting evil. If some of the community perform these duties the responsibility is removed from the rest. These duties promote the welfare of the public by providing the benefit and preventing them from harm. Such results can be achieved with the effort of a few within the community so they do not require the performance of each individual. The performance by a few relieves the others of the responsibility, but if no one performs these duties the whole community falls into sin and is held accountable. Even though communal obligation is the definition of *kifaī wajib*, if there is only one person qualified to carry out this task, the communal duty becomes his individual responsibility (*'aynī wajib*) as he is the only one who can fulfil this duty. An example is medical treatment which is a communal responsibility. Only properly trained medics are able to carry out this duty, therefore the responsibility lies with them and this duty is *'aynī wajib* upon them. The responsibility for this task is upon those who are in a position to fulfil it and this removes the responsibility from other in the community. However, if no one fulfils this duty, the whole community is in sin and responsible for its neglect.

Wajib is further classified into two categories according to whether the task is assigned and clear or optional; *mu'ayyan* (assigned) and *muḫayyar* (optional). If the duty is assigned without potential for the liable person to choose among different options, it is *mu'ayyan wajib*. Examples of this are the Daily Prayers, fasting in Ramadan and paying the rent. The responsibility for these duties lies with the liable person until they have been carried out.

Muḫayyar wajib are those duties where the liable person has options of how to fulfil the duty. In these cases, the Lawgiver has not assigned a specific duty with regards to a law, but has provided options from which the liable person can choose. An example is the compensation of an oath. In this case, the Lawgiver has provided three options of compensation from which the liable person who has broken their oath can choose one to fulfil their duty. The options are freeing a slave, feeding ten poor or dressing them. If the liable person is unable to perform any of these options they must fast for three days. This law is established by the following verse:

> The expiation (for breaking such oaths) is to feed ten destitute persons (or one person for ten days) with the average of the food you serve to your families, or to clothe them, or to set free a slave. If anyone does not find (the means to do that), let him fast for three days.[430]

Each of the three options is *muḫayyar wajib* and the liable person can choose to perform any one of them to compensate his offence, therefore removing the responsibility. By performing one of these options, the liable person removes the responsibility. However, if he does not carry out any of the options he falls into sin and may be punished.

Summary: *Wajib, Fard* (The Obligatory)

1. *Wajib* according to majority of *Uṣūl* scholars is an obligatory duty raised from a definite source or evidence. The Ḫanafī School labels this *farḏ.* For them *wajib* is slightly weaker in that it is raised from speculative evidence that is open to interpretation.
2. Denying *farḏ* (*wajib* in *Uṣūl al-Fiqh*) is disbelief (*kufr*).
3. *Wajib* acts are absolutely binding and it is necessary to perform them or punishment is incurred.
4. *Wajib* acts have been categorised into two types based on time conditions: *mutlaq wajib* (duty unrestricted by time) and *muqayyad wajib* (duty with time restrictions).
5. *Muqayyad wajib* has been further divided into three categories according to the length of the performance time: *muwassa'* (extended)*; mudayyaq* (limited) and *dhush-shabahayn* (similar to the two sides).
6. *Muwassa' wajib* must be performed with a specific intention as of other similar rituals of worship can also be performed during the same time frame but *mudayyaq wajib* does not require a specific intention. The intention for *dhush-shabahayn wajib* is different.

[430] Qur'an, 5: 89.

7. *Wajib* acts have also been classified into two categories according to their amount; *muhaddad* (specific amount) and *ghayr muhaddad* (unspecific amount).
8. *Wajib* duties are again divided into two categories from the view point of the liable person upon which the ruling operates; *'aynī* (personal) which must be fulfilled by all liable people and *kifaī* (communal) which must be fulfilled by some of the community and failure in this results in punishment of the whole community.
9. *Wajib* is further classified into two categories according to whether the task is assigned and clear or optional; *mu'ayyan* (assigned) is a duty that the liable person must perform and *muḫayyar* (optional) is a duty where the liable person has options of how to fulfil the duty.

Mandub (Recommended)

Mandub are the acts that are recommended by the Lawgiver but are not binding. Neglecting *mandub* is not a sin, but their performance incurs reward. *Mandub* acts may exist in the text of *Shari'ah* as recommendations, or they may be given in the nature of a command but the Lawgiver later makes it clear that it is something that can be omitted. The following verses demonstrate this:

> O you who believe! When you contract a debt between you for a fixed term, record it in writing...[431]

> ...But if you trust one another, let him (the debtor) who is trusted fulfil his trust, and let him act in piety and keep from disobedience to God, his Lord (by fulfilling the conditions of the contract)...[432]

The evidence which renders an otherwise binding command a recommendation might arise from textual evidence in the Qur'an and Sunnah, or a general principle of Islamic law. It can also be indicated by the lack of punishment set for the omission of such acts. The first verse above commands that a debt must be recorded in writing when a contract is made. However, there is textual proof that makes this *mandub*; the Lawgiver gives permission to the liable person to omit this act if both parties trust each other. Therefore, recording the debt in writing is recommended but not absolutely binding and blame cannot be apportioned if this is omitted. Another example is the following verse:

---

[431] Qur'an 2:282.

[432] Qur'an 2:283.

> ...And if any of those whom your right hands possess desire to enter into a contract with you to purchase their freedom, make this contract with them if you know that they are honest (and able to earn without begging and be good, free citizens). Help them out of God's wealth which He has granted you...[433]

The verse contains a command to the master to make a contract with the slaves who want to purchase their freedom. Despite being a command, evidence exists which make this *mandub*. One of the principles of Islamic law is that an owner has the right to exercise over the slaves' property, goods and possessions however they wish to. This right cannot be limited and the owner cannot be obliged to do something that is not necessary. Therefore, the command in the verse is understood to be a recommendation but not binding.

Mandub acts are divided into three different types: Sunnah *muakkada*, (the emphasised Sunnah), Sunnah *ghayr-i muakkada* (recommended Sunnah) and Sunnah *zawaid* (the general daily acts of the noble Prophet).

a) Sunnah *muakkada* (emphasised Sunnah); this Sunnah consist of two parts; the first is acts to comply with the *Shari'ah* such as calling the *adhan* and performing the Prayers in congregation. The second is the acts that were consistently performed by the Prophet but sometimes he omitted them to show his followers that they are not binding. For example, rinsing the mouth and nostrils three times when making ablution. Whoever performs emphasised Sunnah is rewarded; omitting it does not incur punishment but it is blameworthy.

b) Sunnah *ghayr-i muakkada* (not emphasised Sunnah but recommended); these acts are classified as obedience in that they were performed by the Prophet but not consistently. He performed these acts many times but omitted them at other times. For example, praying four *rak'ah* before the *'Asr* and *'Isha* Prayers. Those who perform these types of Sunnah deserve reward but omitting them is not a sin or something that can be blamed.

c) Sunnah *zawāid*; this category consists of all the acts of the Prophet pertaining to his ordinary daily life, such as how he dressed, what he chose to eat and drink, etc. It is part of an individual's perfection to strive to imitate the Prophet in all actions; therefore, the people who try to copy these acts in their daily lives will be rewarded for it, whilst those who omit them do not commit a sin and cannot be blamed.

---

[433] Qur'an 24: 33.

Summary: *Mandub* (Recommended)

1. *Mandub* are the acts that are recommended by the Lawgiver and are not binding; neglecting them is not a sin.
2. The evidence which renders an otherwise binding command a recommendation might be a textual authority in the Qur'an and Sunnah, or a general principle of Islamic law, or it could be indicated by the lack of punishment set for the omission of such acts.
3. *Mandub* acts are divided into three different types: Sunnah *muakkada*, (the emphasised Sunnah), Sunnah *ghayr-i muakkada* (recommended Sunnah) and Sunnah *zawāid* (the general daily acts of the noble Prophet).
4. Sunnah *muakkada* were consistently performed by the Prophet. He omitted their performance once or twice to show they were not obligatory. Whoever performs Sunnah *muakkada* is rewarded; omitting it does not incur punishment but it is blameworthy.
5. Sunnah *ghayr-i muakkada* were performed by the Prophet but not consistently. Those who perform these types of Sunnah deserve reward but omitting them is not a sin and is not blameworthy.
6. Sunnah *zawāid* is the daily life habits of the Prophet. People who try to copy these habits in their daily lives will be rewarded for it. However, not copying them is not a sin or blameworthy.

***Haram* (Prohibited)**

Prohibited acts are named *haram* and are absolutely forbidden by the Lawgiver in binding and definite terms. The prohibition may take place in the textual authority in one of the following ways:

a) With the Arabic word *haram* and its derivations.
b) By removing or abrogating the *hálal* (permissible).
c) With general terms of prohibition without allowing interpretation.
d) With a phrase of caution that requires one to omit the act.
e) With the enactment of a punishment for practicing it.

The following texts from the Qur'an and Sunnah demonstrate these forms of prohibition:

> Forbidden to you (O believing men) are your mothers...[434]

[434] Qur'an 4: 23.

The Arabic word *haram* is used in this text to indicate the prohibition of marriage with one's mother.

> It is not lawful for you to become inheritors, against their will of women...[435]

In this verse the expression 'It is not lawful' indicates that the *halal* (permissible) status is removed for the act of inheriting women against their will.

"*...do not kill your children for fear of poverty...*"[436] and "*Do not draw near to any unlawful sexual intercourse...*"[437]

Both verses prohibit the relevant acts with general expressions.

> O you who believe! Intoxicants, games of chance, sacrifices to (anything serving the function of) idols (and at places consecrated for offerings to other than God), and (the pagan practice of) divination by arrows (and similar practices) are a loathsome evil of Satan's doing; so turn wholly away from it so that you may prosper (in both worlds).[438]

In this verse God warns the believers against performing particular acts and this is another form of prohibition.

> Surely those who consume the property of orphans wrongfully, certainly they consume a fire in their bellies; and soon they will be roasting in a Blaze.[439]

This verse indicates a punishment for a certain type of act, therefore it is *haram*.

Haram acts are classified into two categories; *haram li-dhatih* (forbidden for its own sake) and *haram li-ghayrih* (forbidden because of something else).

a) *Haram li-dhatih* is defined as the acts that are forbidden for their own sake such as theft, murder, adultery and performing the Prayers without ablution. All of these examples contain evil and harm and thus they are forbidden. Acts in this category are absolutely forbidden. If someone performs them the act is deemed a sin and invalid. The results of such acts have no legal basis; for example, lineage and inheritance cannot be established through the act of fornication, neither can stealing establish the right of ownership.

---

435 Qur'an 4: 19.
436 Qur'an 6: 151.
437 Qur'an 17: 32.
438 Qur'an 5: 90.
439 Qur'an 4: 10.

b) *Haram li-ghayrih* is defined as the acts that are forbidden because of something else. In other words, the acts themselves are permissible but become forbidden due to external reasons; for example, fasting on the day of Eid. Fasting is a permissible act but on this particular day it becomes *haram.* The day of Eid is the external condition that makes the act of fasting prohibited. Another example is conducting business transactions that contain usury. There are two opposite laws here, one is permissibility for business transactions and the other one is the prohibition of usury. Usury is the external condition that makes this type of business transaction forbidden. These acts are permissible from the aspect of their original state but with the interplay of the external conditions or attributes they are rendered *haram.* According to Ḫanafī jurists, legal results can be established based on these type of acts; they may constitute a means for legal results. For example, business transactions that contain usury are not deemed invalid (*bātil*) but they are considered to be corrupt (*fāsid*). If both parties continue with the transaction, the ownership rights for the goods can be established. However, this ownership cannot be deemed beneficial due to the words of the Lawgiver about usury, therefore, this ownership is considered *haram* and the act is a sin. Similarly, Ḫanafī jurists hold that lineage and inheritance can be established through illicit sexual relationships despite the act being unlawful.

SUMMARY: *HARAM* (PROHIBITED)

1. Prohibited acts are named *haram* and are absolutely forbidden by the Lawgiver in binding and definite terms.
2. Prohibition is recognized in the evidence in various ways: the use of the word *haram;* by abrogating the *halal;* with general terms of prohibition; with cautionary phrases and with the assignment of punishment.
3. There are two categories of *haram* acts: *haram li-dhatih* (forbidden for its own sake) and *haram li-ghayrih* (forbidden because of something else).
4. *Haram li-dhatih* acts are absolutely forbidden because they contain evil and bring harm. If someone performs them the act is deemed a sin and invalid and cannot bring a legal result.
5. *Haram li-ghayrih* is acts that are permissible in themselves but prohibited due to other reasons. Ḫanafī jurists hold that legal results can be established based on this type of act.

Makruh (Disliked)

Makruh acts are those that should be omitted based on evidence. However, the available evidence for these acts is not definite; rather it is open to interpretation. *Makruh* status is established with *dalil ẕannī* (speculative evidence) and is the opposite of *mandub* (recommended). *Makruh* does not constitute a binding law but omission of these acts is preferred. The majority of scholars hold that performing *makruh* does not incur punishment or blame.[440] On the other hand, Ḫanafī jurists maintain that only acts in the *makruh tanzihan* (somewhat disliked) category do not incur punishment or blame but *taḫriman makruh* (prohibitively disliked) acts do incur punishment. Denying *taḫriman makruh* is not disbelief but it is misguidance and worthy of punishment and performing these acts is a sin according to Ḫanafī jurists.

The evidence indicating the status of certain acts as *makruh* can be expressed in different forms:

a) The Lawgiver uses the Arabic word '*karahah*' (the root word of *makruh*) when He demands those liable to avoid certain acts. For example, the noble Prophet said:

> God prohibited disobedience towards parents, burying daughters alive, preventing the rights of others and asking for something that you do not deserve. He also disliked (*makruh*) the following acts for you; gossiping, asking too many questions and wasting the good.[441]

b) The Lawgiver uses the same form as for prohibition but there is evidence indicating that it is not *haram* but *makruh*. For example, in the verse God commanded: "*O you who believe! Do not ask about things which, if made manifest to you, would give you trouble.*"[442] In this verse the *makruh* act is conveyed in the form of prohibition but it only indicates dislike of such act.

c) The Lawgiver discourages the act. For example, the noble Prophet said: "The most disliked of permissible things in the sight of God is divorce."[443]

Ḫanafī jurists divided *makruh* into two types; *tanzihan makruh* (somewhat disliked) and *taḫriman makruh* (prohibitively disliked).

a) *Taḫriman makruh* (prohibitively disliked) is the acts for which there exists a firm command to omit them but they are based on probable evidence (*dalil-i ẕannī*) such as *khabar wāḫid* (reported by a single source), therefore they are not definite but are open to interpretation. For example, making a purchase offer to someone when he is already holding an offer from someone else is *taḫriman makruh*. Similarly, making a marriage offer to a woman who already has an offer

440 Abu Zahrah, *Uṣūl*, p. 36.
441 Bukhari, *Saḫīḫ, Riqaq*, hadith no: 22.
442 Qur'an 5: 101.
443 Tabrizi, *Mishkat*, vol.2, hadith no. 3280.

from another person is also *taḫriman makruh*. Both examples are conveyed by *khabar wāḫid* and do not constitute a definite prohibition but are speculative; for this reason they are not *haram* but *makruh*. Denying *taḫriman makruh* is not disbelief but it is misguidance and worthy of punishment. Performing these types of acts is a sin.

b) *Tanzihan makruh* (somewhat disliked) are acts are not issued by the Lawgiver with binding terms but are acts which it is recommended to avoid. For example, the Prophet instructed his followers to avoid eating raw onion and garlic before attending congregational Prayers. Acting against this recommendation is considered *tanzihan makruh*. Since *tanzihan makruh* are not strictly forbidden acts, performing them is not a sin. One who does not perform these acts is rewarded, while one who does perform them diminishes his rewards but is not deserving of punishment.

Summary: *Makruh* (Disliked)

1. *Makruh* acts are those that should be omitted based on evidence. However, the available evidence for these acts is speculative and open to interpretation.
2. The majority of scholars hold that performing *makruh* does not incur punishment or blame. For Ḫanafī jurists only *makruh tanzihan* (somewhat disliked) acts do not incur punishment or blame but *taḫriman makruh* (prohibitively disliked) acts do incur punishment.
3. Denying *taḫriman makruh* is not disbelief but it is misguidance and worthy of punishment and performing these acts is a sin.
4. The evidence indicating the status of certain acts as *makruh* can be expressed in the following ways: the Lawgiver uses the Arabic word '*karahah*': the Lawgiver uses the same form as for prohibition but there is evidence indicating that it is not *haram* but is *makruh*; the Lawgiver discourages the act.
5. Ḫanafī jurists divided *makruh* into two types; *tanzihan makruh* (somewhat disliked) and *taḫriman makruh* (prohibitively disliked).
6. *Taḫriman makruh* have a firm command to omit them but they are based on probable evidence (*dalil-i ẕannī*) such as *khabar wāḫid* (reported by a single source), therefore they are not definite but are open to interpretation. Performing these types of acts is a sin.
7. *Tanzihan makruh* are not issued by the Lawgiver with binding terms but are acts which it is recommended to avoid. Avoiding these acts is rewarded whilst performing them diminishes rewards but is not deserving of punishment.

Mubah (Permissible)

Mubah are the acts where it is left up to the liable person whether or not to perform them. It is understood from the evidence that the Lawgiver has left the option of action up to the person in regard to specific conducts. *Mubah* can be phrased in different ways:

a) The Lawgiver uses the word for permissibility (*halal*) for certain acts, for example; "*This day (all) pure, wholesome things have been made lawful for you*..."[444] the *mubah* act is conveyed with the word of permissibility (*halal*) in this verse.

b) *Mubah* is conveyed with expressions such as 'There is no sin' or 'There is no blame.' For example:

> He has made unlawful to you only carrion, and blood, and the flesh of swine, and that (the animal) which is offered in the name of other than God. Yet whoever is constrained by dire necessity to eat of them, provided he does not covet (that which is forbidden) nor transgress (the bounds of necessity), no sin shall be on him. Surely God is All-Forgiving, All-Compassionate.[445]

This verse indicates that unlawful things become lawful if one is constrained by dire necessity and this permissibility is conveyed with the expression 'No sin shall be on him.' A similar example is; "*There is no blame on the blind nor any blame on the lame nor any blame on the sick*..."[446]

c) *Mubah* may be conveyed in the form of a demand but it only indicates permissibility, for example; "...*Eat and drink of that which God has provided*..."[447]

d) In the case where no evidence exists for an act, the default legal value is permissibility (*istiṣḫāb baraat*) until the contrary is proved. In Islamic law the main principle is permissibility until otherwise indicated, therefore, if the legal value of a certain act is not clear, it is accepted as *mubah* until otherwise proven.

There is neither sin nor reward for avoiding or performing these acts. The legal value of each is the same with regard to their results.

Summary: *Mubah* (Permissible)

1. *Mubah* are the acts where the evidence shows the liable person can decide whether or not to perform them.

[444] Qur'an 5: 5.
[445] Qur'an 2: 173.
[446] Qur'an 24: 61.
[447] Qur'an 2: 60.

2. *Mubah* can be phrased in different ways: the Lawgiver uses the word for permissibility (*halal*) for certain acts; they are conveyed with expressions such as 'There is no sin' or 'There is no blame'; they may be conveyed in the form of a demand but it only indicates permissibility.
3. In the case where no evidence exists for an act, the default legal value is permissibility (*istiṣḫāb baraat*) until the contrary is proved.
4. There is neither sin nor reward for avoiding or performing these acts.

Aḫkām Wad'iyya (Declaratory Law)

Aḫkām wad'iyya (declaratory law) is a communication from the Lawgiver which renders a cause (*sabab*), a condition (*shart*) or an obstacle (*māni'*) for a ruling. It has been classified into three types; *sabab* (a cause), *shart* (a condition) and *māni'* (an obstacle).

Sabab (a Cause)

The definition for *sabab* (a cause) differs based on whether or not it covers *'illah* (an underlying reason). *Sabab* that covers *'illah* is defined as an attribute that either has or doesn't have a clear relationship with the law (*ḫukm*). It is assigned by the Lawgiver as the indicator of a law in such a way that its presence necessitates the presence of the law and its absence requires the contrary. If there is a clear relationship between an attribute and a law, this is called both *sabab* and *'illah*, however if there is no clear relationship between them it is only called *sabab*. For example, traveling is an attribute which has a clear relationship with the law (*ḫukm*), because the Lawgiver assigned the attribute of traveling as a cause (*sabab*) for not observing the Ramadan fast and the rule of permission is established based on this cause:

> ...Whoever is so ill that he cannot fast or on a journey (must fast the same) number of other days. God wills ease for you, and He does not will hardship for you...[448]

In this case, there is a clear relationship between the law permitting not fasting in Ramadan and the cause for this ruling is travel or being on a journey. Travel brings hardship and the Lawgiver permitted the travellers not to observe the Ramadan fast due to hardship. In this case travel is not only the cause (*sabab*) for this law but it is also the underlying reason (*'illah*).

[448] Qur'an 2: 185.

The following case is an example for *sabab* that does not have a relationship with the law. *Ẕuhr* Prayer becomes obligatory upon those liable to pray when the sun moves from its zenith at midday. The Lawgiver assigned this movement as the cause (*sabab*) for the obligation of the *Ẕuhr* Prayer, and if a person witnesses noon time he is obliged to perform the Prayer. However, there is no clear relationship between the attribute of movement of the sun and the obligation of the *Ẕuhr* Prayer; therefore, it is only *sabab* (a cause) but not *'illah* (an underlying reason) of this law.

Scholars differ in their opinion of whether *sabab* covers *'illah* or not. The scholars, who maintain that *sabab* does not cover *'illah*, define *sabab* as an attribute assigned by the Lawgiver to indicate the law; therefore its presence necessitates the presence of the law and its absence requires the contrary; there is no clear relationship between the law and the attribute. An example of this was mentioned above where the movement of the sun from its zenith is the cause of the obligation of *Ẕuhr* Prayer; however, it is not the underlying reason for the Prayer. Similarly the month of Ramadan is the cause for the obligation of the Ramadan fast but it does not have a clear relationship with the law of fasting.

The first definition of *sabab* is broader than the second; according to it, every *'illah* is also considered a *sabab* but every *sabab* is not deemed an *'illah*. In the second definition, *sabab* and *'illah* are essentially different concepts. For example, the case of not observing the Ramadan fast due to travel cannot be called *sabab* because there is not a clear relationship between the law and travel. An underlying reason has to exist, and this is hardship and difficulty. For these reasons the Lawgiver made it permissible for travellers to refrain from fasting. Conversely, in the case of the *Ẕuhr* Prayer, the movement of the sun and the obligation of *Ẕuhr* Prayer are not logically connected to each other, therefore the concept of *'illah* cannot be used in this case; rather it is only *sabab*.

Sabab has been divided into two categories from the view point of whether it is actionable by the liable person;

a) *Sabab* as an act of the liable person and he is able to perform it: for example, the act of travel is *sabab* for not observing the fast and it is also in the capacity of the liable person. If a person wishes to travel, he does not need to observe the fast.

b) *Sabab* that is beyond the power of the liable person; for example, the movement of the sun is *sabab* for the obligation of *Ẕuhr* Prayer. The obligation of Prayer and the movement of the sun are beyond the power of the liable people; they cannot affect these attributes.

Sabab is further divided into two categories with regards to the result (*mus-abbab*):

a) *Sabab* for *ahkām taklifiyya* (a cause for a defining law); for example, ownership of *nisab* (possessing certain amount of wealth) is *sabab* for the duty of *zakat* and giving a certain amount of charity. The marriage contract is *sabab* that renders a man and woman living together *halal* and divorce is *sabab* that renders this *halal* action *haram* so it is unlawful for them to live together.

b) *Sabab* as a result of an act of a liable person; for example, business transactions are *sabab* for achieving the right of ownership whilst giving property to a charity is *sabab* for losing the right of ownership.

There is one important point here; a law may require more than one condition and cause to exist. In this case, the ruling can only exist if all the conditions and causes are present and there is no obstacle (*māni'*) to it.

Summary: *Sabab* (a Cause)

1. The definition for *sabab* (a cause) differs based on whether or not it covers *'illah* (an underlying reason).
2. *Sabab* that covers *'illah* is defined as an attribute that either has or doesn't have a clear relationship with the law (*hukm*). It is assigned by the Lawgiver as the indicator of a law in such a way that its presence necessitates the presence of the law and its absence requires the contrary.
3. If there is a clear relationship between an attribute and a law, this is called both *sabab* and *'illah*, however if there is no clear relationship between them it is only called *sabab*.
4. Scholars differ in their opinion of whether *sabab* covers *'illah* or not.
5. The scholars, who maintain that *sabab* does not cover *'illah*, define *sabab* as an attribute assigned by the Lawgiver to indicate the law; there is no clear relationship between the law and the attribute.
6. The first definition of *sabab* is broader than the second; according to it, every *'illah* is also considered a *sabab* but every *sabab* is not deemed an *'illah*.
7. In the second definition, *sabab* and *'illah* are essentially different concepts.
8. *Sabab* has been divided into two categories from the view point of whether it is actionable by the liable person: *sabab* as an act of the liable person and he is able to perform it; *sabab* that is beyond the power of the liable person.

9. *Sabab* is further divided into two categories with regards to the result (*musabbab*): *sabab* for *aḫkām taklifiyya* (a cause for a defining law); *sabab* as a result of an act of a liable person.

Rukun (a Pillar)

Rukun is an attribute or pillar which constitutes a part of an act and the existence of this act depends on the presence of its pillars. Similarly the absence of a pillar results in the absence of the act. For example, *qiraat* (reciting the Qur'an) is a pillar of the Prayers and without this pillar the Prayer is invalid. Similarly, *ruqu'* (bowing) is another pillar of the Prayer and its absence results the invalidity of the Prayer. *Rukun* is both a condition and an essential part of an act.

Shart (a Condition)

Shart is an attribute or condition which must be present for an act to be valid, but it is not a part of the act. For example, ablution is *shart* (a condition) for the Prayer but it is not part of the Prayer. Facing *qibla* is a condition of the Prayer, without which the Prayer is invalid, but it is not part of the Prayer.

Rukun and *shart* are similar with regard to the result of the act. If either is missing the act is invalid. However, *rukun* is a part of the act, but *shart* is not part of it.

Shart has been classified into two categories;

a) *Shart* to establish a law. For example, if one is married and commits the sin of fornication the specific punishment is incurred. If one commits this crime whilst single (unmarried) the punishment of *rajm* (stoning) is not applied. Marriage is the condition of this law and without its presence the law cannot be applied. Another example is the case of murder; in order to apply the punishment of the death penalty (*qiṣaṣ*) for the murder case, the murderer must have killed his victim intentionally. If the crime happened unintentionally, the death penalty cannot be applied, because the condition of intentional killing is not present.

b) *Shart* for the validity of the legal law. For example, the testimony of two witnesses in the marriage act is a condition for the validity of the marriage. If the marriage contract is performed without witnesses it is not valid. A condition for being liable to pay *zakat* is the ownership for at least a year of *nisab* (a certain amount of money, gold, silver, etc.). The noble Prophet said: "There is no *zakat* on the items that do not remain in the possession of the liable person for one year."[449] For this reason a liable person is not responsible to give *zakat* when he obtains the amount of *nisab* unless he has possessed it for one year.

Summary: *Shart* (a Condition)

1. *Shart* is an attribute or condition which must be present for an act to be valid, but it is not a part of the act.
2. *Rukun* and *shart* are similar with regard to the result of the act. If either is missing the act is invalid. However, *rukun* is a part of the act, but *shart* is not part of it.
3. *Shart* has been classified into two categories: *shart* to establish a law and *shart* for the validity of the legal law.

Māni' (an Obstacle)

Māni' is an attribute or obstacle whose presence either nullifies the law or the cause for the law. The presence of *māni'* (an obstacle) results in the prevention of the application of the law. For example, killing a close relative intentionally with the view to gaining an early inheritance is an obstacle to the right of inheritance. The necessary conditions for the law of inheritance are present, such as being a close relative or being joined in marriage, but there is an obstacle to the application of the law which is intentional killing. Another example is the menstrual cycle and postnatal bleeding being an obstacle to the obligation of the Daily Prayers. The liable person is present during the set times and the Prayer becomes obligatory on them but because of the obstacle, the result of this conditions (the obligation to pray) is absent. As such, women who are in their menstrual cycles are not obliged to pray.

In some cases, *māni'* removes one of the necessary conditions of liability and a ruling (*ḫukm*) is not applied. For example, one who has money to the amount of *nisab* but has a debt that removes the condition of possessing *nisab* is not obliged to pay *zakat* because there is an obstacle to the application of the law. Indebted people are supposed to clear their debts and only afterwards, if the remaining money amounts to *nisab* are they liable to pay *zakat*.

Summary: *Māni'* (an Obstacle)

1. *Māni'* is an attribute or obstacle whose presence either nullifies the law or the cause for the law.

[449] Abu Dāwud, *Sunan, Zakat*, hadith no: 4.

2. The presence of *māni'* (an obstacle) results in the prevention of the application of the law.
3. In some cases, *māni'* removes one of the necessary conditions of liability and a ruling (*ḫukm*) is not applied.

Saḫīḫ (Valid), *Bātil* (Invalid) and *Fāsid* (Irregular)

These concepts are used to evaluate the acts of the liable person with regard to their validity or invalidity and are used by jurists to assess whether they are performed in the proper manner where the conditions and pillars exist. An act that is obligatory, recommended or permissible may be required to be performed in a certain manner by the Lawgiver. When the act is performed in its right manner it is deemed valid (*saḫīḫ*), otherwise it is null and void (*bātil*).[450] The acts have been classified into two categories; *ibadāt* (devotional acts) such as the five Daily Prayers, *zakat*, fasting, etc. and *muamalāt* (legal acts) such as buying, selling, leasing, business transactions, etc.

The essential pillars (*rukun*) and conditions (*shart*) for the acts of a liable person have been assigned by the Lawgiver and aid the jurists in evaluating the acts. If the essential pillars and conditions are not met by the liable person the act is not deemed valid (*bātil*). On the other hand, if all the conditions and pillars are fulfilled the acts are deemed valid (*saḫīḫ*). For example, the Prayer is a devotional act and has specific conditions and pillars which validate it. It becomes invalid (*bātil*) when one of the conditions or pillars is missing. Similarly, a contract is valid (*saḫīḫ*) when it fulfils all of its necessary conditions; otherwise it becomes void.

Acts are only valid and achieve the desired results if they are performed correctly which necessitates the presence of the pillars and conditions. A liable person who performs devotional (*ibadāt*) duties properly is freed of the responsibility and will be rewarded in the afterlife. Acts in the category of *muamalāt* are only valid if the necessary requirements are fulfilled. For example, a business transaction establishes the right of ownership of the buyer and the entitlement to possess the money of the seller. On completion, both sides are able to use their possessions as they wish. In the absence of any of the requisite pillars or conditions the transaction is rendered null and void.

The majority of scholars hold that an act, whether devotional or legal is either valid or invalid. Similarly, from the view point of the results, they do not separate *rukun* (essential pillar) from *shart* (a condition). Their view is that any defi-

---

450 Sadr al-Shari'ah, *al-Tawḫīd*, vol.1, p. 30.

ciency renders the act invalid (*bātil*). On the other hand, Ḫanafī jurists employ an intermediary category, *fāsid* (irregular), for legal acts between the valid (*saḫīḫ*) and invalid (*bātil*). All scholars agree that if there is a deficiency in the essential requirements of a legal act it is invalid. However, Ḫanafī jurists hold that if a deficiency in a legal act only affects a condition, it is *fāsid* (irregular) but not invalid and still produces some legal consequences despite its deficiency. For example, the marriage contract without witnesses is *fāsid* but not *bātil* and the contract must either be performed again in front of two witnesses to validate it, or it should be dissolved, even if the marriage has been consummated. In this case, the woman retains the right to her dowry and must observe the waiting period before re-marrying. The children of a *fāsid* marriage contract are legitimate but the woman does not have the right of inheritance or maintenance.

Ḫanafī jurists define *fāsid* as legal acts which are lawful but deficient with respect to their conditions. The deficiency can be rectified or the parties of the legal act can dissolve it. For example, selling a merchandise item without specifying the price for it is a *fāsid* contract but it is not void, therefore it has legal consequences. If the buyer receives the merchandise item by mutual agreement despite the price not being specified, he has the right of ownership. However, he is not able to use or benefit from the merchandise until the deficiency in the contract has been rectified.

Summary: *Saḫīḫ* (Valid), *Bātil* (Invalid), and *Fāsid* (Irregular)

1. These concepts are used by jurists to evaluate the acts of the liable person with regard to their validity or invalidity.
2. An act that is obligatory, recommended or permissible may be required to be performed in a certain manner by the Lawgiver. When the act is performed in its proper manner it is deemed valid (*saḫīḫ*) otherwise it is null and void (*bātil*).
3. The acts have been classified into two categories; *ibadāt* (devotional acts) and *muamalāt* (legal acts).
4. If the essential pillars (*rukun*) and conditions (*shart*) for the acts of a liable person are not met the act is not deemed valid (*bātil*). If they are met the act is deemed valid (*saḫīḫ*).
5. A liable person who performs devotional (*ibadāt*) duties properly is freed of the responsibility of these acts and will be rewarded in the afterlife.
6. Acts in the category of *muamalāt* are only valid if the necessary requirements are fulfilled.

7. The majority of scholars hold that an act in either category is either valid or invalid.
8. Ḫanafī jurists employ an intermediary category, *fāsid* (irregular), for legal acts between the valid (*saḫīḫ*) and invalid (*bātil*).
9. All scholars agree that if there is a deficiency in the essential requirements of a legal act it is invalid.
10. Ḫanafī jurists define *fāsid* as legal acts which are lawful but deficient with respect to their conditions. The deficiency can be rectified or the parties of the legal act can dissolve it.

'Aẕimah (Initial Rules) and *Rukhṣah* (Exemptions)

'Aẕimah is an initial ruling or law that the Lawgiver issued for every liable person in every condition but which was followed by an exemption (*rukhṣah*) which was issued to remove difficulty and hardship.[451] For example, drinking wine is prohibited as a general rule for all liable people and is an *aẕimah*. However, in cases of necessity, such as if it will save one from dying of thirst, it is permissible to drink it; this is a *rukhṣah*. According to some jurists, the entire law may be classified into general rules and related exemptions.

Other examples of *aẕimah* are *zakat*, the *Hajj*, fasting and the Daily Prayers which are enjoined by the Lawgiver upon all liable individuals. A law or ruling is considered to be *rukhṣah* if it makes an exemption from the general rule with the intention of bringing ease in difficult circumstances. An example is the Ramadan fast which is obligatory for all liable people and is *aẕimah*. However, the Lawgiver has made some exemptions and brought ease for the traveller, sick and elderly people making it permissible for them not to observe the fast. This brings ease to them and is called *rukhṣah*.

The exemptions remain valid as long as the reasons which bring the *rukhṣah* continue. For example, when the traveller returns home, he is no longer exempt from the fast so he is obliged to begin fasting. Another example is a person under persecution who is forced to denounce his belief; this has been permitted by God in the Qur'an:

> Whoever disbelieves in God after having believed—not him who is under duress, while his heart is firm in and content with faith, but the one who

[451] Sadr al-Shari'ah, *al-Tawḫīd*, vol.2, p. 686.

willingly opens up his heart to unbelief—upon them falls God's anger (His condemnation of them), and for them is a mighty punishment.[452]

It is permissible for a person who is under duress and in fear for his life to use the words of disbelief without intending them in his heart.

Rukhṣah comes after *'azimah*, in other words, without *'azimah rukhṣah* cannot be present. There is an initial command from the Lawgiver and then exemptions follow. For example, eating pork or drinking wine is initially prohibited by the Lawgiver but is made lawful for a dying person in efforts to save their life.

Rukhṣah may occur in four forms;[453] firstly, making unlawful things lawful because of bare necessity, for example, drinking wine at the point of extreme thirst which will lead to death. Secondly, neglecting a *wajib* element if it leads to hardship and difficulty, for example, shortening the Daily Prayers on a journey. Thirdly, validating a transaction which would normally be dissolved, for example, hiring, leasing and early sales are not valid but have been exempted from the general ruling to remove the difficulty upon the people. Lastly, *rukhṣah* occurs in the form of a concession to the Muslim nation from certain severe laws which were enjoined upon previous nations.[454] For example, the whole earth became clean and pure for Muslims enabling them to perform their Prayers on any clean spot of earth rather than having to pray in a *masjid*.[455]

Summary: *'Aẕimah* (Initial Rules) and *Rukhṣah* (Exemptions)

1. *Aẕimah* is an initial ruling or law that the Lawgiver issued for every liable person in every condition but which was followed by an exemption (*rukhṣah*) which was issued to remove difficulty and hardship.
2. Examples of *aẕimah* are *zakat*, the *Hajj*, fasting and the Daily Prayers which are enjoined by the Lawgiver upon all liable individuals.
3. A law or ruling is considered to be *rukhṣah* if it makes an exemption from the general ruling with the intention of bringing ease in difficult circumstances.
4. Exemptions remain valid for as long as the reasons which bring the *rukhṣah* continue.

---

452 Qur'an 16: 106.
453 Hashim Kamali, *Islamic Jurisprudence*, p. 294.
454 Kamali, *Islamic Jurisprudence*, p. 294.
455 Abu Zahrah, *Uṣūl*, p. 50.

5. *Rukhṣah* comes after *'a̱zimah*, in other words, without *'a̱zimah rukhṣah* cannot be present.
6. *Rukhṣah* may occur in four forms: making unlawful things lawful because of bare necessity; neglecting a *wajib* element if it leads to hardship and difficulty; validating a transaction which would normally be dissolved; and in the form of a concession to the Muslim nation.

Chapter 10

The Rules of Interpretation

The Rules of Interpretation

Introduction

A prerequisite for being able to deduce the law from the Qur'an and Sunnah is a detailed knowledge of the language contained within them. Jurists responsible for interpreting and deducing the law from these sources must have sufficient knowledge around the rules of interpretation, which are related to their linguistic aspects and not an essential part of the law itself. For this reason, the phrases contained within both the Qur'an and Sunnah and how they are used have been classified into categories from the aspect of their scope, clarity and level of certainty which directly impact the strength of the law.

The first step to understanding the Qur'an is to understand its language. A language has the same meaning for a text as the bodily features have for a human being in that the essential existence of a text lies in its meaning, as that of a human being lies within his spirit. The bodily features are the externalized form which the spirit of a human being has adopted and serve as a mirror of his character. Similarly, the language and styles of the Qur'an are the form of its meaning and cannot be separated from it.

In cases where the text is clear and the meaning is definite, it is not necessary to apply the rules of interpretation. However, if the text is unclear leaving it open to interpretation these rules are applied to comprehend the correct meaning.

Summary: Introduction

1. It is necessary for jurists to have a detailed knowledge of the language of the Qur'an and Sunnah to be able to interpret them and deduce the law.
2. This knowledge is linguistic and not a part of the law itself.
3. The phrases contained within both the Qur'an and Sunnah and how they are used have been classified into categories determining their impact on the law.
4. These linguistic rules are applied in cases where the text is unclear to be able to comprehend the intended meaning.

Ta'wil (Interpretation)

Ta'wil is the infinitive form of the root word '*a-wa-la*' and means to return.[456] The infinitive form *ta'wil* means to explain, to discover, to interpret, to translate and the result.[457] In Islamic terminology, it means giving one of the possible meanings for the verses[458] or giving the meaning for the verses according to their contexts.[459]

The word '*tafsīr*' is in the infinitive form and comes from either '*fa-sa-ra*' or '*sa-fa-ra.*'[460] The root '*fasara*' means to explain, discover, expose and uncover.[461] The other root '*safara*' means to uncover something that is covered, to enlighten and open.[462] Evidentially, both of these root words are close in meaning and it is possible that the word '*tafsīr*' may be derived from either one of them. Amin al-Khuli alludes to some differences between these two root words. He states that, '*safara*' is to discover something material or the outer dimension of things, but ''*fasara*' is to discover something immaterial or spiritual.[463] *Tafsīr* in the Qur'anic sciences is related to discovering the meanings of the verses.[464] The real explanation is only possible by the author, so the real *tafsīr* of the Qur'an lies in the explanations of God and His Messenger.

The word *ta'wil* is used fifteen times within the verses of the Qur'an. This word has multiple meanings, including; interpretation of the words,[465] the dreams[466] and the actions.[467] As such its use is related to explaining the meanings of the words and phrases, informing about real facts pertaining to events, predicting the results of certain things, and interpreting dreams. All the usages of *ta'wil* in the Qur'an are related to people, but one of them (Surah Ali Imran, verse 7) relates to God.

The Companions of the noble Prophet were hesitant to talk about *tafsīr*, because they understood that it was related to God and His Messenger and were fearful of making mistakes. In their time, *tafsīr* was understood as the explanations of God and the Prophet which were exactly true with no possibility of a

---

[456] Ibn Manzūr, *Lisan'ul 'Arab,* vol.11 p. 32.
[457] *Lisan'ul 'Arab*, vol.11, p. 33.
[458] Zarkashī, al-Burhān, vol. 2, p. 148.
[459] Tabarī, *Jami' al-Bayan*, vol.19, p. 8.
[460] Jawhari, *Siḫaḫ*, vol.2, p. 781.
[461] Rāghib al-Isfahānī, *al-Mufradaat*, p. 380.
[462] Ibn Manzūr, *Lisan'ul 'Arab*, vol.6, p. 369, *Siḫaḫ*, vol.2, p.686.
[463] al-Huli, *at-Tafsīr Maalimu Hayatihi ve Manhaj al-Yawm*, p. 5.
[464] Ibn Manzūr, *Lisan'ul 'Arab*, p. 55.
[465] Qur'an, 3: 7.
[466] Qur'an, 12: 36.
[467] Qur'an, 17: 35.

mistake. The word *ta'wil* is used more often because it implies possible meanings rather than stating exact fact.

Imam Māturidī explains the difference between *tafsīr* and *ta'wil* as follows:

> *Tafsīr* refers to the companions but *ta'wil* refers to Muslim jurists. The companions witnessed the occasions, the history of the verses and they knew the reasons behind the verses very well. For this reason, the explanation of the verses was clear for them and it was the real *tafsīr* of the verses. This type of explanation is like learning something directly from a scholar or witnessing it in person. When a person says 'This is the *tafsīr* of this verse' he means by this statement 'God is my witness and the certain meaning of this verse is as I say.' This is very dangerous and the Prophet warned people about this. He said, 'If any of you makes *tafsīr* on Qur'an based on his opinion (without having necessary conditions for it) he better prepare his place in hell.'[468]
>
> In *ta'wil*, the scholar chooses one of the possible meanings for the verse, but it is very difficult to do this in *tafsīr*. In *ta'wil*, a scholar doesn't invoke God as a witness for his interpretation, nor does he say this is the real meaning of this verse. He does not claim that God's purpose is his interpretation of the verse. The scholar explains that the words are what are usually used in the human language for these meanings and God knows best.[469]

For jurists, *ta'wil* and *tafsīr* are used for the same purpose; to clarify the law and to determine the purpose of the Lawgiver by examining the usage of the words and phrases from a linguistic perspective. We should also bear in mind that in the context of *Uṣūl al-Fiqh*, especially in our discussion of the rules of interpretation, it is *ta'wil* rather than *tafsīr* with which we are primarily concerned.[470]

SUMMARY: *TA'WIL* (INTERPRETATION)

1. *Ta'wil* in Islamic terminology means giving one of the possible meanings for the verses or giving the meaning for the verses according to their contexts.
2. *Tafsīr* in the Qur'anic sciences is related to discovering the meanings of the verses and this lies in the explanations of God and His Messenger.
3. *Ta'wil* is used fifteen times within the verses of the Qur'an and is related to explaining the meanings of the words and phrases, informing about

---

468 Tirmidhi, *Sunan, Kitāb at-Tafsīr*, 2951.

469 Māturidī, *Sarh-u Ta'wilat al-Qur'an*, p. 2.

470 Kamali, *Islamic Jurisprudence*, p. 88.

real facts pertaining to events, predicting the results of certain things, and interpreting dreams.

4. The Companions of the noble Prophet were hesitant to talk about *tafsīr*, because they understood that it was related to God and His Messenger and were fearful of making mistakes.
5. For jurists, *ta'wil* and *tafsīr* are used to clarify the law and to determine the purpose of the Lawgiver by examining the usages of the words and phrases from a linguistic perspective.

Clear and Unclear Words

Words are divided into two categories according to their clarity; clear and unclear words. Clear words convey meaning and do not need any interpretation. Unclear words are ambiguous and require clarification; without applying the rules of interpretation, the law cannot be based on these words. These two main categories have each been subdivided into four further categories which are explained individually.

Clear Words

Clear words have four subcategories based on their level of clarity and the strength of their meaning: *ẕāhir, naṣṣ, mufassar* and *muhkam*.

Ẕāhir (Manifest)

Ẕāhir is a word or phrase conveying a clear meaning which is understood when it is heard. However, the word or phrase does not express the principal meaning of the text and is open to interpretation. In other words, *ẕāhir* conveys the secondary meaning of the text. For example:

> As to those who devour interest, (even though they seem, for a time, to be making a profit), they turn out like one whom Satan has bewitched and confounded by his touch, (and they will rise up (from their graves in the same way before God). That is because they say interest is just like trading, whereas God has made trading lawful, and interest unlawful.[471]

In this verse the principle meaning is the difference between trade and usury and from this aspect this verse is *naṣṣ*. However, the secondary meaning of this verse is that trade is lawful and usury is unlawful, and from this aspect the verse is *ẕāhir*. Another example is the verse:

[471] Qur'an 2: 275.

> If you fear that you will not be able to observe their rights with exact fairness when you marry the orphan girls (in your custody), you can marry, from among other women (who are permitted to you in marriage and) who seem good to you, two, or three, or four. However, if you fear that (in your marital obligations) you will not be able to observe justice among them, and then content yourselves with only one...[472]

The principle meaning of this verse is observing the rights of orphan girls who are in custody, and treating them well. This verse from this aspect is *naṣṣ* because it conveys the principle meaning of the text. However, other meanings can be understood from this verse including the permissibility of polygamy and, if one is afraid of not being just, marrying just one woman. These are not the principle meanings or the essential purpose of this verse but are secondary meanings and therefore *ẕāhir*.

Ẕāhir text conveys binding law and it is obligatory (*wājib*) to act upon it. *Ẕāhir* words can be *āam* (general) and *khās* (specific), and for this reason are open to interpretation and limitation (*takhsis*). They are also open to abrogation (*naskh*) but this was only possible during the lifetime of the noble Prophet.

Naṣṣ (Evident)

Naṣṣ literally means 'a word' and this is usually the term jurists use to refer to the words of the Qur'an and Sunnah. It is defined by the scholars of *uṣūl* as the words which convey the principle meaning of the text, because the essential purpose of the text is understood from *naṣṣ*. As previously explained, in *ẕāhir* the principle meaning and the essential purpose of the text is not understood. In *naṣṣ* however, the jurists understand both the essential purpose of the text and also its principle meaning.

Naṣṣ can be general (*āam*) or specific (*khās*) and it is clearer and stronger than *ẕāhir*, therefore, if there is a conflict between *naṣṣ* and *ẕāhir*, the former is preferred. It is obligatory (*wājib*) to act based on *naṣṣ* words. *Naṣṣ* is open to interpretation and limitation (*takhsis*) and had the possibility of abrogation in the lifetime of the Prophet.

Mufassar (Explained)

Mufassar is the words that clearly convey the meaning and the purpose of the text, including the principle meaning; it is not open to interpretation or limita-

[472] Qur'an 4: 3.

tion. In this way it differs from *naṣṣ* which is open to interpretation. However, *mufassar* words were liable to abrogation during the lifetime of the Prophet. For example in the verse, "*...fight all together against those who associate partners with God just as they fight against you all together...*"[473], the phrase '*those who associate partners with God*' (*mushrikin*) is general and open to interpretation; however, the phrase 'all together' removed this probability and therefore the text is *mufassar*.

Mufassar can be in two forms; firstly, self-explained words or texts and secondly, ambiguous text which is clarified and explained by another text.[474] For example, the Qur'an contains some ambiguous concepts such as the Prayers (*salah*), charity (*zakat*), the greater pilgrimage (*Hajj*) and fasting (*sawm*), etc. Details of these were explained by the Prophet which makes them *mufassar*. The Prophet removed the ambiguity from devotional matters by his practices; 'Perform the Prayers the way you see me performing them'[475], and regarding the *Hajj* 'take from me the rituals of the *Hajj*.' [476]

Mufassar text infers obligation and it is not open to interpretation. In the time of the Prophet there was the possibility of abrogation of this type of text. *Mufassar* is stronger than *naṣṣ*, and in the case of a conflict between them, the *mufassar* is preferred. For example, two different hadiths exist about the status of the ablution of a woman who has chronic vaginal bleeding (*mustaḫada*);

> A woman who is *mustaḫada* (a woman who has chronic vaginal bleeding) must make a new ablution for every Prayer[477] and

> A woman who is *mustaḫada* must make a new ablution at the time of every obligatory Prayer.[478]

The first hadith is *naṣṣ* and is open to interpretation, because it does not make it clear if *mustaḫada* makes ablution for every Prayer regardless of whether the Prayer is *wājib*, *fard* or Sunnah. However, the second hadith clarifies this ambiguity and therefore it is *mufassar*. This hadith explains that one ablution performed during each obligatory time is sufficient for *mustaḫada* and the woman is permitted to perform as many Prayers as she wishes with this ablution until the next obligatory Prayer time.

---

473 Qur'an 9: 36.

474 Abu Zahra, *Uṣūl*, p. 96.

475 Tabrizi, *Mishkat*, vol.1, p. 215, hadith no. 683

476 Shātibī, *Muwafaqaat*, vol.3, p. 178.

477 Abu Dāwud, *Sunan, The Book of Prayer*, hadith no: 294.

478 Abu Dāwud, *Sunan, The Book of Prayer*, hadith no: 304.

Muhkam

Muhkam is a word or text whose meaning is very clear and is not open to interpretation or abrogation. An example of this is the verse: *"Their reward is with their Lord: Gardens of perpetual bliss through which rivers flow, abiding therein forever."*[479] This verse states that the believers will stay in Paradise forever. The expression 'forever' makes this verse *muhkam*, because after this expression the verse cannot be abrogated or interpreted.

There are two types of *muhkam*; the first is a word or text whose meaning is clear and needs no further explanation. For example, the noble Prophet said; "*Jihad* remains valid till the day of resurrection."[480] This hadith clearly states that *jihad* will remain valid forever. The expression 'forever' removes the possibility of abrogation and thus it is *muhkam*. The other type of *muhkam* is *mufassar* words or text that remains the same after the death of the Prophet because the possibility of abrogation is removed. This type became *muhkam* as a result of the Prophet's death but is not *muhkam* in itself. It includes things such as the Prayers, *zakat* and *Hajj*.

It is obligatory to act upon *muhkam* text and it is neither open to interpretation nor abrogation. *Muhkam* is the strongest evidence and in case of a conflict between the previous types, *muhkam* is preferred.

Summary: Clear Words

1. Clear words have four subcategories based on their level of clarity and the strength of their meaning: *ẕāhir, naṣṣ, mufassar* and *muhkam*.
2. *Ẕāhir* (manifest) is a word or phrase conveying a clear meaning but which does not express the principal meaning of the text and is open to interpretation.
3. *Ẕāhir* text conveys binding law and it is obligatory (*wājib*) to act upon it. It can be *āam* (general) and *khās* (specific), and for this reason is open to interpretation and limitation (*takhsis*) and abrogation (*naskh*).
4. *Naṣṣ* (evident) is the words which convey the principle meaning of the text.
5. *Naṣṣ* can be general (*āam*) or specific (*khās*) and it is clearer and stronger than *ẕāhir*,
6. It is obligatory (*wājib*) to act based on *naṣṣ* words. *Naṣṣ* is open to interpretation and limitation (*takhsis*) and abrogation.

[479] Qur'an 98: 8.

[480] Abu Dāwud, *Sunan*, Jihad, hadith no: 702.

7. *Mufassar* (explained) is the words that convey the meaning and the purpose of the text, including the principle meaning, completely clearly; it is not open to interpretation and limitation but was liable to abrogation.
8. *Mufassar* can be in two forms; self-explained words or texts and ambiguous text which is clarified and explained by another text.
9. *Mufassar* text infers obligation and it is not open to interpretation but was open to abrogation.
10. *Mufassar* is stronger than *naṣṣ*.
11. *Muhkam* is a word or text whose meaning is very clear and is not open to interpretation or abrogation.
12. *Muhkam* has two types; a word or text whose meaning is clear in itself and needs no further explanation, and *mufassar* words or text that remains the same after the death of the Prophet because the possibility of abrogation is removed.
13. It is obligatory to act upon *muhkam* text and it is neither open to interpretation nor abrogation.
14. *Muhkam* is the strongest evidence.

Unclear Words

Unclear words are the phrases which are ambiguous and unclear and rely on external aid to uncover the purpose of the text. If the ambiguity of the text is removed by the *ijtihād* of the jurists it is classified as *khafī* (secret) and *mushkil* (difficult). If the ambiguity of the text can only be clarified by the Lawgiver, the words are classified as *mujmal* (brief) and *mutashābih* (complex).[481] The order of the types beginning with the most unclear is *mutashābih* (complex), then *mujmal* (brief), after that *mushkil* (difficult) and lastly *khafī* (secret).

Khafī (Secret)

Khafī is a word or text which, due to external reasons, is ambiguous and this can only be removed by the research of the jurists. In fact, *khafī* has a basic meaning and is clear, but when it comes to its application in some cases it becomes ambiguous and needs further explanation.[482]

An example of this is the penal law for the crime of theft in the Qur'an and Sunnah. It is not clear if this concept covers the crimes of pickpocketing (*nash-*

[481] Khallaf, *'Ilm*, p. 162.
[482] Sarakhsī, *Uṣūl*, vol.1, p. 167.

shal) or theft of the shrouds of the dead (*nabbash*), and due to this ambiguity, the word *sariq* (thief) becomes *khafī* in those cases. In the case of pickpocketing, the crime differs from theft in that the victim is awake during the crime. The difference between ordinary theft and stealing the shrouds of the dead is that the dead cannot protect their goods. Scholars hold different views on the punishments for these two crimes because of the ambiguity in the scope of the word *sariq*. Imam Shāfi'ī and Abu Yusuf hold that the punishment of the thief is applied for a man who steals the shroud of the dead, however, the majority of scholars do not agree. Ḫanafī scholars hold that the punishment for pickpocketing is the same as the punishment for theft.

Mushkil (The Difficult)

Mushkil is more ambiguous than *khafī*; in these cases the meaning of the word is unclear because the word itself is unclear rather than the application of it. In the absence of external evidence it is impossible to understand *mushkil* whereas *khafī* can be understood after some research by the scholars. In both cases there is a need for further explanation to clarify the text.

The reason for the ambiguity of *mushkil* words is that they do not convey a specific meaning, but have two or more meanings and the text does not make it clear which meaning is intended. It is the role of the *mujtahid* to investigate the text and prefer one of the meanings as the purpose of the Lawgiver before implementing the rule.[483]

An example of this is the verse: "*Divorced women shall keep themselves in waiting for three quru.*"[484] The word '*quru*' in this verse has two meanings; menstruation and the clean period and the rule will be different according to which meaning is preferred. Ḫanafī scholars are of the opinion that the correct meaning of *quru* is menstruation whereas Shāfi'ī scholars believe the correct meaning is the clean period. For this reason, words which have more than one meaning and do not clearly indicate which meaning is intended by the text are classified as *mushkil*.

It is obligatory upon the *mujtahid* to investigate the text and choose the correct meaning before issuing the fatwa. After this investigation, it is *wājib* to act upon this ruling.

---

483 Badran, *Uṣūl*, p. 413.

484 Qur'an 2: 228.

Mujmal (Brief)

Mujmal is more ambiguous than *mushkil*.[485] It means an ambiguous word or text whose meaning can only be understood by the explanation of the Lawgiver. In other words, the human intellect cannot clarify the ambiguity of this word; it is only removed by the extra explanation of the Lawgiver. There are three reasons for the ambiguity of the *mujmal*;

a) A word may have more than one meaning and there is no indication as to which is the correct one. For example, the Arabic word '*mawlā*' is a homonym meaning both a freed slave and the master who freed the slave. If a person stipulates in their will that on his death his *mawlā* will get one third of his inheritance the will is invalid, according to the Ḫanafī School, provided that this person has two types of *mawlā*; his freed slave and the master who freed him.

b) The word may be used with a meaning that is different than its literal meaning; for example, *salah* (the Daily Prayers), *zakat* (charity), *Hajj* (pilgrimage) and *sawm* (fasting). Each of these words gained a new concept with the advent of Islam. The Lawgiver used them with a different meaning than had previously been known and which is also different to the literal meaning.

c) The word may be totally unfamiliar. For example, the Arabic word '*halu'an*' is used in the verse; "*Surely human has been created as halu'an.*" If the following verses did not explain the meaning of this word, it would be impossible to understand its meaning; "*Fretful when evil visits him and niggardly when good visits him.*"[486] Based on this explanation, the meaning of *halu'an* is impatient and niggard.

In all of these cases, the only source to remove the ambiguity is the Lawgiver. This category of word remains ambiguous until it is clarified by the Lawgiver and the *mujtahid* cannot take action based on this type of word until it is clarified. When the *mujmal* is explained and the ambiguity is removed, it turns into a *mufassar*. However, if the explanation is incomplete or insufficient to remove the ambiguity, the *mujmal* becomes a *mushkil*. After this, the *mujtahid* investigates the meaning. For example, the word *riba* (usury) remained ambiguous in the text because the explanations of the Lawgiver were insufficient for removing the ambiguity for the goods.[487] The noble Prophet explained six different forms of usury but still the ambiguity about other goods remained requiring further investigation and clarification.

---

485 Taftazani, *Talwīḫ*, vol.1, 127.

486 Qur'an 70: 20–21.

487 Khallaf, *'Ilm*, pp. 173–175.

Mutashābih (Complex)

Mutashābih is a word or text with ambiguous meaning which has not been clarified either by the Lawgiver or by external evidence. This is the most ambiguous category of unclear words.[488]

Mutashābih means;

a) To be similar or resemble.

b) To complement one another.

c) To be doubtful or uncertain in meaning.

d) Difficult to differentiate because of equality in similarities.

In the Qur'anic sciences, *mutashābih* means verses which are not very clear or completely agreed upon, or those that are open to more than one interpretation. In other words, it has many meanings, needs explanation and the meanings cannot be known through the application of reason. Examples in this category are, the time of the Day of Judgment and the *huruf al-muqatta'* (conjecture letters) at the beginning of some *surahs.* One of the verses actually states that some parts of the Qur'an are *mutashābih*;

> It is He Who has sent down on you this (glorious) Book, wherein are verses absolutely explicit and firm: they are the core of the Book, others being *mutashābih*. Those in whose hearts is swerving pursue what is allegorical in it, seeking (to cause) dissension, and seeking to make it open to arbitrary interpretation, although none knows its interpretation save God. And those firmly rooted in knowledge say: "We believe in it (in the entirety of its verses, both explicit and allegorical); all is from our Lord"; yet none derives admonition except the people of discernment.[489]

Mutashābih does not mean that it is impossible to comprehend, rather it means that there are many possible meanings; for this reason, it is difficult to prefer one meaning to others. There are various methods to remove ambiguity in *mutashābih*. One of these methods is to refer *mutashābih* verses to the *muhkam* since *muhkam* text is the essence of the Qur'an. All the religious books sent by God contain both *muhkam* and *mutashābih* parts and the latter always refers to the former, thus the *mutashābih* in the Qur'an's is referred to its *muhkam*.

The *mutashābih* verses are those which, having more than one meaning, require other evidence in order to be understood. The reason for multiple meanings is that time progresses, conditions change, human information increases,

---

[488] Sarakhsī, *Uṣūl*, vol.1, p. 169.

[489] Qur'an, 3: 7.

and the verses accommodate the many levels of intellect existent in humankind. The Qur'an, being the Word of God, addresses all levels of understanding from the time of its revelation to the Day of Resurrection. It utilises metaphors, similes, personifications and parables to explain matters that cannot be easily understood. This form of explanation does not harm the unchanging, essential truths of the religion for God has made clear His demands relating to faith, worship, morality, and the mandatory duties and prohibitions. The *mutashābih* (allegorical) verses contain relative truths which can be understood by considering the relevant verses and with reference to the *muhkam* verses.

Because of the realities of human life in this world, there are more truths than absolute, unchanging ones. To understand this we can use a crystal chandelier as an analogy. Those observing the chandelier will all perceive different colours or lights of varying strengths even though the light remains the same. These differences arise from the different shapes of the crystals in the chandelier, and the different angles of the crystals. In the same way, God included in the Qur'an several allegorical verses to provide unlimited meanings with limited words to all levels of intellect and understanding, to be a guide until the Last Day. In this way, all people of all kinds are invited to reflect on the Book and to be guided to the truth. It should not be forgotten that an exact resemblance is not sought between that which is compared and that to which it is being compared. Since the allegorical verses have multiple meanings, the interpreters of the Qur'an may be able to discover one or more of those meanings. Each of their discoveries can be regarded as being true, provided it is in conformity with the *muhkam* verses and the essentials of Islam, the rules of Arabic, and the rules of the science of interpretation. But, whichever meaning is deduced by the scholar, the exact meaning of these verses is always referred to God, the All-Knowing.[490]

Summary: Unclear Words

1. Unclear words are the words or phrases which are ambiguous and unclear relying on external aid to uncover the purpose of the text. There are four types: *mutashābih* (complex), *mujmal* (brief), *mushkil* (difficult) and *khafī* (secret).
2. *Khafī* (secret) is a word or text which, due to external reasons, is ambiguous and the meaning can only be removed by the research of the jurists.

490 Ünal, *The Qur'an with Annotated Interpretation*, see the footnote for 3:7.

3. *Mushkil* (the difficult) is when the meaning of the word is unclear because the word itself is unclear rather than the application of it.
4. The reason for the ambiguity of *mushkil* words is that they do not convey a specific meaning, but have two or more meanings and the text does not make it clear which meaning is intended.
5. *Mujmal* (brief) means an ambiguous word or text whose meaning can only be understood by the explanation of the Lawgiver, not by human intellect.
6. There are three reasons for the ambiguity of the *mujmal*; a word may have more than one meaning and there is no indication as to which is the correct one; the word may be used with a meaning different than its literal meaning; the word may be totally unfamiliar.
7. When the *mujmal* is explained and the ambiguity is removed, it turns into a *mufassar*. However, if the explanation is incomplete or insufficient to remove the ambiguity, the *mujmal* turns into a *mushkil.*
8. *Mutashābih* (complex) is a word or text with ambiguous meaning which has not been clarified either by the Lawgiver or external evidence.
9. *Mutashābih* means; to be similar or resemble; to complement one another; to be doubtful or uncertain in meaning; difficult to differentiate because of equality in similarities
10. In the Qur'anic sciences, *mutashābih* means verses which are not very clear or completely agreed upon, or those that are open to more than one interpretation.
11. There are various methods to remove ambiguity in *mutashābih* including referring *mutashābih* verses to the *muhkam.*
12. The *mutashābih* verses are those which, having more than one meaning, require other evidence in order to be understood.

The *'Āam* (General) and the *Khās* (Specific)

The words or the text are divided into two categories according to their scope; *āam* (general) and *khās* (specific). This division is conceptual and is very important to identify the value of the law. According to the majority of scholars, the general words do not convey definite meaning but the specific words do.

The *āam* (general) is a word which covers all the instances in its own category and does not impose limitations on the number.[491] In other words, it is used in a general way without specifying any group or number. For example, 'Every

[491] Ghazali, *Muṣtaṣfā*, vol.2, p. 12.

believer enters the paradise' is an *āam* (general) statement, because it covers every believer without specifying a particular number or nation. *Āam* is a word with a single meaning that covers an unlimited number without restrictions. The words remain general if they are not limited or restricted in some way. Similarly the statements of the Qur'an and Sunnah are deemed general by jurists unless a limit or restriction is indicated.[492]

When a word is applied to a limited number, including everything to which it can be applied, for instance, one or two or a hundred, it is referred to as *khās* (specific).[493] *Khās* is applied to a single subject or a specified number of objects; the scope of its application is limited. A word which addresses specific individuals such as Mahmud, Amr, or specific species such as a bird or a horse is considered *khās*.[494] The *khās* word applies to a limited number, be it a genus, or a species, or a particular individual; as long as it applies to a single subject, or a specified number thereof, it is *khās*.[495] Legal rules conveyed by *khās* words or text are definite in their application and not open to interpretation as long as there is no evidence to contradict this.[496] For example, the compensation for breaking an oath is to feed ten destitute people,[497] the number is specific which makes it *khās* and, therefore, it is definite and cannot be changed.

Generality is an attribute because it is an indication of the scope of the words. *Āam* applies to all the members of a specific set, no matter how small or large that set is. Some Qur'anic verses have a very wide, general application including all human beings, or all Muslims, etc. Other verses are restricted in their application to certain special circumstances only.

A word may be *āam* (general) in different ways;

a) By its form: such as women, teachers and believers, "*Prosperous indeed are the believers.*"[498]

b) By its meaning only: such as human and nation, "*Most certainly, human is in loss.*"[499]

---

[492] Badran, *Uṣūl*, p. 375.

[493] Kamali, *Principles of Islamic Jurisprudence*, p. 102.

[494] Abdur Rahim, *Jurisprudence*, p. 79.

[495] Kamali, p. 102.

[496] Pazdawi, *Uṣūl*, vol.1, p. 79.

[497] Qur'an 5: 89.

[498] Qur'an 23: 1.

[499] Qur'an 103: 2.

c) By prefixing pronouns like all, every, entire, etc., to common nouns: "*It is He Who created all that is in the world for you.*"[500]

d) *Nakra* (undefined) words convey a general meaning in prohibition and condition: In the verse, "*There is no compulsion in the Religion*"[501], the word 'compulsion' is *nakra* (undefined) and therefore it covers every kind of compulsion.

e) By pronouncements (*ism mawsul*) such as which, that, whom, etc.: "*To God belongs all that is in the heavens and the earth*"[502] and "*God strengthens in guidance those who have sought and found guidance.*"[503]

f) The condition pronounces; "*Whatever good you spend (in charity and other good causes) is to your own benefit*"[504] and "*whoever of you is present this month, must fast it.*"[505]

g) By using question nouns; "*Who is better in religion than he who has submitted his whole being to God*"[506] and "*Where, now, are those beings that you have deified and invoked apart from God?*"[507]

Āam covers all of the instances that the word is applicable to: the general form of the command is implemented for every member that the general word covers. However, scholars dispute the value of the general words as to whether or not they convey definite evidence.[508] The Maliki, Shāfi'ī and Hanbalī schools hold that *āam* words do not convey definite meaning because evidence covering all instances is speculative (*ẕannī*). There is a possibility of limitation and restriction for *āam* expressions. Most *āam* words have been specified in some way and only a few have remained general without being limited or restricted. Therefore, there is doubt over whether general words include all the instances. The majority of scholars hold that *āam* can be specified (*takhsis*) with speculative (*ẕannī*) evidence which renders conflict between *āam* (general) and *khās* (specific) impossible. In other words, *khās* is applied in its own scope and *āam* is applied in the area that *khās* did not specify. This is because *khās* conveys definite evidence and in case of conflict with *āam*, *khās* is preferred.

500 Qur'an 2: 29.
501 Qur'an 2: 256.
502 Qur'an 2: 284.
503 Qur'an 19: 76.
504 Qur'an 2: 272.
505 Qur'an 2: 185.
506 Qur'an 4: 125.
507 Qur'an 7: 37.
508 Shawkānī, *Irshād al-Fuhūl*, p. 100.

The view of the Ḫanafī School is that *āam* is definite evidence, because it is established for this purpose. In other words, the general words are used by the Lawgiver to include all the instances in them. If there is no evidence to prove their restriction or limitation, *āam* remains as it is and conveys definite evidence. Without proof, *āam* cannot be specified (*takhsis*), the possibility of specification is rare and it does not affect the definite nature of *āam*. Ḫanafī scholars hold that *āam* words cannot be specified with *ẕannī* (speculative) evidence. As speculative proof cannot limit or restrict a definitive proof, there is no conflict between *āam* and *khās,* and both of them are applied separately in their own scope. Based on this criterion, Ḫanafī scholars maintain that it is *haram* (prohibited) to eat meat from an animal that hasn't been slaughtered whilst uttering *basmala* (the Name of God). God declared in the Qur'an;

> Do not eat of that which is slaughtered in the name of other than God and over which God's Name has not been pronounced (at the time of its slaughtering), for that is indeed a transgression."[509]

This verse is *āam* and definite evidence. There is a hadith which is both *khabar wāḫid* (a single source report) and *ẕannī* (speculative) evidence which states that it is lawful to eat from the meat of animal as long as it has been slaughtered by a Muslim; it isn't necessary for them to utter the Name of God as they slaughter. Ḫanafī scholars hold, however, that the verse cannot be limited or restricted in scope by the hadith. Their reasoning is that the hadith is *ẕannī* evidence whereas the verse is *qat'ī* (definitive) and as such, it takes preference. Shāfi'ī scholars hold that the verse can be specified by the hadith, because they believe that both are speculative, therefore one can specify the other. Hence, according to Shāfi'ī scholars it is permissible to eat the meat of animals which are slaughtered by Muslims regardless of whether they utter the Name of God or not.

Another demonstration of the conflict between *āam* and *khās* is the *nisab* (minimum amount to be responsible to give *zakat*) value for agricultural crops and fruits. Ḫanafī jurists hold that there is no minimum value (*nisab*) which constitutes obligation of *zakat* on agricultural crops and fruits, but the majority of scholars hold that the minimum amount is 653 kg (five *wasaq*). The dispute is based on two hadiths declaring the *nisab* amounts for agricultural crops; one is *āam* and the other one is *khās*;

[509] Qur'an 6: 121.

Whatever is watered by the sky is subject to a tithe[510] and

There is no charity in less than five *awsuq* (653 kg).[511]

The first hadith is *āam* and contains a general ruling about agricultural crops, but the second hadith is *khās* and sets a limitation on the amount of agricultural crops subject to *zakat*. The majority of scholars agree that the second hadith restricts the ruling of first hadith. On the other hand, Ḫanafī scholars hold that first hadith abrogated the second because the first hadith was expressed by the Prophet after the second one causing an abrogation. For Ḫanafī scholars, when the *āam* is revealed after the *khās*, the former abrogates the latter completely; therefore, they hold that there is no minimum amount (*nisab*) for the obligation of *zakat* in agricultural crops.

There are three different types of *āam*;

a) The definitive *āam*: this applies to a word or piece of text whose content indicates that there is no possibility of limitation or restriction. For example the verse; "*No living creature is there moving on the earth but its provision depends on God*..."[512] is a general law of God and is unchangeable.

b) *Āam* in wording but *khās* in meaning: this is a word or a piece of text that is expressed in a general way but the meaning is specific. For example; "*Pilgrimage to the House is a duty owed to God by all who can afford a way to it*."[513] The first expression highlights that *Hajj* is duty upon all human beings. However, this injunction is then restricted to only those who can afford it.

c) *Āam* in wording but the text does not indicate whether it is general or specific. This applies to general statements in a variety of different ways. For example the verse; "*Divorced women shall keep themselves in waiting for three menstrual courses*..."[514] does not make it clear if it includes every type of divorced woman such as one whose marriage was not consummated. If there is no evidence to restrict this general rule, it is applied as it is. However, in this case, there is evidence which indicates a specific rule for women whose marriage was not consummated.

[510] Al-Tabrizi, *Mishkat*, vol.1, hadith no: 1794.
[511] Al-Tabrizi, *Mishkat*, vol.1, hadith no: 1797.
[512] Qur'an 11: 6
[513] Qur'an 3: 97.
[514] Qur'an 2: 228.

Āam can be specified or limited within the same text or in another piece of text. If a general word is restricted to its specific meaning only, it includes only those specific instances. There are many examples of *takhsis* (limitation or restriction) in the Qur'an and Sunnah. For Ḫanafī scholars, if *takhsis* occurs in a different location it is only accepted if the two texts are parallel to each other in chronology. If this is not the case, the later *takhsis* abrogates the earlier and it is then categorised as *naskh* (abrogation) rather than *takhsis*.

Takhsis (limitation or restriction) can occur in the form of an exception from a general statement, a condition, a quality, or by indicating the extent of the original proposition. Each of these has the effect of limiting and specifying the scope of the general proposition.[515] For example, the general rule for the documentation of commercial transactions where payment will be made later is restricted by the indication that if both sides trust each other it is not necessary to record it.[516] Similarly, the general rule indicating the share of the husband in the inheritance of his deceased wife is restricted by the condition of the woman not having children. In this case, the man inherits half of his wife's estate.[517]

The majority of scholars agree that the *āam* can be restricted or limited according to independent reasons. Ḫanafī scholars specify three reasons that can restrict the *āam*; the intellect, custom (*'urf*) and textual evidence. They are independent reasons and not part of the *āam* text. The majority of scholars add three more categories; the senses, *ijma'* and the statement of the Companions. Each of these reasons is explained with examples;

a) *Takhsis* by the senses; for example, in the verse: "*...a wind bearing a painful punishment, bound to devastate everything by the command of its Lord...*"[518] we sense that God did not devastate the whole earth and the heavens; He only destroyed the Thamud (the nation of Prophet Salih, peace be upon him) and their dwellings. The general meaning of this verse is restricted by our senses.

b) *Takhsis* by intellect; for example, the commands and prohibitions do not apply to children or insane people because they do not have sound intellect and cannot be held liable for their actions.

c) *Takhsis* by *'urf* (custom); for example, in some countries the word *dirham* is understood by people to mean their own currency and similarly, the word 'food' is understood to mean 'wheat' by the people in certain places.

---

[515] Kamali, *Principles of Islamic Jurisprudence*, p. 106.

[516] Qur'an 2: 282.

[517] Qur'an 4: 12.

[518] Qur'an 46: 24–25.

d) *Takhsis* by *ijma'*; for example, there is an *ijma'* that the Friday Prayer is not obligatory for women and slaves, however, the verse is *āam*; "*O you who believe! When the call is made for the Prayer on Friday, then move promptly to the remembrance of God...*"[519] This general text was restricted by *ijma'* resulting in women and slaves being excluded from the scope of this command.

e) *Takhsis* by the statement of the Companions; Ḫanafī scholars view the statement of the Companions as evidence and prefer it to *qiyāṣ*. The *ijtihāds* of 'Umar are an example for this type of *takhsis*.

f) *Takhsis* by textual proof from the Qur'an or the Sunnah; for example, the period of waiting that a divorced woman has to observe before remarrying is three months. This is a general rule, but it is restricted by other verses: "*For the women who are pregnant (whether divorced or widows), their waiting-period is until they deliver their burden*"[520] and

> O you who believe! When you have made a marriage contract with any of the believing women, and then divorce them before you have touched them, you have no reason to ask them to observe any waiting-period for you.[521]

The scholars usually validate the *takhsis* of the Qur'an by *mutawātir*[522] Sunnah but they disputed over the *takhsis* by *khabar wāḫid*.[523] For the majority, it is permissible to undergo *takhsis* of the Qur'an by *khabar wāḫid* but for Ḫanafī scholars it is neither valid nor permissible.

Summary: The *Āam* (general) and the *Khās* (specific)

1. The words or the text are divided into two categories according to their scope; *āam* (general) and *khās* (specific).
2. The *āam* (general) is a word which covers all the instances in its own category and does not impose limitations on the number.
3. *Āam* is a word with a single meaning that covers an unlimited number without restrictions.

[519] Qur'an 62: 9.

[520] Qur'an 65: 4.

[521] Qur'an 33: 49.

[522] A report that is transmitted by such large group in every generation that is inconceivable to think that they all agreed to perpetrate a lie.

[523] A report that is lower than *mutawātir* and only transmitted by some individuals and therefore it is not definite evidence.

4. The *khās* (specific) is when a word is applied to a limited number, including everything to which it can be applied.
5. *Khās* is applied to a single subject or a specified number of objects; the scope of its application is limited.
6. Legal rules conveyed by *khās* words or text are definite in their application and not open to interpretation as long as there is no evidence to contradict this.
7. *Āam* applies to all the members of a specific set, no matter how small or large that set is.
8. A word may be *āam* (general) in different ways; by form, meaning, prefixing pronouns, undefined words, pronouncements, conditions and by using question nouns.
9. *Āam* covers all of the instances that the word is applicable to: the general form of the command is implemented for every member that the general word covers.
10. The Maliki, Shāfi'ī and Hanbalī schools hold that *āam* words do not convey definite evidence because evidence covering all instances is speculative (*ẕannī*).
11. The Ḫanafī School holds that *āam* is definite evidence, because it is established for this purpose.
12. There are three different types of *āam*: definitive *āam*; *āam* in wording but *khās* in meaning; *āam* in wording but the text does not indicate whether it is general or specific.
13. *Āam* can be specified or limited within the same text or in another piece of text.
14. *Takhsis* (limitation or restriction) can occur in the form of an exception from a general statement, a condition, a quality, or by indicating the extent of the original proposition.
15. The majority of scholars agree that the *āam* can be restricted or limited accordingly to independent reasons.
16. Ḫanafī scholars specify three reasons that can restrict the *āam*; the intellect, custom (*'urf*) and textual evidence.
17. The majority of scholars add three more categories; the senses, *ijma'* and the statement of the Companions.
18. The scholars usually validate the *takhsis* of the Qur'an by *mutawātir* Sunnah and all except Ḫanafī scholars accept *takhsis* of the Qur'an by *khabar wāḫid*.

Mutlaq (The Absolute) and *Muqayyad* (The Qualified)

Mutlaq is a word or text which conveys absolute meaning without being qualified. For example, the words 'man', 'book', 'bird', 'student', etc. are *mutlaq* words because they stand alone without their meaning being qualified. In other words, *mutlaq* conveys a meaning which is neither qualified nor limited in its application. The *mutlaq* (absolute) is different from the *āam* (general), in that the *āam* includes all the instances to which it can be applied, whereas the *mutlaq* can apply to any one of them, but not to all.

Some words or texts related to rulings (*aḫkām*) are absolute in meaning and free from any conditions or circumstances (*mutlaq*), whilst others are bound (*muqayyad*) to special conditions or situations, and apply only therein. The *āam* applies to all types that are included in its meanings simultaneously and without exception, whereas the *mutlaq* can only apply to one member of its meaning. In other words, the *āam* applies to all the members of a specific set, whereas *mutlaq* only applies to any one of that set. An example for *mutlaq* is the command of God for expiation of the following case;

> Those who declare their wives unlawful for them (by using of them that abhorred expression) and thereafter wish to go back on the words they have uttered must free a slave before they (the spouses) touch each other. This is what you are urged to do. And God is fully aware of what you do[524]

The condition or quality of the slave is not specified which makes the word *mutlaq* (absolute). If the verse was about freeing all slaves, it would be *āam*. In another verse, the expiation for an offense is specified; "*...He who has killed a believer by mistake must set free a believing slave...*"[525] This verse specifies that the slave to be freed by the offender should be Muslim, so the ruling is *muqayyad*; Islam is the quality specified by the word.

If there is no evidence to qualify the *mutlaq* it remains absolute. However, in the existence of evidence the word becomes *muqayyad* (qualified).[526] For example, the ruling prohibiting marriage with the mothers of wives is conveyed in *mutlaq* wording.[527] There is no evidence to qualify it in any way; therefore, it is applied in its absolute term. If the *mutlaq* is qualified, it is necessary to act upon it. An example is the two texts about the ruling of blood; one is worded in abso-

---

524 Qur'an 58: 3.

525 Qur'an 4: 92.

526 Taftazani, *Tawdih*, vol.1, p. 63.

527 Qur'an 4: 23.

lute terms, the other is qualified. The verses state; "*...Unlawful to you (for food) are carrion, and blood...*"[528] and "I do not find in what has been revealed to me anything made unlawful to one who would eat except it be carrion or *blood outpoured.*"[529] Both texts are ruling a prohibition on the same subject; blood. In cases of this type, the *muqayyad* prevails over the *mutlaq*.[530]

However, if there are two texts regarding the same issue, one absolute and the other qualified, but they differ in their rulings or causes, or in both, then neither is qualified by the other and each operates as it stands.[531] For example, God commanded the believers to wash their hands up to the elbows for ablution.[532] This command is conveyed in qualified terms (*muqayyad*) specifying the elbows as the border. There is another command about *tayammum* ablution which is conveyed in absolute (*mutlaq*) terms; "*...if you can find no water, then betake yourselves to pure earth, passing with it lightly over your face and hands...*"[533] This verse did not qualify the border of the face and hands that need to be rubbed with the soil. Both commands have the same cause which is the performance of ablution, but there is a difference between them regarding the ruling; one is washing with water and the other is wiping with soil. Consequently, according to the Ḥanafī and Maliki schools, the first verse cannot qualify the second verse and they are applied accordingly, independent of each other.

Another example of two texts conveying the same ruling is that regarding witnesses; one is *mutlaq* and the other one is *muqayyad* and they differ in respect of their causes. The first verse is; "*...bring two witnesses from among your men...*"[534] This verse is about business transactions and is conveyed in absolute form without qualifying the conditions for the witness. The second verse; "*...divorce them in a fair manner and in observance of their rights and call upon two men of probity from among you as witnesses...*" qualifies the witnesses; only men of probity are accepted as witnesses for the case of divorce. Both cases state the same requirement; two witnesses must be brought, however, the causes are different. The cause of the first case is business transactions and the cause of the second case is divorce. According to Ḥanafī scholars, the second verse cannot qualify the first because the causes are different; Shāfi'ī scholars however, hold that the second

[528] Qur'an 5: 3.
[529] Qur'an 6: 145.
[530] Khallaf, *'Ilm*, p. 193.
[531] Kamali, p. 111.
[532] Qur'an 5: 6.
[533] Qur'an 4: 43.
[534] Qur'an 2: 282.

verse qualifies and prevails over the first. As a result, in both cases the witnesses must be upright and just.[535]

Summary: *Mutlaq* (the Absolute) and *Muqayyad* (the Qualified)

1. *Mutlaq* is a word or text which conveys absolute meaning without being qualified.
2. The *mutlaq* (absolute) is different from the *āam* (general), in that the *āam* includes all the instances to which it can be applied, whereas the *mutlaq* can apply to any one of them, but not to all.
3. Some words or texts related to rulings (*aḫkām*) are absolute in meaning and free from any conditions or circumstances (*mutlaq*), whilst others are bound (*muqayyad*) to special conditions or situations, and apply only therein.
4. The *āam* applies to all types that are included in its meanings simultaneously and without exception, whereas the *mutlaq* can only apply to one member of its meaning.
5. If there is no evidence to qualify the *mutlaq* it remains absolute. However, in the existence of evidence the word becomes *muqayyad* (qualified).
6. If there are two texts regarding the same issue, one absolute and the other qualified, but they differ in their rulings or causes, or in both, then neither is qualified by the other and each operates as it stands.

Ḫaqiqī (The Literal) and *Majāzī* (The Metaphorical)

The original and primary intent of the words refers to their real and literal meanings. If a word is used in its literal meaning it is called *ḫaqiqī* (the literal). If a word is used metaphorical context, the meaning or connotation is not the primary use of the word, it is called *majāzī* (the metaphorical). There is a logical connection between the literal and the metaphorical meanings of a word, but this relationship forms thirty possibilities.[536] The *majāzī* usage of a word means to transfer the meaning of the word from literal to metaphorical based on a connection between the two usages. However, both meanings cannot be referred to by jurists at the same time; they have to choose just one of them for the basis of their legal opinions.

If a word is used in a way which can be understood both literally and metaphorically, the literal meaning is always preferred, because the law is usually

[535] Badran, *Uṣūl*, p. 354.

[536] Shawkānī, *Irshād*, pp. 23–24.

established on the literal meaning of the words. *Ḥaqiqī* and *majāzī* are used by the Lawgiver with their respective meanings. For example; "*Lower to them the wing of humility out of mercy, and say: 'My Lord, have mercy on them even as they cared for me in childhood'*"[537] In this verse the expression '*lower to them the wing of humility*' is a metaphorical expression and is not meant literally. "*Inquire in the township where we were, and the caravan with whom we travelled hither. We are certainly telling the truth.*"[538] It is not possible for one to obtain information from a town, only from those who live within the town; therefore, this verse is used in the metaphorical sense.

If a word has both a literal and a metaphorical meaning and the metaphorical meaning is well known and prevalent, it is preferred over the literal meaning. For example, the literal meaning of the word '*talaq*' is 'to free' and can be used for marriage, slavery or ownership. However, this word was used metaphorically to mean 'divorce' and this meaning became well-known. For this reason, instances of the word '*talaq*' in the text are understood according to the metaphorical meaning if there is no evidence to imply the literal meaning. Another example is the word '*salah*' which literally means supplication and beseeching God. However, in the Qur'an it has been used to mean the prescribed five Daily Prayers and the metaphorical meaning has prevailed over the literal meaning.

Ḥaqiqī and *majāzī* words are classified into two types according to the clarity of the intention of the speaker; *ṣarīh* (clear) and *kināyah* (allusive). If a word is used in a way that clearly indicates the intention of the speaker it is called *ṣarīh* (clear). On the other hand, if the usage of the word does not clearly indicate the intention of the speaker it is called *kināyah* (allusive). For example, 'Zayd bought a car' is a clear statement and the intention of the speaker is understood, however, 'Adam and Eve ate from the tree' is allusive as the real meaning is that they ate from the fruit of the tree. When *ṣarīh* words are used, such as 'You are divorced', it is not necessary to investigate the intention of the speaker; in this case the utterance results in the end of the marriage contract. However, in the case of *kināyah* (allusive) words being used it is necessary to ascertain the true intention of the speaker. For example, a man who instructs his wife to leave and go to her parent's house is not ending his marriage contract unless that is what he intended with his words.[539] Legal rulings require absolute certainty and if there is a doubt, they are not applied. Similarly, for the application of penal law

[537] Qur'an 17: 24.

[538] Qur'an 12: 82.

[539] Badran, *Uṣūl*, p. 398.

the crime must be fully ascertained, but it cannot be proved by allusive expressions. If a man confesses to a crime using allusive words such as 'I touched a woman' the respective punishment for fornication cannot be applied, because it is not certain whether he committed this crime or whether he literally just touched her.

Jurists agree that a word may be used metaphorically while still retaining its literal meaning, however, they disagree as to whether both meanings can be applied simultaneously. Ḫanafī scholars are of the opinion that the two meanings cannot be applied simultaneously whereas Shāfi'ī scholars hold that they can be. For this reason, for Shāfi'ī scholars the literal action of touching a woman invalidates ablution. They support their view with the verse; "*...but if you have had contact with women...*"[540] The metaphorical meaning of 'contact' is sexual intercourse and based on this, Ḫanafī scholars ruled that only sexual intercourse, but not literal touching, invalidates the ablution.

Summary: *Ḫaqiqī* (the Literal) and *Majāzī* (the Metaphorical)

1. *Ḫaqiqī* (the literal) is a word used in the context of its literal meaning.
2. *Majāzī* (the metaphorical) is a words used in a metaphorical context.
3. The *majāzī* usage of a word means to transfer the meaning of the word from literal to metaphorical based on a connection between the two usages. However, both meanings cannot be referred to by jurists at the same time.
4. If a word is used in a way which can be understood both literally and metaphorically, the literal meaning is always preferred.
5. If a word has both a literal and a metaphorical meaning and the metaphorical meaning is well-known and prevalent, it is preferred over the literal meaning.
6. *Ḫaqiqī* and *majāzī* words are classified into two types according to the clarity of the intention of the speaker; *ṣarīh* (clear) and *kināyah* (allusive).
7. When *ṣarīh* words are used it is not necessary to investigate the intention of the speaker.
8. When *kināyah* words are used it is necessary to ascertain the true intention of the speaker.
9. Jurists agree that a word may be used metaphorically while still retaining its literal meaning, however, they disagree as to whether both meanings can be applied simultaneously.

---

[540] Qur'an 4: 43.

10. Ḥanafī scholars are of the opinion that the two meanings cannot be applied simultaneously whereas Shāfi'ī scholars hold that they can be.

The *Mushtarak* (The Homonym)

The *mushtarak* (homonym) is a word that has two or more meanings. The Arabic word '*ayn*' has several meanings including; eye, water-spring, gold, spy, etc. and is a good example of a *mushtarak* (homonym). Similarly, the Arabic word '*quru*' has two meanings; menstruation, and the clean period between two menstruation periods.[541]

There are various reasons behind the existence of homonym words in the Arabic language, including;

a) In some cases the different tribes ascribed different meanings to the same word, resulting in it becoming a homonym. For example, the word '*yad*' was used by one tribe to mean the arm up until the elbow, whilst another tribe used it to mean the wrist and another to mean the hand. These various meanings were transmitted to further generations without indicating the differences.

b) In some cases the use of a word changed over time and came to include two meanings due to the connection between them. This is the case with some words that were used both literally and metaphorically; over time, people forgot the difference between them and accepted both meanings resulting in a homonym. For example, the literal meaning of '*mawlā*' is 'a helper' but is has, over time, also come to mean 'a freed slave' and also 'a master who frees a slave.'

c) Other homonyms occurred through the metaphorical meaning becoming prevalent over the literal meaning of the word. Over time, people forgot that it was metaphorical and both meanings are accepted as the literal meaning. For example, '*sayyara*' means 'the caravan' but later it also attained the meaning of 'a car.' This meaning prevailed over the original and became known as the original meaning of the word.

d) Some words have both a literal and a customary meaning and the frequent use of the customary meaning results in it being used as a homonym. *Salah* (the Prayer), *zakat* (charity) and *talaq* (divorce), etc. are examples of this type of homonym.

---

541 Abu Zahra, *Uṣūl*, p. 132.

Ḥanafī scholars accept that in the case of *mushtarak* only one meaning can be accepted for legal rulings. If a homonym is used in the Qur'an or Sunnah, it conveys one meaning alone; the Lawgiver does not intend for a word to have more than one meaning at the same time in legal matters; the language of law is clear regarding commands and prohibitions. Where a homonym is used, it is the duty of the *mujtahid* to investigate the original intent of the Lawgiver using two criteria; the context of how the word is used in the text and the meaning of the word at the time of the revelation. In this way, the *mujtahids* can determine the original intent of the Lawgiver from the homonym words.

If, in Shari'ah, a word gains a different meaning, such as *salah*, the *shar'ī* (religious) meaning prevails unless there is an indication in the text implying the literal meaning. For example:

> Surely God and His angels bless the Prophet. O you who believe, invoke the blessings of God on him, and pray to God to bestow His peace on him, greeting him with the best greeting[542]

In this verse the word '*salah*' is used but the *shar'ī* meaning is not intended, because neither God nor the angels perform the prescribed Prayers for the noble Prophet. Also, the believers perform the prayer for God but not for the Prophet, therefore, it can be clearly understood that the literal meaning of '*salah*' is meant in this context. However, the same word can have different connotations when used by different speakers. If '*salah*' is used by God it means blessing; when used by the angels it means asking forgiveness from God for the Prophet and when it is used by the believers it means praying for the Prophet.

Sometimes the context in which a word is used can help the *mujtahid* identify the original intent of the homonym word. For example, in the verse; "*They also ask you about (the injunctions concerning) menstruation...*"[543] the word '*mahid*' is a homonym with two meanings; the menstruation time and the menstruation place. In this context, however, it can be understood to mean the menstruation time or cycle.

On occasion, textual evidence may help the *mujtahid* identify the intended meaning of the homonym. For example, in the verse; "*For the thief, male or female: cut off their hands as a recompense for what they have earned, and an exemplary deterrent punishment from God.*"[544] The word '*yad*' is a homonym with three pos-

[542] Qur'an 33: 56.
[543] Qur'an 2: 222.
[544] Qur'an 5: 38.

sible meanings; the hand from the tip of the fingers up to the wrist, or up to the elbow, or up to the shoulder. However, by way of his practical Sunnah, the Prophet explained this verse enabling *mujtahids* to derive the meaning as the right hand up to the wrist.

Summary: The *Mushtarak* (The Homonym)

1. *Mushtarak* is a word that has two or more meanings.
2. Homonyms exist in Arabic for various reasons: different tribes ascribed different meanings to the same word; the use of a word changed over time and came to include two meanings; the metaphorical meaning of a word became prevalent over the literal meaning of the word; a word has both a literal and a customary meaning.
3. Ḥanafī scholars accept that in the case of *mushtarak* only one meaning can be accepted for legal rulings.
4. Where a homonym is used, it is the duty of the *mujtahid* to investigate the original intent of the Lawgiver using two criteria; the context of how the word is used in the text and the meaning of the word at the time of the revelation.
5. If, in Shari'ah, a word gains a different meaning, such as *salah*, the *shar'ī* meaning prevails unless there is an indication in the text implying the literal meaning.
6. Sometimes the context in which a word is used can help the *mujtahid* identify the original intent of the homonym word.
7. On occasion textual evidence may help the *mujtahid* identify the intended meaning of the homonym.

Chapter 11

Command and Prohibition

Command and Prohibition

Introduction

The first step to understanding the Qur'an is to understand its language and its expressive forms. It is unique in the way it phrases its subjects according to the content and addressees. The most important aspect of Islamic law is commands and prohibitions and for valid *ijtihād,* it is essential that *mujtahid* understand the textual interpretations. As well as conveying commands and prohibitions and their consequences, the Qur'an appeals to the hearts of people. It convinces them intellectually by both warning those who violate the rulings about the consequences of their acts and giving good tidings to those who obey the guidance. Legislation will not be successful without satisfying the hearts and minds of individuals compelling them to comply. For this reason, Islamic law is not only set of rulings for people but also an education to encourage them to perfect their human values.

There are various methods in which commands and prohibitions are communicated in the Qur'an; they are not always conveyed in the imperative form. On occasion injunctions are declared in the past tense; for example, "*O you who believe! Prescribed for you is the Fast, as it was prescribed for those before you, so that you may deserve God's protection and attain piety.*"[545] In other instances, the legislation is indicated by blaming the conduct; for example, "*Do not spy (on one another), nor backbite (against one another). Would any of you love to eat the flesh of his dead brother?*"[546] The following section deals with commands and prohibitions separately.

Summary: Introduction

1. The most important aspect of Islamic law is commands and prohibitions and for valid *ijtihād* it is essential that *mujtahid* understand the textual interpretations.

---

[545] Qur'ān 2: 183.
[546] Qur'ān 49: 12.

2. Islamic law is not only set rulings for the liable person but it is also education for human beings to perfect their moral values.
3. Commands and prohibitions are communicated in various ways in the Qur'an including the imperative form, injunctions in the past tense and blaming certain types of behaviour.

Amr (Command)

A command (*amr*) is an act that is compulsory for liable people which is issued as a command by a valid authority. For example; "*Establish the Prayer, and pay the Prescribed Purifying Alms* (*zakat*)"[547] in this text, the expression 'Establish the Prayer' and 'Pay the *zakat'* is a command issued by the Lawgiver. A command is a verbal demand referring to a certain act from the Lawgiver to His servants.[548]

Command differs from supplication and request in that it is issued from a superior authority to an inferior one. Supplication and request are the opposite; issued from the inferior to the superior authority. *Amr* can convey obligation but also recommendations and permissibility. Islamic scholars disputed the nature of *amr,* in particular the main themes or principal meanings of commands. Some scholars believe that *amr* encompasses commands, recommendations and permissibility whilst others are of the opinion that it only covers obligation and recommendation, but not permissibility. Another group maintains that *amr* indicates permission for certain acts which cover all three forms.[549]

The majority view is that a command by itself conveys a demand as long as there are no other indications; if there are, then the command may become permissibility or a recommendation. For example, in the verse; "*Eat and drink*'[550] the command, '*Eat and drink*' conveys permissibility only, because they are essential elements of life which don't need to be commanded by the Lawgiver.

The majority use the following arguments to support their view: 'a command by itself conveys a demand only':

> (Remember) when your Lord said to the angels: "I am creating a mortal out of clay (to set him on the earth as vicegerent). When I have fashioned him fully and breathed into Him out of My Spirit, then fall down prostrating before him (as a sign of respect for him and his superiority)." So

[547] Qur'ān 2: 43.
[548] Badran, *Uṣūl*, p. 360.
[549] Shawkānī, *Irshād*, p. 91.
[550] Qur'ān 7: 31.

> the angels prostrated all of them together, But Iblis did not (in defiance of God's explicit order to him); he grew arrogant and displayed himself as an unbeliever. (God) said: "O Iblis! What prevents you from prostrating before the being whom I have created with My two Hands? Are you too proud (to bow down before any created being in defiance of My command), or are you (of those who think themselves) so high in honour (that they cannot be ordered to prostrate before anyone)?" (Iblis) answered: "I am better than him. You have created me from fire and him You have created from clay." (God) said: "Then get you down out of it; surely You are one eternally rejected (from My Mercy). And My curse is on you until the Day of Judgment.[551]

God commanded the angels to prostrate before Adam, peace be upon him, and all of them complied except Iblis (Satan) who rejected this command. God then condemned and cursed Iblis because he did not comply with the demand from his Lord. If a command did not convey a binding demand, Iblis would not have been cursed or punished. Further supporting evidence are the verses:

> So, let those who go against the Messenger's order beware lest a bitter trial befall them or a painful punishment afflict them.[552]

> Whoever disobeys God and His Messenger and exceeds His bounds, God will admit him into a Fire, to abide therein, and for him is a shameful, humiliating punishment[553]

> When they are told, 'Bow down (before God in humility and worship Him)!' they do not bow down. Woe on that Day to those who deny![554]

All these verses contain warnings to the people if they do not fulfil a command and set a punishment for disobedience. This proves that the command itself conveys a binding demand as long as there is no other implication. The believers were ordered to obey God and His Prophet without recourse to any other option.

> When God and His Messenger have decreed a matter, it is not for a believing man and a believing woman to have an option insofar as they themselves are concerned. Whoever disobeys God and His Messenger has evidently gone astray.[555]

551 Qur'ān 38: 71–78.
552 Qur'ān 24: 63.
553 Qur'ān 4: 14.
554 Qur'ān 77: 48–49.
555 Qur'ān 33: 36.

The Arabic language has two forms which are used to clearly convey commands: the first is a direct command for those who are present (*amr khādir*) such as 'Perform the Prayer' or 'Pay the *zakat*'; the second is a command for those who are absent (*amr ghāyib*) such as "...whoever of you is present this month, must fast it..." The expression 'must fast it' conveys this type of command. In addition to these two forms, there are other Arabic words used to convey commands despite not being of imperative form:

a) '*Amr*' and its derivations. For example; "*God commands you to deliver trusts to those entitled to them; and when you judge between people, to judge with justice*"[556] In this text the expression 'God commands' (*ya'muru*) is used in the present tense but it conveys command and obligation. The word '*amr*' is used in this verse to make a demand of the believers.
b) '*Kitāb*' (book, prescription) and its derivations. For example; "*O you who believe! Prescribed for you is the Fast, as it was prescribed for those before you...*"[557] The expression 'prescribed' (*ku-ti-ba*) in this verse conveys command and obligation and is used to demand observation of the fast during Ramadan.
c) A sentence conveyed in the informative mode but which actually conveys a command. For example; "*Divorced women shall keep themselves in waiting for three menstrual courses.*"[558] The expression 'shall keep themselves in waiting' is in the informative mode but it conveys a command and obligation. Divorced women are commanded to wait three menstrual courses before re-marrying. There are also other forms of command in this category.
d) A statement which conveys an implied threat, such as the word of God to the unbelievers; "*Do what you wish*"[559] and "*Lead to destruction those that you can.*"[560]
e) A statement which indicates debasement, such as the word of God to the unbelievers; "*Taste [the torture], you mighty and honourable.*"[561]

The majority of scholars agree that if a certain thing is prohibited first and then commanded later by the Lawgiver it conveys permissibility rather than an

[556] Qur'ān 4: 58.
[557] Qur'ān 2: 183.
[558] Qur'ān 2: 228.
[559] Qur'ān 24: 33.
[560] Qur'ān 17: 64.
[561] Qur'ān 44: 47.

obligation; for example, in the verse, "*O you who believe! When the call is made for the Prayer on Friday, then move promptly to the remembrance of God and leave off business*"[562] the prohibition for leaving business is followed by the command to make business; "*When the Prayer is done, then disperse in the land and seek of God's bounty.*"[563] The command in this verse conveys permissibility because it came after the prohibition. Another example is the prohibition of hunting whilst in *iḥrām* (the special attire for the *Hajj* and *umrah* rituals); "*Unlawful (for you is) hunted game when you are in the state of pilgrim sanctity.*"[564] This verse conveys that the usually permissible act of hunting is prohibited due to being in *iḥrām* , however, when the rituals of *Hajj* or *umrah* are completed the believers are commanded to hunt; "*But once you leave your pilgrim you hunt.*"[565] The command is declared using the imperative form but it only conveys permissibility because it came after a prohibition.

According to majority of scholars, unless otherwise indicated, a command demands that it is carried out once by those liable; this is the minimum requirement of a command. However, if there are conditions attached, it must be repeated whenever the conditions are present. For example, making ablution is required before performing the obligatory Prayers and must be repeated whenever the condition is present; "*If you are impure then clean yourselves.*"[566] The state of impurity requires a new ablution at every obligatory Prayer time. Similarly, the command for the Daily Prayers is conveyed in conditional terms and so it must be repeated: "Perform the Prayer at the decline of the sun." When the cause for the Prayer (the specific time set for each Prayer) is repeated, then the command also comes into effect again.[567]

The majority of scholars agree that where there is a command to do something, there is an implication that the opposite is prohibited, regardless of whether the opposite is a single act or multiple acts. The practical result of this debate is whether a person who commits the opposite of a command must be punished, and if so, to what extent. It is only possible to determine the answer by regarding the circumstances and the state of mind of the individual concerned alongside the

[562] Qur'ān 62: 9.
[563] Qur'ān 62: 10.
[564] Qur'ān 5: 1.
[565] Qur'ān 5: 2.
[566] Qur'ān 5: 6.
[567] Shawkānī, *Irshād*, pp. 98–99.

general objectives of the Lawgiver (or the commanding authority) that can be ascertained in a given command.[568]

Summary: Command (*Amr*)

1. A command (*amr*) is an act that is compulsory for liable people issued as a command by a valid authority.
2. Command differs from supplication and request in that it is issued from a superior authority to an inferior one.
3. *Amr* can convey obligation but also recommendations and permissibility.
4. The majority of scholars hold that a command by itself conveys a binding demand as long as there are no other indications; if there are then the command may become permissibility or a recommendation.
5. The Arabic language conveys commands directly for those who are present (*amr khādir*) and indirectly for those who are absent (*amr ghāyib*).
6. Additional ways of conveying commands in Arabic include: the word *amr* and its derivations; the word *kitāb*' and its derivations; a sentence conveyed in the informative mode but which actually conveys a command; a statement which conveys an implied threat; and a statement which indicates debasement.
7. The majority of scholars are in agreement that if a certain thing is prohibited first and then commanded later by the Lawgiver, it conveys permissibility rather than an obligation.
8. According to majority of scholars, unless otherwise indicated, a command demands that it is carried out once by those liable; this is the minimum requirement of a command. However, if there are conditions attached, it must be repeated whenever the conditions are present.
9. The majority of scholars agree that where there is a command to do something, there is an implication that the opposite is prohibited, regardless of whether the opposite is a single act or multiple acts.

Nahy (Prohibitions)

Prohibition is a demand issued from a superior authority to an inferior one to avoid committing a certain act.[569] A prohibition can only be made by the Lawgiver who has the authority both to issue a prohibition and to punish violations there-

[568] Kamali, *Islamic Jurisprudence*, p. 134.

[569] Badran, *Uṣūl*, p. 366.

of. For example, the verse; "*Do not draw near to any unlawful sexual intercourse...* "[570] issues a binding prohibition for all individuals using the expression '*Do not draw near.*'

The Arabic language has two typical forms for conveying prohibitions: the first is a direct prohibition for those who are present (*nahy khādir*) such as the expression '*Do not draw near*' in the previous verse. The second form is prohibition for those who are absent (*nahy ghāyib*) such as "*Tell the believing women that they should restrain their gaze and guard their private parts...*"[571] The prohibition in this verse is conveyed in the form of *nahy ghāyib*. Besides these two forms, there are some other Arabic words that can be used to infer prohibition, the most important of which are mentioned below:

a) Words which have the meaning 'abandon', 'leave off', 'refrain', etc.' for example; "*O you who believe! When the call is made for the Prayer on Friday, then move promptly to the remembrance of God and leave off business.*"[572] In this verse the word 'leave off' conveys prohibition.

b) Words which mean forbid. For example; "*...God forbids you indecency, wickedness and vile conduct...*"[573] In this verse the Arabic word '*yanha*' (forbids) conveys prohibition.

c) The Arabic word *haram* (prohibited/unlawful) and its derivations. For example; "*God prohibited usury but made trade lawful*"[574] In this verse the Arabic word '*harrama*' (prohibited) is an example this form of prohibition.

d) Expressions declaring something as unlawful. For example; "*...They are not (being believers) lawful (as wives) for the unbelievers nor are the unbelievers lawful (as husbands) for them...*"[575] In this verse the expression 'unlawful' conveys the prohibition.

e) Words used to threaten and warn. For example;

> Those who hoard up gold and silver and do not spend it in God's cause (to exalt His cause and help the poor and needy): give them (O Messenger) the glad tidings of a painful punishment.[576]

---

[570] Qur'ān 17: 32.
[571] Qur'ān 24: 31.
[572] Qur'ān 62: 9.
[573] Qur'ān 16: 90.
[574] Qur'ān 2: 175.
[575] Qur'ān 60: 10.
[576] Qur'ān 9: 34.

This text clearly expounds that the act of hoarding gold and silver rather than spending it for the cause of God is prohibited and incurs punishment.

f) Cases where the Lawgiver has assigned a certain punishment for an act. For example; "*For the thief, male or female: cut off their hands as a recompense for what they have earned, and an exemplary deterrent punishment from God*"[577] In this verse the assigned punishment for the thief indicates the prohibition of the act of theft.

Scholars disputed the precise meaning of prohibition and whether it conveys prohibition only or also has other meanings. The principle meaning of prohibition is unlawfulness but some argue that it may also convey dislike (*makruh*), guidance, reprimand or supplication. Some scholars argue that prohibition conveys the meaning of dislike and *haram* together and that it is up to the *mujtahid* to determine which is meant based on indications in the text. Other scholars maintain that the principle meaning of prohibition is dislike and other meanings can be obtained from indications in the text or from other evidence. The majority of scholars hold that a prohibition by itself establishes the meaning of *haram* only if there is no other indication. For example; "*Do not kill any soul, which God has made forbidden...*"[578] Killing any soul is prohibited in this text because there is no other implication or evidence that conveys any other meaning. However, in other cases a verse may be conveyed in terms of prohibition but the actually meaning is that the act is disliked due to an indication in the text. For example; "*O you who believe! Do not ask about things which, if made manifest to you, would give you trouble...*"[579] In this verse, a prohibition "do not ask" is immediately followed by permissibility "if made manifest" making the act disliked rather than prohibited; "*...if you ask about them while the Qur'an is being sent down, they will be made manifest to you....*"[580]

Scholars used the following verse as evidence for their argument that prohibition by itself only conveys *haram* if there is no other indication; "*...Whatever the Messenger gives you accept it willingly, and whatever he forbids you, refrain from it...*"[581] This verse clearly demands the believers avoid things which are prohibited. This proves that the principle meaning of prohibition is *haram*.

---

577 Qur'ān 5: 38.
578 Qur'ān 17: 33.
579 Qur'ān 5: 101.
580 Qur'ān 5: 101.
581 Qur'ān 59: 7.

A prohibition can be used to give moral guidance, for example; "*Do not turn your face from people in scornful pride, or move on earth haughtily*..."[582] It can also be used to encourage supplication; "*Our Lord, condemn us not if we forget.*"[583]

Prohibitions demand immediate compliance by avoiding certain acts. The liable person must refrain from prohibited acts as soon as the prohibition is issued. For this reason, when the command about the prohibition of adultery was revealed, adultery immediately became unlawful.

The reason for prohibitions in the law is to prevent harm. For this reason they should be continuous as the removal of the prohibition will result in harm being inflicted. The consequence for violating prohibitions is punishment in the afterlife. Some violations, such as adultery and theft, also require punishment in this world, but if there is no penal law about a certain act, the punishment is postponed until the afterlife.

Another important issue is the validity types regarding the conduct of liable people and the related legal results. As mentioned earlier, there are three concepts used to evaluate the conduct of the liable person; *saḫīḫ* (valid), *bātil* (void) and *fāsid* (irregular). To be able to assess the result of prohibited conduct regarding devotional matters (*ibadāt*) or the conduct and transactions between people (*muamalāt*), it is necessary to understand the reasons behind the prohibitions. A prohibition can be issued due to unlawfulness or harm in its essence (*rukun*), harm in its attribute or harm in its conditions.

Where there is a prohibition about the essential qualities of something, a person in violation of the prohibition cannot resort to legal recourse; his conduct is invalid. This is the case whether it is related to devotional or legal matters. For example, the right of paternity cannot be established as a result of adultery or fornication, but the person who has violated this prohibition is liable to punishment. Similarly, the right of ownership cannot be established by one who has violated the prohibition of theft.

Similarly, the majority of scholars agree that if the object of prohibition is an act prohibited because of a specific attribute rather than its essential qualities, the act is invalid regardless of whether it is related to *ibadāt* (devotional matters) or *muamalāt* (legal matters) and it does not produce legal effects. Ḫanafī scholars, however, hold that in *muamalāt* matters such acts are *fāsid* (irregular) rather than *bātil* (void) and they do produce legal results even though the acts

---

[582] Qur'ān 31: 18.

[583] Qur'ān 2: 286.

are sinful. In their view, the act is deficient and should be abolished or rectified where possible. For example, if a person conducts business transactions involving usury, the transaction is void for Shāfi'ī scholars but *fāsid* (irregular) for Ḥanafī scholars. Ḥanafī scholars hold that a transaction can be rectified by removing the usury whereby the transaction becomes valid. If the usury element remains, the transaction must be revoked. In the case of prohibitions related to *ibadāt* matters, scholars agree that there is no difference between *fāsid* and *bātil* in terms of the result; the act of *ibadāt* becomes void and it does not produce any legal result. For example, fasting on the day of Eid is *fāsid* and must be terminated by its doer because it is a sin to fast on this day and there can be no reward for it. If a person starts fasting on that day and breaks his fast before sunset, he does not have to compensate it as *qada* (make up).

If the prohibition is due to external conditions or factors, for example, a transaction made during the time of the Friday Prayer, this act is a sin but it does produce legal effects according to the majority of the scholars. Any trade which is concluded during the time of the Friday Prayer does result in ownership rights for the buyer.[584]

Summary: *Nahy* (Prohibition)

1. Prohibition is a demand issued from a superior authority to an inferior one to avoid committing a certain act.
2. Prohibitions are generally conveyed in two forms in the Arabic language; through a direct prohibition for those who are present (*nahy khādir*) and secondly for those who are absent (*nahy ghāyib*).
3. Other Arabic words are also used to convey prohibitions such as: words which have the meaning 'abandon', 'leave off', 'refrain', etc.; words which mean forbid; the word *haram* (prohibited/unlawful) and its derivations; expressions declaring something as unlawful; words used to threaten and warn; and cases where the Lawgiver has assigned a certain punishment for an act.
4. Scholars disputed the precise meaning of prohibition and whether it conveys prohibition only or also has other meanings such as dislike (*makruh*), guidance, reprimand or supplication.
5. The majority of scholars hold that a prohibition by itself establishes the meaning of *haram* only if there is no other indication.

---

584 Shawkānī, *Irshād*, p. 110.

6. A prohibition can be used to give moral guidance and to encourage supplication.
7. Prohibitions demand immediate compliance by avoiding certain acts.
8. Prohibitions exist within the law to prevent harm and therefore must be continuous.
9. Where there is a prohibition about the essential qualities of something, a person in violation of the prohibition cannot resort to legal recourse; their conduct is invalid. This is the case whether it is related to *ibadāt* or *muamalāt* matters.
10. If the object of prohibition is an act prohibited because of a specific attribute rather than its essential qualities, the act is invalid regardless of whether it is related to *ibadāt* or *muamalāt* and it does not produce legal effects.
11. Ḫanafī scholars, however, hold that in *muamalāt* matters this act is *fāsid* (irregular) rather than *bātil* (void) and it does produce legal results even though the act is sin.
12. In the case of prohibitions related to *ibadāt* matters, scholars agree that there is no difference between *fāsid* and *bātil* in terms of the result; the act of *ibadāt* becomes void and it does not produce any legal result.
13. If the prohibition is due to external conditions or factors the act is a sin but it does produce legal effects according to the majority of the scholars.

Naskh (Abrogation)

Introduction

Naskh literally means obliteration, to remove, to abolish, to abrogate, to replace, to supersede, to transcribe (*istinsakh*) or to copy. In the Qur'anic sciences, *naskh* means the abrogation (suspension or replacement) of one Shari'ah ruling by another with the conditions that the latter is of a subsequent origin and the two rulings are enacted separately from one another.[585] Based on evidence, some of the verses related to commands (*amr*) or prohibitions (*nahy*) were totally abrogated or superseded by other verses. A verse whose ruling has been abrogated is called '*mansūkh*' and the abrogating verse which brings the new regulation is called '*nāsikh*.' Knowledge in this area of *nāsikh-mansūkh* is important to enable *mujtahids* to deduce the correct rulings concerning liable believers.

---

[585] Sayyid Sharif Jurjani, *Tārifāt*, p. 163.

The usage of *naskh* can also be seen in the familiar Arabic expressions, '*tanasukh al-arwah*' (reincarnation), and '*tanasukh al-mawarith*', the transfer of inheritance from persons to persons. According to the majority view, however, obliteration (*al-raf wa al-izalah*) is the primary meaning, and transcription or transfer is the secondary meaning of *naskh*.[586] In terms of Qur'an and Sunnah *naskh* could only be applied during the lifetime of the noble Prophet.

The word '*naskh*' and its derivations are used in the Qur'an with different meanings, such as writing, transcribing and copying;

> "This is Our Book (the record of your deeds that We prepared), speaking the truth against you. Assuredly We have had transcribed what you used to do (in the world)"[587]

> Never did We send a Messenger or a Prophet before you but that when he recited (God's Revelations to the people) Satan would make insinuations (about these Revelations, prompting people to misconstrue them in many wrong senses, rather than the right one). But God abrogates whatever insinuations Satan may make, and then He confirms and establishes His Revelations. God is All-Knowing, All-Wise[588]

In this verse, the word '*fayansakhu*' is used to mean 'to remove' and 'to abrogate.'

> (Though they would exploit the abrogation of some rules of secondary degree to challenge your authority, the truth is that) We do not abrogate any verse or omit it (leaving it to be forgotten) but We bring one better than it or the like of it (more suited to the time and conditions in the course of perfecting religion and completing Our favour upon you). Do you not know (and surely you do know) that God has full power over everything?[589]

Scholars interpret this verse to mean that God abrogates the rulings conveyed in some verses by bringing other verses to replace them. He supersedes the original rulings with new ones without removing the former ones from the Qur'an. *Naskh* brings change not in *'ilm* (knowledge of God) but in *ma'lum* (what is known to us). In other words, it is not a change in the Creator's knowledge; it is only a change for humankind regarding the rulings related to them.

---

586 Ghazali, *Muṣtaṣfā*, vol.1, p. 69; Āmidī, *Aḥkām*, vol.3, p. 102.

587 Qur'ān 45: 29.

588 Qur'ān 22: 52

589 Qur'ān 2: 106.

The Qur'anic revelations are related to various subjects, including, but not limited to, beliefs, history, tales of the Prophets, the Day of Judgment, Paradise and Hell. Particularly important are revelations conveying the *aḫkām* (legal rulings), because they prescribe God's Will regarding the nature of the conduct of people. While the basic message of Islam remains the same, the legal rulings have varied throughout the ages, with many Prophets prior to Prophet Muhammad, peace and blessings be upon him, bringing particular codes of law (*shari'ah*) to their respective communities.[590]

Islamic law encompasses three forms of legislation:

a) It retained the commandments that pre-dated it, including rulings from previous revelatory books, traditional customs and the practises of the community in which Islam appeared which did not contradict the essential principles of Islam.
b) It corrected or amended existing rulings that were not in conformity with its principles.
c) It introduced new legislation.

In establishing new legislation, both life's essential (unchanging) and temporal (changing) aspects were considered. Secondly, rulings were laid down that could be revised when necessary, according to the time and conditions and in conformity with the essentials of faith, worship, and morality; and legal principles were established to maintain this process. The same procedure was also followed in the time of the Prophet himself, during which the Qur'an was revealed. The Lawgiver abrogated some verses, either with the injunction contained in their wording or with both their wording and the command they contained. This process is called *naskh*; the verses that were abrogated are known as *mansūkh*; and the new verses substituting the previous verses are known as *nāsikh*.[591]

Naskh is one of the most controversial topics among the scholars. Whilst most accept the notion of *naskh,* others do not accept it at all. Some use the term '*naskh*' with a broad meaning, including *āam-khās, mutlaq-muqayyad* and *bayān*. The term *bayān* refers to clarity after being ambiguous and coming into existence after non-existence whilst *khās* refers to limitation of general statement; therefore neither term is related to the notion of '*naskh*.'

The message of Islam was presented to the Arabs in stages. It was new and very different from their accustomed way of life, therefore changes were intro-

---

[590] Von Denffer, *'Ulūm al-Qur'ān*, 102.

[591] Ali Ünal, *The Qur'ān with Annotated Interpretation*, footnote for 2:106.

duced gradually to give people time to internalise and practice the new rulings. For example, there are three verses in the Qur'an[592] concerning the drinking of wine. Wine drinking was widespread and highly esteemed in pre-Islamic Arabia, despite being a social evil. The three verses which finally led to the prohibition of intoxicating substances were revealed in stages.[593]

Naskh indicates that the first ruling contradicts the later rulings and therefore the first ruling should be completely abrogated. The conditions for *naskh* to occur are: there must be a pre-existing ruling on exactly the same subject which is then abrogated by a later ruling; there should be *fasila/tarakhi* (intervals) between the rulings of *mansūkh* and *nāsikh*.

During the formative period of Islam there were various words to refer to *naskh*. Imam Shāfi'ī was the first to limit the meaning of the word to abrogation. Other scholars consider *naskh* to mean *bayān* (explanation), *khitāb* (discourse) or *raf'* (omit). Each of these is close to the meaning of *naskh* (to abrogate the previous *ḥukm* with the new one), but none of them are *naskh*. This is important to know when looking at statements from the scholars from the first three generations of Islam. If they claim that a particular verse was 'abrogated' (*nasakha*) by another verse it cannot immediately be taken as an example of *naskh*. This has been one of the greatest causes of confusion regarding the number of *nāsikh/ mansūkh* verses in the Qur'an.[594]

Naskh is only valid in legal matters and cannot occur in regard to matters of belief such as the Names and Attributes of God, the Day of Judgment, and other matters related to the fundamentals of belief. *Naskh* cannot occur with respect to *ijma'* (general consensus) or *qiyāṣ* (analogy), but only in the Qur'an and Sunnah. It happened only during the lifetime of the Prophet when there was no need for *ijma'* and *qiyāṣ*. The Qur'an and Sunnah have the authority to abrogate the rulings of some verses but *ijtihād* (personal reasoning), *qiyāṣ* or any other sources of Islamic law cannot abrogate a ruling from the Qur'an or Sunnah. Therefore, it is important to note that *naskh* happened primarily in Medina where Islamic law was finalised.

The knowledge of *nāsikh* and *mansūkh* is important because it concerns the correct and exact application of Islamic law. It is specifically concerned with legal revelations and is one of the important pre-conditions for exegesis of the Qur'an. It is one of the important pre-conditions for the understanding and application

592 Qur'ān, 4: 43, 2: 219; 5: 93–94.

593 Von Denffer, *'Ulūm al-Qur'ān*, 103.

594 Qadhi, *the Sciences of the Qur'ān*, p. 234.

of Islamic law. It also sheds light on the historical development of the Islamic legal code and helps scholars to understand the immediate meanings of the verses concerned.

Evidence for *naskh* must be based on reliable hadith reports going back to the noble Prophet and his Companions, and cannot be accepted upon mere personal opinion. The evidence must clearly state which part of the revelation is abrogating and which is abrogated. There are three types of evidence for *naskh*: a) report from the Prophet or Companions, b) *ijma'* (consensus of the *mujtahids* upon *naskh*) and c) knowledge of the chronology of the Qur'anic revelation. The vast majority of scholars accepted the existence of *naskh* in the Qur'an and Sunnah. Three verses refer to the reality of *naskh*:

> (Though they would exploit the abrogation of some rules of secondary degree to challenge your authority, the truth is that) We do not abrogate any verse or omit it (leaving it to be forgotten) but We bring one better than it or the like of it (more suited to the time and conditions in the course of perfecting religion and completing Our favour upon you). Do you not know (and surely you do know) that God has full power over everything?[595]

> When We put a Revelation in place of another Revelation (in the course of perfecting the Religion and completing Our favour upon you),—and God knows best what He sends down—they say: "You are but a forger!" No, rather, most of them do not know[596]

> O (most illustrious) Prophet! Rouse the believers to fighting. If there be twenty of you who are steadfast, they will vanquish two hundred; and if there be of you a hundred, they will vanquish a thousand of those who disbelieve, for they (the disbelievers) are a people who do not ponder and seek to penetrate the essence of matters in order to grasp the truth. For now (while you lack in necessary equipment and training), God has lightened your burden, for He knows that there is weakness in you. So if there be a hundred of you who are strong-willed and steadfast, they will vanquish two hundred; and if there be a thousand of you, they will vanquish two thousand by God's leave. God is with those who are steadfast.[597]

[595] Qur'ān 2: 106.
[596] Qur'ān 16: 102.
[597] Qur'ān 8: 65–66.

Further evidence supporting the existence of *naskh* is the statement of the Prophet; "I used to forbid you to visit graves, but now you may freely do so, for they remind you of death."[598]

A'isha reported the Holy Qur'an revealed that ten clear sucklings make the marriage unlawful, then it was abrogated (and substituted) by five sucklings and God's Messenger died and it was before that time (found) in the Holy Qur'an (and recited by the Muslims).[599]

Summary: Introduction

1. In the Qur'anic sciences, *naskh* means the abrogation (suspension or replacement) of one Shari'ah ruling by another.
2. The abrogating ruling must be of a subsequent origin and the two rulings are enacted separately from one another.
3. A verse whose ruling has been abrogated is called '*mansūkh*' and the abrogating verse which brings the new regulation is called '*nāsikh*.'
4. *Naskh* could only be applied during the lifetime of the Prophet.
5. The word '*naskh*' and its derivations are used in the Qur'an with different meanings.
6. Islamic law encompasses three forms of legislation: it retained the commandments that pre-dated it if they didn't contradict the essentials of Islam; it corrected or amended existing rulings when they contradict its essentials; and it introduced new legislation.
7. *Naskh* is one of the most controversial topics among the scholars. Whilst most accept the notion of *naskh*, others do not accept it at all.
8. The message of Islam was presented to the Arabs in stages. It was so new and different from their accustomed way of life, therefore changes were introduced gradually to give people time to internalise and practice the new rulings.
9. *Naskh* indicates that the first ruling contradicts the later and therefore the first ruling should be completely abrogated.
10. The conditions for *naskh* to occur are: there must be a pre-existing ruling on exactly the same subject which is then abrogated by a later ruling; there should be *fasila/tarakhi* (intervals) between the rulings of *mansūkh* and *nāsikh*.

---

[598] Tabrizi, *Mishkat*, vol. 1, hadith no: 1762.

[599] Muslim, *Saḥīḥ*, vol. 2, hadith no: 3421.

11. Scholars from the first three centuries of Islam used various words to refer to *naskh* some of which were close in meaning but which weren't actually *naskh*, therefore their statements on this topic cannot immediately be taken as an example of *naskh*.
12. *Naskh* is only valid in legal matters and cannot occur in regard to matters of belief.
13. *Naskh* cannot occur with respect to *ijma'* (general consensus) and *qiyāṣ* (analogy) but only in the Qur'an and Sunnah and only during the lifetime of the noble Prophet. It primarily took place in the Medinian period.
14. The knowledge of *nāsikh* and *mansūkh* is important because it concerns the correct and exact application of Islamic law and is one of the important pre-conditions for exegesis of the Qur'an.
15. Evidence for *naskh* must be based on reliable hadiths or reports going back to the Prophet and his Companions.
16. There are three types of evidence for *naskh*: a) report from the Prophet or Companions, b) *ijma'* (consensus of the *mujtahids* upon *naskh*) and c) knowledge of the chronology of the Qur'anic revelation.

Classification of *Naskh*

Legal rulings affected by *naskh* can be classified with respect to the sources, with respect to their existence or non-existence in the Qur'an, or with respect to the rulings of the *mansūkh* (abrogated) in comparison with the *nāsikh* (abrogating).

With respect to the sources *naskh* can be classified as follows:

a) The Qur'an abrogates the Qur'an. For example, the verses regarding the stages of the prohibition of alcohol.

b) The Qur'an abrogates the Sunnah. For example, when the Prophet came to Medina, he performed the daily-prescribed Prayers toward Jerusalem for 17 months, after that God abrogated this practise by the following verse;

> Certainly We have seen you (O Messenger) often turning your face to heaven (in expectation of a Revelation. Do not worry, for) We will surely turn you towards a direction that will please and satisfy you. (Now the time has come, so) turn your face towards the Sacred Mosque...[600]

c) The *mutawātir* (most strong and authentic hadith) Sunnah abrogates the Qur'an. For example, the following verses;

---

600 Qur'ān 2: 144.

> Prescribed for you, when any of you is visited by death, if he leaves behind wealth, is to make testament in favour of his parents and near relatives according to customary good and religiously approvable practice—a duty for the truly God-revering, pious[601]

> God commands you in (the matter of the division of the inheritance among) your children: for the male is the equivalent of the portion of two females...[602]

In the second verse, each legal heir is assigned their portion from the inheritance without needing to make a testament in favour of his parents and near relatives. For this reason, the majority of scholars hold that the first ruling legislating bequests to relatives is abrogated by the verse of inheritance. They use the following hadith to support their view; "God has assigned a portion to all who are entitled. Hence there shall be no bequest to legal heirs."[603]

d) The Sunnah abrogates the Sunnah: this category contains a few subdivisions such as *mutawātir* abrogates *mutawātir* Sunnah and *āḥād* abrogates the *āḥād* Sunnah. For example;

> I had forbidden you from storing away the sacrificial meat because of the large crowds. You may now store it as you wish[604]

> I had forbidden you from visiting the graves. Nay, visit them, for they remind you of the Afterlife.[605]

Abrogation may either be explicit or implicit. Explicit abrogation occurs when the abrogating text clearly repeals one ruling and substitutes another in its place.[606] Implicit abrogation is when the abrogating text does not clearly state that the other text is in conflict with it. If this is the case, the *mujtahids* investigate all the indications and the chronological order of the revelation to reach their conclusion.

SUMMARY: CLASSIFICATION OF *NASKH*

1. Legal rulings affected by *naskh* can be classified by source, by their existence or non-existence in the Qur'an, or by comparing the *mansūkh* (abrogated) with the *nāsikh* (abrogating).

---

601 Qur'ān 2: 180

602 Qur'ān 4: 11.

603 Abu Dāwud, *Sunan*, vol.2, hadith no: 808.

604 Ghazali, *Muṣtaṣfā*, vol.1, p. 83.

605 Tabrizi, *Mishkat*, vol. 1, hadith no: 1762.

606 Kamali, *Principles of Islamic Jurisprudence*, p. 143.

2. Classification by source includes: the Qur'an abrogating the Qur'an; the Qur'an abrogating the Sunnah; the *mutawātir* (most strong and authentic hadith) Sunnah abrogating the Qur'an; the Sunnah abrogating the Sunnah.
3. Explicit abrogation occurs when the abrogating text clearly repeals one ruling and substitutes another in its place.
4. Implicit abrogation is when the abrogating text does not clearly state that the other text is in conflict with it.

Difference between *Naskh* (Abrogation) and *Takhsis* (Specification)

Naskh and *takhsis* are similar to each other in that they both limit or specify a previous law in some way. The two have been the subject of some confusion among scholars and it is essential that the two concepts should be clear. *Naskh* differs from *takhsis* in the following ways:

1) *Takhsis* contains no conflict; it is a specification or limitation of a general concept in the text and one text completes the other in meaning. In the case of *naskh* there is an irreconcilable conflict between two texts.
2) *Naskh* can occur in both general (*āam*) and specific (*khās*) rulings whereas *takhsis* only occurs with general rulings.
3) *Naskh* only takes place with regards to rulings (*aḫkām*); however *takhsis* may occur with respect to other matters that are not directly related to the law.
4) *Naskh* only occurs in the Qur'an or Sunnah but *takhsis* can happen by means of rationality and circumstantial evidence such as *qiyāṣ*, *khabar wāḫid*, (single source report) *'urf* (custom), etc. In the case of *naskh*, a definite ruling can only be abrogated by another definite ruling.[607]
5) There is no time restriction for *takhsis* whereas with *naskh* the abrogating text must have been revealed after the abrogated one. If the chronological order is unknown or the two rulings were revealed in the same timeframe, *naskh* cannot occur. This is not a requirement of *takhsis*.
6) *Naskh* is a total abolishment of the previous ruling, whereas *takhsis* is a limitation in the scope of the ruling.

Islamic scholars dispute the actual number of abrogated verses in the Qur'an as can be seen in the table below.

[607] Āmidī, *Iḫkām*, vol.3, p. 113.

Scholar's name	Number of verses
Abu Ja'far Nahhas	20
Makkī b. Abi Tālib	200
Ibn Ḫazm	214
Abu Bakr b. al-Arabi	105
Ibn al-Jawzī	22
Al-Suyūtī	20
Shah Wali Allah al-Dahlawi	5

This difference occurs due to many verses being considered examples of *naskh*, when in fact they are examples of *takhsis* or do not fall under *naskh* at all.

There are many wisdoms as to why *naskh* occurred in Islam and why it is important to know it, including;

a) It sheds light on the historical development of the Islamic legal code.
b) It helps scholars to understand which verse was revealed first and which one was last.
c) It helps scholars to understand the immediate meaning of the verses concerned.
d) It supports the gradual progress and education of the Muslim community.

Naskh declares the expiration of a ruling contained within the Qur'an or Sunnah. Although the religious practise changes there is no change to the knowledge of God.

The prominent contemporary scholar Fethullah Gülen approaches the notion of *naskh* in a unique and outstanding way;

> We see that the Qur'an sometimes temporarily takes into consideration the understanding of its first addressees and the conditions at the time of the revelation to prepare them for the universal values which will be revealed later. Even so, there exists no conflict or contradiction from the beginning of the revelation to its end. It seems that one verse is the preparation for another verse, in a sense pioneering what is to come; in turn, the other verse is the compliance for the previous one. Even in the verses of *nāsikh-mansūkh*, there is a miracle of the Qur'an. [608]

Summary: Difference between *Naskh* (Abrogation) and *Takhsis* (Specification)

1. *Naskh* and *takhsis* are similar to each other in that they both limit or specify a previous law in some way.

[608] Gülen, *Kur'ân'ın Altın İkliminde*, pp. 128–132.

2. *Naskh* differs from *takhsis* in the following ways:
3. *Takhsis* contains no conflict; it is a specification or limitation of a general concept.
4. *Takhsis* only occurs with general rulings.
5. *Naskh* only takes place with regards to rulings (*aḫkām*); however *takhsis* may occur with respect to other matters that are not directly related to the law.
6. *Naskh* only occurs in the Qur'an or Sunnah but *takhsis* can happen by means of rationality and circumstantial evidence.
7. There is no time restriction for *takhsis.*
8. *Naskh* is a total abolishment of the previous ruling, whereas *takhsis* is a limitation in the scope of the ruling.
9. Islamic scholars dispute the actual number of abrogated verses in the Qur'an.
10. Even though the law changes through *naskh* the knowledge of God does not change.

Dalālah (Textual Implications)

The law requires compliance, both with the explicit meaning of the text and also with the implicit meanings, indirect indications and inferences that can be drawn from it.[609] Ḫanafī scholars divided the textual meanings into four categories; *ibārah naṣṣ*, *ishārah naṣṣ*, *dalālah naṣṣ* and *iktizā naṣṣ*, each of which is explained separately.

Ibārah Naṣṣ (The Explicit Meaning)

Ibārah naṣṣ is the direct meaning of the text which is derived from its words. In other words, whether it is the primary or secondary intent of the words, the meaning can immediately be understood. Every *shar'ī* text conveys a meaning. This meaning could be the original intention of the Lawgiver or it could be a secondary intention.[610] The difference between the two is explained with the example: "*...God has made trading lawful, and interest unlawful...*"[611] The principal meaning of this verse is that trading is lawful and usury is unlawful. In the verse, the two are separated from each other to answer the people of ignorance (pre-Islam-

[609] Kamali, *Principles of Islamic Jurisprudence*, p. 118.
[610] Sarakhsī, *Uṣūl*, vol.1, p. 236.
[611] Qur'an 2: 275.

ic) and the Jews who argued that usury and trade were the same. The primary intent of this verse was to reject this argument and the secondary intention to declare the ruling about trade and usury. This meaning is also immediately understood from the words of the text.

Ibārah naṣṣ usually conveys the principal theme and purpose of the text. This classification is important in identifying the original intent of the Lawgiver in cases where the text contains more than one meaning. The Qur'an and Sunnah usually convey the law with *ibārah naṣṣ* (the explicit meaning) and it takes priority over other types of indications. For example;

> If you fear that you will not be able to observe their rights with exact fairness when you marry the orphan girls (in your custody), you can marry, from among other women who seem good to you, two, or three, or four. However, if you fear that (in your marital obligations) you will not be able to observe justice among them, and then content yourselves with only one.[612]

This verse has main and subsidiary themes. The main theme of this verse is protecting the rights of orphan girls who are under someone's custody. Other themes are the legality of marriage, the permission for polygamy and limiting polygamy to the maximum of four wives. In pre-Islamic times polygamy was not limited; Islam provided these limiṭs and specified that one must remain monogamous if he is unable to be equally just towards multiple wives. All these themes are conveyed explicitly and are directly understood from the text.

Ibārah naṣṣ indicates a definite ruling on without the need for further external evidence to clarify the law. However, if the text is *āam* (general), there is the possibility of restriction and limitation, so this type of text is speculative (*ẕannī*) evidence only.[613]

Ishārah Naṣṣ (The Alluded Meaning)

Ishārah naṣṣ (the alluded meaning) is a meaning which is not immediately understood from the words of the text but is obtained through further investigation. *Ishārah naṣṣ* does not convey the principal theme of the text but is a contributing factor in extracting the ruling; it is necessary to more clearly comprehend the main theme of the text. For example, the verse; "*It is made lawful for you to go in*

[612] Qur'an 4: 3.

[613] Badran, *Uṣūl*, pp. 419–420.

to your wives on the night of the fast..."[614] conveys using *ibārah* (actual words) that it is lawful to have sexual intercourse with the wife in every segment of the night until dawn. Similarly, this verse also indicates through *ishārah* (alluded meaning) that it is permissible to spend the night as *junub* (with major impurity after sexual intercourse). This implication is understood because if it is permissible to have intercourse up until dawn, it is permissible to still be *junub* at this time as couples won't have time to shower before then. This meaning in the text is not explicit but alluded to.

A further example is the verse; "*...It is incumbent upon him who fathered the child to provide the mothers with sustenance and clothing according to customary good and religiously approvable practice...*"[615] which conveys with its *ibārah* (actual words) the meaning that the maintenance of mothers is incumbent upon the fathers. Similarly, it implies with *ishārah* (alluded meaning) that the maintenance of children is the duty of the fathers alone because the children's descent is only attributed to their fathers. Moreover, fathers can use the wealth of their children in case of necessity based on the alluded meaning of the text, because if children belong to the father, their wealth also belongs to him. This is only valid from the view point of morality but does not affect the right of property. The noble Prophet said; "You and your property both belong to your father."[616] As a result, the *ishārah naṣṣ* constitute the basis of obligation, unless there is evidence to suggest otherwise.

Dalālah Naṣṣ (The Inferred Meaning)

Dalālah naṣṣ (the inferred meaning) is not derived from the words of the text or from the alluded meaning of the words; it is obtained from the effective cause of the ruling (*'illah*) or from the rationale basis of the law (*manāt*). It is not possible to derive the inferred meaning from the text, it comes from external indications such as through the identification of an effective cause (*'illah*); for example, if there are two cases which have a common *'illah* and the commonality can be understood without resorting to *ijtihād*. Imam Shāfi'ī equated *dalālah naṣṣ* with analogical deduction, namely *qiyāṣ jalī* (clear analogy).

The following examples help to understand *dalālah naṣṣ* (the inferred meaning):

[614] Qur'an 2: 187.
[615] Qur'an 2: 233.
[616] Tabrizi, *Mishkat*, vol.2, hadith no: 3354.

"Surely those who consume the property of orphans wrongfully, certainly they consume a fire in their bellies and soon they will be roasting in a Blaze."[617] This verse conveys in *ibārah* (actual words) that it is *haram* to consume the property of orphans wrongfully, it also indicates with *dalālah* (inferred meaning) that using the property of orphans for charity or to help other people is also *haram*. The inferred meaning is obtained through analogy because in both cases there is a common *'illah*; wrongfully consuming the property of orphans. Another example is the verse:

> Divorced women shall keep themselves in waiting for three menstrual courses, and it is not lawful for them, if they believe in God and the Last Day, to conceal what God has created in their wombs...[618]

The text conveys in *ibārah* (actual words) that it is obligatory for divorced women to wait until three menstrual courses have passed to be sure they are not pregnant; the *'illah* of the waiting period clarity around pregnancy. Similarly, a divorced woman who married without two witnesses but consummated the marriage has to wait three menstrual courses for the same reason. This meaning is obtained through *dalālah naṣṣ*. The final example:

> Your Lord has decreed that you worship none but Him alone, and treat parents with the best of kindness. Should one of them, or both, attain old age in your lifetime, do not say 'Ugh!' to them (as an indication of complaint or impatience), nor push them away, and always address them in gracious words.[619]

This verse conveys through *ibārah* that it is *haram* to say 'ugh!' to parents. Through *dalālah* (inferred meaning) it also conveys that it is *haram* to insult, to yell, and to harm them physically, because these acts are worse than saying 'ugh!', therefore, if the Lawgiver prohibited the minimum offense it is clear that the maximum offense is strongly *haram*.

Iktizā Naṣṣ (The Required Meaning)

Iktizā naṣṣ refers to cases where a required part of the meaning is not included in the text but is necessary to comprehend the true intention. For example, the expression; *"Ask the town where we were in..."*[620] does not sound valid without

---

[617] Qur'an 4: 10.
[618] Qur'an 2: 228.
[619] Qur'an 17: 23.
[620] Qur'an 12: 83.

clarifying that it means asking the people in the town. This meaning is required for the text to make sense. Also, the verse; *"Unlawful to you are your mothers and your daughters..."*[621] does not mention the word 'marriage' but this is required to complete the meaning of the text. Similarly, the verse; *"Unlawful to you (for food) are carrion, and blood ..."* does not include the word 'consuming' but it is required to complete the meaning that the prohibition is related to their consumption.

In conclusion, a text may be interpreted through the application of any of the four textual implications and the meaning that is arrived at may be indicated in the words of the text, by the signs which occur therein, by inference, or by the supplementation of a missing element.[622] In the case of a conflict between *ibārah naṣṣ* (explicit meaning) and *ishārah naṣṣ* (alluded meaning) the former is preferred.

SUMMARY: *DALĀLAH* (TEXTUAL IMPLICATIONS)

1. Ḫanafī scholars divided the textual meanings into four categories; *ibārah naṣṣ, ishārah naṣṣ, dalālah naṣṣ* and *iktizā naṣṣ.*
2. *Ibārah naṣṣ* (the explicit meaning) is the direct meaning of the text which is derived from its words. In other words, whether it is the primary or secondary intent of the words, the meaning can immediately be understood.
3. *Ibārah naṣṣ* usually conveys the principal theme and purpose of the text. This classification is important in identifying the original intent of the Lawgiver in cases where the text contains more than one meaning.
4. *Ibārah naṣṣ* indicates a definite rule on without the need for further external evidence to clarify the law. However, if the text is *āam* (general), there is the possibility of restriction and limitation, so this type of text is speculative (*ẕannī*) evidence only.
5. *Ishārah naṣṣ* (the alluded meaning) is a meaning which is not immediately understood from the words of the text but is obtained through further investigation into the implied meaning.
6. *Ishārah naṣṣ* does not convey the principal theme of the text but is a contributing factor in extracting the ruling.
7. *Dalālah naṣṣ* (the inferred meaning) is obtained from the effective cause of the rule (*'illah*) or from the rational basis of the law (*manāt*). It is not possible to derive the inferred meaning from the text.

---

[621] Qur'an 4: 22.

[622] Kamali, *Principles of Islamic Jurisprudence*, p. 122.

8. *Iktizā naṣṣ* (the required meaning) refers to cases where a required part of the meaning is not included in the text but is necessary to comprehend the true intention.
9. A text may be interpreted through the application of any of the four textual implications and the meaning that is arrived at may be indicated in the words of the text, by the signs which occur therein, by inference, or by the supplementation of a missing element.

Chapter 12

Ijtihād (Personal Reasoning)

Ijtihād (Personal Reasoning)

Introduction

Ijtihād literally means exercising the utmost effort to reach something or to obtain a certain result. *Ijtihād* involves hardship and the usage of the whole capacity to carry a heavy load. In a juridical sense, the heavy burden is the intellectual duty that the *mujtahid* should fulfil. Thus, *ijtihād* is defined by the scholars of *Uṣūl* as a jurist engaging all his mental faculties to extract the rules of Islamic law from the sources and apply them to particular cases.[623] There are two parts to *ijtihād*; extracting the rules from their sources and explaining them and then applying them to particular issues.

Ijtihād is an important source of Islamic law and is the dynamic component which continued after the death of the Prophet when the revelation ended. It is necessary to interpret the Qur'an and Sunnah through the application of *ijtihād* ensuring their relevance to the time and conditions. The validity of *ijtihād* is based on its harmony with the Qur'an, Sunnah and the main principles of Islamic law as the revelation is the ultimate source of the law. In other words, the revelation is essential and personal reasoning is a tool to clarify its ambiguity and make it applicable to all times and conditions.

Time is an important criterion in solving problems, explaining issues and applying Islamic law in the correct way. There are some issues in the Qur'an and Sunnah that are left to the *ijtihād* of the *mujtahids* because their explanations and interpretations are dependent on the time and the conditions present. It is important that, when confronted with this type of problem, the *mujtahid* knows whether there is an existing regulation in the Qur'an or Sunnah. It is not valid for the *mujtahid* to make *ijtihād* on an issue that is already addressed in a definite way in the Qur'an or Sunnah. Similarly, if there is an *ijma'* on a specific matter, it is not permissible for a *mujtahid* to make *ijtihād* on that area. If both the primary sources and *ijma'* contain no evidence for a contemporary problem, the *mujtahid* analyses it according to the principles of Islamic law and gives a personal judgment

[623] Abu Zahra, *Uṣūl*, p. 301.

on the matter. As well as being fully equipped to make *ijtihād*, the *mujtahid* must fear uttering a word that may contradict the word of God and His objectives. If a *mujtahid* rules based on his own ideas and comfort, his *ijtihād* is void regardless of whether or not he is qualified to make *ijtihād*.

Ijtihād is the personal reasoning of *mujtahids* that consists of speculative inference. In other words, it is not definite and binding on everyone. *Ijtihād* is speculative and does not convey definitive knowledge; therefore, it could be right or wrong. Thus, the clear and definite rulings of the Qur'an or Sunnah are outside of the scope of *ijtihād*. There is a difference between issuing fatwa[624] and making *ijtihād*. A person who is well-versed in Islamic law and qualified to issue fatwa is not necessarily able to perform *ijtihād*. An example is muftis (clergy). They have a detailed knowledge of Islamic law but they are not qualified as *mujtahid*. The definition of *ijtihād* conveys that a *mujtahid* is a *fāqih* (jurist) who fulfils all the conditions to be able to extract the rulings regarding the conducts of the liable persons from the primary and secondary sources of Islamic law. It is not possible for a scholar to reach the level of *mujtahid* merely by learning from other *mujtahids* and reading their books.

The detailed evidences found in the Qur'an and Sunnah are divided into four types;[625]

1) Evidence which is decisive with respect to both its authenticity and meaning.
2) Evidence which is authentic but speculative in meaning.
3) Evidence which is of doubtful authenticity, but is definite in meaning.
4) Evidence which is speculative in both its authenticity and meaning.

Ijtihād does not apply to the first category which includes things such as the clear textual evidences concerning prescribed penalties, but it can validly operate with regard to any of the other three categories of evidence.[626]

Summary: Introduction

1. *Ijtihād* is defined by the scholars of *Uṣūl* as a jurist engaging all his mental faculties to extract the rulings of Islamic law from the sources and apply them to particular cases.

---

624 Fatwa are issued explaining the rulings that have already been addressed by the *mujtahids* without establishing new methodology. A mufti may know the fatwa of the *mujtahids* but he is not qualified to establish his own methodology in Islamic law to extract the rulings from their sources.

625 Kamali, *Principles of Islamic Jurisprudence*, pp. 316–317.

626 Ibid.

2. There are two parts to *ijtihād*; extracting the rules from their sources and explaining them and then applying them to particular issues.
3. It is necessary to interpret the Qur'an and Sunnah through the application of *ijtihād* ensuring their relevance to the time and conditions.
4. There are some issues in the Qur'an and Sunnah that are left to the *ijtihād* of the *mujtahids* because their explanations and interpretations are dependent on the time and the conditions present.
5. The *mujtahid* must know whether a regulation already exists in the Qur'an or Sunnah. It is not valid for the *mujtahid* to make *ijtihād* on an issue that is already addressed in the Qur'an or Sunnah or *ijma.'*
6. *Ijtihād* is the personal reasoning of *mujtahids* that consists of speculative inference and is not definite and binding on everyone.
7. A *mujtahid* is *fāqih* who has the capacity to extract the rulings regarding the conducts of the liable persons from the primary and secondary sources of Islamic law.
8. The detailed evidences found in the Qur'an and Sunnah are divided into four types: decisive in authenticity and meaning; authentic but speculative in meaning; doubtful in authenticity but definite in meaning; speculative in both authenticity and meaning.
9. *Ijtihād* applies to the last three types of evidence.

The Proof Value of *Ijtihād*

The application of personal reasoning by the capable *mujtahid* is valid based on the Qur'an, Sunnah and intellect. Scholars support this argument with some verses, however the verses are speculative (*ẕannī*) rather than definite evidence in regards to the validity of the application of *ijtihād*. Some of the verses are;

> And the believers should not go forth to war all together. But why should not a party from every community of them mobilize to acquire profound, correct knowledge and understanding of religion and warn their people when they return to them so that they may beware (of wrongful attitudes)?[627]

Devotion to the study of religion is the essence of *ijtihād* and it is a duty upon the Muslim community to fulfil this mission. The religion must be taught and

---

[627] Qur'ān 9: 122.

applied correctly and this task can be done only by the *mujtahids* who have valid and comprehensive knowledge and understanding of the religion.

> Those (on the other hand) who strive hard for Our sake, We will most certainly guide them to Our ways Most assuredly, God is with those devoted to doing good, aware that God is seeing them.[628]

There are many ways to find the truth and the duty of *mujtahids* is to struggle with their utmost effort to find it.

> O you who believe! Obey God and obey the Messenger, and those from among you who are invested with authority; and if you are to dispute among yourselves about anything, refer it to God and the Messenger, if indeed you believe in God and the Last Day. This is the best (for you) and fairest in the end.[629]

The implementation of this verse requires knowledge of the Qur'an, the Sunnah and the objectives of the Lawgiver and only one with those qualities can use them to adjudicate on and resolve problems and disputes.[630]

The scholars also use the following hadiths to support the validity of *ijtihād*;

> When the Messenger of Allah intended to send Mu'adh ibn Jabal to the Yemen, he asked: How will you judge when the occasion of deciding a case arises? He replied: I shall judge in accordance with Allah's Book. He asked: (What will you do) if you do not find any guidance in Allah's Book? He replied: (I shall act) in accordance with the Sunnah of the Messenger of Allah. He asked: (What will you do) if you do not find any guidance in the Sunnah of the Messenger of Allah and in Allah's Book? He replied: I shall do my best to form an opinion and I shall spare no effort. The Messenger of Allah then patted him on the breast and said: Praise be to Allah Who has helped the messenger of the Messenger of Allah to find something which pleases the Messenger of Allah.[631]

The hadith; "When a judge exercises *ijtihād* and gives a right judgment, he will have two rewards, but if he makes mistakes in his judgment, he will still earn one reward"[632] clearly outlines that a *mujtahid* will be rewarded for his efforts regard-

---

[628] Qur'ān 29: 69.
[629] Qur'ān 4: 59.
[630] Kamali, *Principles of Islamic Jurisprudence*, p. 321.
[631] Abu Dāwud, *Sunan, Kitāb Al-Aqdiya*, hadith no: 3585.
[632] Abu Dāwud, *Sunan, Kitāb Al-Aqdiya*, hadith no. 3567.

less of the result of his *ijtihād*. The noble Prophet encouraged scholars to be *mujtahids* and carry out this vital mission on behalf of the Muslim community.

"When God favours one of His servants, He enables him to acquire profound knowledge in religion."[633] *Ijtihād* is an essential part of learning the religion and applying the law correctly according to the time and conditions. The Prophet praised those who are willing and able to accept and carry out this important responsibility.

In their search for solutions to new problems, the Companions of the Prophet first looked to the Qur'an and Sunnah for answers. If they were unable to find a solution it is reported through *mutawātir* reports that they would then resort to *ijtihād*.[634] Rationally, it can be argued that as textual evidence is limited and new experiences and problems will continually arise in the Muslim community, *ijtihād* is an essential tool for the learned members of the community to be able to fulfil their duty effectively.[635]

Summary: The Proof Value of *Ijtihād*

1. The application of personal reasoning by the capable *mujtahid* is valid based on the Qur'an, Sunnah and intellect.
2. Devotion to the study of religion is the essence of *ijtihād* and it is a duty upon the Muslim community to fulfil this mission: this task can be done only by the *mujtahids*.
3. There are many ways to find the truth and the duty of *mujtahids* is to struggle with their utmost effort to find it.
4. The Prophet encouraged scholars to be *mujtahids* and carry out this vital mission on behalf of the Muslim community.
5. In their search for solutions to new problems, the Companions of the Prophet first looked to the Qur'an and Sunnah for answers. If they were unable to find a solution it is reported through *mutawātir* reports that they would then resort to *ijtihād*.

Conditions of *Ijtihād*

There are certain qualifications the *mujtahid* must possess in order to carry out *ijtihād*:

---

633 Bukhari, *Saḫīḫ*, vol.1, hadith no: 25–26.
634 Ghazali, *Muṣtaṣfā*, vol.2, p. 106.
635 Kamali, p. 322.

1) Scholars agree that the *mujtahid* must have an exemplary command of Arabic. Arabic is the language of the religion and it is essential to understanding both the evidence and the purpose of God. Without this knowledge it is impossible to extract the meanings from the texts and interpret them correctly. Additionally, the *mujtahid* must possess the particular knowledge of the language of the Qur'an and Sunnah. The Qur'an was revealed in the most eloquent manner and this particular knowledge is necessary in order to deduce the rulings through textual interpretation. The capacity of deducing the rulings from their sources is directly related to the knowledge of Arabic. Imam Shātibī holds that a beginner in the Arabic language is also a beginner in deducing the rulings from their sources. Similarly, if they have a medium understanding of Arabic, their understanding of the sources is also medium. Those with the highest level of understanding of Arabic language can have a high understanding of the Qur'an and Sunnah comparable to the understanding of the Companions. Anyone with a deficiency in their understanding of the language of the Qur'an and Sunnah cannot be deemed *mujtahid*.[636] Since the *mujtahid* performs a religious duty and his *ijtihād* is evidence for the layman, he must be well-versed in the language of the Qur'an.

2) A *mujtahid* must have a detailed knowledge of the Qur'an and its related sciences such as the notion of abrogation (*naskh*), *āam-khās, mutlaq-muqayyad, mafhum-mantuq*, *ibārah*, *ishārah*, *iktizā* and *dalālah,* etc. The *mujtahid* must also know the Makkī (Mecca) and the Madanī (Medina) contents of the Qur'an, the occasions of its revelation and the incidences of abrogation therein. The *mujtahid* must specifically know the legal contents of the Qur'an which means the five hundred *aḫkām* verses that detail legislation.[637] Additionally, the *mujtahid* must know the general content of the Qur'an, because the knowledge of the *aḫkām* verses is strongly interrelated with the knowledge of the general content.

3) Knowledge of Sunnah. Scholars agree that *mujtahid* must know the verbal, practical and the affirmative Sunnah, especially the part of Sunnah which is directly related to *ijtihād*. For some scholars, *mujtahid* must know all the Sunnah regardless of its content including the abrogated-abrogating verses, the general-specific, the absolute-qualified and the reliability level of the hadiths.[638] Scholars produced many works to separate the weak from the authentic hadiths and

---

[636] Shātibī, *Muwafaqaat*, vol.4, p. 114.

[637] Ghazali, *Muṣtaṣfā*, vol.2, p. 101.

[638] Abu Zahrah, *Uṣūl*, p. 304.

they set the criteria for this work. *Mujtahid* must be familiar with the hadiths which are directly related to the rulings.[639]

4) A *mujtahid* must have knowledge of the issues that have been solved previously by general consensus. If previous *mujtahids* have reached a general consensus on a matter it is not permissible for a later *mujtahid* to make *ijtihād* on the same issue.[640] Abū Ḫanīfa said that the most learned of people is also one who is the most knowledgeable of the differences among people.[641]

5) According to Imam Shāfi'ī, *ijtihād* is the knowledge of all forms of *qiyāṣ*.[642] For this reason the *mujtahid* must know *qiyāṣ* and its application in new cases. As previously described, *qiyāṣ* is extending the rule of the original text to new cases based on common *'illah* (effective cause) between the two. For some scholars, *qiyāṣ* and *ijtihād* are identical, but *ijtihād* is a broader concept than *qiyāṣ*, because it covers other reasoning methods such as *istiḫsan*, *maslaḫah mursala* and *sadd dharā'ī.'*[643]

6) A *mujtahid* must know the objectives of Islamic law and the purpose of the Lawgiver. There are three main objectives in Islamic law; *ḏaruriyyāt* (five essential values such as protecting religion, intellect, lineage and property, life), *ḫājiyyāt* (necessary regulations to complete the first category of objectives) and *taḫsiniyyāt* (the embellishments). The *mujtahid* must also know the general maxims of Islamic law in order to distinguish the harmful from the beneficial; to provide the *maslaḫah* for the public and prevent them from harm.[644] Shātibī holds that *mujtahid* must know the objectives of Islamic law (*maqāsid Shari'ah*) as well as the sources of the rulings and the methods of deduction.[645]

7) A *mujtahid* must have a sound intellect and the capacity to understand the matters correctly. This condition is related to logical reasoning which is necessary to make reasoning valid; however, this condition is not mandatory as this science was developed after the Companions time.[646]

8) A *mujtahid* must be an upright person with a sincere intention. He is one who fears contradicting the objectives of Lawgiver. If a person seeks his own

639 Shawkānī, *Irshād*, p. 251.
640 Ibid.
641 Abu Zahrah, *Uṣūl*, p. 305.
642 Shāfi'i, *Risāla*, p. 477.
643 Shawkānī, *Irshād*, p. 252.
644 Badran, *Uṣūl*, p. 208.
645 Shātibī, *Muwafaqaat*, vol.4, p. 56.
646 Abu Zahrah, *Uṣūl*, pp. 308–309.

pleasure and comfort, his *ijtihād* is void regardless of his capabilities.[647] A *mujtahid* represents the noble Prophet and therefore should be righteous, God-fearing, pious and one who refrains from committing sins.

These are the required conditions for a *mujtahid* who is fully qualified to make *ijtihād* in every matter of *Shari'ah*. However, for the scholars who accept divisions in *ijtihād*, only relevant conditions are necessary for particular cases. This subject will be discussed separately.

Summary: Conditions of *Ijtihād*

1. There are certain qualifications the *mujtahid* must possess in order to carry out *ijtihād*:
2. The *mujtahid* must have an exemplary command of Arabic; particularly the language of the Qur'an and Sunnah. Without this it is impossible to extract the meanings from the texts and interpret them correctly.
3. A *mujtahid* must have a detailed knowledge of the Qur'an and its related sciences; the Makkī (Mecca) and the Madanī (Medina) contents; the occasions of its revelation and the incidences of abrogation; the legal contents and the general content.
4. The *mujtahid* must know the verbal, practical and the affirmative Sunnah, especially the part of Sunnah which is directly related to *ijtihād*.
5. The *mujtahid* must have knowledge of the issues that have been solved previously by general consensus as it is not permissible for a later *mujtahid* to make *ijtihād* on these issues.
6. The *mujtahid* must know *qiyāṣ* and its application in new cases.
7. A *mujtahid* must know the objectives of Islamic law and the purpose of the Lawgiver. They must also know the general maxims of *fiqh* in order to distinguish the harmful from the beneficial; to provide the *maslaḫah* for the public and prevent them from harm.
8. A *mujtahid* must have a sound intellect and the capacity to understand the matters correctly.
9. A *mujtahid* must be an upright person with a sincere intention.

The Matter of Division in *Ijtihād*

The division of *ijtihād* into categories enables *mujtahid* to specialise in specific areas of the *Shari'ah* whilst leaving others. Scholars debated the validity of this

[647] Ghazali, *Muṣtaṣfā*, vol.2, p. 101.

with most agreeing the necessity of being *mujtahid* on all areas of the law, both penal and devotional, as all the parts of Islamic jurisprudence are strongly interrelated. Scholars agreed that if the *mujtahid* fulfils the conditions mentioned previously, he is capable of performing *ijtihād* in every part of the *Shari'ah* because one person cannot be a *mujtahid* and a *muqallid* (imitator) at the same time.[648] The majority of scholars defend their opinion saying if a *mujtahid* is ignorant in some areas it will result in misunderstanding in other areas resulting in mistakes. They also argue that a true *mujtahid* does not follow other people in legal matters, he makes *ijtihāds* and forms his own opinions.[649]

Hanbalī, Ẕahirī and some Maliki scholars hold that *ijtihād* can be divided and that a person well-versed in a specific area can just make *ijtihād* in that area only. According to this view, a person can be a *mujtahid* and a *muqallid* (imitator) at the same time. For example, Imam Mālik expressed his insufficiency in some areas but this does not remove his title as *mujtahid*.[650] Ghazali holds that if a person is knowledgeable in the area of *qiyāṣ* he can practice *ijtihād* in this area even though he may not be an expert in the field of hadith. If knowledge of all the parts of Islamic law were necessary for the application of *ijtihād*, few scholars would meet this requirement and consequently the duty of *ijtihād* would be abandoned.[651] In view of the sheer bulk of information and the rapid pace of its growth in modern times, specialisation in any major area of knowledge would seem to hold the key to originality and creative *ijtihād*, therefore division in *ijtihād* would seem to be in greater harmony with the conditions of research in modern times.[652]

Summary: The Matter of Division in *Ijtihād*

1. The division of *ijtihād* into categories enables *mujtahid* to specialise in specific areas of the *Shari'ah* whilst leaving others.
2. The validity of this is the subject of debate amongst scholars.
3. Scholars agreed that if the *mujtahid* fulfils the conditions mentioned previously, he is capable of performing *ijtihād* in every part of the *Shari'ah.*
4. The majority of scholars believe that if a *mujtahid* is ignorant in some areas it will result in misunderstanding in other areas resulting in mistakes.

---

[648] Shawkānī, *Irshād*, p. 254.
[649] Āmidī, *Iḥkām*, vol.4, p. 204.
[650] Badran, *Uṣūl*, p. 486.
[651] Ghazali, *Muṣtaṣfā*, vol.2, p. 103.
[652] Kamali, *Principles of Islamic Jurisprudence*, p. 326.

5. Hanbalī, Ẕahirī and some Maliki scholars hold that *ijtihād* can be divided and that a person well-versed in a specific area can just make *ijtihād* in that area only.
6. Ghazali holds that if a person is knowledgeable in the area of *qiyāṣ* he can practice *ijtihād* in this area even though he may not be an expert in the field of hadith.
7. If knowledge of all the parts of Islamic law were necessary for the application of *ijtihād*, few scholars would meet this requirement and consequently the duty of *ijtihād* would be abandoned.

Truth and Fallacy of *Ijtihād*

Scholars unanimously agree that there is only one truth regarding the essentials of belief such as unity of God, afterlife, the Prophethood, angels, etc. One who disagrees with this becomes a disbeliever.[653] On the other hand, it is possible to have different views regarding judicial matters and this is the focus of a discussion. Scholars debate about the different rulings on the same topic resulting from *ijtihāds* of different legal schools as to which one is true. Is it possible to have several solutions for a particular problem and accept all the *ijtihāds* as truth? If the rulings are clearly addressed by the Qur'an, Sunnah or *ijma'* there is only one truth and the *mujtahid* cannot rule against this. However, if the matters are left to *ijtihād* the scholars may have different views. We will mention one of the most comprehensive explanations for this matter from Bediüzzaman Said Nursi:

> Laws change over time. Prior to Prophet Muhammad, different Prophets were sent to different people with different laws in even one age. As the Prophet's most comprehensive Shari'ah suffices for all people in every age, there has been left no need for different Laws. However, various secondary matters showed that different legal schools were needed. Just as clothes are changed seasonally and cures may differ according to temperaments, rules governing secondary matters may differ, as they are based on time's passage and people's characters and capacities. This allows them to answer newly arising questions and situations.
>
> The same water functions in five different ways when given to five sick people. It will cure the first person's illness, and so, according to the science of medicine, it is necessary. It will be like poison for the second person, making him even sicker, and therefore is medically forbidden. It will be slightly harmful for the third person, and therefore should be avoid-

[653] Shawkānī, *Irshād*, p. 259.

ed. It will be beneficial for the fourth person, and thus medicine advises it. It will be neither harmful nor beneficial for the fifth person, and because he can drink it with good health it is medically permissible. Thus all five approaches are valid. Can you argue that water is only a cure, and that it must be consumed regardless of its effect?

Similarly, Divine Wisdom requires that Divine ordinances of secondary importance should differ according to those who follow them. This results in different schools, all of which are right. For example, most members of the Shāfi'ī school are closer to village life and less familiar with the social life that makes the community like a single body. This is why, in a congregational Prayer, each one recites Surah Fatiha behind the imam to unburden themselves at the Court of the Dispenser of needs and relate their private wishes. This is right and pure wisdom. However, since over time the majority of Islamic governments have adopted the Ḥanafī school of law as their official code, those who follow this school have been closer to civilization and city life and more inclined to social life. As social, civilized life makes a community like a single individual, one person can speak for the community. Therefore, since all people affirm and support the leader with their hearts and his word becomes the word of all, Ḥanafī congregations do not recite Surah Fatiha behind the imam. This is also right and pure wisdom.[654]

Summary: Truth and Fallacy of *Ijtihād*

1. Scholars unanimously agree that there is only one truth regarding the essentials of belief such as unity of God, afterlife, the Prophethood, angels, etc.
2. It is possible to have different views regarding judicial matters and this is the focus of a discussion.
3. Scholars debate whether it is possible to have several solutions for a particular problem and accept all the *ijtihāds* as truth.
4. Bediüzzaman Said Nursi explains that differences between different schools are permissible and correct because different times and the condition of people changes bringing new challenges. Different reflections of the same rules are necessary to meet the needs of everyone. All of them are correct because each takes into account the needs of the people at that time.

[654] Nursi, *The Words*, pp. 504–505.

Restrictions on *Ijtihād*

After the 11th Century, scholars of *Uṣūl al-Fiqh* imposed restrictions on *ijtihād* due to specific circumstances. At the beginning of the formation of Islamic law, *ijtihād* was applied in two forms by the imams of the different legal schools: deducing the law from its sources; and interpreting and applying it to different cases according to a specific methodology. During the first three centuries of Islam, these imams produced legal solutions for the contemporary problems. After this, some scholars believed that they were the real *mujtahids* and no one could replace them in establishing a new legal school. They declared that the gate of *ijtihād* was closed. Said Nursi summarizes the reasons for this in a clear and comprehensive way;

> The door to *ijtihād* is open, but six obstacles block the way to it. Under the onslaught of a mighty flood, making openings in a wall to repair it leads to being drowned. So, at this time of the un-Islamic and even anti-Islamic practices, the onslaught of customs from Europe, the legion of religious innovations and the destruction of misguidance, to open new holes and invasion routes in the citadel of Islam in the name of *ijtihād* is a crime against Islam.
>
> The essentials of Islam are not subject to *ijtihād*. They are specified and definite, and are like basic food and sustenance without which life is impossible. At present, they are abandoned and neglected. We must strive to restore and revitalize them with all our strength.
>
> Various products are sought in the marketplace according to season and demand. This is also true of humanity's social life and civilization as well. During the early generations of Islam, the most sought-after "product" was learning from the Word of the Creator of the heavens and the earth what He approves of and wants from us, and how to obtain eternal happiness in the world of the Hereafter, the doors of which had been opened so widely by the light of Prophethood and the Qur'an that they could not be closed. But now European civilization is dominant. We face naturalistic philosophy's heavy pressure, and the conditions of modern life scatter our minds and hearts and divide our efforts and cares. Our minds are estranged from spiritual issues.
>
> A living body has an inherent tendency to expand and grow. Since this tendency is inherent in or comes from within the body, it serves for the body's development and perfection. If this tendency is an external intervention, it will tear up the body's skin and destroy it; it is not a growth and development. Similarly, if, like the pious, righteous early generations,

those who have entered the sphere of Islam through the door of perfect piety, righteousness and God's consciousness, and conform to Islam's essentials strictly have the inclination to expand and the desire to engage in *ijtihād*, it is a virtue and serves for perfection. But this inclination and desire in those who neglect Islam's essentials, prefer the world over the afterlife, and occupy themselves with materialistic philosophy destroys Islam's body and leads to breaking away from the Shari'ah.

The Law of Islam is heavenly and revealed, however, three factors now make *ijtihād* worldly: first, the cause for establishing a rule differs from the wisdom and benefit expected of it. Wisdom or benefit is the reason for its preference, while the cause requires its existence. In our day, however, people substitute wisdom or benefit for the cause and act accordingly. Second, People now give priority to worldly happiness; the Shari'ah gives absolute priority to otherworldly eternal happiness, since the present viewpoint is alien to the Sharia's spirit, it cannot exercise *ijtihād* in the Sharia's name. Third, the principle that absolute necessity makes permissible what the Shari'ah forbids is not always valid, regardless of time and place. If the necessity does not arise from a forbidden act, it may be the cause for permission. But if it arises from a misuse of willpower and unlawful acts, it cannot be the means for any dispensation. These days, many things that are not necessary for people's life have become necessary and an addiction because of people's voluntary misuse of their willpower, unlawful inclinations, and forbidden acts. Thus they cannot be the means for a dispensation or making the unlawful lawful. Those who favour exercising *ijtihād* in the present circumstances build their reasoning on such "necessities," and so their *ijtihād* is worldly, the product of their fancies, and under the influence of modern trends of thought.

Respected mujtahids who lived close to the time of the Prophet and the Companions (the Age of Light and Truth) were purified by that light and exercised *ijtihād* with pure intentions. Their modern counterparts look at the Qur'an from such a great distance and from behind so many veils that it is very hard for them to see even its clearest letter.[655]

Summary: Restrictions on *Ijtihād*

1. After the 11th Century, scholars of *Uṣūl al-Fiqh* imposed restrictions on *ijtihād*.
2. Previously, *ijtihād* was applied in two forms by the imams of the different legal schools: deducing the law from its sources; and interpreting and applying it to different cases according to a specific methodology.

---

655 Nursi, *The Words*, pp. 499–502.

3. After this some scholars declared that the gate of *ijtihād* was closed.
4. Said Nursi summarizes the reasons for this as being:
5. There are six obstacles to *ijtihād.*
6. Un-Islamic and anti-Islamic practices combined with religious innovation, misguidance and the influence of European customs make *ijtihād* impossible.
7. The essentials of Islam have been abandoned and neglected and must be restored.
8. In the early days of Islam, people demanded knowledge of the Creator and the obligations of humankind. However, other philosophies have become dominant, modern life has imposed other priorities and the mind has been estranged from spiritual issues.
9. *Ijtihād* performed in any way other than the true way, by those who neglect Islam's essentials will lead to the destruction of Islam and the Shari'ah.
10. *Ijtihād* is worldly in that it is performed by people. It cannot be performed by those who substitute wisdom and benefit for worldly issues.
11. The respected *mujtahids* lived at a time that was close to the noble Prophet and his Companions and benefited from this closeness. Today people are far from the Qur'an and cannot interpret it clearly.

The Classification of *Mujtahids*

Scholars of *Uṣūl* have classified the *mujtahids* and jurists into seven different categories. The first four are deemed *mujtahid* while the rest are *muqallid* (imitator) and unable to reach the level of *ijtihād.* Each group will be explained regarding their capacity for making *ijtiḥād.*

1) A *mujtahid* in *Shari'ah*; or in other words, the *mujtahids* who are fully qualified to make *ijtihād.* This group meets all the previously mentioned conditions and are the highest rank of those able to make *ijtihād.* They can extract the rulings from their sources without following any legal school or their methodology. In other words, they can deduce the rulings from the Qur'an, Sunnah, *ijma', qiyāṣ, maslaḥah mursala, istiḥsān, 'urf, sadd dharā'ī,* etc. This group is capable of utilizing all the sources for deducing the legal rulings and they do not imitate anyone in this work. They have their own methodology to make *ijtihād* and they apply it to new cases to identify their legal values. Examples in this category are; Abu Ḥanīfa, Shāfi'ī, Awza'i, Lays ibn Sa'd, Sufyan Thawrī and Imam Malik. There is a dispute as to whether the disciples of Abū Ḥanīfa, Abū Yusuf and Muhammad are *mujtahids*

in this category or in the second category where they are dependent in *uṣūl* but independent in *furu'* (detailed rulings). Ibn Ābidīn accepts them in the second category but Abu Zahra criticizes this view and ranks them in the first category.[656]

There is a question that needs to be answered here; is this type of *ijtihād* still possible or has its era come to an end? The majority of scholars hold that this type of *ijtihād* is no longer possible whereas Hanbalī scholars hold the opposite view that *ijtihād* regardless of its form is still possible. They believe that every era must have *mujtahid* because *ijtihād* is a duty upon the Muslim community and is not fulfilled by means of limited *ijtihād* or by the issuance of fatwa alone.[657] Some Ḫanafī scholars are of the opinion that the *mujtahid* Kamalud-Din ibn Humam belongs in the first category and this is evidence that independent *ijtihād* has not finished.[658]

2) A *mujtahid* in a legal school. This group is second in rank in terms of *ijtihād*. They are dependent *mujtahids* in regard to *uṣūl*, methodology and the principles of each legal school, but they are independent in terms of detailed rulings (*furu'*); this means that they may disagree with their imams in some cases. In other words, *mujtahids* at this level expound the law within the limits of a specific school while following the principles established by their imams.[659] These *mujtahids* follow their imams in *Uṣūl* but may disagree with them in *furu'* and they may reach different result in their *ijtihāds*. However, in practise they usually arrive at the same conclusion in the *ijtihāds* because they have studied together for so long and use the same principles of methodology. Examples in this group are Imam Zufar and Ḫasan ibn Ziyad from the Ḫanafī school, al-Muzani, Ibn Salah, Suyūtī from the Shāfi'ī school, Ibn Abd al-Barr, Ibn 'Arābī from the Maliki school and Ibn Taymiyyah and Ibn Qayyim al-Jawziyyah from the Hanbalī school.

3) *Mujtahids* in specific matters. These *mujtahids* follow their imams in both *uṣūl* and *furu.'* They make *ijtihāds* in areas that their imams didn't address, explaining them and identifying the rulings using the methodology of their imams. They do not oppose the *ijtihāds* of their imams, rather they elaborate the law and apply it in new cases. In short, their *ijtihāds* consist of two forms; summarizing and deducing the methodology of the *ijtihāds* of the imams and making *ijtihāds* on new cases. Examples in this category are; Karkhī and Taḫawī from the Ḫanafī school, Abū

---

[656] Abu Zahrah, *Uṣūl*, p. 310.
[657] Kamali, *Principles of Islamic Jurisprudence*, p. 334.
[658] Abu Zahra, p. 311.
[659] Abu Zahra, Uṣūl, p. 312.

Bakr al-Anbari from the Maliki school, Marwazi and Shirazi from the Shāfi'ī school and Husayn al-Khiraqi from the Hanbalī school.

4) A *mujtahid* who is capable of making preferences between different *ijtihāds* in the same legal school. *Mujtahids* in this group do not make new *ijtihāds*, they remove the ambiguity between different *ijtihāds* and prefer one over the others, explaining why it is the most suitable with respect to the time and conditions.[660] They evaluate the reasoning and evidences of each *mujtahid* and choose one of them as the more suitable *ijtihād* for the followers of this legal school.

5) The *mujtahids* who are capable of evaluating all the different views, reports and *ijtihāds* of their school and classifying them as the correct, preferred and the agreed upon *ijtihāds*. There is no clear difference between this and the previous category. Examples are 'Ala' al-Din Kāshānī and Burhān al-Din Marghinanī from the Ḫanafī school, Qurtubī in Maliki and Nawawī from the Shāfi'ī school and Ibn Qudamah from the Hanbalī schools.

6) The jurists who have learned and memorized the *ijtihāds* of their legal school in great detail. They are considered *muqallid* (imitator) not *mujtahid*. These jurists distinguish the reports of the previous *mujtahids* as strong and exceptional or rare. They know the views of the fourth and fifth category of *mujtahids* and their books only contain the sound reports.

7) The imitators (*muqallid*). This is the lowest rank of jurist. They can understand the law books but they cannot make preferences or distinguish between the reports or the *ijtihāds*.[661]

Summary: The Classification of *Mujtahids*

1. Scholars of *Uṣūl* have classified the *mujtahids* and jurists into seven different categories. The first four are deemed *mujtahid* while the rest are *muqallid* (imitator) and unable to reach the level of *ijtihād*.
2. A *mujtahid* in *Shari'ah*; they can extract the rulings from their sources without following any legal school or their methodology. The majority of scholars hold that this type of *ijtihād* is no longer possible whereas Hanbalī scholars hold the opposite view that *ijtihād* regardless of its form is still possible.
3. A *mujtahid* in a legal school; dependent *mujtahids* in regard to *uṣūl*, methodology and the principles of each legal school, but independent in terms of detailed rulings (*furu'*).

---

[660] Ibid., p. 315.

[661] Ibid., p. 316.

4. *Mujtahids* in specific matters; they follow the imams in both *uṣūl* and *furu'* and make *ijtihāds* in areas that their imams didn't address.
5. A *mujtahid* who is capable of making preferences between different *ijtihāds* in the same legal school.
6. The *mujtahids* who are capable of evaluating all the different views, reports and *ijtihāds* of their school.
7. The jurists who have learned and memorized the *ijtihāds* of their legal school; they are considered *muqallid* (imitator) not *mujtahid*.
8. The imitators (*muqallid*). They can understand the law books but they cannot make preferences or distinguish between the reports or the *ijtihāds*.

Taqlid (Imitation)

Taqlid is derived from '*qilada*' and means necklace. Jurists define it as imitating the views of other people without having any evidence or proof. In other words, *taqlid* is following someone blindly without knowledge of whether the followed one is right or wrong. For example, applying the *ijtihād* of a jurist without knowing its validity is *taqlid*.

Taqlid is controversial in Islam because it is blind imitation and can result in bias and prejudice from the imitators. Scholars dispute its legal validity as it isn't possible for every *mujtahid* to reach the highest levels of *ijtihād*. Some scholars hold that *taqlid* is not permissible and each liable person must learn the means of *ijtihād* and reach the level of *mujtahid*. Other scholars hold that *taqlid* is permissible for everyone. The middle view is that *taqlid* is permissible for those who cannot reach the level of *ijtihād* but it is not permissible for the *mujtahid*.

The liable person is required to obey God and His Messenger and this concept is supported by many verses: for example;

> Obey God and the Messenger, so that you may be shown mercy[662]
>
> Whatever the Messenger gives you accept it willingly, and whatever he forbids you, refrain from it[663]
>
> But no! By your Lord, they do not (truly) believe unless they make you the judge regarding any dispute between them, and then find not the

[662] Qur'ān 3: 132.
[663] Qur'ān 59: 7.

> least vexation within themselves over what you have decided, and surrender in full submission[664]

Based on these verses, it is *fard aynī* for each individual to obey God and His Messenger, and this duty can be fulfilled by the knowledge of commands, prohibitions, permissible acts, etc. Liable people can learn these duties by studying first the Qur'an and Sunnah and then the high objectives and main principles of Islamic law. However, following this method and identifying the rulings for the conducts of the liable person requires a broad knowledge and the capacity of *ijtihād*. This capacity is undefined and changes according to the person and the conditions. If a liable person cannot identify the rulings regarding their conduct through *ijtihād* because they have not reached that level, they can apply to the *mujtahid* who is an expert. God declared in Qur'an; "*If you (O people) do not know, then ask the people of expert knowledge*"[665] so *taqlid* is permissible for the layman in legal matters. Individuals can ask any capable scholar about the rulings related to their conducts or they can even learn them through reading legal books. God does not overburden people with more than they are capable. It is almost impossible for most Muslims to perform the duty of *ijtihād*, thus it is up to the *mujtahids* to extract the rulings from their sources. The *mujtahids* are qualified to perform this duty on behalf of the Muslims so those unable to make their own *ijtihād* can follow that of the *mujtahid.*

Legal schools were established to address the needs of the laymen. The imams did not invite people to follow their views, they were accepted by the people as trustworthy and knowledgeable and the people began to follow their opinions. Over time, many legal schools have been established but some of them disappeared after people stopped following them; others have survived until the present time. It is permissible to follow these legal schools as long as they follow the Qur'an and Sunnah. Due to the ignorance of people and the non-existence of independent *mujtahids* it is of vital importance that the legal schools are followed to avoid deviation through deficient people making their own *ijtihād*.

Summary: *Taqlid* (Imitation)

1. *Taqlid* is following someone blindly without knowledge of whether the followed one is right or wrong.

---

[664] Qur'ān 4: 65.

[665] Qur'ān 16: 43.

2. Scholars are divided over whether *taqlid* is permissible; some hold that each liable person must learn the means of *ijtihād* and reach the level of *mujtahid*; others hold that *taqlid* is permissible for everyone; the middle view is that *taqlid* is permissible for those who cannot reach the level of *ijtihād* but it is not permissible for the *mujtahid*.
3. It is *fard aynī* for each individual to obey God and His Messenger, and this duty can be fulfilled by the knowledge of commands, prohibitions, permissible, acts, etc.
4. Identifying the rulings for the conducts of the liable person requires a broad knowledge and the capacity of *ijtihād*. Only a *mujtahid* can fulfil this condition.
5. Legal schools were established to address the needs of the laymen. It is permissible to follow these legal schools as long as they follow the Qur'an and Sunnah.

Ta'arud al-Adillah (The Conflicts of the Evidences)

The Arabic word *ta'arud* (conflict) derives from *'urd* meaning a side, a direction and a course. If one word prevents the meaning of another it is expressed as *muta'arid kalam* in Arabic.[666] Jurists define *ta'arud* as a conflict of evidence; when two evidences of equal strength require the opposite of each other.[667] For example, where there are two evidences of equal strength, one conveying a positive result and the other conveying a negative result, there is a conflict because one cannot be preferred over the other. Similarly, if one piece of evidence conveys something as *halal* whilst the other conveys it as *haram* a conflict arises. The following cases demonstrate *ta'arud*;

According to the following verse, a woman who loses her husband must wait until one year passes before re-marrying; "*Those of you who (are about to) die leaving behind wives should make testament in their favour of one year's provision without expulsion.*"[668] A different verse contradicts this waiting time; "*Those among you who die, leaving behind their wives: they (the wives) shall keep themselves in waiting for four months and ten days...*"[669] This verse states that a woman who loses her husband has to wait four months and ten days regardless of whether or not she is pregnant. A further verse states that the waiting period for a

---

[666] Shawkānī, *Irshād*, p. 241.
[667] Sarakhsī, *Uṣūl*, vol.2, p. 12.
[668] Qur'ān 2: 240
[669] Qur'ān 2: 234.

pregnant woman is when she delivers her baby; *"As for the women who are pregnant (whether divorced or widows), their waiting-period is until they deliver their burden."*[670] These three verses contradict each other regarding the waiting period for a woman who loses her husband. This conflict is removed through abrogation and *takhsis*: the second verse abrogates the first verse and the third verse limits (*takhsis*) the scope of the second verse because it was revealed after it.

There cannot be a valid conflict between definite and speculative evidence nor between the Qur'an and *ijma'*, or *ijma'* and *qiyāṣ* because in each case the stronger evidence is preferred thereby removing the conflict. Conflict however, may occur between the following sources: two texts of the Qur'an; two rulings of hadith; between a Qur'anic *ayah* and a *mutawātir* hadith; between two non-*mutawātir* hadiths; or between two rulings of *qiyāṣ*.[671]

In the opinion of the four imams and the majority of scholars there is no real conflict between evidence because God is all-wise and conflict cannot occur in His words, rather the conflict is in the assumptions of the *mujtahids*. The rulings of Islam were introduced gradually by the Lawgiver to give the Muslim community time to adapt to the new way of life. In some cases, temporary rulings were conveyed. These prepared Muslims gradually for the final law which, when issued, abrogated the previous temporary rulings. Similarly, on occasion the Lawgiver established general rulings (*āam*) first and then limited (*takhsis*) their scope later. However, the *mujtahids* may not be able to uncover these facts and assume there is a conflict in the evidence.

On encountering an apparent conflict in the evidence, the first priority of the *mujtahid* is to try to reconcile and apply both of them first. If this is not possible, he must investigate if one of the evidences is abrogated by another. If this is not clear, he abandons both of the evidences.[672] Ḫanafī scholars hold that the definite evidences contain no conflict and it is not permissible to accept that there is. However, speculative evidence may contain conflicts as the Lawgiver set out the rulings for the benefit of the people and sometimes left them open to interpretation. The benefit is that they are not required to follow one legal school or one form of conduct; rather they have various options in how to meet their needs through legal schools. It is permissible to act upon speculative evidence and the conflict between them does not harm the objectives of Islamic law.[673]

---

670 Qur'ān 65: 4.

671 Kamali, *Principles of Islamic Jurisprudence*, p. 307.

672 Khudari, *Uṣūl*, p. 359.

673 Shawkānī, *Irshād*, p. 24.

There are certain conditions that must be met in order to accept conflicts between two evidences. Both evidences must be equal in strength in every aspect, otherwise the stronger is preferred. The other conditions are;

1) Both evidences must be related to the same topic or issue; if the subject of the evidence is different the conflict cannot be raised.
2) Conflict only occurs in evidence that was issued during the same time frame. If the time frame is different, the later evidence is preferred. For example there is no conflict among the verses about consuming alcohol, because they were revealed in different time frames.
3) The evidences must convey opposite rulings to each other; one may contain a command to do something and the other one may prohibit the act. However if the prohibited act is permitted in a specific time segment there is no real conflict between them. For example, during the Ramadan fast, eating, drinking and sexual intercourse are prohibited. However, the Lawgiver gave permission for these acts during the night time. As the two evidences are not addressing same time segment there is no conflict between them.
4) If the evidences are related to same subject but they elaborate on it from different aspects there is no conflict between them. For example, there are many verses about the Daily Prayers and each touches upon a different aspect of the Prayer but none of them conveys an opposite ruling. As such, there is no conflict between the verses about the Prayer. Only if the evidences convey an opposite meaning to each may a conflict arise.

If the evidences are general and one opposes the other in ruling the *mujtahid* may resort to interpretation to reconcile the evidences. For example, the following two hadiths are in conflict regarding their rulings:

> Should I inform you who makes the best of witnesses? The Companions said, 'Yes O Messenger of God', thereupon the Prophet said, 'It is one who gives testimony before he is requested to do so'[674]

> The best generation is the one in which I live, then the generation after that and then the next one, but after that there will be people who will give testimony although they are not invited to give it.[675]

There is an apparent conflict between these two hadiths; one recommends the testimony while the other deters it. Since both hadiths are general and not specified in any way, the best course for reconciling them is interpretation. The

674 Muslim, *Sahīh*, hadith no: 1059.
675 Tabrizi, *Mishkat*, hadith no: 6001

first hadith is related to the right of God and the second hadith is related the rights of the servants, therefore, the conflict is removed by way of interpretation.[676]

If the conflicting evidences cannot be reconciled, the next step is to prefer one of them over the other. This may be in the form of clarification and explanation between the evidences such as *ibārah* and *ishārah*, *ṣarīh* and *kināyah*, *muhkam* and *mufassar*, *naṣṣ* and *ẕāhir*. In all these examples the first takes priority over the second because it is stronger and more explicit.

The hadiths are classified as *mutawātir*, *mashhūr*, and *āḫād* according to their strength therefore, *mutawātir* is preferred over other two, *mashhūr* prevails over *āḫād* and the report of a transmitter who is *fāqih* is preferred to the report of a transmitter who is not.[677] Hadith scholars deem that reports from *kutub sitta* (the most authentic six hadith books) are preferable over other hadiths and this is another way of removing the conflict between the evidences.

Scholars of *Uṣūl* prefer affirmative evidence over negative if both are in conflict on the same issue. The jurists hold that if a slave woman is freed while married to a slave man, she has the option to either continue or end the marriage. For example, there are two reports about the case of Barirah who was a slave of A'isha. The first relates that A'isha emancipated Barirah whilst her husband was still a slave and Barirah ended the marriage. The second report relates that her husband was freed but still Barirah finished the marriage.[678] These reports contradict each other regarding the husband's status however, the evidence is definite that he was a slave and speculative that he was freed at that time, so the first report is preferred.

If two evidences on the same subject conflict with each other regarding prohibition and permission, the prohibition report is favoured and the conflict is removed. If this fails to reconcile the evidence abrogation must be investigated by the *mujtahid.* The chronological order of the texts and the occasions behind the revelations must be looked at to establish abrogated and abrogating texts. If this cannot be ascertained, the *mujtahid* abandons both evidences and applies to other sources to extract the ruling for the issue.

SUMMARY: *TA'ARUD AL-ADILLAH* (THE CONFLICTS OF THE EVIDENCES)

1. Jurists define *ta'arud* as a conflict of evidence; when two evidences of equal strength require the opposite of each other.

[676] Badran, *Uṣūl*, p. 466.

[677] Kamali, p. 311.

[678] Abu Dāwud, *Sunan*, hadith no: 601–602.

2. There cannot be a valid conflict between definitive and speculative evidence nor between the Qur'an and *ijma'*, or *ijma'* and *qiyāṣ* because in each case the stronger evidence is preferred thereby removing the conflict.
3. Conflict can occur between two texts of the Qur'an; two rulings of hadith; between a Qur'anic *ayah* and a *mutawātir* hadith; between two non-*mutawātir* hadith; or between two rulings of *qiyāṣ*.
4. On encountering an apparent conflict in the evidence, the first priority of the *mujtahid* is to try to reconcile and apply both of them first. If this is not possible, he must investigate if one of the evidences is abrogated by another. If this is not clear, he abandons both of the evidences.
5. There are certain conditions that must be met in order to accept conflicts between two evidences.
6. Both evidences must be equal in strength in every aspect, otherwise the stronger is preferred. The other conditions are:
7. Both evidences must be related to the same topic or issue.
8. Conflict only occurs in evidence that was issued during the same time frame.
9. The evidences must convey opposite rulings to each other.
10. If the evidences are related to same subject but they elaborate on it from different aspects there is no conflict between them.
11. If the evidences are general and one opposes the other in ruling the *mujtahid* may resort to interpretation to reconcile the evidences.
12. If the conflicting evidences cannot be reconciled, the next step is to prefer one of them over the other.
13. The hadiths are classified as *mutawātir*, *mashhūr*, and *āḫād* according to their strength therefore, *mutawātir* is preferred over other two, *mashhūr* prevails over *āḫād* and the report of a transmitter who is *fāqih* is preferred to the report of a transmitter who is not.
14. Scholars of *Uṣūl* prefer affirmative evidence over negative if both are in conflict on the same issue.
15. If two evidences on the same subject conflict with each other regarding prohibition and permission, the prohibition report is favoured.

Glossary

'adl: justice, upright and just.
'adālah: justice, uprightness of character.
adillah: proofs, evidences, indications.
āḫād: solitary hadith, report by a single person or by odd individuals.
aḫkām (pl. of *hukm*): laws, values and ordinances.
ahliyyah: legal capacity.
ahliyyah al-edā: active legal capacity that can incur rights as well as obligations.
ahliyyah wujub: receptive legal capacity which is good for receiving but cannot incur obligations.
'amalī: practical.
āam: general.
amr: command.
'aql: intellect, rationality, reason.
arkan: pillars, essential requirements.
asl: root, origin, source.
athar: impact, trace, vestige; also deeds and precedents of the Companions of the noble Prophet.
'aẕimah: strict or unmodified law which remains in its original rigour due to the absence of mitigating factors.
bātil: invalid.
bayān: explanation, clarification.
dalālah: meaning, implication.
dalil: proof, indication, evidence.
fāqih: jurist.
far'i: a branch or a sub-division, and a new case.
fard: obligatory.
fard 'ayn: personal obligation.
fard kifaī: collective obligation.
fāsid: irregular.
hadd: prescribed penalty.
Hajj: the once-in-a-lifetime obligation of pilgrimage to the holy Ka'ba.
ḫaqiqī: literal.

hijrah: the Prophet's migration from Mecca to Medina, signifying the beginning of the Islamic calendar.
ḫukm shar'ī: law, value, or ruling of *Shari'ah.*
al-ḫukm al-taklifiyya: defining law.
ḫukm al-wad'iyya: declaratory law
ibārah al-naṣṣ: explicit meaning of a given text which is borne out by its words.
iḫrām: Special attire that pilgrims put on when performing pilgrimage (hajj-umrah)
ijma': consensus.
ijtihād: the effort of a jurist to deduce the law from its sources.
'illah: effective cause.
iktizā al-naṣṣ: the required meaning of a given text.
ishārah al-naṣṣ: an alluded meaning that can be detected in a given text.
istiḫsān: juristic preference.
istiṣḫāb: presumption of continuity.
junub: major impurity which needs bath to be cleaned.
kaffārah: compensation, expiation.
karahah: dislike.
khabar: news, report.
khabar wāḫid: single source report.
khās: specific.
madhhab: juristic/theological school.
makruh: dislike.
mandub: recommended.
māni': hindrance, obstacle.
mansukh: abrogated.
maqāsid: objectives.
mashhūr: well-known.
maslaḫah: considerations of public interest.
mawdu': fabricated, forged.
mubah: permissible.
mufassar: explained.
mukallaf: a liable person.
muhkam: perspicuous.
mujmal: ambiguous.
munasib: appropriate.
muqayyad: qualified.
mursal: the hadith with a broken chain of transmission: the Companion is missing in the chain.
mushkil: complicated.

mushtarak: homonym.
mustaḫada: chronic vaginal bleeding.
mutashābih: intricate word or a text.
mutlaq: absolute, unqualified.
nahy: prohibition.
naqlī: transmitted evidences.
nāsikh: the abrogating text or evidence.
naskh: abrogation.
naṣṣ: a clear textual ruling.
qat'ī: definitive.
riwāyah: narration.
rukhṣah: easiness due to the presence of difficulties.
rukun: pillar.
sabab: cause.
Saḫābah: Companions of Prophet Muhammad, peace and blessings be upon him.
saḫīḫ: valid, authentic.
sanad: basis, proof, authority.
shart: condition.
Tabi'in: Successors, second generation after the Companions.
taḫrima: prohibition.
ta'līl: causation, search for the effective cause of a ruling.
ta'wil: allegorical interpretation.
takhsis: limiting the general.
taklif: liability, obligation.
taqlid: imitation, following the views and opinions of others.
tashri': legislation.
tawātur-mutawātir: continuous testimony.
tayammum: ablution with clean sand/earth in the event where no water can be found.
'Umrah: Lesser pilgrimage that consists of turning around the Ka'ba and walking between two hills called Safa and Marwa.
waḫy: divine revelation.
wajib: obligatory.
wajib 'aynī: personal obligation.
wajib kifaī: collective obligation of the entire community.
wasf: attribute, adjective.
wudu: ablution.
wujub: obligation, rendering something obligatory.
ẕann: speculation.
ẕannī: speculative, doubtful.
ẕāhir: manifest.

Bibliography

Āmidī, Sayf al-Din 'Ali b. Muhammad, *al-Iḫkām fi Uṣūl al-Aḫkām* 4 vols. ed. 'Abd al-Razzaq 'Afifi, 2nd edn. Beirut: al-Maktab al-Islamī, 1982.

Ibn al-'Arābī, Abu Bakr b. 'Abd Allah, *Aḫkām al-Qur'an*. Cairo: Matba'ah Dar al-Sa'adah, 1330 AH.

Azami, Muhammad Mustafa. *Studies in Hadith Methodology and Literature*. Indianapolis: American Trust Publications, 1977.

Badran, Abu al-'Aynayn Badran, *Uṣūl al-Fiqh al-Islamī*, Alexandria: Mu'assasah Shabab al-Jami'ah, l984.

_____ *Bayan al-Nusus al- Tashri'iyyah*: Turuquh wa-Anwa'uh. Alexandria: Mu'assasah Shabab al-Jami'ah, l982.

al-Bayḫaqī, Abu Bakr Ahmad b. al-Husayn, *Al-Sunan al-Kubra*, 10 vols. Beirut: Dar al-Fikr, n.d.

al-Bukhari, Muhammad b. Isma'il, *Saḫīḫ al-Bukhari*, 8 vols. İstanbul: al-Maktabah al-Islamiyyah, 1981.

_____ *Sahih Bukhari*. Eng. trans. Muhammad Muhsin Khan. 9 vols. Lahore: Kazi Publications, 1979.

al-Bukhari, 'Ala' al-Dln 'Abd al-'Aziz, *Kashf al-Asrār 'ala al-Bazdawī*, İstanbul, 1307 AH.

al-Dārimī, Muhammad, *Sunan al-Dārimī*, 2 vols. Beirut: Dar al-Kutub al-'Ilmiyyah, n.d.

Abu Dāwud al-Sijistani, *Sunan Abu Dāwud*, Eng. trans. Ahmad Hasan. 3 vols. Lahore: Ashraf Press, 1984.

Denffer, Ahmad Von. *Ulūm al-Qur'an*: *An Introduction to the Sciences of the Qur'an*. Leicester: The Islamic Foundation, 1983.

Fuad, Muhammad Abdul Baqi, *Al-Mu'ajam al Mufharras Li Alfazil Qur'ān al-Kareem*. Cairo, 1988.

al-Ghazali, Abu Hamid Muhammad, *Al-Muṣtaṣfā min 'Ilm al-Uṣūl*, Cairo: al-Maktabah al-Tijariyyah. 2 vols. 1937.

_____ *Ihyâ al-'ulūm ad-Din*, Beirut: Dar al-Ma'rifah, 1980–1993.

Gülen, M. Fethullah, *Kur'ân'ın Altın İkliminde*, İzmir, Nil Yayınları, 2011.

_____ *Reflections on the Qur'ān*, trans. Ayşenur Kaplan and Harun Gültekin, New Jersey, Tughra Books, 2012.

_____ *Kendi Dünyamıza Doğru*, Nil Yayınları, İstanbul, 2008.

Goldziher, Ignaz, *Introduction to Islamic Theology and Law*, trans. Andras and Ruth Hamori, Princeton (New Jersey): Princeton University Press, 1981.

Ibn al-Hājib, Jamal al-Din Abu 'Amr, *Mukhtasar al-Muntaha*, Constantinople: al-Maktabah al-Islamiyyah, 1310 AH.

Haythami, 'Ali b. Abū Bakr, *Majma' az-Zawiz'id*, 10 vols. Cairo, 1352.

Haji Khalifa, Mustafa b. 'Abdullah: *Kasha z-Zunun* 3rd ed. Tehran, 1967.

Ḫākim, Muhammad b. 'Abdullah: *al-Mustadrak*, ed. M.A. 'Ata', Beirut, 1990.

Hallaq, Wael B. *'The Gate of Ijtihād: A Study in Islamic Legal History.'* Ph.D. dissertation (University of Washington), 1985.

Ibn Hajar al-'Asqalani, Ahmad b. 'Ali, *Fath al-Bari*, ed. F. 'Abdul-Baqi, 13 vols. Cairo, 1380–1390.

______ *Al Isaba fi Tamyiz as-Sahaba*, 4 vols. Beirut, no date [reprint of first ed. Cairo, 1328.

Ibn Hanbal, Ahmad, *Musnad al-Imam Ahmad ibn Hanbal*, 6 vols. Beirut: Dar al-Fikr, n.d.

Ibn Ḫazm, Abu Muhammad 'Ali b. Ahmad, *al-Itqān fi Uṣūl al-Aḫkām*, ed. Ahmad Muhammad Shakir. 4 vols. Beirut: Dar al-Afaq al-Jadidah, 1980.

Ibn Hishām: *Sīrah*, ed. M. Saqqa et al, 4 vols. 2nd ed. Cairo, 1955.

Ibn Khaldun, *The Muqaddima, An Introduction to History*, trans. Franz Rosenthal, 3 vols, New York, 1958; 2nd revised ed, Princeton, NJ: Princeton University Press, 1967.

Ibn Manzur, *Lisan al-Arab*, Beirut: Dar Sadir; Dar Beirut, 1955–1956.

Ibn Sa'd, Muhammad: *Kitab at-Tabaqat al-Kubra*, ed. E. Sachau et al, 9 vols. Leiden, 1905–1917.

Iqbal, Muhammad, *The Reconstruction of Religious Thought in Islam*, Lahore: Sh. Muhammad Ashraf, 1982.

Isfahani, Imam Raghib, *Mufradaat al Qur'ān*, Able hadith Academy Lahore- 1971.

al-Isnawi, Jamal al-Din Abu Muhammad 'Abd al-Rahimm. *Al-Tamhid fi Takhrīj al-Furu' ala'l Uṣūl*, Ed. Muhammad Hasan Hitu. 3rd edn. Beirut: Mu'assasah al-Risalah, 1984.

Kamali, Mohammad Hashim, *Principles of Islamic Jurisprudence*, 3rd edn, Islamic Text Society, Cambridge, 2003.

Kassab, al-Sayyid 'Abd al-Latif, *Adwa Hawl Qadiyyah al-Ijtihad fi al-Shari'ah al-Islamiyyah*, Cairo: Dar al-Tawfiq, 1984.

Khadduri, Majid, *Islamic jurisprudence: Al-Shafi'i's Risalah*, Baltimore: John Hopkins University Press, 1961. Cambridge: The Islamic Texts Society, 1987.

Khallaf, 'Abd al-Wahhab, *'Ilm Uṣūl al-Fiqh*, 12th edn. Kuwait: Dar al-Qalam, 1978.

al-Khudari, Shaykh Muhammad, *Uṣūl al-Fiqh*, 7th edn. Cairo: Dar al-Fikr, 1981.

Ibn Majah, Muhammad b. Yazid al-Qazwini, *Sunan Ibn Majah*, İstanbul: Çağrı Yayınları, 2 vols. 1981.

Malik b. Anas, *Al-Muwatta*, ed. M.F. Cairo: 'Abdul-Baqi, 1951.

Makdisi, John, "Legal Logic and Equity in Islamic Law," *American Journal of Comparative Law*, 33 (1985), 63–92.

al-Marghinanī, Burhān al-Din, *Hidayah*, Eng. trans. Hamilton. Lahore: Premier Book House, 1982.

The Mejelle, Eng. trans. C. R. Tyser. Lahore: Law Publishing Co., 1979.

Ibn al-Muqaffa' 'Abd Allah, *Risalah fi al-Sahabah*. In Muhammad Kurd 'Ali (ed.), *Risalah al-Bulagha*. 4th edn. Cairo, n.p., 1954.

Muslim, Abu al-Husayn ibn al-Hajjaj al-Nishaburi, *Mukhtasar Saḫīḫ Muslim*, Ed. Muhammad al-Albani, 4th edn. Beirut: al-Maktab al-Islamī, 1982.

al-Nawawī, Muhyi al-Din Abu Zakariya Yahya ibn Sharaf, *Minhaj al- Talibin*, Eng. trans. E. C. Howard. Lahore: Law Publishing Company, n.d.

Nursi, Said, *The Words*, trans. Hüseyin Akarsu, Light, New Jersey, 2005.

al-Qarafi, Shihab al-Din, *Kitāb al-Furuq*, Cairo: Dar al-Kutub al-'Arabiyyah, 1346 AH.

al-Qattan, Manna' Khalil, *al-Tashri' wa'l-Fiqh fi'l-Islam: Tarikhan wa Manhajan*, 4th edn. Beirut: Mu'assasah al-Risalah, 1985.

Ibn Qayyim al-Jawziyyah, 'Abd Allah Muhammad b. Abu Bakr. *al-Turuq al-Hukmiyyah fi'l-Siyasah al-Shari'iyyah*. Cairo: Mu'assasah al-'Arabiyyah li'l-Tiba'ah, 1961.

_____ *I'lam al-Muwaqqi'in 'an Rabb al-'Alamin*, Ed. Muhammad Murur al-Dimashqi. Cairo: Idarah al-Tiba'ah al-Muniriyyah. 4 vols., n.d.

The Qur'an, Text, Translation and Commentary by Ali Ünal, Light, New Jersey, 2005.

al-Qurtubi, Abu 'Abd Allah Muhammad b. Ahmad, *Al-Jami' li-Aḫkām al-Qur'an* 3rd edn. Cairo: Dar al-Kutub al-'Arabiyyah, 1967.

al-Qurtubi, Muhammad b. Ahmad b. Rushd, *Bidayah al-Mujtahid*, Cairo: Mustafa al-Babi al-Halabi, 1981.

Rahim, Abdur, *Principles of Muhammadan Jurisprudence*, London: Luzac and Co. 1911.

al-Rāzī, Fakhr al-Din b. 'Umar, *Al- Tafsir al-Kabir*, Beirut: Dar al-Fikr, 1978.

Sadr al-Shari'ah, 'Ubayd Allah ibn Mas'ud al-Mahbubi, *al- Tawdih fi Hall al-Ghawamid al-Tanqih*, Cairo: Dar al-'Ahd al-Jadid li'l Taba'ah, 1957.

Salih, Subhi, *Mabahith fi 'Ulum al-Qur'an*, 15th edn. Beirut: Dar al-'Ilm li al-Malayin, 1983.

al-Sarakhsī, Shams al-Din Muhammad, *Uṣūl al-Sarakhsī*, Ed. Abu'l Wafa al-Afghani. Cairo: Matba'ah Dar al-Kitab al-'Arabi, 1372 AH.

Sha'ban, Zaki al-Din, *'Uṣūl al-Fiqh al-Islamī*. 2nd edn. Beirut: Dar al-Kitāb, 1971.

Shāfi'i, Muhammad b. Idris, *Kitāb al-Umm*, 7 vols. Cairo: Dar al-Sha'b, 1321 AH.

_____ *Al-Risalah*, Ed. Muhammad Sayyid Kilani, 2nd edn. Cairo: Mustafa al-Babi al-Halabi, 1983.

Shaltut, Mahmud, *Al-Islam, 'Aqidah wa-Shari'ah*, Kuwait: Matabi' Dar al-Qalam, I966.

Al-Shātibī, Abu Ishaq Ibrahim, *Al-Muwafaqaat fi Uṣūl al-Aḫkām*, Ed. Muhammad Hasanayn Makhluf Cairo: al-Matba'ah al-Salafiyyah, 1341 AH.

_____ *Al-Muwafaqaat fi Usul al-Shari'ah*, Ed. Shaykh 'Abd Allah Diraz, Cairo: al-Maktabah al-Tijariyyah al-Kubra, n.d.

_____ *Al-I'tisām*, Cairo: Matba'ah al-Manar, 1914.

al-Shawkānī, Yahya b. 'Ali. *Irshād al-Fuhūl min Taḫqīq al-Haqq ila 'Ilm al-Uṣūl*, Cairo: Dar al-Fikr, n.d.

al-Shirazi, Abu Ishaq, *Al-Luma fi Uṣūl al-Fiqh*, Cairo: Dar al-'Arābī, 1970.

al-Sijistani, Abu Dāwud, *Sunan*, Eng. trans. Ahmad Hasan, 3 vols. Lahore: Ashraf Press, 1984.

al-Suyūtī, Jalal al-Din, *Itqān fi 'Ulūm al-Qur'an*, Beirut: Maktabah al-Thaqafiyyah, 1973.

Tabarī, Abu Ja'far Muhammad b. Jarir, *Jami al-Bayan 'an Ta'wil al-Qur'an*. Cairo: Dar al-Ma'rifah, 1374 AH.

Tahawi, Abū Ja'far Ahmad, *Sharh Mushkil al-Athar*, ed. by Shu'ayb Arnawud, Muassasah ar-Risalah, Beirut. 1994.

al-Tabrizi, Muhammad b. 'Abd Allah al-Khatib, *Mishkat al-Masabih*, Ed. Muhammad al-Din al-Albani. 3 vols. 2nd edn. Beirut: al-Maktabah al-Islami, 1979.

Taftazani, Sa'd al-Din Mas'ud b. 'Umar, *Al- Talwih 'ala'l-Tawdih*, Cairo: 'Isa al-Babi al-Halabi, 1957.

Ibn Taymiyyah, Taqi al-Din, *Mas'alah al-Istiḫsān*, trans. and ed. George Makdisi as '*Ibn Taymiyyah's Manuscript on istiḫsān*', in G. Makdisi (ed.). Arabic and Islamic Studies in Honour of Hamilton A.R. Gibb. Leiden: E.J. Brill, 1965.

Ünal, Ali, *The Qur'ān with Annotated Interpretation in Modern English*, New Jersey: Tughra Books, 2008.

Yıldırım, Suat, *Anahatlarıyla Kur'an-ı Kerim ve Kuran İlimlerine Giriş*, İstanbul: Ensar, 2013.

Abu Yusuf, Ya'qub b. Ibrahim, *Kitāb al-Kharaj*, 2nd edn. Cairo: al-Matba'ah al-Salafiyyah, 1352 AH.

Abu Zahrah, Muhammad, *Uṣūl al-Fiqh*, Cairo: Dar al-Fikr al-'Arābī, 1958.

al-Zarkashī, Badr al-Din Muhammad b. Bahadur, *Al-Bahr al-Muhit Uṣūl al-Fiqh*, ed. 'Umar Sulayman al-Ashqar. 2nd edn. Cairo: Dar al-Sahwah, 1992.

al-Zarqa, Mustafa Ahmad, *Al-Madkhal al-Fiqḫ al-'Āam*, 3 vols. 6th edn. Damascus: Dar al-Fikr.

Zaydan, 'Abd al-Karim, *Al-Wajiz fi Uṣūl al-Fiqh*, Baghdad: Maktabah al-Quds, 1976.

al-Zuhayli, Wahbah, *Uṣūl al-Fiqh al-Islamī*, Damascus: Dar al-Fikr li'l-Tib''ah wa'l-Tawzi', 1986.